Fundamental Problems in Philosophy

Edited by
OSWALD HANFLING
at The Open University

BASIL BLACKWELL
in association with
THE OPEN UNIVERSITY PRESS

ISBN (cased edition) 0 631 14450 1
       (paperback edition) 0 631 14460 9

Printed in Great Britain by
Western Printing Services Ltd, Bristol

Contents

List of Acknowledgements   ix

Editor's Introduction   xi

BODY AND MIND   1

1. Jerome Shaffer: Consciousness and the Body (1968)   1
2. Jerome Shaffer: Machines and the Mind-Body Problem (1965)   24
3. Bertrand Russell: The Argument from Analogy (1948)   31
4. A. J. Ayer: The Analysis and Justification of Statements about other Minds (1956)   35

PERSONAL IDENTITY   43

5. David Hume: Of Personal Identity (1738)   43
6. J. McT. E. McTaggart: The Self as Substance (1927)   51
7. C. A. Campbell: Self-consciousness, Self-identity and Personal Identity (1957)   56
8. Peter Geach: The Fallacy of 'Cogito ergo sum' (1957)   59
9. David Pears: Hume on Personal Identity (1963)   62
10. Bernard Williams: The Self and the Future (1970)   69

ARITHMETIC, LOGIC AND PROOF   89

11. J. S. Mill: Demonstration and the Science of Number (1843)   89
12. G. Frege: The Foundations of Arithmetic: Introduction (1884)   101

13. D. Hilbert: On the Foundations of Logic and
    Arithmetic (1904)   109

MORAL PHILOSOPHY   115

14. Philippa Foot: Moral Beliefs (1958, 1967)   115

15. D. Z. Phillips and H. O. Mounce: On Morality's
    having a Point (1965)   135

POLITICAL PHILOSOPHY   149

16. J. J. Rousseau: The First Societies (1762)   149

17. Immanuel Kant: The Kingdom of Ends (1785)   151

18. S. I. Benn and R. S. Peters: Justice and
    Equality (1959)   154

19. Bernard Williams: The Idea of Equality (1962)   159

CAUSE AND EFFECT   181

20. David Hume: Of the Idea of Necessary
    Connexion (1748)   181

21. William Kneale: Natural Laws and Natural
    Necessity (1949)   182

22. R. B. Braithwaite: Laws of Nature and Causality (1953)   186

23. J. S. Mill: The Real Cause of a Phenomenon (1843)   199

24. H. L. A. Hart and A. M. Honoré: Causation and
    Common Sense (1959)   201

FREEDOM AND DETERMINISM   211

25. Thomas Hobbes: My Opinion about Liberty and
    Necessity (1652)   211

26. David Hume: Of Liberty and Necessity (1748)   216

27. J. L. Austin: Ifs and Cans (1956)   219

28. David Pears: Freedom and the Will (1963)   231

TRUTH   239

29. G. E. Moore: Propositions, Facts and Truth (1910–11)   239

30. Alfred Tarski: Truth and Proof (1969)   261

31. W. V. Quine: Meaning and Truth (1970)   287

KNOWLEDGE AND BELIEF   303

32. Plato: The Sun, the Line and the Cave (427–347 B.C.)   303

33. Aristotle: Knowledge, Error and Opinion
    (384–322 B.C.)   314

34. Aristotle: Knowledge, Experience and Understanding
    (384–322 B.C.)   319

35. Gilbert Ryle: Knowing How and Knowing That (1949)   321

36. William Kneale: Knowledge, Opinion and Probability
    (1949)   329

PERCEPTION   343

37. Galileo: The Falsity of the Accepted Notion of
    Heat (1623)   343

38. René Descartes: Knowledge of Corporeal Objects (1642)   344

    The Three Grades of Perception (1642)   346

    The Representative Theory of Perception (1637)   347

39. John Locke: Primary and Secondary Qualities (1690)   351

    Sensation and Judgement in Perception (1690)   355

    Knowledge of Exterior Causes of Sensations (1690)   356

40. George Berkeley: Immaterialism (1710)   360
    Heat and Pain (1713)   364

41. J. S. Mill: The Meaning of 'White' (1843)   367

UNIVERSALS AND REALITY   379

42. H. F. Cherniss: The Philosophical Economy of the
    Theory of Ideas (1936)   379

43. J. L. Austin: Are there Universals? (1939)   390

PHILOSOPHY OF LANGUAGE 397

44. John Locke: Of Words (1690) 397

45. Peter Geach: Abstractionism and Concept-
    Formation (1957) 400

Index 417

List of Acknowledgements

The Editor wishes to acknowledge with gratitude the permission given by the following publishers and editors for the use of the extracts reprinted in this volume as follows. The full details of each source are given at the end of the relevant passages.

George Allen & Unwin and Collier Books for permission to use items 3, 7, 18 and 29;

the Editor of the *American Philosophical Quarterly* and Professor Jerome Shaffer for item 2;

the Editor of The Aristotelian Society for item 14: © 1959, The Aristotelian Society;

Cambridge University Press for items 6, 22 (Braithwaite, R. B.: *Scientific Explanation*, © 1953 Cambridge University Press), and 38 (ii);

Collier-Macmillan and The Macmillan Company of New York for item 25, *Body, Man and Citizen* by Thomas Hobbes, Edited and with an Introduction by Richard S. Peters;

W. H. Freeman & Company, San Francisco, for item 30: Reprinted with permission. Copyright © 1969 by Scientific American Inc. All rights reserved. Harvard University Press and B. G. Teubner, Stuttgart, for item 13: Cambridge, Mass.: Harvard University Press, Copyright 1967, by the President and Fellows of Harvard College;

Hutchinson Publishing Group Limited for item 17, and Hutchinson and Barnes & Noble Books of New York for item 35;

the Editor of the *Journal of Philology* for item 43;

St. Martin's Press and Macmillan London and Basingstoke for items 4, 9 and 28;

Thomas Nelson & Sons Limited for items 38 (i), 38 (iii), 40 (i) and 40 (ii);

A. D. Peters and Company for item 16;

the Editor of *The Philosophical Review* and Professor Bernard Williams for item 10;

the *Editor of Philosophy* and Professor D. Z. Phillips and Mr H. O. Mounce for item 15;
Routledge & Kegan Paul Limited and Humanities Press Inc. for items 8, 37 and 45;
Professor Bernard Williams for item 19;
Item 1—Jerome A. Shaffer, *Philosophy of Mind*, © 1968, and item 31—W. V. Quine, *Philosophy of Logic*, © 1970, are reprinted by permission of Prentice-Hall Inc., Englewood Cliffs, New Jersey.
Items 5, 20, 21, 24, 26, 27, 32, 33, 34, 36, 39, 43, 44, and the Appendix to item 14 are reprinted by permission of The Clarendon Press, Oxford.

Editor's Introduction

The readings in this volume have been selected by members of the Open University 'Problems of Philosophy' Course Team. The course, which aims to introduce the student to most of the central topics in Philosophy, created a need to bring together a set of essential readings in one volume. The scope and nature of the volume is such that it should prove of value for anyone interested in Philosophy, whether or not they enrol for the 'Problems of Philosophy' course.

The beginnings of Philosophy stretch back into antiquity. In almost every period there have been persons who engaged in philosophical speculation about man's nature and his place in the universe. The output of philosophical literature through the ages —and especially since the 17th and 18th centuries—has been vast. No single volume could possibly claim to be representative in anything like a comprehensive sense. Necessarily the selections printed here reflect to some extent the interests of the members of the Course Team. Nevertheless the book can fairly be regarded as representative of philosophical literature in a number of ways. In period it ranges from Plato to the present day—though most of the contributions date from the time since Descartes, who is widely held to have begun a new era in philosophical enquiry. The main headings given on the contents page would, I think, be generally regarded by present-day philosophers as covering most of the central topics in Philosophy; though here again opinions would vary as to the most important questions within each topic. Many of the sections have been so arranged as to juxtapose alternative and often conflicting views of a given problem, thus bringing out the essentially controversial and 'open-ended' nature of philosophical enquiry.

It is sometimes suggested that philosophers are more interested in creating problems than in solving them. There is some truth in this: although the problems are real enough, it is in the nature of philosophical enquiry that one cannot hope to find definitive solutions. Why this should be so is itself, I suppose, a philosophical question. It is not, however, one that I shall try to answer here. I believe, in any case, that the best way of approaching it is by seeing how philosophers do in fact go about their business; and this is revealed, to a considerable extent, by the writings printed in this volume.

We have thought it important, both in planning our course and in devising this volume, that the student should become acquainted with the original works of philosophers, as opposed to commentaries and summary treatments of the 'Philosophy made simple' variety. Philosophy is not simple. Any attempt to gloss over its difficulties can only lead to superficiality and distortion. We have therefore included only writings by philosophers who had, in our opinion, something original and important to say. Apart from the conflict in conclusions which is a characteristic feature of philosophising, the reader, if he is unfamiliar with philosophical literature, may well be astonished at the great variety of styles with which different philosophers approach a given problem. Although our selections have been made primarily on the basis of their philosophical content, the reader may also be agreeably surprised at the high literary quality of many of the contributions.

In making this selection we have avoided items which would require a previous knowledge of philosophy or which make extensive use of special terminology.

The volume begins with a group of topics which certainly belong to one of the central areas of philosophical enquiry. 'Body and Mind', 'The Problem of Other Minds' and 'Personal Identity' are all concerned, in one way or another, with the nature of a person or 'Self', and the relationship of that 'Self' with the rest of the world. The topics which follow have been ordered in a coherent pattern which takes account of the relationships between them. We do not pretend, however, that it is necessarily the best or most logical order. In Philosophy one is constantly coming up against overlaps and interrelations between the various topics. For this reason there cannot be an ordering of topics which could properly be claimed as being 'the right' one.

Again, although the division of Philosophy under separate topic headings is obviously required for practical purposes, the way in which it is done is bound to be to some extent arbitrary and artificial. The reader will often find that an extract under one heading has important implications for a problem treated under another. This again is a characteristic feature of philosophical enquiry. In spite of its many facets, the whole philosophical enterprise has somehow a recognisable unity and continuity. As Wittgenstein wrote (in a somewhat different context) in his *Philosophical Investigations*: 'We see a complicated network of similarities overlapping and criss-crossing. As in spinning a thread we twist fibre on fibre. And the strength of the thread does not reside in the fact that some one fibre runs through its whole length, but in the overlapping of many fibres.'

O.H.

February 1972

BODY AND MIND

1 Consciousness and the Body (1968)

JEROME SHAFFER

The third-person account

When we ask of a man who has been hit on the head whether he is *conscious*, what do we mean? Well, what do we expect to find if we are told he is not conscious, and what do we expect to find if we are told that he is conscious? We expect that if he is not conscious, he will not respond to certain stimuli; for example, he will not flinch at a loud noise nearby. On the other hand, we expect that if he is conscious, he will flinch at the noise. That is, we expect certain kinds of behavior under certain stimuli. For example, we expect he will open his eyes when he is spoken to, perhaps try to get up, ask what happened to him, and so on. If he has not suffered bodily injury, then we will expect even more complex behavior. If, on request, he is able to get up, walk around without bumping into things, reply to questions, follow commands, then it would be absurd for anyone to wonder if he is conscious yet. Just that kind of behavior is exactly the sort of behavior we have in mind when we say that a person has regained consciousness. This fact might lead us to say that 'consciousness' is to be defined in terms of the kind of bodily behavior elicited by certain sorts of stimuli. [...]

Now it must be said at the outset that this third-person account does indeed do considerable justice to a great many of the concepts applicable exclusively to conscious beings. If we say of a person that he is ingenious or witty, resourceful or industrious, ambitious or considerate, we are referring predominantly to what he says and does. And the same goes for knowing Latin, reminiscing, studying the behavior of a cat, and flying into a rage. The

1

crucial tests for the application of these terms and, indeed, their
basic content, lie in behavior and behavioral dispositions.[1]

For example, *to know Latin* is to be able to perform in prescribed ways under certain circumstances. At the very least, one
must be able to translate a goodly number of sentences into and
out of Latin, and it is even better if one can explain *why* he uses
the constructions he does. *To be greedy* is to jump at opportunities to increase one's acquisitions, or at least be strongly inclined
to jump at them, far beyond actual need. And to *exercise reason*
or *intelligence* is to do things in sensible and efficacious ways,
avoiding pitfalls and surmounting obstacles with a minimum of
effort.

It might be said in general that the third-person account is
applicable to what can be classified as qualities of mind, personality and character, of skills, abilities and capacities (or the
absence thereof), of habits, tendencies, propensities and bents, of
attitudes and outlooks, and of moods, frames of mind and humors;
and to whatever is an exercise or expression of them.

Why is it that the third-person account is especially applicable
to the analysis of these concepts? It is no accident. This can be
seen when we ask what entitles someone to apply any one of
these concepts to himself. Consider, for example, knowing Latin.
My opinion that I know Latin has no special weight, balanced
against another's opinion. Anyone who claims I know Latin must
have *evidence*, and that includes me. The kind of evidence that
is relevant is the kind that not only I but anyone could have. So
others are typically in as good a position as I am to say of me that
I know Latin. In the case of some concepts, such as *ambition*,
others often are in an even better position to know, for they may
look more objectively at my behavior than I do.

The fact that, in principle, I am in no better position to describe
my own state indicates that even when I do describe my state, I
take an essentially *third-person* approach to myself, taking account
of the sorts of things any third person would when he makes a
judgment. So the third-person account would be naturally well
suited to the analysis of such states and would furnish an appropriate analysis.

Note that even for the concepts most amenable to behavioristic
analysis, it is out of the question that we should be able to give a

[1] It is one of the great merits of Gilbert Ryle's *The Concept of Mind*
(Hutchinson, 1949) that he demonstrates this thesis over and over for an
astonishing range of expressions involving a reference to consciousness.

precise dispositional *definition*. We cannot say in detail just what dispositions are involved. From that fact, some would conclude that the third-person account is inadequate even here. But a supporter of that account would remind us that this is a general feature of dispositional terms.

Whether the third-person account does justice to all of the concepts involving consciousness remains to be seen. Let us turn to a set of cases notorious for the difficulties they offer to a proponent of the third-person account.

Some difficulties of the third-person account

We may bring out the important feature of such cases by noting a peculiarity of cases favorable to the third-person account, cases such as knowing Latin or being ambitious. It may very well be true of a person who is *sound asleep* that he knows Latin or is greedy; it is not necessary that there be anything, as we say, *going on before his mind* or *occupying his consciousness*. When it comes to the exercise or expression of these states, he must, typically, be awake (I say 'typically,' because one might argue that a person speaking Latin in his sleep is exercising his knowledge of Latin, and the person crying out in his sleep 'I want the whole cake!' is giving expression to his greed). Although it is not easy to see this point, reflection will show that it is not necessary even in the standard case of being awake that there be anything particular *going on before his mind or occupying his consciousness* when he gives expression to his knowledge of Latin or his greed. He may recite a Latin poem automatically or reach out and grab the whole cake on impulse, without any thought. To be sure, he *might* be inwardly reciting the poem in addition to reciting it outwardly, and he *might* be inwardly enjoying the thought of eating the whole cake as he grabs it. But such inward experiences are not essential. The essence of the expression of the knowledge or the greed consists in what is done *outwardly*, not what is done *inwardly*.

To find cases that offer difficulty to the third-person account, we must look for those cases in which the essence lies in what happens *inwardly*. It is the thesis of adherents of the third-person account that there are *no* such cases, that anything involving consciousness can be analyzed in terms of publicly observable behavior or dispositions toward such behavior.

Let us turn to those cases in which it appears that an essential feature of the case is the *inner* occurrence of something, as we say, 'going on before the person's mind' or 'occupying his consciousness.' The most plausible candidates are sensations (e.g., feeling pain), mental images (e.g., visualizing a scene), and thoughts (e.g., having the thought, upon awakening, that today is a holiday). Let us concentrate on having sensations; for example, a *sensation of pain*. We see a heavy object fall on someone's foot. We see him turn pale, grimace, cry out, clutch his foot, jump up and down, call for help, and limp about. He is obviously feeling pain. But what is it to feel pain? On the third-person account it is just to behave in these ways under these circumstances, or at least to be disposed so to behave. That is all that is observable in principle, and so that is all that is involved in feeling pain.

But does not such an analysis leave out just the essential feature, the sharp, highly unpleasant *sensation* so forcibly there in the forefront of consciousness and so agonizingly distressful? Surely it is the inner sensation which is the immediate cause of the outward behavior of grimacing, crying out, and limping about. That inner cause is left out in the third-person account. Particular behavior or dispositions to behave are neither necessary nor sufficient conditions for sensations. Not necessary because one can imagine a pain so paralyzingly great or so trivially slight that there is no disposition to behave; and one can imagine stoics who have so trained themselves that they have exterminated any such dispositions. And not sufficient because one can imagine such dispositions arising from other causes such as the desire to call attention to oneself, to deceive others, or imitate a person in pain; and you can imagine even that suddenly and unaccountably you might be overcome by a desire to grimace, cry out, and limp about, *for no reason at all*. Such an occurrence would be very puzzling, and we might not know what to make of it, but surely it might occur. Others might be taken in and believe that you were feeling pain. But *you* would know that you were not feeling pain, even if you could not explain *why* you behaved as though you were in pain. So feeling pain is one thing, and being disposed to behave in certain ways is another. The feeling may produce the disposition to behave, but we cannot say they are identical, nor even that the one is a necessary or sufficient condition for the other.

One might try to deal with this objection by broadening the definition of sensations beyond behavior. One way in which this might be done while still remaining consistent with the third-person account is to bring into the picture a publicly observable *cause*; e.g., the heavy object falling on his foot and causing his disposition to grimace, cry out, and limp around. We can define the feeling of pain as the disposition to behave in the relevant ways *as a result of* a particular sort of injury to the body. In this way, we would rule out those cases in which the disposition to behave is caused by a desire (e.g., to imitate a person in pain) or in which the disposition to behave has no known cause at all.

The difficulty with this attempt to bolster the third-person account is that it makes the cause a part of the *definition* of 'sensation,' and the proposition that every sensation has a cause becomes a tautology. But it is clearly *not* a tautology that every sensation has a cause; it is an empirical hypothesis. Since speaking of a sensation without any cause is not a contradiction in terms, this suggested analysis, which would make it a contradiction, must be rejected.

A way of getting around this difficulty is proposed by David K. Lewis.[2] He suggests that we define the sensation in terms of its typical causes and effects, and admit that there may be a small residue of atypical cases. This suggestion, however, commits us to the view that the proposition that *most sensations have causes* is a tautology. And I am inclined to think that even though it is highly likely, perhaps even certain, that most sensations have causes, it is not a tautology. Take headaches, for instance; is it not logically possible that they should occur randomly? That most headaches have causes is surely an empirical hypothesis. Hence we cannot bring in their causes, not even typical causes, to define the term 'headache.'

I conclude, then, that such third-person accounts will not give us a correct account of mental events such as sensations. There seems to be a purely contingent connection between such mental events and their causal antecedents, their behavioral effects, and even behavioral dispositions. And therefore the third-person account, as broadened, still will not do as an analysis of consciousness. [. . .]

Materialism

Materialism is one of the very oldest theories. It was a familiar

2 *Journal of Philosophy* (1966), pp. 17–25.

doctrine to the ancient Greeks of the fourth and fifth centuries
B.C. The spokesman for this view, Democritus, held that nothing
exists but material atoms and the void and that everything in the
world is nothing but the interactions of these atoms as they move
through the void. Even the most complex behavior of human
beings can be resolved into interactions between the atoms. A
modern materialist would allow a more complicated picture than
'atoms and the void.' He would bring in subatomic particles and
antiparticles, electromagnetic waves, a relativized view of 'the
void,' various kinds of forces and energies, and the rest of the
conceptual apparatus of contemporary physics. But he would still
hold that nothing exists but such physical phenomena; if such
terms as 'thought,' 'feeling,' 'wish,' etc., have any meaning at all,
they must refer in the last analysis to physical phenomena. So-
called mental events are really nothing but physical events
occurring to physical objects. [. . .]

The last version of materialism we shall consider, and currently
the most seriously discussed, is known as the identity theory. It
is the theory that thoughts, feelings, wishes, and the rest of so-
called mental phenomena are identical with, one and the same
thing as, states and processes of the *body* (and, perhaps, more
specifically, states and processes of the nervous system, or even of
the brain alone). Thus the having of a thought is identical with
having such and such bodily cells in such and such states, other
cells in other states.

In one respect the identity theory and behaviorism are very
much alike. This comes out when we ask ourselves what the 'dispositions' of the behaviorist are. If an object has a 'disposition,'
then *it is in a particular state* such that when certain things happen
to it, other things will happen to it. Thus if an object is brittle, it
is in a particular state such that when subject to a sudden force it
will shatter. And similarly dispositions of a body to behave in
particular ways are *states of that body*. So it is fair to say that
both identity theorists and behaviorists identify the mental with
bodily states. But one important way in which they differ concerns how those states are to be defined or characterized. As we
have seen, behaviorists wish to define those states in terms of
what changes they result in when certain specifiable conditions
obtain. Identity theorists wish to define them in terms of identifiable structures of the body, ongoing processes and states of the
bodily organs, and, in the last analysis, the very cells which go to
make up those organs.

There is another important respect in which the identity theory differs from behaviorism. The behaviorist offered his notion of dispositions to behave in certain ways as an analysis of the very meaning of mentalistic terms. But the identity theorist grants that it is wildly implausible to claim that what I *mean* when I say, for example, that I just had a particular thought is that certain events were going on in my nervous system. For I have no idea what those events are, nor does even the most advanced neurophysiologist at the present time, and yet I know what I mean when I say I just had a particular thought. So, since I know what I mean by those words, I cannot mean by them something I know nothing about (viz., unknown events in my nervous system). Hence the identity theory is not intended to be an analysis of the *meanings* of mentalistic terms as behaviorism purports to be. What, then, is the theory that mental phenomena are 'identical' with the body intended to be?

The sense of 'identity' relevant here is that in which we say, for example, that the morning star is 'identical' with the evening star. It is not that the expression 'morning star' means the same as the expression 'evening star'; on the contrary, these expressions mean something different. But the object referred to by the two expressions is one and the same; there is just one heavenly body, namely, Venus, which when seen in the morning is called the morning star and when seen in the evening is called the evening star. The morning star is identical with the evening star; they are one and the same object.

Of course, the identity of the mental with the physical is not exactly of this sort, since it is held to be simultaneous identity rather than the identity of a thing at one time with the same thing at a later time. To take a closer example, one can say that lightning is a particularly massive electrical discharge from one cloud to another or to the earth. Not that the word 'lightning' *means* 'a particularly massive electrical discharge . . .'; when Benjamin Franklin discovered that lightning was electrical, he did not make a discovery about the meaning of words. Nor when it was discovered that water was H_2O was a discovery made about the meanings of words; yet water is identical with H_2O.

In a similar fashion, the identity theorist can hold that thoughts, feelings, wishes, and the like are identical with physical states. Not 'identical' in the sense that mentalistic terms are synonymous in meaning with physicalistic terms but 'identical' in the sense that the actual events picked out by mentalistic terms are one and the same events as those picked out by physicalistic terms.

It is important to note that the identity theory does not have a chance of being true unless a particular sort of correspondence obtains between mental events and physical events, namely, that whenever a mental event occurs, a physical event of a particular sort (or at least one of a number of particular sorts) occurs, and vice versa. If it turned out to be the case that when a particular mental event occurred it seemed a matter of chance what physical events occurred or even whether any physical event at all occurred, or vice versa, then the identity theory would not be true. So far as our state of knowledge at the present time is concerned, it is still too early to say what the empirical facts are, although it must be said that many scientists do believe that there exists the kind of correspondences needed by identity theorists. But even if these correspondences turn out to exist, that does not mean that the identity theory will be true. For identity theorists do not hold merely that mental and physical events are correlated in a particular way but that they are one and the same events, i.e., not like lightning and thunder (which are correlated in lawful ways but not identical) but like lightning and electrical discharges (which always go together because they are one and the same).

What are the advantages of the identity theory? As a form of materialism, it does not have to cope with a world which has in it both mental phenomena and physical phenomena, and it does not have to ponder how they might be related. There exist only the physical phenomena, although there do exist two different ways of talking about such phenomena: physicalistic terminology and, in at least some situations, mentalistic terminology. We have here a dualism of language, but not a dualism of entities, events, or properties.

Some difficulties in the identity theory

But do we have merely a dualism of languages and no other sort of dualism? In the case of Venus, we do indeed have only one object, but the expression 'morning star' picks out one phase of that object's history, where it is in the mornings, and the expression 'evening star' picks out another phase of that object's history, where it is in the evenings. If that object did not have these two distinct aspects, it would not have been a *discovery* that the morning star and the evening star were indeed one and the same body, and, further, there would be no point to the different ways of referring to it.

Now it would be admitted by identity theorists that physical-istic and mentalistic terms do not refer to different phases in the history of one and the same object. What sort of identity is intended? Let us turn to an allegedly closer analogy, that of the identity of lightning and a particular sort of electrical pheno-menon. Yet here again we have two distinguishable aspects, the appearance to the naked eye on the one hand and the physical composition on the other. And this is also not the kind of identity which is plausible for mental and physical events. The appearance *to the naked eye* of a neurological event is utterly different from the experience of having a thought or a pain. *So what ?*

It is sometimes suggested that the physical aspect results from looking at a particular event 'from the outside,' whereas the mental results from looking at the same event 'from the inside.' When the brain surgeon observes my brain he is looking at it from the outside, whereas when I experience a mental event I am 'looking' at my brain 'from the inside.'

Such an account gives us only a misleading analogy, rather than an accurate characterization of the relationship between the mental and the physical. The analogy suggests the difference between a man who knows his own house from the inside, in that he is free to move about within, seeing objects from different perspectives, touching them, etc., but can never get outside to see how it looks from there, and a man who cannot get inside and therefore knows only the outside appearance of the house, and perhaps what he can glimpse through the windows. But what does this have to do with the brain? Am I free to roam about inside my brain, observing what the brain surgeon may never see? Is not the 'inner' aspect of my brain far more accessible to the brain surgeon than to me? He has the X rays, probes, electrodes, scalpels, and scissors for getting at the inside of my brain. If it is replied that this is only an analogy, not to be taken literally, then the question still remains how the mental and the physical are related.

Usually identity theorists at this point flee to even vaguer accounts of the relationship. They talk of different 'levels of analysis,' or of different 'perspectives,' or of different 'conceptual schemes,' or of different 'language games.' The point of such suggestions is that the difference between the mental and the physical is not a basic, fundamental, or intrinsic one, but rather a difference which is merely relative to different human purposes or standpoints. The difference is supposed to exist not in the thing itself but in the eye of the beholder.

But these are only hints. They do not tell us in precise and literal terms how the mental and the physical differ and are related. They only try to assure us that the difference does not matter to the real nature of things. But until we are given a theory to consider, we cannot accept the identity theorist's assurance that some theory will do only he does not know what it is.

One of the leading identity theorists, J. J. C. Smart, holds that mentalistic discourse is simply a vaguer, more indefinite way of talking about what could be talked about more precisely by using physiological terms. If I report a red afterimage, I mean (roughly) that something is going on which is like what goes on when I really see a red patch. I do not actually *mean* that a particular sort of brain process is occurring, but when I say something is going on I refer (very vaguely, to be sure) to just that brain process. Thus the thing referred to in my report of an afterimage is a brain process. Hence there is no need to bring in any non-physical features. Thus even the taint of dualism is avoided.

Does this ingenious attempt to evade dualistic implications stand up under philosophical scrutiny? I am inclined to think it will not. Let us return to the man reporting the red afterimage. He was aware of the occurrence of something or other, of some feature or other. Now it seems to me obvious that he was not necessarily aware of the state of his brain at that time (I doubt that most of us are ever aware of the state of our brain) nor, in general, necessarily aware of any physical features of his body at that time. He might, of course, have been incidentally aware of some physical feature but not insofar as he was aware of the red afterimage as such. Yet he was definitely aware of something, or else how could he have made that report? So he must have been aware of some nonphysical feature. That is the only way of explaining how he was aware of anything at all.

Of course, the thing that our reporter of the afterimage was aware of might well have had further features which he was *not* aware of, particularly, in this connection, physical features. I may be aware of certain features of an object without being aware of others. So it is not ruled out that the event our reporter is aware of might be an event with predominantly physical features—he just does not notice those. But he must be aware of some of its features, or else it would not be proper to say he was aware of *that* event. And if he is not aware of any physical features, he must be aware of something else. And that shows that we cannot get rid of those nonphysical features in the way that Smart suggests.

One would not wish to be dogmatic in saying that identity theorists will never work out this part of their theory. Much work is being done on this problem at the present time, for it arises in other areas of philosophy as well as in the philosophy of mind. In particular philosophers of science are concerned with the problem. We saw that the identity theory used such analogies as the identity of lightning with electrical phenomena and the identity of water with molecules consisting of hydrogen and oxygen. But the question to be raised is what kind of identity we are dealing with in such cases. Do we have mere duality of terms in these cases, duality of features, properties, or aspects, or even duality of substances? Very similar issues arise. So it is quite possible that further work on this problem of identity will be useful in clarifying the identity theory of the mental and the physical. But at the present the matter is by no means as clear as it should be.

Even if the identity theorist could clarify the sense of 'identity' to be used in his theory, he would still face two other problems. These concern coexistence in time and space. Coexistence in time and space are conditions that must be met if there is to be identity. That is to say, for two apparently different things to turn out to be one and the same, they must exist at the same time and in the same location. If we could show that Mr. A existed at a time when Mr. B did not, or that Mr. A existed in a place where Mr. B did not, then this would show that Mr. A and Mr. B were different men. It is by virtue of these facts about identity that an alibi can exonerate a suspect: if Mr. A was not in Chicago at the time, then he could not be one and the same with the man who stole the diamonds in Chicago.

So if mental events are to be identical with physical events, then they must fulfill the conditions of coexistence in time and space. The question is, Do they?

So far as coexistence in time is concerned, very little is known. The most relevant work consists in direct stimulation of an exposed part of the brain during surgery. Since only a local anesthetic is necessary in many such cases the patient may well be fully conscious. Then, as the surgeon stimulates different parts of his brain, the patient may report the occurrence of mental events—

memories, thoughts, sensations. Do the physical events in the brain and the mental events occur at precisely the same time? It is impossible to say. All that would be required is a very small time gap to prove that the physical events were not identical with the mental events. But it is very difficult to see how the existence of so small a time gap could be established. And even if it were, what would it prove? Only that the mental event was not identical with just that physical event; it would not prove it was non-identical with any physical event. So it could well be that co-existence in time is present or is not. I do not think that we shall get much decisive information from empirical work of the sort here described. The identity theorist, then, does not have to fear refutation from this quarter, at least not for a long time.

How about coexistence in space? Do mental events occur in the same place the corresponding physical events occur? This is also a very difficult question to answer, for two reasons. First our present ignorance of neurophysiology, especially concerning the brain and how it functions, allows us to say very little about the location of the relevant physical events. This much does seem likely: they are located in the brain. Much more than that we do not at present know, although as the time passes, we should learn much more. The second reason for our difficulty in telling if there is coexistence in space has to do with the location of mental events. Where do thoughts, feelings, and wishes occur? Do they occur in the brain? Suppose you suddenly have the thought that it is almost supper-time; where does that occur? The most sensible answer would be that it occurs wherever you are when you have that thought. If you are in the library when you have that thought, then the thought occurs in the library. But it would be utterly unnatural to ask where inside your body the thought occurred; in your foot, or your liver, or your heart, or your head? It is not that any one of these places is more likely than another. They are all wrong. Not because thoughts occur somewhere *else* within your body than your foot, liver, heart, or head—but because it *makes no sense at all* to locate the occurrence of a thought at some place within your body. We would not understand someone who pointed to a place in his body and claimed that it was *there* that his entertaining of a thought was located. Certainly, if one *looked* at that place, one would not *see* anything resembling a thought. If it were replied to this that pains can be located in the body without being seen there, then it should be pointed out that one *feels* the pain there but one hardly feels a thought in the body.

The fact that it makes no sense at all to speak of mental events as occurring at some point within the body has the result that the identity theory cannot be true. This is because the corresponding physical events do occur at some point within the body, and if those physical events are identical with mental events, then those mental events must occur at the same point within the body. But those mental events do not occur at any point within the body, because any statement to the effect that they occurred here, or there, would be senseless. Hence the mental events cannot meet the condition of coexistence in space, and therefore cannot be identical with physical events.

Our inability to give the location within the body of mental events is different from our inability to give the location of the corresponding physical events within the body. In the latter case, it is that we do not know enough about the body, particularly the brain. Some day, presumably, we will know enough to pin down pretty exactly the location of the relevant physical events. But in the case of mental events it is not simply that at present we are ignorant but that someday we may well know. What would it be like to discover the location of a thought in the brain? What kind of information would we need to be able to say that the thought occurred exactly *here*? If by X rays or some other means we were able to see every event which occurred in the brain, we would never get a glimpse of a thought. If, to resort to fantasy, we could so enlarge a brain or so shrink ourselves that we could wander freely through the brain, we would still never observe a thought. All we could ever observe in the brain would be the *physical* events which occur in it. If mental events had location in the brain, there should be some means of detecting them there. But of course there is none. The very idea of it is senseless.

Some identity theorists believe this objection can be met. One approach is to reply that this objection begs the question: if the identity theory is true, and mental events are identical with brain events, then, paradoxical as it may sound, mental events do indeed have location, and are located precisely where the physical events are located. Another approach is to reply that the relevant physical events should be construed as events which happen to the body as a whole, and therefore occur where the body as a whole is located; then it is not so paradoxical to give location to the mental events, for they would be located where the body is located but would not be located in any particular part of the body. [. . .]

Dualistic theories

It would seem to be a familiar fact that states of consciousness can be produced, eliminated, or modified by physical changes. (We will soon see that this apparently 'familiar fact' is open to various interpretations.) Consider visual phenomena. By covering the eyes we can eliminate or at least sharply curtail visual content, and by uncovering them we can restore it. We can cause ourselves to see double by pushing at the hollow under the eye. We can produce spots before the eyes or afterimages by looking at certain things for certain lengths of time. Illnesses like jaundice make things look different, i.e., yellowish. We know that flashes of light may be seen when we bump our heads severely or suffer a migraine attack or an epileptic seizure. Marijuana and mescaline may make things look as if they were glowing or moving, and whiskey may make it look as if the bugs were crawling up our legs again. Similar examples of physical causation can be cited for other states of consciousness, such as having sensations, emotional feelings, thoughts, images, etc. It would seem to be a familiar fact, then, that physical phenomena can affect mental phenomena.

It would also seem to be a familiar fact that mental phenomena can affect the physical world in various ways. My feeling of great terror may cause me to turn ashen, tremble, or fall down in a faint. My having the thought that it is too dark to read may lead me to turn on the lights. My 'seeing bugs' may cause me to scream. My decision to start a fire may lead to the destruction of the whole city.

These, then, are apparently familiar facts which indicate an intimate relation between consciousness and physical phenomena. Since the physical phenomena most directly relevant are states and changes in the *body* (it is through our bodies that external physical phenomena affect our consciousness and it affects them), we can ignore the physical changes in the rest of the world and confine our attention to the relation between consciousness and the *body*.

The most obvious theory to describe the 'facts' as we have stated them is known as psychophysical interactionism. It holds that (1) states of consciousness can be causally affected by states of the body and (2) states of the body can be causally affected by states of consciousness; thus the mind and the body can interact.

The paragraphs above contain respective illustrations of the two kinds of causal action.

Why have we hedged by speaking of 'apparently familiar facts'? Because it is not absolutely clear that the facts are as we have stated them. Consider the 'fact' that we can affect visual experience by covering the eyes. What do we really know in such cases? We know that when the eyes get covered, visual content becomes curtailed, and that when the covering is removed, visual content is restored. In other words, we know that there is a *correlation* between covering the eyes and curtailing visual content. Similarly for the second set of 'facts' above, such as that my feeling of terror causes me to turn ashen. We know that when a person feels great terror, certain physical changes like turning ashen, trembling, or falling down in a faint are often correlated with it. In general we know that usually or always, depending upon the case, a particular state of consciousness is correlated with a particular physical state. But do we know any more than that? Do we know that one is the *cause* of the other?

There are two main rivals to interactionism, and each proposes a somewhat different interpretation of the 'facts.' Psychophysical parallelism accepts the fact of correlation but denies that there is any direct causal action between the mental and the physical; there is *mere* correlation. The following analogy is often proposed: if there were two clocks, each keeping perfect time, then each state of the one would always be *correlated* with a corresponding state of the other, but neither would in any way *cause* the other.

The other rival to interactionism is epiphenomenalism, the theory that there is a causal connection, but that it goes one way, from the physical to the mental but not from the mental to the physical. Mental states and events, on this theory, are nothing but by-products or side-effects of physical processes and themselves can have no effect on those physical processes. Physical phenomena are like the fingers moving in front of a light source and mental phenomena are like the shadows cast on the wall, produced by the moving fingers but unable to affect those fingers in any way.

Why have some philosophers turned to one of these rather curious theories rather than accept at face value the apparent fact of interaction? We will consider each of these alternative theories in turn.

Parallelism

Proponents of parallelism have refused to allow that there could be a *causal* connection between events which differ so radically in type. So they theorize that there is the kind of *correlation without direct causal connection* which we have in the case of the two perfect clocks. At the heart of this issue is the concept of *cause.* It would be nice if we could start off by giving a definition of 'cause' and proceed from there, but there does not exist at present an adequate definition of that term. David Hume claimed that constant conjunction was *all* there was, objectively speaking, but that does not seem adequate, as the example of the two clocks shows. In that example we can distinguish between the constant (but *accidental*) correlation of the various phases of the *two* clocks and the constant (but *causally* connected) correlation of the successive phases in *each individual* clock. And the parallelist himself, like his rival theorists, accepts the distinction between constant correlation and causal connection; he allows causal connection between successive physical events and between successive mental events, although he rejects causal connection between physical and mental events.

Some philosophers, following a further suggestion of Hume's, hold that the cause must be at least a necessary condition. This idea can be expressed negatively and counterfactually as follows: 'If the first object had not been, the second never had existed' either.[3] But this is refuted by the existence of 'back-up systems' which ensure that if a result is not brought about in one way then the same result will be brought about in another way; a simple example of this is leaving your car on a downhill slope in 'Park' with the emergency brake on and with the front wheels jammed against the curb. In such cases, if the actual cause had not existed, the same result would still have been brought about. So the cause is not a necessary condition for the effect.

The best we can say is that to call one event the cause of the other is to say that the first is a *sufficient* condition for the second, in the sense that if the former occurs, then, given the circumstances, the latter *must* occur. But such an account does not get us anywhere, for we would still have to say what kind of 'must' is involved here. It is obviously not the logical 'must,' which states

[3] David Hume, *An Inquiry Concerning Human Understanding,* Sec. 7, Pt. 2.

that the occurrence of the former logically entails the occurrence of the latter. The most that can be said is that it is the causal 'must,' which brings us back to where we began. And that is pretty much where the analysis of causality is at the present time.

At any rate, proponents of parallelism accept the concept of causality. They allow that there is causal connection between bodily events, so that a bodily event like a cut on the hand could produce another *bodily* state, for example, stimulation in the nerves leading from the hand to the brain. And they allow that one *mental* event, say, feeling a sharp pain, could affect another *mental* event, say, the thought that I'd better do something about that pain. But they deny that a *physical* event like the stimulation of certain nerves, a public matter of electrochemical occurrences in tiny cells, could produce a *mental* event like a sensation of pain, private to the individual concerned and utterly different in character from electrochemical cellular phenomena. And similarly, they deny that a mental event like a sensation of pain could produce an electrochemical change in cells. The events in question are so utterly dissimilar, they argue, that it is inconceivable that events of one type should produce events of the other type.

It might be thought that the present difference in kind between the mental and physical will be closed by future physiological or psychological discoveries of some sort of 'bridge' between the mental and the physical. But it must be admitted that that is a pipe dream. All that we can expect from future research is a more precise determination of the mental and physical events involved. We will still be left with the basic difference in type between some sort of mental event on the one hand and some sort of physical event on the other. And that would still leave us with the problem how such different sorts of events could affect each other.

The hypothesis of psychophysical parallelism presents rather considerable problems of its own, however. The situation with respect to the two clocks, the basic analogy of parallelism, is clear enough; each clock has its own internal mechanism which accounts for its own successive states, and the perfection of each mechanism keeps the two always in phase. But the situation in the case of mind and body does not seem analogous. For while there may be a way of accounting for the various succeeding states of the body in purely physical terms, there does not seem to be a way of accounting for the various succeeding states of the mind in purely mental terms. Consider a person asleep who is

awakened by a fire alarm. His mind is suddenly filled with a wailing, clamorous noise. Now if the parallelist is right, the occurrence
of that mental event, the hearing of the noise, can be explained
simply within the realm of mental events, by some prior mental
event. But surely hearing that wailing noise cannot be explained
simply by appealing to some prior mental state or event. The only
obvious candidate for the prior cause of the hearing is the ringing
of the alarm, and that is ruled out as a cause on the parallelist
thesis. So all that the parallelist can say of this case is that when
the alarm rings, then at the same time there just happens to be
the accompanying mental event of the hearing of the alarm and
that this is a mere correlation without causal connection. But then
it is *completely inexplicable* why that correlation should occur,
whereas in the case of the two clocks it was entirely explicable
why the correlations should occur. So the analogy breaks down
here. The mental does not comprise a self-enclosed and causally
self-sufficient system in the way that each clock in the analogy
does. Therefore on the parallelist theory the undeniable fact of
correlation of mental and physical is left completely miraculous
and inexplicable.

In attempting to deal with this difficulty, the French seventeenth century philosopher Malebranche introduced a theory
(called occasionalism) to the effect that, on the occasion when the
alarm rings, *God* produces in the mind the hearing of the alarm.
But this desperate attempt to explain the correlation of mental
and physical without resorting to direct causal action between
them has never appealed to the modern mind. There is not much
difference between saying that the correlation which exists between the ringing of the alarm and the hearing of that ringing is
totally inexplicable and saying that the correlation is miraculously
produced by the action of the divine will.

Why does the parallelist resist what seems to be so obvious a
conclusion, namely that the ringing *causes* the hearing? Because
the events involved are so utterly different in their natures. But
what is the source of this resistance? After all, are there not many
cases in which the cause and effect differ utterly? Consider a very
cold piece of ice which is gradually heated, so that we eventually
turn it from ice to a liquid to a gas. Here we have the *same* cause
throughout the application of heat. First we have the effect that
the ice melts into water; then that the water increases in temperature; then that the water begins to boil; then that the water
begins to vaporize; and then that the vapor increases in

temperature. How utterly different these effects are one from the other and how utterly different each is from the cause! Yet it would be rash indeed to say that there can be no causal connection, only correlation, because the alleged cause and effects are so different from each other. Cause and effect are where we find them, and it would be in violation of the principles of scientific reasoning if we rejected some apparent causal connections on the a priori ground that the events were 'too different' to be causally connected.

Why might a person be inclined to think that the difference in type between mental events and physical events would rule out a causal connection? One possible source of this inclination is the feeling that there should be some sort of *intelligible connection* between the cause and the effect, that one should be able to discern in the cause the coming of the effect, that the effect should be contained in the cause in some way and should emerge forth from the cause. This feeling is strongly present in Spinoza, a classic case of a philosopher who denied the possibility of interaction between the mental and the physical. He held that the effect follows from the cause in the way that the propositions in a geometrical system follow from the definitions and axioms and therefore that 'if two things have nothing in common with one another, one cannot be the cause of the other.'[4] On such reasoning it becomes plausible to hold that the mental and physical cannot causally affect each other.

It was Hume who pointed out with such force that this picture of causality is incorrect. He maintained that no scrutiny of the cause, no matter how searching, would tell us prior to experience what the effect would be. It is only by waiting to see what happens that we can determine what causes give rise to what effects. After a suitable amount of experience we may be able to infer from the existence of a particular event that it will have a particular effect, but such an inference is based merely on the knowledge that in the past the two have been correlated. And if events of two kinds have been correlated in the past, then it becomes likely that they are causally related, no matter how different in character they may be. [...]

---

[4] *Ethics*, Part I, Prop. III.

so he is an interactionist

Epiphenomenalism

The epiphenomenalist holds that there is a causal connection between the mental and the physical but that it only goes in one direction, from the physical to the mental, so that mental events always are the *effects* of physical changes and never are *causes* of physical changes. Mental events are, as it were, a shadow cast by physical processes and incapable of affecting those physical processes. The epiphenomenalist accepts the first set of familiar facts indicated at the beginning of this chapter, an example of which is that we can causally affect visual content by a physical change like covering the eyes. But he rejects what seems to be an equally familiar set of facts in which mental events causally affect the physical. Why?

The epiphenomenalist believes that a consideration of the development of the physical sciences will show a steady increase in the number of physical phenomena which can be explained in purely physical terms. In case after case, the postulation of nonphysical causes of physical phenomena has proved fruitless, whereas the postulation of physical causes has yielded important results. We no longer believe that immaterial spirits affect the weather, the productivity of crops, or animal fertility; we can explain these in purely physical terms. We have found that kinds of abnormal behavior, e.g., epileptic seizures, are caused by brain malfunctioning; we no longer need appeal to possession by demons. And ghosts, poltergeists, and other spirits no longer play the role they used to in explanation of physical phenomena. It is not an unreasonable extrapolation to postulate that the *whole* of physical phenomena is, in the end, explicable in purely physical terms. This seems to be the direction in which science is moving. We may never come to the time when we can, in fact, explain everything in purely physical terms, but, argues the epiphenomenalist, there is no reason to think that there is some nonphysical agency which must be postulated to explain any physical phenomena. And the whole history of science goes against such postulations.

But what does the epiphenomenalist make of the apparently familiar cases in which the mental seems to affect the physical? A man cuts his hand and the feeling of pain, we are inclined to say, causes him to wince. For the epiphenomenalist what really happens is this. The cut produces a series of events in the nerves which lead to his brain, resulting in the occurrence of a *brain state* which causes the physical movement we call a wince. That brain state also causes the sensation we call the feeling of pain; the sensation is merely a *by-product* of a chain of physical events, which starts with the cut and ends with the wince; in itself the sensation has no effect on any part of the series. Similarly for my thought that it is too dark to read, which ostensibly causes me to turn on the light. It is a mere by-product of a purely physical causal sequence which starts with a particular physical stimulation of my sense organs, produces a particular brain state, and results in my hand moving out and turning on the light; the thought itself has no effects on the sequence of physical events. It is an *illusion* that mental events have effects, just as it is an illusion that the moving hands of a clock cause the clock to strike the hour.

The paradox of epiphenomenalism

If it is only an *illusion* that mental events have effects, then human affairs must be conceived quite differently from the way they are ordinarily conceived. Historians like to attribute events to human decisions, emotions, thoughts, and sensations. All of that would be in error on this theory. And our ordinary, everyday explanations of human behavior in those terms would also be in error. The epiphenomenalist would have us believe that the Pyramids and the Empire State Building were erected without the aid of a single thought, that the greatest works of art were created without the effect of a single feeling, that wars have been declared and nuclear weapons employed, but not as the result of a single human deliberation or decision. Since his view is that mental events have no consequences, the epiphenomenalist would have us believe that the whole of human history would have developed in just the way that it did even if there had never been a single thought, feeling, sensation, decision, or other mental event. Everything would have gone on just the same, even if *everyone had always been completely unconscious.* Even our language, with all its mentalistic expressions, would have existed, and, most astonishing of all, all the verbal interchanges which represent our discussions about the very existence and nature of mental events would have occurred. If there had never been a mental event, men still would have believed in their existence, or

if belief itself is a mental phenomenon, men still would have
spoken and acted as if there were mental events!

Many philosophers have found these paradoxical implications
of epiphenomenalism too incredible to accept. Yet they must be
accepted if epiphenomenalism is correct. For, on that theory,
mental events themselves have no consequences, produce no
effects, and nothing else would have been different if they had
never occurred. They are, in the words of a twentieth century
epiphenomenalist, George Santayana, 'a lyric cry in the midst of
business' and a cry which could in no way affect the course of
business.

In all fairness to the epiphenomenalist position, it must be
pointed out that the theory is not quite so incredible as it appears;
the appearance of wild paradox can be to some degree dissipated.
When the epiphenomenalist says that all would have gone on in
exactly the same way even if no man had ever been conscious, he
is not suggesting that the Pyramids could have been built by men
in their sleep, or in deep comas, or in profound swoons, or with
vacant stares. And when he says that they could have done these
things without thoughts, feelings, decisions, etc., he is not suggesting that they did them impulsively, numbly, or at random. We
must picture men moving skillfully about, poring over plans,
scratching their heads or resting them on their hands, gesticulat-
ing animatedly—in short, men behaving with the full range of
that behavior which is typical of consciousness. What any
observer would see if he were to witness the scene would be
exactly the same as what he would see in the actual case where
men do have mental events. The only thing left out would be the
mental events. And since they are private and invisible, their
absence would never be noticed. So we are not envisioning anything so paradoxical after all.

If we concluded that epiphenomenalism is true, would we have
to stop saying such things as 'The pain made him scream' or 'He
screamed from the pain,' remarks which appear pointedly inter-
actionistic? It might be argued that we could continue truthfully
to say such things, understanding them to mean the same as the
more theoretically neutral remark, *'He screamed with pain.'* After
all, a sympathizer might argue, we still say 'The sun set at 6 p.m.,'
even if we no longer accept the Ptolemaic view that the sun
moves around the earth. But I think it would be a mistake to
argue in this way. For 'The sun set at 6 p.m.' is *genuinely neutral*
between astronomical theories; it simply describes the vanishing

of the sun from view, and does not commit one to an explanation of that vanishing by virtue of the relative movement of the earth and the sun or the rotational movement of the earth upon its axis. But 'The pain made him scream' is not neutral in the same way. It says clearly and explicitly that the feeling causes the behavior. And if epiphenomenalism turns out to be true, then this expression of ordinary language is simply false; plain men might continue to use it but they would always be wrong when they did.

Psychophysical interactionism

How does epiphenomenalism compare with its primary rival, interactionism? Interactionism agrees with epiphenomenalism in holding that physical occurrences can have mental effects, but goes beyond it by holding in addition that *mental occurrences can have physical effects*. Thus the interactionist accepts as genuine fact the apparent facts cited [*see above*, page 14]; it thereby comes closest to the commonsense view of the man in the street (and that is neither in its favor nor against it). But we have seen that these 'facts' which seem to establish interaction are actually open to either an epiphenomenalist or interactionist interpretation.

In trying to decide between these two theories the crucial question to be determined is whether mental events ever have effects. Now, there is a difficulty which arises in trying to answer that question which does *not* arise when we try to determine whether *physical* events can have mental effects. We can, by experiment, introduce an exclusively physical change and see whether it has mental effects or not. For example, we can ring a bell and determine that the ringing affects a person's body and subsequently produces the mental event which consists in the person's hearing the bell. We can show beyond a reasonable doubt that both the physical bodily effects and the mental effects were caused by the physical event of ringing the bell. And thus we can answer conclusively by experiment the question whether physical events can have mental effects. But whether mental events can be causes and have effects is more difficult to determine. It would be easy if we could introduce an exclusively mental change and see whether it has effects; if this exclusively mental change were followed by events which could be explained only by appeal to that mental change, then that would show that mental events can be causes. But, unfortunately, we cannot set up an experimental situation in which it is clear that we have produced an exclusively mental change. The only mental events we can experimentally manipulate are those of creatures having complex and ever active nervous systems. Any mental change will be accompanied by innumerable concomitant physical changes in the nervous system. So even if the mental change were followed by some other event it would always be open to the epiphenomenalist to say that the subsequent event had been produced not by the mental event but by some *physical* event concomitant with that mental event. For example, suppose we produce the consciousness of pain which is followed by a wince; how could it be known that it was the *mental* event of feeling pain rather than the brain events concomitant with the consciousness of pain which produced the wince? [. . .]

Source: Jerome Shaffer, *Philosophy of Mind* (Prentice-Hall), Chs. 2, 3 and 4. (Extracts.)

2 Machines and the Mind–Body Problem (1965)

JEROME SHAFFER

In recent times much attention has been devoted to the very close analogy between the workings of the mind and the workings of certain sorts of mechanical devices. Two sorts of mechanical devices have been especially important: servomechanisms and computers. Servomechanisms can achieve and maintain some predetermined state by use of feedback; here we have something very similar to purposeful human behavior. Computers can start with a set of characters and finish with a new set of characters by performing sequences of operations; here we have something very similar to human reasoning. And in purposeful behavior and reasoning we have features which have been traditionally taken to be at the very heart of the mental. So it has been argued by many that the solution to the mind–body problem is to be found in the consideration of such machines. [. . .]

A. M. Turing raised the following question: Could there be, in theory, a computer which would so answer questions put to it that the answers would be indistinguishable from those a man would give?[1] Here the criterion concerns not the origin, composition, or design of the machine but its capacities, or, if you like, its behavior, or, if you wish to be very strict, its 'output.'

Much of the discussion in recent times has concerned the question whether there are any discernible differences in the output of humans and possible machines. One stumbling block has been that many descriptions of human activities make no sense at all when applied to nonliving systems, e.g., giggling. Probably most of the expressions currently used to describe the output of machines, 'computing,' 'receiving information,' 'remembering,' 'adding and subtracting,' 'making deductions,' 'playing chess,' 'writing checks,' etc., involve a shift of meaning when applied to machines. But it is a perfectly natural shift in these cases (whereas I find it difficult to imagine a computer contemplated at present which might be intelligibly said to be able to giggle). As Turing pointed out with reference to the applicability of the word, 'think,' to computers:

> The original question 'Can machines think?' I believe to be too meaningless to deserve discussion. Nevertheless I believe that at the end of the century the use of words and general educated opinion will have altered so much that one will be able to speak of machines thinking without expecting to be contradicted.[2]

So far as machine performance is concerned, there have been extraordinary achievements in the last decade. Engineers report that 'at present, we have or are currently developing, machines that prove theorems, play games with sufficient skill to beat their inventors, recognize spoken words, translate text from one language to another, speak, read, write music, and learn to improve their own performance when given training.'[3]

Have we reached the point yet where the answers a machine would give to questions put to it would be indistinguishable from human answers? Turing's question has already prompted some

---

[1] 'Computing Machinery and Intelligence,' *Mind* 1950, pp. 433–60.

[2] *Ibid.*, p. 442.

[3] T. Marill, 'Human Factors in Electronics,' *Transactions of the Institute of Radio Engineers*, 1961.

empirical testing. For example, a machine has been programmed which will conduct an intelligent conversation about the weather.[4] The machine program is comparatively small, containing about 800 instructions; yet the machine replies to most remarks or questions about the weather appropriately and intelligently. Occasionally, but surprisingly infrequently, the machine generates replies that do not make sense. An experiment was performed to see how close the computer came to simulating ordinary conversation.[5] Twenty-five comments and questions taken more or less at random from a large number of actual conversations about the weather were fed into the machine. The reply of the machine to each comment was mixed with the responses of nine ordinary people to the comment and a different group of people was asked to judge which of the ten replies to each comment was produced by the computer. If they had been just guessing at random they would have gotten 10 per cent right. Actually they got 16.8 per cent right. This indicates that most of the responses of the machine were indistinguishable from those generated by intelligent humans. And it would not have been difficult to add to the program so as to improve the performance of the machine.

Conversations about the weather do not require *very much* intelligence (hence their frequency), but we do see here the possibility of constructing programs for conducting more profound conversations. It is such achievements as this which lead many experts today to think that in a few years it will be possible to construct a machine such that 'it will be impossible for a human being in another room to tell whether he is conversing with a computer or with a human being.'[6] This was what Turing was inclined to say,[7] and many contemporary philosophers would agree with this.[8]

---

[4] See Edmund C. Berkeley: *The Computer Revolution* (New York, 1962), pp. 87–110.

[5] The experiment was carried out by Patrick J. McGovern and reported in *Computers and Automation*, Sept. 1960.

[6] Edmund C. Berkeley, *ibid.*, p. 110.

[7] A. C. Turing, *op. cit.*, p. 442.

[8] The following articles support this contention: D. M. MacKay, 'Mindlike Behavior in Artifacts,' *British Journal for the Philosophy of Science*, vol. 2 (1951), pp. 105–21; W. Ross Ashby, 'Can a Mechanical Chess-Player Outplay Its Designer?' *ibid.*, vol. 3 (1952), pp. 44–57; D. M. MacKay, 'Mentality in Machines, III,' *Proceedings of the Aristotelian Society, Supplementary Volume XXVI* (1952), pp. 61–86; Michael Scriven, 'The Compleat Robot,' *Dimensions of Mind (op. cit.)*, pp. 113–33; Hilary Putnam, 'Minds and Machines,' *ibid.*, pp. 138–64.

How about emotions and motives? Many have argued that it is in this area that the crucial differences are to be found:

> People get bored; they drop one task and pick up another, or they may just quit work for a while. Not so the computer program; it continues indomitably.[9]

But if we remember that at this point in our discussion we are concerned only with machine *output*, with answers to questions that are put to the machine, then it is reasonable to think that machines, can be programmed to exhibit boredom, restlessness, shifts in attention, sulkiness, rage, etc.[10] Could a machine make jokes? Here one seems to come to something so characteristically human that it is hard to imagine a machine able to do it. But this arises, I think, from the fact that we do not understand very well what humor is. If machines can write tolerable poetry and compose tolerable music, why should they not be able to make jokes also? But could a machine *enjoy* poetry or jokes? Could it *feel* boredom or rage? With these questions we go beyond the Turing formulation in terms of *output* to questions of internal states. [. . .]

The Machine and Mental Events

If performance were the logically decisive factor in determining whether something did or did not have a mind or consciousness, then there would be little question that, in theory at least, we could build machines with consciousness. There would still be important differences, to be sure, certainly in origin and composition and probably in design. But such differences are not relevant to whether something was an intelligent or purposive performance. When we say that something was done intelligently or stupidly, on purpose or by accident, we do not commit ourselves to what the immediate origin of the thing was or what it was composed of or what its internal structure was. So if output were all that mattered, there would be no difference in principle between man and machine.

However, there is a further item of crucial importance, *mental events*. Could machines have sensations, feelings, or thoughts?

[9] Ulric Neisser, 'The Imitation of Man by Machine,' *Science*, vol. 139 (1963), p. 194.

[10] See Silvan S. Tomkins and Samuel Messick, *Computer Simulation of Personality* (New York, 1963).

Could a machine feel an ache or a smart; could it feel remorseful, proud, or angry; could it suddenly dawn on a machine that . . . or could a machine have the experience of realizing that . . . ?

Of course a machine could be programmed to *simulate* the having of mental events. It could print out reports on its inner condition ('Tube 37541 just blew out') or its progress in solving a problem ('Just thought up a well-formed formula which is neither an axiom nor an already proven theorem.'). Or it might be programmed to print out such reports only on demand; otherwise it would keep its internal state to itself. Still, this is only simulation, only similarity of *output*. The question would remain whether the machine actually had feelings and thoughts in the sense in which we do.

It is tempting to look for some well-known feature of the machine and *identify* that with mental events, so that it becomes obvious that machines have mental events. Hilary Putnam argues that mental states in the machine are identical with what he calls the 'logical states' of the machine.[11] Any machine is composed of various pieces of hardware, and as it operates the hardware goes through a succession of states; Putnam calls them 'structural states.' But the machine is also going through a succession of states in another sense. Its operations can be described in an abstract, logical way; the machine table or program gives such a description. Symbols in various locations may be replaced by symbols from other locations and in this way a sum may be worked out. Physically any number of structural states may serve to realize this logical operation. Putnam argues that the mind-body problem in the machine is simply the problem of the relation of the logical states to the structural states of that machine.

Illuminating as this is, it does not remove our further question whether machines have mental events. We can see this plainly if we apply Putnam's distinction to a human being, solving an arithmetic problem at the blackboard, for example. The structural states will be physical states of his body (and, in this case, the resulting changes on the blackboard, etc.). The logical states will be the adding, subtracting, etc., and the sub-operations which they require, carrying certain numbers from one column to another, moving decimal points, etc. All of these logical states could be specified in such a way that a machine or person could work out the problem by 'mechanically' following the steps. However, there would still be the question: What *mental events*

11 Hilary Putnam, 'Minds and Machines,' *op. cit.*

occurred? Did the person doing the sum have any thoughts while doing it? Perhaps, if very practiced, he had no thoughts at all as he worked out the problem. Perhaps he was thinking what a boring problem it was. Perhaps he was thinking the rules ('carry the three,' 'drop the decimal point,' etc.) as he did the operation. So in addition to Putnam's 'structural' and 'logical' operations there could also occur mental operations, in the sense in which I have been talking of mental events. Our question, so far as machines are concerned, is precisely whether there might not be these additional mental events.

Some philosophers have tried to dismiss such questions as meaningless, but it seems to me that they are quite meaningful. If you are inclined to think that it is a contradiction to speak of a *machine* having feelings or thoughts, then we can reformulate the question to ask whether there might be things just like people in all respects except that they were made in the electronics laboratory. Imagine computers getting better and better at more and more, as theory and technology improve, until (in principle at least) they behave just like people. Might they not have mental events then too? Could not an extremely complex organization of transistors, tapes, magnetic cores, photo-electric cells, etc., turn out to have sensations, feelings, and thoughts just like ours? Is this not a real possibility? Some are inclined to rule this out:

> A machine made out of vacuum tubes, diodes, and transistors cannot be expected to have consciousness. I do not here offer a proof for this statement, except that it is obvious according to well-disciplined common sense.[12]

But I know of no argument to show this.

The crucial question is how we could tell. Here we have the Other Minds problem with a vengeance. So far as behavior is concerned, our contemplated machine's output matches that of a human. However, its constituents and design are utterly different from that of a human. Does it have mental events or not? If it does, we now have the analog of the mind-body problem, the mind-machine problem: How are the mental events related to the machine? Are they mere concomitants, or mere by-products, or able to produce changes in the machine? We have exactly the same possibilities as in the traditional mind-body problem, and

[12] Satosi Watanabe, 'Comments on Key Issues,' *Dimensions of Mind (op. cit.)*, p. 136.

the same considerations are relevant in both cases. For example,
[...] suppose it turns out that our machine occasionally comes
up with solutions to problems and we cannot explain in terms of
machine mechanics how it came up with these solutions, but we
can explain if we hypothesize causally efficacious nonphysical
events. Could it not happen that in the case of certain sorts of
problems the machine idles for a while and then suddenly starts
printing out a solution? We might say there was a mechanical
explanation which we had not yet found or we might say that
there was a randomness in the machine which resulted in a lucky
outcome. But might we not also speculate that the machine had
had insightful thoughts which produced the solution? Might
there not be circumstances such that this speculation would offer
the best explanation?

Since there is no difference in principle between the mind-body
problem and the mind-machine problem, we shall postpone discussion of these issues. [...] The relevant question here is still
how we could tell whether machines have mental events at all. I
shall discuss only one recent attempt to answer this, the ingenious
suggestion of Michael Scriven that we so design our computer so
that it cannot tell lies and then simply *ask* it if it has mental
events. The problem is how to put our question to the machine.
This is done by feeding into the machine both our ordinary language of mental predication and also behaviorist language so that
it can distinguish as well as we can between a person's being in
pain as opposed to merely behaving as if he were. Then:

> having equipped it with all the performatory abilities of
> humans, fed into its banks the complete works of great poets,
> novelists, philosophers, and psychologists, we now ask it
> whether it has feelings. And it tells us the truth since it can do
> no other.[13]

The trouble with this is that it begs the question by assuming
that the machine will understand the question in the sense we
intend. Might it not take the distinction between having a mental
event and merely acting as if one did as the distinction between
two sorts of behavior, the former more consistent and extensive
and the latter less consistent or extensive? That would not be *our*
concept. Our concept involves more than a certain sort of behavior; to understand the more involved requires having had the

---

[13] Michael Scriven, *op. cit.*, p. 132.

experience itself, or an analogous one at least. So whether the machine understands our question in our sense or not itself depends upon the prior question whether it has feelings itself. If it has not had feelings then it does not even understand what *we* mean when we ask it if it has feelings. The real question is whether the machine could understand our question. Scriven's reply to objections of this sort is that 'we have every good reason for thinking that it does understand, as we have for thinking this of other *people*.' But this is not true since machines would have the further differences from people of origin, composition, and, perhaps, design. And these differences make the Other Minds inference much tougher in the case of machines. [. . .]

Source: 'Recent work on the Mind-Body Problem', *American Philosophical Quarterly*, 1965. (Extract.)

3 The Argument from Analogy (1948)

BERTRAND RUSSELL

The postulates hitherto considered have been such as are required for knowledge of the physical world. Broadly speaking, they have led us to admit a certain degree of knowledge as to the space-time structure of the physical world, while leaving us completely agnostic as regards its qualitative character. But where other human beings are concerned, we feel that we know more than this; we are convinced that other people have thoughts and feelings that are qualitatively fairly similar to our own. We are not content to think that we know only the space-time structure of our friends' minds, or their capacity for initiating causal chains that end in sensations of our own. A philosopher might pretend to think that he knew only this, but let him get cross with his wife and you will see that he does not regard her as a mere spatio-temporal edifice of which he knows the logical properties but not a glimmer of the intrinsic character. We are therefore justified in inferring that his scepticism is professional rather than sincere.

The problem with which we are concerned is the following. We observe in ourselves such occurrences as remembering, reasoning, feeling pleasure and feeling pain. We think that stocks and stones do not have these experiences, but that other people do. Most of us have no doubt that the higher animals feel pleasure and pain, though I was once assured by a fisherman that 'fishes have no sense nor feeling'. I failed to find out how he had acquired this knowledge. Most people would disagree with him, but would be doubtful about oysters and starfish. However this may be, common sense admits an increasing doubtfulness as we descend in the animal kingdom, but as regards human beings it admits no doubt.

It is clear that belief in the minds of others requires some postulate that is not required in physics, since physics can be content with a knowledge of structure. My present purpose is to suggest what this further postulate may be.

It is clear that we must appeal to something that may be vaguely called 'analogy'. The behaviour of other people is in many ways analogous to our own, and we suppose that it must have analogous causes. What people say is what we should say if we had certain thoughts, and so we infer that they probably have these thoughts. They give us information which we can sometimes subsequently verify. They behave in ways in which we behave when we are pleased (or displeased) in circumstances in which we should be pleased (or displeased). We may talk over with a friend some incident which we have both experienced, and find that his reminiscences dovetail with our own; this is particularly convincing when he remembers something that we have forgotten but that he recalls to our thoughts. Or again: you set your boy a problem in arithmetic, and with luck he gets the right answer; this persuades you that he is capable of arithmetical reasoning. There are, in short, very many ways in which my responses to stimuli differ from those of 'dead' matter, and in all these ways other people resemble me. As it is clear to me that the causal laws governing my behaviour have to do with 'thoughts', it is natural to infer that the same is true of the analogous behaviour of my friends.

The inference with which we are at present concerned is not merely that which takes us beyond solipsism, by maintaining that sensations have causes about which *something* can be known. This kind of inference, which suffices for physics, has already been considered. We are concerned now with a much more specific kind of inference, the kind that is involved in our knowledge of the thoughts and feelings of others—assuming that we have such knowledge. It is of course obvious that such knowledge is more or less doubtful. There is not only the general argument that we may be dreaming; there is also the possibility of ingenious automata. There are calculating machines that do sums much better than our schoolboy sons; there are gramophone records that remember impeccably what So-and-so said on such-and-such an occasion; there are people in the cinema who, though copies of real people, are not themselves alive. There is no theoretical limit to what ingenuity could achieve in the way of producing the illusion of life where in fact life is absent.

But, you will say, in all such cases it was the thoughts of human beings that produced the ingenious mechanism. Yes, but how do you know this? And how do you know that the gramophone does *not* 'think'?

There is, in the first place, a difference in the causal laws of observable behaviour. If I say to a student 'write me a paper on Descartes' reasons for believing in the existence of matter', I shall, if he is industrious, cause a certain response. A gramophone record might be so constructed as to respond to this stimulus, perhaps better than the student, but if so it would be incapable of telling me anything about any other philosopher, even if I threatened to refuse to give it a degree. One of the most notable peculiarities of human behaviour is change of response to a given stimulus. An ingenious person could construct an automaton which would always laugh at his jokes, however often it heard them; but a human being, after laughing a few times, will yawn, and end by saying 'how I laughed the first time I heard that joke'.

But the differences in observable behaviour between living and dead matter do not suffice to prove that there are 'thoughts' connected with living bodies other than my own. It is probably possible theoretically to account for the behaviour of living bodies by purely physical causal laws, and it is probably impossible to refute materialism by external observation alone. If we are to believe that there are thoughts and feelings other than our own, that must be in virtue of some inference in which our own thoughts and feelings are relevant, and such an inference must go beyond what is needed in physics.

I am of course not discussing the history of how we come to believe in other minds. We find ourselves believing in them when we first begin to reflect; the thought that Mother may be angry or pleased is one which arises in early infancy. What I am discussing is the possibility of a postulate which shall establish a rational connection between this belief and data, e.g. between the belief 'Mother is angry' and the hearing of a loud voice.

The abstract schema seems to be as follows. We know, from observation of ourselves, a causal law of the form 'A causes B', where A is a 'thought' and B a physical occurrence. We sometimes observe a B when we cannot observe any A; we then infer an unobserved A. For example: I know that when I say 'I'm thirsty', I say so, usually, because I am thirsty, and therefore, when I hear the sentence 'I'm thirsty' at a time when I am not thirsty, I assume that some one else is thirsty. I assume this the more readily if I see before me a hot drooping body which goes on to say 'I have walked twenty desert miles in this heat with never a drop to drink'. It is evident that my confidence in the 'inference' is increased by increased complexity in the datum and also by increased certainty of the causal law derived from subjective observation, provided the causal law is such as to account for the complexities of the datum.

It is clear that, in so far as plurality of causes is to be suspected, the kind of inference we have been considering is not valid. We are supposed to know 'A causes B', and also to know that B has occurred; if this is to justify us in inferring A, we must know that *only* A causes B. Or, if we are content to infer that A is probable, it will suffice if we can know that in most cases it is A that causes B. If you hear thunder without having seen lightning, you confidently infer that there was lightning, because you are convinced that the sort of noise you heard is seldom caused by anything except lightning. As this example shows, our principle is not only employed to establish the existence of other minds, but is habitually assumed, though in a less concrete form, in physics. I say 'a less concrete form' because unseen lightning is only abstractly similar to seen lightning, whereas we suppose the similarity of other minds to our own to be by no means purely abstract.

Complexity in the observed behaviour of another person, when this can all be accounted for by a simple cause such as thirst, increases the probability of the inference by diminishing the probability of some other cause. I think that in ideally favourable circumstances the argument would be formally as follows:

From subjective observation I know that A, which is a thought or feeling, causes B, which is a bodily act, e.g. a statement. I know also that, whenever B is an act of my own body, A is its cause. I now observe an act of the kind B in a body not my own, and I am having no thought or feeling of the kind A. But I still believe, on the basis of self-observation, that only A can cause B; I therefore infer that there was an A which caused B, though it was not an A that I could observe. On this ground I infer that other people's bodies are associated with minds, which resemble mine in proportion as their bodily behaviour resembles my own.

In practice, the exactness and certainty of the above statement must be softened. We cannot be sure that, in our subjective experience, A is the only cause of B. And even if A is the only cause of B in our experience, how can we know that this holds outside our experience? It is not necessary that we should know this with any certainty; it is enough if it is highly probable. It is the assumption of probability in such cases that is our postulate. The postulate may therefore be stated as follows:

If, whenever we can observe whether A and B are present or absent, we find that every case of B has an A as a causal antecedent, then it is probable that most B's have A's as causal antecedents, even in cases where observation does not enable us to know whether A is present or not.

This postulate, if accepted, justifies the inference to other minds, as well as many other inferences that are made unreflectingly by common sense.

Source: Human Knowledge: Its Scope and Limits (Allen & Unwin), Pt. VI, Ch. VIII.

4 The Analysis and Justification of Statements about other Minds (1956)

A. J. AYER

It is maintained by some philosophers that there is a radical difference in the analysis of 'mental' facts, according as they relate to other people or to oneself. The suggestion is that if I say of myself that I am in pain I am referring to a feeling of which I alone am conscious; if my statement is true it may be that I also show certain outward signs of pain, but I do not imply that this is so: it is not part of what my statement means. Or even granting that it is part of what my statement means, it is not all that it means. But if I say of someone else that he is in pain, all that my statement is supposed to mean is that he displays signs of pain, that his body is in such and such a state, or that he behaves, or is disposed to behave, in such and such ways. For this is all that I can conceivably observe.[1]

An obvious objection to this thesis is that it entails that the statements which I make about my feelings cannot have the same meaning for any other person as they have for me. Thus, if someone asks me whether I am in pain and I answer that I am, my reply, as I understand it, is not an answer to his question. For I am reporting the occurrence of a certain feeling; whereas, so far as he was concerned, his question could only have been a question about my physical condition. So also, if he says that my reply is false, he is not strictly contradicting me: for all that he can be denying is that I exhibited the proper signs of pain, and this is not what I asserted; it is what he understood me to be asserting but not what I understood myself. In so far as there is a regular connection between such conscious states and the physical manifestations by which they are defined for others, this discrepancy might not be practically important. But the connection is not perfect; and the fact that it might not obtain is itself sufficient for our argument.

Moreover, in the form in which it is usually held, the theory is inconsistent.[2] For a philosopher who maintains it does not merely wish to argue that the statements which he makes about his own feelings have a different meaning for him from that which they can have for anyone else. He wishes his theory to have a general application: it is supposed to be true of all of us that when we talk about our own mental states, we are referring to experiences of which we can be directly aware, but when we talk about the mental states of others we are referring to their physical condition or behaviour. But if the theory were correct, this distinction between the mental and the physical, between what is private and what is public, could not be made in any case but one's own. If I cannot distinguish between another person's feelings and their physical expression, I cannot suppose that he distinguishes them.

[1] Cf. my *Language, Truth and Logic*, ch. 7.
[2] Martin Shearn, *A Study of Analytical Behaviourism*, Ph.D. thesis in the University of London.

Or rather, if I do suppose that he distinguishes them, I can be supposing only that he is guilty of a logical error, that he is taking two forms of expression to refer to different things when they in fact refer to the same. I cannot both admit the distinction that he makes and say that it has no meaning for me. The picture which this theory tries to present is that of a number of people enclosed within the fortresses of their own experiences. They can observe the battlements of other fortresses, but they cannot penetrate them. Not only that, but they cannot even conceive that anything lies behind them. All their discourse about other fortresses, as opposed to their own, is limited to a description of the battlements. But the philosopher who paints this picture is, by the terms of the theory, himself immured in such a fortress. If he talks about the fortresses of others, he can be doing no more than describing their battlements. Thus, if his picture were accurate he could not paint it. He could not even imagine that other people were in the same situation as himself.

So long as he does not attempt to generalize his thesis, our philosopher may indeed hold that only he can have experiences. But since I do have experiences, I know that this view is false if the philosopher be any other than myself. And since I can surmise that another philosopher holds it, I myself concede that it is false. But this does not dispose of the problem. Let it be granted that in the sense in which we severally claim to have experiences we can also attribute them to others. There is still the philosophical question how this is possible.

The source of the difficulty, here again, is that one is postulating the existence of something that one could not conceivably observe. But, once more, it is necessary to distinguish between statements which are unverifiable by anyone and those that are unverifiable by some particular person. We saw, in the case of statements about the past, that the fact that they were made by persons who could not observe the events to which they referred did not entail that these events were altogether unobservable. Might not the same apply to statements about 'other minds'?[3]

There is, however, a special difficulty in the case of statements about other minds, which differentiates them from statements about the past. It can be argued that one's inability to observe a past event is due to the accident of one's position in time: we have seen that the fact that a person lives at such and such a date

[3] Cf. my 'One's Knowledge of Other Minds', *Theoria*, vol. xix. Reprinted in *Philosophical Essays*.

is not essential to his being the person that he is. But it is not an accident that one is not someone else. One might indeed be a very different sort of person from the person that one is: one might be very much more like some other person than one is in fact. But it is not even logically possible that one should be identical with another person. It is possible that there should have been only one of us and not two, that one or other of us should not have existed; but this is not to say that we might have been, or that we might become, identical. Thus, if my inability to observe what goes on in the mind of another is due to our being separate persons, there is no possible adjustment of my situation by which it could be overcome.[4]

Nevertheless, there is a way in which the parallel still holds. In the sense in which there is no special class of statements about the past, so there is no special class of statements about other minds. The use of pronouns, such as 'you' or 'he', may indicate that the person referred to is someone other than the speaker, just as the use of tenses may indicate that the event is earlier than the time at which the statement is made; but the meaning of a statement which refers to a person's experiences is not affected by the fact that it is made by someone other than the person himself, any more than the meaning of a statement which refers to an event occurring at a certain position in time is affected by the fact that it is made at a subsequent time. In either instance, the statement may be formulated in such a way as to convey information about the circumstances in which it is expressed, but this information is not part of what it states. In the case of a statement, which is in fact about 'another mind', what is stated is, in effect, that someone who answers to a certain description has such and such an experience. To understand it, one must therefore know what it would be like to answer to the description and to have the experience in question. Now, if I am not the person to whom the statement refers, it is not possible that I, being the person that I am, should answer to the description: or rather, if I could answer to it, this would prove only that the description chosen was not a sufficient identification; for if the description does sufficiently identify the person in question, it is impossible that any other person should answer to it, while continuing to answer to the descriptions which sufficiently identify himself. It does not follow, however, that I cannot conceive of myself as answering to it.

[4] John Watling, 'Ayer on Other Minds', *Theoria*, vol. xx, nos. 1–3, and Shearn, *op. cit.*

Suppose, for example, that I am told of the experiences of a child, who is described in a way that, for all I know, could apply to myself. I may come to believe that I was the child in question. Later, I may discover that I was not: but I do not then cease to understand the statement about the child's experiences, nor do I attach a different meaning to it. Admittedly, if I then think of myself as someone to whom the description does not apply, I cannot also suppose that it does. I cannot consistently conceive of myself both as being a person of a certain sort and as being a person of a different sort. But I am not logically obliged to think of myself as satisfying any particular description: and so long as I do not limit the possibilities by forming a picture of myself with which anything that I imagine has to be reconciled, I can conceive of having any consistent set of characteristics that you please. All that is required is that the possession of these characteristics be something that is in itself empirically verifiable. The fact that I do not have the characteristics chosen, or even that I could not have them, being the person that I am, does not therefore entail that I cannot know what it would be like to have them. And if I can know what it would be like to satisfy a certain set of descriptions and to have a certain experience, then I can understand a statement to the effect that someone who satisfies these descriptions is having that experience, independently of the question whether that person is, or could be, myself.

But if it be allowed that one can attach a meaning to statements which refer to the experiences of others, and, what is more, the same meaning as is attached to them by those to whom the experiences are ascribed, then it becomes open to us to justify our acceptance of such statements by an inductive argument. On the basis of my own experience I form a general hypothesis to the effect that certain physical phenomena are accompanied by certain feelings. When I observe that some other person is in the appropriate physical state, I am thereby enabled to infer that he is having these feelings; feelings which are similar to those that in similar circumstances I have myself. The objection taken by some philosophers to this argument is that its conclusion is unverifiable; but I have tried to show that this objection can be met.

Even so, the argument does not seem very strong. The objection that one is generalizing from a single instance can perhaps be countered by maintaining that it is not a matter of extending to all other persons a conclusion which has been found to hold for only one, but rather of proceeding from the fact that certain properties have been found to be conjoined in various contexts to the conclusion that they remain conjoined in further contexts. Thus I have discovered, for example, that when I have an infected tooth I feel considerable pain and that I tend to express this feeling in certain characteristic ways. And I have found that these connections hold independently of other circumstances such as the place where I happen to be, the way in which I am dressed, the state of the weather, the nature of my political opinions, and so forth. On the other hand, I have found that it is not independent of the state of my nervous system. So when I observe that some other person is similarly afflicted and that he acts in a similar way, I may infer that a similar feeling is also present, unless there is something in the circumstances that would make the connection fail. If I knew that he had been anaesthetized, for instance, I might conclude that he did not feel pain; that, although he behaved as if he felt it, he was only pretending. But other features of the context, the colour of his hair, the date of his birth, the number of his children, and many other items among those that went to make him 'another person', I should rightly dismiss as irrelevant. So the question that I put is not: Am I justified in assuming that what I have found to be true only of myself is also true of others? but: Having found that in various circumstances the possession of certain properties is united with the possession of a certain feeling, does this union continue to obtain when the circumstances are still further varied? The basis of the argument is broadened by absorbing the difference of persons into the difference of the situations in which the psycho-physical connections are supposed to hold.

This way of presenting the argument makes it stronger, but it may still be objected that it hardly makes it strong enough. For the variety of conditions in which I can in fact test any of these psycho-physical hypotheses is extremely limited. There are a great many properties of which I cannot divest myself and a great many that I cannot acquire; and among them are properties which are peculiar to me, or peculiar to some other person. Might it not be that the possession of one such property, say the property of having been born at the exact time and place at which I was, is necessary for being conscious? Or that having just those finger-prints that my neighbour has is a barrier to consciousness? These suggestions seem absurd, but what right have I to dismiss them?[5] My neighbour's having the finger-prints he has does not prevent

[5] Shearn, *op. cit.*

him from behaving like anybody else. He displays every sign of consciousness when one would expect him to. But this is not disputed. What is in question is my right to infer the existence of something 'behind' this behaviour. I distinguish my own states of consciousness from their physical expressions and I wish to do the same for others. But then the possibility that they differ from me, or from one another, just in this respect, has a claim to be considered seriously.

Moreover, if my belief in other minds depended on this inductive argument, its strength should be proportionate both to the variety of my own experiences and to the extent to which I had discovered physical resemblances between other people and myself. I should need to vary my own attributes as much as possible, in order to increase the range over which my psychophysical hypotheses were known to hold, and I should have to examine other people to see how far the analogy could be made to extend. The further I could extend it, the more confident I should be in ascribing consciousness to them. But in fact it does not seem that I need make any such experiments in order to discover that other people are conscious.[6] Their consciousness is expressed in their demeanour; in their manner of acting, in their use of language. If I discovered that someone who exhibited these signs of consciousness was physiologically very different from myself, that he had, for example, a different type of nervous system, I should not conclude that the signs were fallacious, that he was not conscious after all. I should conclude rather that I had been mistaken in supposing that in order to be conscious it was necessary to have a nervous system like my own.

This is not to say that the resemblances which I observe between myself and others do not supply the foundation for my belief in the existence and character of their experiences. If I did not know that I had thoughts and feelings and sensations and that I revealed them in characteristic ways, I should have no basis at all for ascribing them to others. Neither in saying that the fact that people are conscious comes out in their demeanour do I wish to imply that the two are to be identified. It is rather that their displays of thought and feeling afford the best evidence that I can have for the existence of what they are said to manifest. Consideration of the physiological resemblances between myself and others plays a secondary rôle.

But still the sceptic can maintain that if this is the best evidence,

[6] Cf. Watling, *op. cit.*

he has no reason to be convinced: it does not even measure up to the standards of scientific proof. And in a way he is right. He is right on the subject of other minds just as he is right on the subject of the past. If it is required of an inductive argument that the generalization to which it leads should be based on a wide variety of experienced instances, both candidates fail the test. One has only a limited experience of the connection of 'inner' states with their outer manifestations; and one has no experience at all of the connection of a present with a past event. But these are not ordinary limitations; what is suspect about them is that they are logically necessary. As we have several times remarked, it is by insisting on an impossible standard of perfection that the sceptic makes himself secure.

This being so, we must be content with what we have. In any particular case, if one's claim to know what some other person is feeling be put in question, one can uphold it by appealing to the evidence. What we cannot do is to vindicate such claims in general, any more than we can give a general vindication of our trust in memory or in any form of record of the past. Or rather, the general vindication comes out only in the way in which the evidence is found to be sufficient in particular instances. Further than this we cannot go: it is enough if we can rebut the sceptic's arguments which are designed to show that we cannot even go so far. Neither is this a purely negative achievement; a matter of running hard in order to stay in the same place. Our reward for taking scepticism seriously is that we are brought to distinguish the different levels at which our claims to knowledge stand. In this way we gain a clearer understanding of the dimensions of our language; and so of the world which it serves us to describe.

Source: The Problem of Knowledge (Macmillan), Ch. V. (Extract.)

PERSONAL IDENTITY

5 Of Personal Identity (1738)

DAVID HUME

There are some philosophers, who imagine we are every moment intimately conscious of what we call our SELF; that we feel its existence and its continuance in existence; and are certain, beyond the evidence of a demonstration, both of its perfect identity and simplicity. The strongest sensation, the most violent passion, say they, instead of distracting us from this view, only fix it the more intensely, and make us consider their influence on *self* either by their pain or pleasure. To attempt a farther proof of this were to weaken its evidence; since no proof can be deriv'd from any fact, of which we are so intimately conscious; nor is there any thing, of which we can be certain, if we doubt of this.

Unluckily all these positive assertions are contrary to that very experience, which is pleaded for them, nor have we any idea of *self*, after the manner it is here explain'd. For from what impression cou'd this idea be deriv'd? This question 'tis impossible to answer without a manifest contradiction and absurdity; and yet 'tis a question, which must necessarily be answer'd, if we wou'd have the idea of self pass for clear and intelligible. It must be some one impression, that gives rise to every real idea. But self or person is not any one impression, but that to which our several impressions and ideas are suppos'd to have a reference. If any impression gives rise to the idea of self, that impression must continue invariably the same, thro' the whole course of our lives; since self is suppos'd to exist after that manner. But there is no impression constant and invariable. Pain and pleasure, grief and joy, passions and sensations succeed each other, and never all

43

exist at the same time. It cannot, therefore, be from any of these impressions, or from any other, that the idea of self is deriv'd; and consequently there is no such idea.

But farther, what must become of all our particular perceptions upon this hypothesis? All these are different, and distinguishable, and separable from each other, and may be separately consider'd, and may exist separately, and have no need of any thing to support their existence. After what manner, therefore, do they belong to self; and how are they connected with it? For my part, when I enter most intimately into what I call *myself*, I always stumble on some particular perception or other, of heat or cold, light or shade, love or hatred, pain or pleasure. I never can catch *myself* at any time without a perception, and never can observe any thing but the perception. When my perceptions are remov'd for any time, as by sound sleep; so long am I insensible of *myself*, and may truly be said not to exist. And were all my perceptions remov'd by death, and cou'd I neither think, nor feel, nor see, nor love, nor hate after the dissolution of my body, I shou'd be entirely annihilated, nor do I conceive what is farther requisite to make me a perfect non-entity. If any one upon serious and unprejudic'd reflexion, thinks he has a different notion of *himself*, I must confess I can reason no longer with him. All I can allow him is, that he may be in the right as well as I, and that we are essentially different in this particular. He may, perhaps, perceive something simple and continu'd, which he calls *himself*; tho' I am certain there is no such principle in me.

But setting aside some metaphysicians of this kind, I may venture to affirm of the rest of mankind, that they are nothing but a bundle or collection of different perceptions, which succeed each other with an inconceivable rapidity, and are in a perpetual flux and movement. Our eyes cannot turn in their sockets without varying our perceptions. Our thought is still more variable than our sight; and all our other senses and faculties contribute to this change; nor is there any single power of the soul, which remains unalterably the same, perhaps for one moment. The mind is a kind of theatre, where several perceptions successively make their appearance; pass, re-pass, glide away, and mingle in an infinite variety of postures and situations. There is properly no *simplicity* in it at one time, nor *identity* in different; whatever natural propension we may have to imagine that simplicity and identity. The comparison of the theatre must not mislead us. They are the successive perceptions only, that constitute the mind; nor have we the most distant notion of the place, where these scenes are represented, or of the materials, of which it is compos'd.

What then gives us so great a propension to ascribe an identity to these successive perceptions, and to suppose ourselves possest of an invariable and uninterrupted existence thro' the whole course of our lives? In order to answer this question, we must distinguish betwixt personal identity, as it regards our thought or imagination, and as it regards our passions or the concern we take in ourselves. The first is our present subject; and to explain it perfectly we must take the matter pretty deep, and account for that identity, which we attribute to plants and animals; there being a great analogy betwixt it, and the identity of a self or person.

We have a distinct idea of an object, that remains invariable and uninterrupted thro' a suppos'd variation of time; and this idea we call that of *identity* or *sameness*. We have also a distinct idea of several different objects existing in succession, and connected together by a close relation; and this to an accurate view affords as perfect a notion of *diversity*, as if there was no manner of relation among the objects. But tho' these two ideas of identity, and a succession of related objects be in themselves perfectly distinct, and even contrary, yet 'tis certain, that in our common way of thinking they are generally confounded with each other. That action of the imagination, by which we consider the un-interrupted and invariable object, and that by which we reflect on the succession of related objects, are almost the same to the feeling, nor is there much more effort of thought requir'd in the latter case than in the former. The relation facilitates the transition of the mind from one object to another, and renders its passage as smooth as if it contemplated one continu'd object. This resemblance is the cause of the confusion and mistake, and makes us substitute the notion of identity, instead of that of related objects. However at one instant we may consider the related succession as variable or interrupted, we are sure the next to ascribe to it a perfect identity, and regard it as invariable and uninterrupted. Our propensity to this mistake is so great from the resemblance above-mention'd, that we fall into it before we are aware; and tho' we incessantly correct ourselves by reflexion, and return to a more accurate method of thinking, yet we cannot long sustain our philosophy, or take off this biass from the imagination. Our last resource is to yield to it, and boldly assert that these different related objects are in effect the same, however inter-rupted and variable. In order to justify to ourselves this absurdity,

we often feign some new and unintelligible principle, that connects the objects together, and prevents their interruption or
variation. Thus we feign the continu'd existence of the perceptions
of our senses, to remove the interruption; and run into the notion
of a *soul*, and *self*, and *substance*, to disguise the variation. But
we may farther observe, that where we do not give rise to such a
fiction, our propension to confound identity with relation is so
great, that we are apt to imagine[1] something unknown and
mysterious, connecting the parts, beside their relation; and this I
take to be the case with regard to the identity we ascribe to plants
and vegetables. [. . .]

We now proceed to explain the nature of *personal identity*,
which has become so great a question in philosophy, especially
of late years in *England*, where all the abstruser sciences are
study'd with a peculiar ardour and application. And here 'tis
evident, the same method of reasoning must be continu'd, which
has so successfully explain'd the identity of plants, and animals,
and ships, and houses, and of all the compounded and changeable
productions either of art or nature. The identity, which we ascribe
to the mind of man, is only a fictitious one, and of a like kind with
that which we ascribe to vegetables and animal bodies. It cannot,
therefore, have a different origin, but must proceed from a like
operation of the imagination upon like objects.

But lest this argument shou'd not convince the reader; tho' in
my opinion perfectly decisive; let him weigh the following reasoning, which is still closer and more immediate. 'Tis evident, that
the identity, which we attribute to the human mind, however
perfect we may imagine it to be, is not able to run the several
different perceptions into one, and make them lose their characters
of distinction and difference, which are essential to them. 'Tis
still true, that every distinct perception, which enters into the
composition of the mind, is a distinct existence, and is different,
and distinguishable, and separable from every other perception,
either contemporary or successive. But, as, notwithstanding this
distinction and separability, we suppose the whole train of perceptions to be united by identity, a question naturally arises
concerning this relation of identity; whether it be something that

---

[1] If the reader is desirous to see how a great genius may be influenc'd by
these seemingly trivial principles of the imagination, as well as the mere
vulgar, let him read my Lord *Shaftesbury's* reasonings concerning the uniting
principle of the universe, and the identity of plants and animals. See his
Moralists; or, *Philosophical Rhapsody*.

really binds our several perceptions together, or only associates their ideas in the imagination. That is, in other words, whether in pronouncing concerning the identity of a person, we observe some real bond among his perceptions, or only feel one among the ideas we form of them. This question we might easily decide, if we wou'd recollect what has been already prov'd at large, that the understanding never observes any real connexion among objects, and that even the union of cause and effect, when strictly examin'd, resolves itself into a customary association of ideas. For from thence it evidently follows, that identity is nothing really belonging to these different perceptions, and uniting them together; but is merely a quality, which we attribute to them, because of the union of their ideas in the imagination, when we reflect upon them. Now the only qualities, which can give ideas an union in the imagination, are these three relations above-mention'd. These are the uniting principles in the ideal world, and without them every distinct object is separable by the mind, and may be separately consider'd, and appears not to have any more connexion with any other object, than if disjoin'd by the greatest difference and remoteness. 'Tis, therefore, on some of these three relations of resemblance, contiguity and causation, that identity depends; and as the very essence of these relations consists in their producing an easy transition of ideas; it follows, that our notions of personal identity, proceed entirely from the smooth and uninterrupted progress of the thought along a train of connected ideas, according to the principles above-explain'd.

The only question, therefore, which remains, is, by what relations this uninterrupted progress of our thought is produc'd, when we consider the successive existence of a mind or thinking person. And here 'tis evident we must confine ourselves to resemblance and causation, and must drop contiguity, which has little or no influence in the present case.

To begin with *resemblance;* suppose we cou'd see clearly into the breast of another, and observe that succession of perceptions, which constitutes his mind or thinking principle, and suppose that he always preserves the memory of a considerable part of past perceptions; 'tis evident that nothing cou'd more contribute to the bestowing a relation on this succession amidst all its variations. For what is the memory but a faculty, by which we raise up the images of past perceptions? And as an image necessarily resembles its object, must not the frequent placing of these resembling perceptions in the chain of thought, convey the imagination more easily from one link to another, and make the whole seem like the continuance of one object? In this particular, then, the memory not only discovers the identity, but also contributes to its production, by producing the relation of resemblance among the perceptions. The case is the same whether we consider ourselves or others.

As to *causation;* we may observe that the true idea of the human mind, is to consider it as a system of different perceptions or different existences, which are link'd together by the relation of cause and effect, and mutually produce, destroy, influence, and modify each other. Our impressions give rise to their correspondent ideas; and these ideas in their turn produce other impressions. One thought chaces another, and draws after it a third, by which it is expell'd in its turn. In this respect, I cannot compare the soul more properly to any thing than to a republic or commonwealth, in which the several members are united by the reciprocal ties of government and subordination, and give rise to other persons, who propagate the same republic in the incessant changes of its parts. And as the same individual republic may not only change its members, but also its laws and constitutions; in like manner the same person may vary his character and disposition, as well as his impressions and ideas, without losing his identity. Whatever changes he endures, his several parts are still connected by the relation of causation. And in this view our identity with regard to the passions serves to corroborate that with regard to the imagination, by the making our distant perceptions influence each other, and by giving us a present concern for our past or future pains or pleasures.

As memory alone acquaints us with the continuance and extent of this succession of perceptions, 'tis to be consider'd, upon that account chiefly, as the source of personal identity. Had we no memory, we never shou'd have any notion of causation, nor consequently of that chain of causes and effects, which constitute our self or person. But having once acquir'd this notion of causation from the memory, we can extend the same chain of causes, and consequently the identity of our persons beyond our memory, and can comprehend times, and circumstances, and actions, which we have entirely forgot, but suppose in general to have existed. For how few of our past actions are there, of which we have any memory? Who can tell me, for instance, what were his thoughts and actions on the first of *January* 1715, the 11th of *March* 1719, and the 3d of *August* 1733? Or will he affirm, because he has entirely forgot the incidents of these days, that the present self is not the same person with the self of that time; and by that means overturn all the most establish'd notions of personal identity? In this view, therefore, memory does not so much *produce* as *discover* personal identity, by shewing us the relation of cause and effect among our different perceptions. 'Twill be incumbent on those, who affirm that memory produces entirely our personal identity, to give a reason why we can thus extend our identity beyond our memory.

The whole of this doctrine leads us to a conclusion, which is of great importance in the present affair, *viz.* that all the nice and subtile questions concerning personal identity can never possibly be decided, and are to be regarded rather as grammatical than as philosophical difficulties. Identity depends on the relations of ideas; and these relations produce identity, by means of that easy transition they occasion. But as the relations, and the easiness of the transition may diminish by insensible degrees, we have no just standard, by which we can decide any dispute concerning the time, when they acquire or lose a title to the name of identity. All the disputes concerning the identity of connected objects are merely verbal, except so far as the relation of parts gives rise to some fiction or imaginary principle of union, as we have already observ'd.

What I have said concerning the first origin and uncertainty of our notion of identity, as apply'd to the human mind, may be extended with little or no variation to that of *simplicity*. An object, whose different co-existent parts are bound together by a close relation, operates upon the imagination after much the same manner as one perfectly simple and indivisible, and requires not a much greater stretch of thought in order to its conception. From this similarity of operation we attribute a simplicity to it, and feign a principle of union as the support of this simplicity, and the center of all the different parts and qualities of the object. [...]

APPENDIX

I had entertain'd some hopes, that however deficient our theory of the intellectual world might be, it wou'd be free from those contradictions, and absurdities, which seem to attend every explication, that human reason can give of the material world.

But upon a more strict review of the section concerning *personal identity*, I find myself involv'd in such a labyrinth, that, I must confess, I neither know how to correct my former opinions, nor how to render them consistent. If this be not a good *general* reason for scepticism, 'tis at least a sufficient one (if I were not already abundantly supplied) for me to entertain a diffidence and modesty in all my decisions. I shall propose the arguments on both sides, beginning with those that induc'd me to deny the strict and proper identity and simplicity of a self or thinking being.

When we talk of *self* or *substance*, we must have an idea annex'd to these terms, otherwise they are altogether unintelligible. Every idea is deriv'd from preceding impressions; and we have no impression of self or substance, as something simple and individual. We have, therefore, no idea of them in that sense.

Whatever is distinct, is distinguishable; and whatever is distinguishable, is separable by the thought or imagination. All perceptions are distinct. They are, therefore, distinguishable, and separable, and may be conceiv'd as separately existent, and may exist separately, without any contradiction or absurdity. [. . .]

So far I seem to be attended with sufficient evidence. But having thus loosen'd all our particular perceptions, when I proceed to explain the principle of connexion, which binds them together, and makes us attribute to them a real simplicity and identity; I am sensible, that my account is very defective, and that nothing but the seeming evidence of the precedent reasonings cou'd have induc'd me to receive it. If perceptions are distinct existences, they form a whole only by being connected together. But no connexions among distinct existences are ever discoverable by human understanding. We only *feel* a connexion or determination of the thought, to pass from one object to another. It follows, therefore, that the thought alone finds personal identity, when reflecting on the train of past perceptions, that compose a mind, the ideas of them are felt to be connected together, and naturally introduce each other. However extraordinary this conclusion may seem, it need not surprize us. Most philosophers seem inclin'd to think, that personal identity *arises* from consciousness; and consciousness is nothing but a reflected thought or perception. The present philosophy, therefore, has so far a promising aspect. But all my hopes vanish, when I come to explain the principles, that unite our successive perceptions in our thought or consciousness. I cannot discover any theory, which gives me satisfaction on this head.

In short there are two principles, which I cannot render consistent; nor is it in my power to renounce either of them, viz. *that
all our distinct perceptions are distinct existences*, and *that the
mind never perceives any real connexion among distinct existences*.
Did our perceptions either inhere in something simple and individual, or did the mind perceive some real connexion among
them, there wou'd be no difficulty in the case. For my part, I must
plead the privilege of a sceptic, and confess, that this difficulty is
too hard for my understanding. I pretend not, however, to pronounce it absolutely insuperable. Others, perhaps, or myself, upon
more mature reflexions, may discover some hypothesis, that will
reconcile those contradictions.

Source: A Treatise of Human Nature, Bk. I, Pt. IV, Sec. VI, and
Appendix. (Extracts.)

6 The Self as Substance (1927)

J. McT. E. McTAGGART

. . . What then do we mean by a self? I should say that the quality
of being a self is a simple quality which is known to me because
I perceive—in the strict sense of the word—one substance as
possessing this quality. This substance is myself. And I believe
that every self-conscious being—that is, every self who knows that
he is a self—directly perceives himself in this manner. [. . .]

The reasons which have led me to accept the view that the self
is known to itself by direct perception were suggested to me by a
passage of Mr. Russell's article 'Knowledge by Acquaintance and
Knowledge by Description.' Mr Russell did not work out his
position in detail—which was not essential for the main design of
his paper. And he has now ceased to hold the position at all. I
remain, however, convinced of the truth of the view, the first
suggestion of which I owe to him.

The argument is as follows. I can judge that I am aware of
certain things—for example, of the relation of equality. I assert,
then, the proposition 'I am aware of equality.' This proposition,
whether true or false, has certainly a meaning. And, since I know
what the proposition means, I must know each constituent of it.

I must therefore know 'I.' Whatever is known must be known by acquaintance or by description. If, therefore, 'I' cannot be known by description, it must be known by acquaintance, and I must be aware of it.

Now how could 'I' be described in this case? The description must be an exclusive description . . . since I do not know 'I' by description unless I know enough about it to distinguish it from everything else. Can I describe 'I' as that which is aware of equality? But it is obvious that this is not an exclusive description of 'I.' It could not be an exclusive description of 'I' unless I was the only person who was ever aware of equality. And it is obvious that this is not certain, and that it is possible that some one besides me was, is, or will be aware of equality. (In point of fact, I have, of course, overwhelming empirical evidence for the conclusion that some other persons *are* aware of equality.) Thus we cannot get an exclusive description of 'I' in this way. [. . .]

An attempt has been made to describe 'I' in another manner. It is no longer described as that which is aware of something, or which has a mental state. It is described as a whole of which certain mental states are parts. The classical statement of this view is Hume's. 'I may venture to affirm of . . . mankind, that they are nothing but a bundle or collection of different perceptions which succeed each other with an inconceivable rapidity and are in a perpetual flux or movement.'

This gives, of course, a very different view of the self from that which is generally held. In the first place, the knowledge of the self is logically subsequent to the knowledge of the mental states. We can know the states without knowing the self, but we can only know the self by means of our knowledge of the states. In the second place, it would seem that the theory holds that this relation of knowledge corresponds to a relation in the things themselves. The ultimate realities are the mental states, and the selves are only secondary, since they are nothing but aggregates of the states. In the third place we must no longer say that the self perceives, thinks, or loves, or that it has a perception of thought or an emotion. We can only say that the bundle includes a perception, a thought, or an emotion, as one of its parts.

On this theory, then, when I use the word 'I,' I know what 'I' means by description, and it is described as meaning that bundle of mental states of which my use of the word is one member. Is this satisfactory?

In the first place we must note that it is by no means every

group of mental states which is a bundle in Hume's sense of the
word, that is to say, an aggregate of mental states which form a
self. For any two mental states form a group by themselves. And
there are an infinite number of groups, of each of which both *G*
and *H* are members. All these groups are not bundles. The
emotions of James II on the acquittal of the seven Bishops, and
the volitions of William III at the Boyne, are to be found together
in an infinite number of groups. But no one supposes—neither
Hume nor anyone else—that they belong to the same self. They
are therefore not in the same bundle.

But, since every group is not a bundle, we say nothing definite
when we say that two mental states are in the same bundle,
unless we are able to distinguish bundles from other groups. How
is this to be done? Can we distinguish them by saying that the
members of bundles have relations to one another which the
members of groups which are not bundles do not have? But what
would such relations be?

They could not be spatial relations, nor relations of apparent
spatiality. For in many cases—as with emotions and abstract
thoughts—the states have no special relation to anything which
is or appears as spatial. And in cases in which they do have those
relations, I can judge, for example, that I have seen Benares and
Piccadilly and that Jones has seen Regent Street. Or again I can
judge that I have seen Piccadilly and Regent Street, and that
Smith has seen Benares. Thus perceptions of sensa which appear
as related to objects close together may be in the same bundle or
in different bundles, and the same is true of sensa which appear as
related to objects distant from one another.

Neither can they be temporal relations, or relations of apparent
temporality. For some cases we say that experiences separated by
years belong to the same bundle, and in some cases to different
bundles. And in some cases we say that simultaneous experiences
belong to the same bundle, and in some cases to different bundles.

They cannot be relations of similarity or dissimilarity. For in
every bundle there are states which are similar and dissimilar to
other states in that bundle, and which are similar and dissimilar
to states in other bundles. Nor can it be causation. For my
happiness today may have no causal connection with my misery
yesterday, whereas, if I am malignant, it may be caused by the
misery of Jones today.

Again the relation cannot be the relation of knowledge. For I
can know both my own misery and that of Jones. Nor can it be

the relation of apparent perception. For, of my state of misery yesterday and my state of happiness today, neither apparently perceives the other. Nor can they be apparently perceived by the same state, for one has ceased some time before the other began.

The relation we are looking for, then, cannot be any of these. Nor do I see any other *direct* relation between the states which could determine the bundle to which they belong. There seems only one alternative left. The relation must be an indirect relation, and it must be through the self. We must say that those states, and those only, which are states of the same self, form the bundle of parts of that self.

There is no difficulty about this, if, as I have maintained, a self is aware of himself by perception. But it is fatal to the attempt to know 'I' by description. It would obviously be a vicious circle if I described 'I' as being that bundle of states of which my use of the word is a member, and then distinguished that bundle from other groups by describing it as that group of mental states which are states of 'I.'

One more attempt to know 'I' by description must be considered. It might be admitted that, if we adhered to a purely presentationist position like Hume's, the bundles could not be described except by their relations to selves. But, it might be said, if we admit the existence of matter (or of some substance which appears as matter), they could be described in another way. For then, it might be considered, we could say that states belong to the same self when, and only when, the same living body (or what appears as such) stands in a certain relation of causality to both of them. In that sense the meaning of 'I am angry' would be that the same living body stood in that relation of causality both to the state of anger and to the judgment about it.

I have said 'a certain relation of causality' because it is clear that not all relations of causality would do. The movements of an actor's body may cause aesthetic emotions in each of a thousand spectators, but these emotions admittedly belong to different selves. It might perhaps suffice if we say that the relation between the living body and the mental state must not be mediated by the intervention of any other living body.

The view that *every* mental state has a cerebral state which stands in such a relation to it, is by no means established, and is rejected by many eminent psychologists. But, even if it were accepted, the theory which we are here considering would break down.

It is to be noticed that all that makes states part of the same self is the indirect relation through the body. It is not any direct relation between the states, which is *caused* by the indirect relation, but which would perhaps be perceived even if the indirect relation was not known. It could not be this, for we have seen that no direct relation can be found such that each state in a self has it to all other states in the self and to no other states.

But if there is no relation but the indirect relation, then no man has any reason to say that any two states belong to the same self unless he has a reason to believe them to be caused by the same body. And this means that the vast majority of such statements as 'I was envious yesterday' are absolutely untrustworthy. In the first place, by far the greater number of them have been made by people who have never heard of the doctrine that emotions and judgments are caused by bodily states. They could not, therefore, have any reason to believe that the envy and the judgment were caused by the same body. And therefore they could have no reason to believe that they belong to the same self. But, as we have seen, in asserting 'I was envious yesterday' I am asserting that the envy and the judgment belong to the same self.

In the second place, even those people who have heard of the doctrine that all mental states are caused by bodily states and who accept it, do not, in far the greater number of cases, base their judgments that two states belong to the same self on a previous conviction that they are caused by the same body. And, indeed, in the case of an emotion and a judgment it is impossible that they should do so. For it would be impossible for any man to observe his brain, and to observe it in two states which he could identify as the causes of the emotion and the judgment respectively. And his only ground for believing that they were caused by the same living body would depend on his recognizing them as belonging to the same self. It is impossible therefore that he can legitimately base his belief that they belong to the same self on the ground that they were caused by the same body.

Thus this theory would involve that every judgment of the type 'I am *x*,' or 'I was *x*,' or 'I did *x*,' where *x* is anything that a substance can be or do, is totally untrustworthy. Such scepticism, even if not absolutely self-contradictory, which I think it is, is so extreme that it may be regarded as a *reductio ad absurdum*.

But we may go further. 'I was envious yesterday' has no meaning for anyone who does not know the meaning of 'I.' Now if 'I' can only be known by description, and the only description which is true of it is 'that group of mental states, caused by the same living body, of which the envy and my judgment are members,' it follows that anyone who does not describe 'I' in that way, will not know what 'I' means, and so will mean nothing when he says 'I was envious yesterday.' But the assertion that the meaning of 'I was envious yesterday' depends on the acceptance, by the man who makes it, of the doctrine of the cerebral causation of all mental states, is clearly preposterous.

We may now, I think, conclude that the meaning of 'I' cannot be known by description, and that, since the meaning of 'I' is certainly known—or all propositions containing it would be meaningless—it must be known by acquaintance. Each self, then, who knows the meaning of 'I' (it is quite possible that many selves have not reached this knowledge), must do it by perceiving himself.

Source: The Nature of Existence (C.U.P.), Vol. II, Ch. 36. (Extract.)

7 Self-consciousness, Self-identity and Personal Identity (1957)

C. A. CAMPBELL

[. . .] Cognition of *any* kind—not merely in remembering—implies a subject conscious of its own identity in its different apprehensions.

The standard argument for this doctrine is so exceedingly well-worn as almost to require apology for its repetition, and I shall expound it in very summary fashion. It derives, of course, from Kant. What follows will perhaps serve as a sufficient reminder of its general character.

Cognition is never of an atomic simple. It is always of a related plurality *as* a related plurality. This is self-evident if all cognition involves judgment, for in all judgment there must be at least the differences of subject and predicate and the affirmation or denial of their union. But we need not invoke the judgment theory to establish our point. It is clear enough, on reflection, that an

'object' which stands in no apprehended relation to other objects
of our experience—'an atomic simple'—can have no significance
for us, and is thus not an object of cognition at all. Even a 'this' is,
for cognition, a 'this-not-that'; apart from its apprehended distinction from, and therefore relation to, a 'that' it could not be
cognised as 'this'. But it seems gratuitous to pursue further a
point which has so often received classic expression in post-
Kantian philosophy. The critic may be challenged to produce a
single instance of cognition, or 'meaningful apprehension', where
the object does *not* consist in a related plurality.

What is cognised, then, is never bare A, but always A in some
sort of relationship to B (C, D, etc.). But unless the subject to
which B (C, D, etc.) is present is the same subject as that to
which A is present, no relationship, obviously, could be apprehended between B (C, D, etc.) and A. To take the very familiar
example of our cognition of succession in time, perhaps the most
basic of all cognitions. If event B is cognised as sequent upon
event A, clearly A must, in some form, be present to the same
subject as that to which B is present. Otherwise A and B would
simply fall apart into separate worlds of experience, and no discerned relationship—not even that of apartness, let alone that of
temporal sequence—would be possible.

Does cognition imply not merely a subject identical in different
cognitions, but a subject *conscious* of its identity in different
cognitions? Some philosophers who are firmly persuaded of the
subject's self-identity show a certain diffidence about pressing for
the subject's consciousness of that identity. Nevertheless I would
suggest that this must be pressed. For let us suppose that the
subject, though in *fact* identical in two different apprehensions, is
in no wise aware of its own identity in them. This subject, let us
further suppose, has an apprehension of A, and then an apprehension of B. Now for an outside observer apprised, if that were
possible, of the two apprehensions, A and B could be seen to be
related, inasmuch as they could be seen both to be objects to the
same subject. But for the *subject himself,* unaware (according to
our supposition) that the self to whom B is present is the same
being as the self to whom A was formerly present, the two apprehensions must fall apart into separate 'worlds' just as surely and
completely as though he, the self-same subject, were in fact *two
different* subjects; and the discernment by him of any *relationship*
between A and B (such as that of temporal sequence) must then
become impossible. The *prius* of any discernment by the subject

of a specific relation between A and B is surely that the subject is aware of A and B as having at least that general relationship to one another which consists in their both being objects for *him*, the one self. He must, in other words, be conscious of his own identity in the different apprehensions.

The point is apt to be as elusive as it is certainly important, and a further illustration may be helpful.

Suppose I hear Big Ben striking. A moment later I—the same subject—hear it striking again. Now is my being 'the same subject' sufficient in itself to enable me to apprehend the second stroke *as* the second stroke, as *sequent upon* the first? Not, surely, unless by 'the same subject' we *mean* a subject conscious of its self-sameness. I may be in so advanced a state of senility that my memory-span is no longer adequate to bridge the gulf between the two strokes, so that, having forgotten the first when I hear the second, I cannot relate the two to one another. It is a pre-condition of my apprehending the second stroke *as* the second stroke that I remember having heard the first. But then I do not 'remember' having heard the first (and here is the crucial point) unless I am aware that it was *I*, the being who now hears the second stroke, who heard the first stroke; unless, in other words, I am not merely the same subject, but also conscious of my self-sameness, in the two experiences.

It seems to me, therefore, that while the identity of the cognising subject is a necessary, it is not, without consciousness of that identity, a sufficient, condition of cognitive awareness.

The point we have now reached (re-tracing, for the most part, familiar lines of argument) is that all cognition implies a subject that is conscious of itself, and that this self of which we are conscious in cognition is a being which is identical with itself throughout—and in despite of—the diversity of its cognitions. [. . .]

Source: On Self-hood and God-hood (Allen & Unwin), pp. 75–7.

8 The Fallacy of *'Cogito ergo sum'* (1957)

PETER GEACH

It is worth while to show what is really wrong with the Cartesian *'cogito ergo sum'*. Many people find this part of Cartesianism attractive when they begin studying philosophy; and many un-philosophical people think that such uses of 'I' as in 'I am feeling hungry, and remembering what I was thinking about yesterday' can enable us straightway to understand such a question as 'shall I still be conscious after the destruction of my body?' The idea is that introspection can give the word 'I' a special sense which each of us can learn on his own account. 'I' in this sense would not mean the man P.T.G., when P.T.G. used it; for nobody would wish to know whether the man P.T.G. was still there after his body was destroyed. What is supposed is that P.T.G. can use 'I' to express knowledge of something distinct from the man P.T.G., which is directly discernible to one who gazes within himself.

Let us begin by reminding ourselves how 'I' is used in ordinary life with psychological verbs. If P.T.G. says 'I see a spider' or 'I feel sick', people will ordinarily think that the speaker who says this, P.T.G., sees a spider or feels sick. The word 'I', spoken by P.T.G., serves to draw people's attention to P.T.G.; and if it is not at once clear who is speaking, there is a genuine question 'Who said that?' or 'Who is "I"?' Now consider Descartes brooding over his *poêle* and saying: 'I'm getting into an awful muddle— but who then is this "I" who is getting into a muddle?' When 'I'm getting into a muddle' is a soliloquy, 'I' certainly does not serve to direct Descartes's attention to Descartes, or to show that it is Descartes, none other, who is getting into a muddle. We are not to argue, though, that since 'I' does not refer to the man René Descartes it has some other, more intangible, thing to refer to. Rather, in this context the word 'I' is idle, superfluous; it is used only because Descartes is habituated to the use of 'I' (or rather, of *'je'* and *'moi'*) in expressing his thoughts and feelings to other people. In soliloquy he could quite well have expressed himself without using the first-person pronoun at all; he could have said: 'This is really a dreadful muddle!', where 'This' would refer back to his previous meditations.

Moreover, what is going to count as an allowable answer to the question 'What is this "I"?' or 'Who then am I?'? These questions might have a good clear sense in certain circumstances— e.g. if Descartes had lost his memory and wanted to know who he was ('Who am I?' 'You are René Descartes'), or if he knew that somebody had said 'I'm in a muddle' but not that it was himself ('Who is this "I"—who said he was in a muddle?' 'You did'). The states of mind that would give the questions sense are queer and uncommon, but they do occur. But no such rare circumstance was involved in Descartes's actual meditation; in the actual conditions, it is simply that the questions 'Who am I?' 'Who is this "I"?' are deprived of any ordinary use and no new use has yet been specified.

When William James tried to pose Descartes's question to himself, and to answer it, he came out with the answer that what he meant by 'I', his 'Self of selves', was a collection of feelings in his head and throat. Now of course 'I am getting into an awful muddle', said as a soliloquy, did not mean to William James 'These head-and-throat feelings are getting into an awful muddle'. But how did he manage to make such a mistake? Unlike Descartes, William James was a skilled and trained professional psychologist; how did he manage to miss his own genuine 'Self of selves' when he took an inward look, and only happen upon head-and-throat feelings? If even a professional psychologist can make such a gross mistake, who can be sure of avoiding such mistakes? Who can give directions to make it at least likely that my inward glance will hit upon my real 'Self of selves'? How shall I know when I have glimpsed it? How do I know that you have discerned yours? Am I to take your word for it? And why should I take your word? I may be sure you are not deliberately deceiving me; but may you not, like William James, be honestly mistaken?

What I maintain is that if William James said to himself 'I am very puzzled about this problem', his soliloquy would not mean either that the man William James was very puzzled or that certain head-and-throat feelings were very puzzled; 'I' would not be serving to show *who* was puzzled. The use of 'I' in such soliloquies is derivative from, parasitic upon, its use in talking to others; when there are no others, 'I' is redundant and has no special reference; 'I am very puzzled at this problem' really says no more than 'This problem *is* puzzling'. Similarly 'I have (had) frightful pain' really says no more than 'That pain is (was) frightful'; the question *whose* pain it is does not arise if the remark is a soliloquy.

If you insist that the soliloquistic 'I' is not redundant in this fashion, and likewise does not stand for the human being who is speaking, then it is up to you to explain your use of 'I'; not only do I not yet understand it, but I have positive grounds for suspecting that your own apparent understanding of it is a familiar philosophical illusion. People have had the oddest ideas about words having to stand for something; 'nothing' has been quite often regarded as naming an entity, or rather nonentity (*cf.* the fourth of the *Meditations, ad init.*); and I even once read an author maintaining that 'there' in the idiom 'there is' signifies Reality—'there is a snake in the bath' would mean 'Reality has the characterization snake-in-bath'! For all I know, a German philosopher has written something like this about the '*es*' referred to in '*es gibt*':[1] '*das Es steht vor Allem, auch vor Gott; denn das Es gibt ja auch Gott, wenn es einen Gott gibt*'. When you look for something, other than the human being who speaks, to be the reference of the soliloquist's 'I', you are surely just falling into this ancient trap.

These are the sort of arguments I should deploy against somebody who thought the Cartesian '*Cogito ergo sum*' afforded a way for him to grasp some immaterial part of his make-up, signified by 'I'. I have not said, nor do I think, that the only way of getting at a concept of *soul* or *spirit* is the '*Cogito*'; I just wanted to show that the '*Cogito*' at least is a blind alley.

Source: Mental Acts (Routledge & Kegan Paul), Ch. 26.

[1] 'Es gibt' (literally, 'it gives') is German for 'there is'. The argument attributed by Geach to his 'German philosopher' plays on the presence of the 'it' in the German for 'There is a God'—i.e. 'It gives a God'.—Ed.

Thinking thing is puzzled ~

9 Hume on Personal Identity (1963)

DAVID PEARS

A person is sometimes said to have no strong sense of his own identity. What that usually means is that he lacks some of the things that give inner stability and continuity to a human life: for instance, he may be uncertain about his beliefs, feelings and desires; he may not know the sort of person that he is, or the sort of person that he wants to be. But there is also another way in which a person may lose the sense of his own identity: he may be afflicted with amnesia and simply forget who he is. Someone in this situation would probably need the help of the police in order to re-establish his own identity, and, of course, he would want them to tell him not only the sort of person that he was, but also the particular person that he was. These two pieces of information are connected with one another, and in Nigel Dennis's novel *Cards of Identity* the victims are deprived of both at once. But it is easy to see that they are different things, and the philosophical problem of personal identity is in fact concerned with only one of them—particular identity.

Most people know their own particular identities. I know who I am, and I can produce enough facts to establish who I am. Anyone who wonders what these facts would be in his own case has only to imagine himself being questioned by the police. But what about other people? Every day I see a great number of other people whose particular identities are unknown to me. So there is a striking contrast between one's knowledge of one's own particular identity and one's knowledge of the particular identities of other people. But it is not such a complete contrast as it seems to be at first sight. For though I know enough facts to establish my own particular identity, there are also a great many facts of this kind that I do not know. For example, I know my name, address and telephone number, but I do not know whether I am the person who walked through the gate of this college exactly twenty-nine minutes ago.

The philosophical problem of personal identity is concerned

with particular identities. It begins when one asks how such statements of personal identity are established. But that is only the beginning. For suppose that some philosopher gave a completely satisfactory account of the criteria that we use in order to establish that these statements are true. Then it would still be possible for someone to argue, in a sceptical way, that those criteria were inadequate, because they did not really add up to anything that could properly be called identity. This is how Hume's treatment of the problem develops. And other developments are possible: for instance, it might be argued that the real person is the soul, and that the real criteria of personal identity have nothing to do with the body. But whatever happens in the end, we can at least insist that any philosophical treatment of this subject should begin with a realistic account of the ways in which we ask and answer questions about the particular identities of people. After all, that is what it is all about.

Hume's treatment of the subject is surprisingly unrealistic. His account of the way in which questions of personal identity are asked and answered is out of touch with the familiar facts which ought to have been its starting-point. In everyday life one asks questions not only about one's own identity but also about the identities of other people. But Hume only considers questions about his own identity. It is true that he intends that what he says about himself should be applied by his readers to themselves. But this does not alter the situation. For each of his readers will consider the problem only in its application to his own case, as Hume himself does. So though Hume's use of the pronoun 'I' is, in a way, impersonal, it always excludes consideration of other people. That is very unrealistic. So too is his account of the way in which questions of personal identity are answered. For he never mentions the fact that we use physical criteria in answering them, but always confines himself to facts about the inner life of the person concerned. We might take the example that I gave just now and use it again in order to show how crippling these two limitations are. Suppose that I wish to establish that I am not the person who walked through the gate of this college exactly twenty-nine minutes ago. Then Hume would perhaps allow that I might do it by recalling what time it was when I entered this college. But this is not the only way of establishing that I am not that person. For I might get someone else to testify that my body has been in this room for more than twenty-nine minutes, and thus establish an alibi. And this alibi would bring in both the things that are missing in Hume's account—the use of physical criteria in answering identity-questions, and the posing of identity-questions about other people (since my witness poses an identity-question about me).

When Hume looked in his own mind for the criteria of his identity as a person, he found only a succession of impressions and ideas, related to one another in various ways. He failed to find any impression of the self that is supposed to have these impressions and ideas. He took this failure to be of the utmost importance. For he assumed that, if his adversaries were correct in thinking that the self is a mental substance, perhaps a soul, in which impressions and ideas inhered, then there would have to be a separate impression of the self. But there is no such impression, and therefore the continued identity of a person could only consist in certain relations between the impressions and ideas that were the contents of his mind.

These relations between impressions and ideas were, according to him, similarity and causation. It sounds very odd to our ears when we hear Hume saying that the continued identity of a person consists in the fact that his impressions and ideas form a series in which many of the elements are related by similarity and causation. But we have to remember that he is speaking from the eighteenth century in antique psychological terms. If we express his thesis in a different terminology, it sounds less odd. For it is quite natural to say that the continued identity of a person consists in the fact that his mental life contains many repetitions, and that its development is governed by causal laws.

How would these facts be used by someone who was trying to answer a question about the particular identity of a person? Perhaps it is not immediately clear how he would use them. If he were asking the other question that I mentioned at the beginning of this essay, the question whether a person's life had inner stability and continuity, it is very obvious how he would use them. For stability and continuity depend, to a large extent, on recurrent patterns and consistent developments of thought and feeling. But suppose that I were wondering about a question of particular identity; for example, whether a man talking to me on a railway journey was the man who talked to me several weeks ago in the station buffet. How would I use Hume's two factors? I think that they would make some contribution towards the solution of my problem. For example, the man might say things that fitted the character revealed in the earlier conversation. If he did, that would not *prove* that he was the same man, since two different people can have similar characters and views. In fact, the possibility of very extensive similarities, both psychological and psychical, between two different people creates a difficulty which can be completely overcome only by appealing to space, time and motion, as is done by people who produce alibis. Nevertheless consistency of character is some help in answering questions of particular identity.

Hume was dissatisfied with his two factors, but the reason for his dissatisfaction was not the difficulty that is presented by the possibility of extensive similarities, and so he was not led to recognise the importance of space, time, and motion which are, of course, involved in the physical criteria of personal identity. His reason for feeling dissatisfied was not that a statement of particular identity might turn out to be false in spite of the fact that his two criteria had been fulfilled—for example, that the travelling companion might not be the same man again after all— but rather that, whoever the man was, there would be something inadequate about his psychological history. For he thought that, though what he had said about the psychological history of a person was the very most that a careful empiricist could say, nevertheless it was inadequate, since it did not add up to anything that could properly be called identity. All that he had found was a series of impressions and ideas. Although the series itself lasted as long as the life of the person, it contained no permanent element; indeed, all its elements were so brief as to be almost momentary. It is true that the series as a whole exhibited various kinds of pattern and structure, but it had no background and no observer, rather like a piece of music in empty space. And Hume did not think that this was enough to deserve the name 'personal identity.' It might, indeed, be *called* personal identity, but only by courtesy and as a kind of fiction.

Now it might be thought that Hume was not entirely sincere when he expressed himself dissatisfied with his own theory of personal identity. For it is characteristic of his philosophy to take a generally accepted idea and to demonstrate that its foundation in human experience is inadequate. Of course, if it had no foundation at all, he would reject it completely. But what usually happens is that he finds adequate support only for a very reduced version of the original idea. And when he expresses dismay at the difference between the reduced idea, which is well founded, and the original idea, which is ill founded, he is usually being ironical, and he is implying that the original idea is largely pretentious nonsense. This kind of irony is very noticeable in his account of perception, and in his treatment of causal necessity. And it might be thought that there is a good deal of the same irony in his expression of dissatisfaction with his theory of personal identity, particularly since the theory was in conflict with an accepted religious doctrine. But this would be a complete misinterpretation. In the appendix to the *Treatise* he makes it absolutely clear that he regards his account of personal identity as totally unsatisfactory; and yet he confesses that he has nothing better to put in its place.

His total withdrawal of his theory of personal identity is neglected by some commentators, who talk as if he had made up his mind on the subject once and for all. But the withdrawal is a fact, and an important one. For if we look at his philosophy as a whole, we see that it has a serious consequence. His philosophy is, for the most part, neither abstract nor remote from human interests. It ranges very widely over morality, politics, aesthetics and religion. In all this he constantly appeals to the idea of the self. But the idea of the self was precisely the idea that he was unable to place on an adequate foundation. So there is an important weakness, a weakness which he himself admits, in the theoretical basis of his science of human nature.

What exactly was the weakness? Hume gave his account of it in the appendix to the *Treatise*. But it is arguable that his diagnosis was wrong, and that the weakness was really something other than what he took it to be. So in the remainder of this essay I shall be occupied with two things. First, I shall try to explain Hume's version of what was wrong with his theory of personal identity: and then I shall argue that what is really wrong with it is something else, which he himself did not recognise.

First let us look at his own diagnosis of his failure. Now it is an important fact about him that he wished to achieve in the science of human nature what Newton had achieved in astronomy. Where Newton used mechanics, he would use what we now call psychology, and he compares his law of the association of ideas with Newton's law of gravitation. I think that the fact that he regarded his work in this way really explains why he was willing to reduce the accepted idea of causal necessity and the accepted idea of a material object, and yet could not bring himself to reduce the accepted idea of personal identity. For he was prepared, or at least half prepared, to reduce the external world to phenomena in the human mind. But this meant that his theory of the self had to bear a great weight, and so it was essential that it should remain strong and unreduced. But when he reviewed it in the appendix to the *Treatise*, it seemed to him to be too thin and weak. He said that, if the self were a substance in which impressions and ideas inhered, or if there were a real connexion between impressions and ideas, he would be satisfied. But since neither of these two things was the case, he remained dissatisfied.

But would he really have been in a better position if he had been able to say that the self is a substance, or that there is a real connexion between impressions and ideas? Certainly he might have claimed to have justified the sense that we have of the stability and continuity of our lives. On the other hand, perhaps he would not have felt the need for some unattainable kind of connexion between the elements in our psychological histories if he had realised the importance of intentional connexions, instead of being so preoccupied with mechanical ones. However, suppose that he had succeeded in establishing one of the two things which, according to him, could not be established. Would that have helped him to solve the philosophical problem of the particular identity of persons? As I pointed out earlier, some of the factors that give stability and continuity to a human life can be used by a person who asks himself a question of particular identity. So this might be true of the two factors that Hume wished that he could find, but admitted that he could not find. Whether it would in fact be true is a difficult question, which I shall not attempt to answer here.

In any case, there is another deficiency in Hume's theory. He not only does not find adequate criteria for answering questions of particular identity, but also fails to provide a setting in which such questions can even be asked. This came about in the following way. When he asked himself a question about his own particular identity, he always confined himself to earlier impressions and ideas, and did not consider earlier speech, behaviour and actions. Perhaps he could have avoided this restriction, but it was at least very natural for a philosopher who admitted that he could give no rational account of our belief in the physical world. Anyway, the consequence was that he would ask himself whether, for example, he was the person who had a certain idea, which was not expressed in words, on New Year's Day 1735. But the trouble with this kind of question was that, if he had any reason to believe that the idea occurred at all, he could not fail to believe that it occurred in the series that was himself, David Hume. For only his own unaided memory vouched for the occurrence of the idea. Consequently he could never be in a position in which he could ask himself whether he was the person who . . .: if he had any doubt about the answer, he would equally doubt whether the question was properly framed.

This situation can be avoided only if questions of particular identity are framed in such a way that they make some reference to speech, behaviour and actions, or, more generally, to the body and its history. It is exceedingly important that this is so even when the identity-question is one that a person asks about himself. For example, when I ask myself whether I am the person who walked through the gate of this college at a particular moment today, I must have some way of knowing that there was such a person even if he was not myself. And that means that I must be able to use something other than my memory of my own psychological history. Otherwise there will be no possibility of my knowing that there was such a person unless he was myself. Questions of particular personal identity presuppose the existence of other people. If other people did not exist, there would be nobody for me not to be. And I must have some way of knowing that other people exist.

Now we are aware of other people only through their bodies. Whether this is a contingent fact or a necessary fact, it is the human predicament. And since we are in this predicament, any philosophical theory of personal identity must be based on our physical existence in space and time. That is absolutely essential. But what Hume tried to do was to work out a theory of personal identity that did not rely on our knowledge of the external world or on our awareness of other people. In this he necessarily failed, not only because he could not explain completely how questions of personal identity are answered, but because he could not explain at all how they are asked.

Hume was not a solipsist, but he suffered from a tendency to solipsism. As always happens in such a case, the attempt to describe the internal world without the external world led to a curious distortion. For Hume's impressions and ideas gradually began to take over the characteristics of material objects. In his discussion of personal identity he talked as if they could exist in isolation, floating in a kind of impersonal medium. And his version of the theory that the self is a substance, which he is reluctantly forced to reject, is based on obvious analogies with the body.

When the external world is neglected, it usually makes itself felt in this way.

Earlier in this essay I said that Hume's theory of personal identity is unrealistic. That is true. It is unrealistic because it fails to take account of the fact that we live together in space and time, and communicate through our bodies. But though this is a true judgement about Hume's theory, it is an inadequate one. For it is not as if he simply overlooked these obvious facts through carelessness. If that were so, his theory would be of little interest. What makes it interesting is that it is a careful attempt to work out a theory of personal identity within an egocentric framework. The attempt failed, conspicuously and avowedly, because Hume was more consistent and clear-sighted than others who tried to do the same thing. That kind of failure is important. What it probably shows is that the thing cannot be done.

Source: David Hume—A Symposium, ed. David Pears (Macmillan). (Extract.)

10 The Self and the Future (1970)

BERNARD WILLIAMS

Suppose that there were some process to which two persons, A and B, could be subjected as a result of which they might be said—question-beggingly—to have *exchanged bodies.* That is to say—less question-beggingly—there is a certain human body which is such that when previously we were confronted with it, we were confronted with person A, certain utterances coming from it were expressive of memories of the past experiences of A, certain movements of it partly constituted the actions of A and were taken as expressive of the character of A, and so forth; but now, after the process is completed, utterances coming from this body are expressive of what seem to be just those memories which previously we identified as memories of the past experiences of B, its movements partly constitute actions expressive of the character of B, and so forth; and conversely with the other body.

There are certain important philosophical limitations on how such imaginary cases are to be constructed, and how they are to be taken when constructed in various ways. I shall mention two principal limitations, not in order to pursue them further here, but precisely in order to get them out of the way.

There are certain limitations, particularly with regard to character and mannerisms, to our ability to imagine such cases even in the most restricted sense of our being disposed to take the later performances of that body which was previously A's as expressive of B's character; if the previous A and B were extremely unlike one another both physically and psychologically, and if, say, in addition, they were of different sex, there might be grave difficulties in reading B's dispositions in any possible performances of A's body. Let us forget this, and for the present purpose just take A and B as being sufficiently alike (however alike that has to be) for the difficulty not to arise; after the experiment, persons familiar with A and B are just *overwhelmingly struck* by the B-ish character of the doings associated with what was previously A's body, and conversely. Thus the feat of imagining an exchange of bodies is supposed possible in the most restricted sense. But now there is a further limitation which has to be overcome if the feat is to be not merely possible in the most restricted sense but also is to have an outcome which, on serious reflection, we are prepared to describe as A and B having changed bodies—that is, an outcome where, confronted with what was previously A's body, we are prepared seriously to say that we are now confronted with B.

It would seem a necessary condition of so doing that the utterances coming from that body be taken as genuinely expressive of memories of B's past. But memory is a causal notion; and as we actually use it, it seems a necessary condition on x's present knowledge of x's earlier experiences constituting memory of those experiences that the causal chain linking the experiences and the knowledge should not run outside x's body. Hence if utterances coming from a given body are to be taken as expressive of memories of the experiences of B, there should be some suitable causal link between the appropriate state of that body and the original happening of those experiences to B. One radical way of securing that condition in the imagined exchange case is to suppose, with Shoemaker,[1] that the brains of A and of B are transposed. We may not need so radical a condition. Thus suppose it were possible to extract information from a man's brain and store it in a device while his brain was repaired, or even renewed,

[1] *Self-Knowledge and Self-Identity* (Ithaca, N. Y., 1963), p. 23 f.

the information then being replaced: it would seem exaggerated to insist that the resultant man could not possibly have the memories he had before the operation. With regard to our knowledge of our own past, we draw distinctions between merely recalling, being reminded, and learning again, and those distinctions correspond (roughly) to distinctions between no new input, partial new input, and total new input with regard to the information in question; and it seems clear that the information-parking case just imagined would not count as new input in the sense necessary and sufficient for 'learning again.' Hence we can imagine the case we are concerned with in terms of information extracted into such devices from A's and B's brains and replaced in the other brain; this is the sort of model which, I think not unfairly for the present argument, I shall have in mind.

We imagine the following. The process considered above exists; two persons can enter some machine, let us say, and emerge changed in the appropriate ways. If A and B are the persons who enter, let us call the persons who emerge the *A-body-person* and the *B-body-person*: the A-body-person is that person (whoever it is) with whom I am confronted when, after the experiment, I am confronted with that body which previously was A's body—that is to say, that person who would naturally be taken for A by someone who just saw this person, was familiar with A's appearance before the experiment, and did not know about the happening of the experiment. A non-question-begging description of the experiment will leave it open which (if either) of the persons A and B the A-body-person is; the description of the experiment as 'persons changing bodies' of course implies that the A-body-person is actually B.

We take two persons A and B who are going to have the process carried out on them. (We can suppose, rather hazily, that they are willing for this to happen; to investigate at all closely at this stage why they might be willing or unwilling, what they would fear, and so forth, would anticipate some later issues.) We further announce that one of the two resultant persons, the A-body-person and the B-body person, is going after the experiment to be given \$100,000, while the other is going to be tortured. We then ask each A and B to choose which treatment should be dealt out to which of the persons who will emerge from the experiment, the choice to be made (if it can be) on selfish grounds.

Suppose that A chooses that the B-body-person should get the pleasant treatment and the A-body-person the unpleasant treatment; and B chooses conversely (this might indicate that they thought that 'changing bodies' was indeed a good description of the outcome). The experimenter cannot act in accordance with both these sets of preferences, those expressed by A and those expressed by B. Hence there is one clear sense in which A and B cannot both get what they want: namely, that if the experimenter, before the experiment, announces to A and B that he intends to carry out the alternative (for example), of treating the B-body-person unpleasantly and the A-body-person pleasantly—then A can say rightly, 'That's not the outcome I chose to happen,' and B can say rightly, 'That's just the outcome I chose to happen.' So, evidently, A and B before the experiment can each come to know either that the outcome he chose will be that which will happen, or that the one he chose will not happen, and in that sense they can get or fail to get what they wanted. But is it also true that when the experimenter proceeds *after* the experiment to act in accordance with one of the preferences and not the other, then one of A and B will have got what he wanted, and the other not?

There seems very good ground for saying so. For suppose the experimenter, having elicited A's and B's preference, says nothing to A and B about what he will do; conducts the experiment; and then, for example, gives the unpleasant treatment to the B-body-person and the pleasant treatment to the A-body-person. Then the B-body-person will not only complain of the unpleasant treatment as such, but will complain (since he has A's memories) that that was not the outcome he chose, since he chose that the B-body-person should be well treated; and since A made his choice in selfish spirit, he may add that he precisely chose in that way because he did not want the unpleasant things to happen to *him*. The A-body-person meanwhile will express satisfaction both at the receipt of the $100,000, and also at the fact that the experimenter has chosen to act in the way that he, B, so wisely chose. These facts make a strong case for saying that the experimenter has brought it about that B did in the outcome get what he wanted and A did not. It is therefore a strong case for saying that the B-body-person really is A, and the A-body-person really is B; and therefore for saying that the process of the experiment really is that of changing bodies. For the same reasons it would seem that A and B in our example really did choose wisely, and that it was A's bad luck that the choice he correctly made was not carried out, B's good luck that the choice he correctly made was carried out. This seems to show that to care about what happens to me in the future is not necessarily to care about what happens to *this* body (the one I now have); and this in turn might be taken to show that in some sense of Descartes's obscure phrase, I and my body are 'really distinct' (though, of course, nothing in these considerations could support the idea that I could exist without a body at all).

These suggestions seem to be reinforced if we consider the cases where *A* and *B* make other choices with regard to the experiment. Suppose that *A* chooses that the *A*-body-person should get the money, and the *B*-body-person get the pain, and *B* chooses conversely. Here again there can be no outcome which matches the expressed preferences of both of them: they cannot both get what they want. The experimenter announces, before the experiment, that the *A*-body-person will in fact get the money, and the *B*-body-person will get the pain. So *A* at this stage gets what he wants (the announced outcome matches his expressed preference). After the experiment, the distribution is carried out as announced. Both the *A*-body-person and the *B*-body-person will have to agree that what is happening is in accordance with the preference that *A* originally expressed. The *B*-body-person will naturally express this acknowledgment (since he has *A*'s memories) by saying that this is the distribution he chose; he will recall, among other things, the experimenter announcing this outcome, his approving it as what he chose, and so forth. However, he (the *B*-body-person) certainly does not like what is now happening to him, and would much prefer to be receiving what the *A*-body-person is receiving—namely, $100,000. The *A*-body-person will on the other hand recall choosing an outcome other than this one, but will reckon it good luck that the experimenter did not do what he recalls choosing. It looks, then, as though the *A*-body-person had gotten what he wanted, but not what he chose, while the *B*-body-person has gotten what he chose, but not what he wanted. So once more it looks as though they are, respectively, *B* and *A*; and that in this case the original choices of both *A* and *B* were unwise.

Suppose, lastly, that in the original choice *A* takes the line of the first case and *B* of the second: that is, *A* chooses that the *B*-body-person should get the money and the *A*-body-person the pain, and *B* chooses exactly the same thing. In this case, the experimenter would seem to be in the happy situation of giving both persons what they want—or at least, like God, what they have chosen. In this case, the *B*-body-person likes what he is receiving, recalls choosing it, and congratulates himself on the wisdom of (as he puts it) his choice; while the A-body-person does not like what he is receiving, recalls choosing it, and is forced to acknowledge that (as he puts it) his choice was unwise. So once more we seem to get results to support the suggestions drawn from the first case.

Let us now consider the question, not of A and B choosing certain outcomes to take place after the experiment, but of their willingness to engage in the experiment at all. If they were initially inclined to accept the description of the experiment as 'changing bodies' then one thing that would interest them would be the character of the other person's body. In this respect also what would happen after the experiment would seem to suggest that 'changing bodies' was a good description of the experiment. If A and B agreed to the experiment, being each not displeased with the appearance, physique, and so forth of the other person's body; after the experiment the B-body-person might well be found saying such things as: 'When I agreed to this experiment, I thought that B's face was quite attractive, but now I look at it in the mirror, I am not so sure'; or the A-body-person might say 'When I agreed to this experiment I did not know that A had a wooden leg; but now, after it is over, I find that I have this wooden leg, and I want the experiment reversed.' It is possible that he might say further that he finds the leg very uncomfortable, and that the B-body-person should say, for instance, that he recalls that he found it very uncomfortable at first, but one gets used to it: but perhaps one would need to know more than at least I do about the physiology of habituation to artificial limbs to know whether the A-body-person would find the leg uncomfortable: that body, after all, has had the leg on it for some time. But apart from this sort of detail, the general line of the outcome regarded from this point of view seems to confirm our previous conclusions about the experiment.

Now let us suppose that when the experiment is proposed (in non-question-begging terms) A and B think rather of their psychological advantages and disadvantages. A's thoughts turn primarily to certain sorts of anxiety to which he is very prone, while B is concerned with the frightful memories he has of past experiences which still distress him. They each hope that the experiment will in some way result in their being able to get away from these things. They may even have been impressed by philosophical arguments to the effect that bodily continuity is at least a necessary condition of personal identity: A, for example, reasons that, granted the experiment comes off, then the person who is bodily continuous with him will not have this anxiety, while the other person will no doubt have some anxiety—perhaps in some sense his anxiety—and at least that person will not be he. The experiment is performed and the experimenter (to whom A and B previously revealed privately their several difficulties and hopes) asks the A-body-person whether he has gotten rid of his anxiety. This person presumably replies that he does not know what the man is talking about; he never had such anxiety, but he did have some very disagreeable memories, and recalls engaging in the experiment to get rid of them, and is disappointed to discover that he still has them. The B-body-person will react in a similar way to questions about his painful memories, pointing out that he still has his anxiety. These results seem to confirm still further the description of the experiment as 'changing bodies.' And all the results suggest that the only rational thing to do, confronted with such an experiment, would be to identify oneself with one's memories, and so forth, and not with one's body. The philosophical arguments designed to show that bodily continuity was at least a necessary condition of personal identity would seem to be just mistaken.

Let us now consider something apparently different. Someone in whose power I am tells me that I am going to be tortured tomorrow. I am frightened, and look forward to tomorrow in great apprehension. He adds that when the time comes, I shall not remember being told that this was going to happen to me, since shortly before the torture something else will be done to me which will make me forget the announcement. This certainly will not cheer me up, since I know perfectly well that I can forget things, and that there is such a thing as indeed being tortured unexpectedly because I had forgotten or been made to forget a prediction of the torture: that will still be a torture which, so long as I do know about the prediction, I look forward to in fear. He then adds that my forgetting the announcement will be only part of a larger process: when the moment of torture comes, I shall not remember any of the things I am now in a position to remember. This does not cheer me up, either, since I can readily conceive of being involved in an accident, for instance, as a result of which I wake up in a completely amnesiac state and also in great pain; that could certainly happen to me, I should not like it to happen to me, nor to know that it was going to happen to me. He now further adds that at the moment of torture I shall not only not remember the things I am now in a position to remember, but will have a different set of impressions of my past, quite different from the memories I now have. I do not think that this would cheer me up, either. For I can at least conceive the possibility, if not the concrete reality, of going completely mad, and thinking perhaps that I am George IV or somebody; and being told that something like that was going to happen to me would have no tendency to reduce the terror of being told authoritatively that I was going to be tortured, but would merely compound the horror. Nor do I see why I should be put into any better frame of mind by the person in charge adding lastly that the impressions of my past with which I shall be equipped on the eve of torture will exactly fit the past of another person now living, and that indeed I shall acquire these impressions by (for instance) information now in his brain being copied into mine. Fear, surely, would still be the proper reaction: and not because one did not know what was going to happen, but because in one vital respect at least one did know what was going to happen—torture, which one can indeed expect to happen to oneself, and to be preceded by certain mental derangements as well.

If this is right, the whole question seems now to be totally mysterious. For what we have just been through is of course merely one side, differently represented, of the transaction which we considered before; and it represents it as a perfectly hateful prospect, while the previous considerations represented it as something one should rationally, perhaps even cheerfully, choose out of the options there presented. It is differently presented, of course, and in two notable respects; but when we look at these two differences of presentation, can we really convince ourselves that the second presentation is wrong or misleading, thus leaving the road open to the first version which at the time seemed so convincing? Surely not.

The first difference is that in the second version the torture is throughout represented as going to happen to *me*: 'you,' the man in charge persistently says. Thus he is not very neutral. But should he have been neutral? Or, to put it another way, does his use of the second person have a merely emotional and rhetorical effect on me, making me afraid when further reflection would have shown that I had no reason to be? It is certainly not obviously so. The problem just is that through every step of his predictions I seem to be able to follow him successfully. And if I reflect on whether what he has said gives me grounds for fearing that I shall be tortured, I could consider that behind my fears lies some principle such as this: that my undergoing physical pain in the future is not excluded by any psychological state I may be in at the time, with the platitudinous exception of those psychological states which in themselves exclude experiencing pain, notably (if it is a psychological state) unconsciousness. In particular, what impressions I have about the past will not have any effect on whether I undergo the pain or not. This principle seems sound enough.

It is an important fact that not everything I would, as things are, regard as an evil would be something that I should rationally fear as an evil if it were predicted that it would happen to me in the future and also predicted that I should undergo significant psychological changes in the meantime. For the fact that I regard that happening, things being as they are, as an evil can be dependent on factors of belief or character which might themselves be modified by the psychological changes in question. Thus if I am appallingly subject to acrophobia, and am told that I shall find myself on top of a steep mountain in the near future, I shall to that extent be afraid; but if I am told that I shall be psychologically changed in the meantime in such a way as to rid me of my acrophobia (and as with the other prediction, I believe it), then I have no reason to be afraid of the predicted happening, or at least not the same reason. Again, I might look forward to meeting a certain person again with either alarm or excitement because of my memories of our past relations. In some part, these memories operate in connection with my emotion, not only on the present time, but projectively forward: for it is to a meeting itself affected by the presence of those memories that I look forward. If I am convinced that when the time comes I shall not have those memories, then I shall not have just the same reasons as before for looking forward to that meeting with the one emotion or the other. (Spiritualism, incidentally, appears to involve the belief that I have just the same reasons for a given attitude toward encountering people again after I am dead, as I did before: with the one modification that I can be sure it will all be very nice.)

Physical pain, however, the example which for simplicity (and not for any obsessional reason) I have taken, is absolutely minimally dependent on character or belief. No amount of change in my character or my beliefs would seem to affect substantially the nastiness of tortures applied to me; correspondingly, no degree of predicted change in my character and beliefs can unseat the fear of torture which, together with those changes, is predicted for me.

I am not at all suggesting that the *only* basis, or indeed the only rational basis, for fear in the face of these various predictions is how things will be relative to my psychological state in the eventual outcome. I am merely pointing out that this is one component; it is not the only one. For certainly one will fear and otherwise reject the changes themselves, or in very many cases one would. Thus one of the old paradoxes of hedonistic utilitarianism; if one had assurances that undergoing certain operations and being attached to a machine would provide one for the rest of one's existence with an unending sequence of delicious and varied experiences, one might very well reject the option, and react with fear if someone proposed to apply it compulsorily; and that fear and horror would seem appropriate reactions in the second case may help to discredit the interpretation (if anyone has the nerve to propose it) that one's reason for rejecting the option voluntarily would be a consciousness of duties to others which one in one's hedonic state would leave undone. The prospect of contented madness or vegetableness is found by many (not perhaps by all) appalling in ways which are obviously not a function of how things would then be for them, for things would then be for them not appalling. In the case we are at present discussing, these sorts of considerations seem merely to make it clearer that the predictions of the man in charge provide a double ground of horror: at the prospect of torture, and at the prospect of the change in character and in impressions of the past that will precede it. And certainly, to repeat what has already been said, the prospect of the second certainly seems to provide no ground for rejecting or not fearing the prospect of the first.

I said that there were two notable differences between the second presentation of our situation and the first. The first difference, which we have just said something about, was that the man predicted the torture for *me*, a psychologically very changed 'me'. We have yet to find a reason for saying that he should not have done this, or that I really should be unable to follow him if he does; I seem to be able to follow him only too well. The second difference is that in this presentation he does not mention the other man, except in the somewhat incidental role of being the provenance of the impressions of the past I end up with. He does not mention him at all as someone who will end up with impressions of the past derived from me (and, incidentally, with

$100,000 as well—a consideration which, in the frame of mind appropriate to this version, will merely make me jealous).

But why *should* he mention this man and what is going to happen to him? My selfish concern is to be told what is going to happen to me, and now I know: torture, preceded by changes of character, brain operations, changes in impressions of the past. The knowledge that one other person, or none, or many will be similarly mistreated may affect me in other ways, of sympathy, greater horror at the power of this tyrant, and so forth; but surely it cannot affect my expectations of torture? But—someone will say—this is to leave out exactly the feature which, as the first presentation of the case showed, makes all the difference: for it is to leave out the person who, as the first presentation showed, will be you. It is to leave out not merely a feature which should fundamentally affect your fears, it is to leave out the very person for whom you are fearful. So of course, the objector will say, this makes all the difference.

But can it? Consider the following series of cases. In each case we are to suppose that after what is described, A is, as before, to be tortured; we are also to suppose the person A is informed beforehand that just these things followed by the torture will happen to him:

- (*i*) A is subjected to an operation which produces total amnesia;
- (*ii*) amnesia is produced in A, and other interference leads to certain changes in his character;
- (*iii*) changes in his character are produced, and at the same time certain illusory 'memory' beliefs are induced in him; these are of a quite fictitious kind and do not fit the life of any actual person;
- (*iv*) the same as (*iii*), except that both the character traits and the 'memory' impressions are designed to be appropriate to another actual person, B;
- (*v*) the same as (*iv*), except that the result is produced by putting the information into A from the brain of B, by a method which leaves B the same as he was before;
- (*vi*) the same happens to A as in (*v*), but B is not left the same, since a similar operation is conducted in the reverse direction.

I take it that no one is going to dispute that A has reasons, and fairly straightforward reasons, for fear of pain when the prospect is that of situation (*i*); there seems no conceivable reason why this should not extend to situation (*ii*), and the situation (*iii*) can surely introduce no difference of principle—it just seems a situation which for more than one reason we should have grounds for fearing, as suggested above. Situation (*iv*) at least introduces the person *B*, who was the focus of the objection we are now discussing. But it does not seem to introduce him in any way which makes a material difference; if I can expect pain through a transformation which involves new 'memory'-impressions, it would seem a purely external fact, relative to that, that the 'memory'-impressions had a model. Nor, in (*iv*), do we satisfy a causal condition which I mentioned at the beginning for the 'memories' actually being memories; though notice that if the job were done thoroughly, I might well be able to elicit from the *A*-body-person the kinds of remarks about his previous expectations of the experiment—remarks appropriate to the original *B* —which so impressed us in the first version of the story. I shall have a similar assurance of this being so in situation (*v*), where, moreover, a plausible application of the causal condition is available.

But two things are to be noticed about this situation. First, if we concentrate on *A* and the *A*-body-person, we do not seem to have added anything which from the point of view of his fears makes any material difference; just as, in the move from (*iii*) to (*iv*), it made no relevant difference that the new 'memory'-impressions which precede the pain had, as it happened, a model, so in the move from (*iv*) to (*v*) all we have added is that they have a model which is also their cause: and it is still difficult to see why that, to him looking forward, could possibly make the difference between expecting pain and not expecting pain. To illustrate that point from the case of character: if *A* is capable of expecting pain, he is capable of expecting pain preceded by a change in his dispositions—and to that expectation it can make no difference, whether that change in his dispositions is modeled on, or indeed indirectly caused by, the dispositions of some other person. If his fears can, as it were, reach through the change, it seems a mere trimming how the change is in fact induced. The second point about situation (*v*) is that if the crucial question for *A*'s fears with regard to what befalls the *A*-body-person is whether the *A*-body-person is or is not the person *B*,[2] then that condition has not yet been satisfied in situation (*v*): for there we have an undisputed *B*

---

[2] This of course does not have to be the crucial question, but it seems one fair way of taking up the present objection.

in addition to the A-body-person, and certainly those two are not the same person.

But in situation (*vi*), we seemed to think, that is finally what he is. But if A's original fears could reach through the expected changes in (*v*), as they did in (*iv*) and (*iii*), then certainly they can reach through in (*vi*). Indeed, from the point of view of A's expectations and fears, there is less difference between (*vi*) and (*v*) than there is between (*v*) and (*iv*) or between (*iv*) and (*iii*). In those transitions, there were at least differences—though we could not see that they were really relevant differences—in the content and cause of what happened to him; in the present case there is absolutely no difference at all in what happens to him, the only difference being in what happens to someone else. If he can fear pain when (*v*) is predicted, why should he cease to when (*vi*) is?

I can see only one way of relevantly laying great weight on the transition from (*v*) to (*vi*); and this involves a considerable difficulty. This is to deny that, as I put it, the transition from (*v*) to (*vi*) involves merely the addition of something happening to *somebody else*; what rather it does, it will be said, is to involve the reintroduction of A himself, as the B-body-person; since he has reappeared in this form, it is for this person, and not for the unfortunate A-body-person, that A will have his expectations. This is to reassert, in effect, the viewpoint emphasized in our first presentation of the experiment. But this surely has the consequence that A should not have fears for the A-body-person who appeared in situation (*v*). For by the present argument, the A-body-person in (*vi*) is not A; the B-body-person is. But the A-body-person in (*v*) is, in character, history, everything, exactly the same as the A-body-person in (*vi*); so if the latter is not A, then neither is the former. (It is this point, no doubt, that encourages one to speak of the difference that goes with [*vi*] as being, on the present view, the *reintroduction* of A.) But no one else in (*v*) has any better claim to be A. So in (*v*), it seems, A just does not exist. This would certainly explain why A should have no fears for the state of things in (*v*)—though he might well have fears for the path to it. But it rather looked earlier as though he could well have fears for the state of things in (*v*). Let us grant, however, that that was an illusion, and that A really does not exist in (*v*); then does he exist in (*iv*), (*iii*), (*ii*), or (*i*)? It seems very difficult to deny it for (*i*) and (*ii*); are we perhaps to draw the line between (*iii*) and (*iv*)?

Here someone will say: you must not insist on drawing a line—borderline cases are borderline cases, and you must not push our concepts beyond their limits. But this well-known piece of advice, sensible as it is in many cases, seems in the present case to involve an extraordinary difficulty. It may intellectually comfort observers of *A*'s situation; but what is *A* supposed to make of it? To be told that a future situation is a borderline one for its being myself that is hurt, that it is conceptually undecidable whether it will be me or not, is something which, it seems, I can do nothing with; because, in particular, it seems to have no comprehensible representation in my expectations and the emotions that go with them.

If I expect that a certain situation, S, will come about in the future, there is of course a wide range of emotions and concerns, directed on S, which I may experience now in relation to my expectation. Unless I am exceptionally egoistic, it is not a condition on my being concerned in relation to this expectation, that I myself will be involved in S—where my being 'involved' in S means that I figure in S as someone doing something at that time or having something done to me, or, again, that S will have consequences affecting me at that or some subsequent time. There are some emotions, however, which I will feel only if I will be involved in S, and fear is an obvious example.

Now the description of S under which it figures in my expectations will necessarily be, in various ways, indeterminate; and one way in which it may be indeterminate is that it leave open whether I shall be involved in S or not. Thus I may have good reason to expect that one out of us five is going to get hurt, but no reason to expect it to be me rather than one of the others. My present emotions will be correspondingly affected by this indeterminacy. Thus, sticking to the egoistic concern involved in fear, I shall presumably be somewhat more cheerful than if I knew it was going to be me, somewhat less cheerful than if I had been left out altogether. Fear will be mixed with, and qualified by, apprehension; and so forth. These emotions revolve around the thought of the eventual determination of the indeterminacy; moments of straight fear focus on its really turning out to be me, of hope on its turning out not to be me. All the emotions are related to the coming about of what I expect: and what I expect in such a case just cannot come about save by coming about in one of the ways or another.

There are other ways in which indeterminate expectations can be related to fear. Thus I may expect (perhaps neurotically) that something nasty is going to happen to me, indeed expect that when it happens it will take some determinate form, but have no range, or no closed range, of candidates for the determinate form to rehearse in my present thought. Different from this would be the fear of something radically indeterminate—the fear (one might say) of a nameless horror. If somebody had such a fear, one could even say that he had, in a sense, a perfectly determinate expectation: if what he expects indeed comes about, there will be nothing more determinate to be said about it after the event than was said in the expectation. Both these cases of course are cases of *fear* because one thing that is fixed amid the indeterminacy is the belief that it is to me to which the things will happen.

Central to the expectation of S is the thought of what it will be like when it happens—thought which may be indeterminate, range over alternatives, and so forth. When S involves me, there can be the possibility of a special form of such thought: the thought of how it will be for me, the imaginative projection of myself as participant in S.[3]

I do not have to think about S in this way, when it involves me; but I may be able to. (It might be suggested that this possibility was even mirrored in the language, in the distinction between 'expecting to be hurt' and 'expecting that I shall be hurt'; but I am very doubtful about this point, which is in any case of no importance.)

Suppose now that there is an S with regard to which it is for conceptual reasons undecidable whether it involves me or not, as is proposed for the experimental situation by the line we are discussing. It is important that the expectation of S is not *indeterminate* in any of the ways we have just been considering. It is not like the nameless horror, since the fixed point of that case was that it was going to happen to the subject, and that made his state unequivocally fear. Nor is it like the expectation of the man who expects one of the five to be hurt; his fear was indeed equivocal, but its focus, and that of the expectation, was that when S came about, it would certainly come about in one way or the other. In the present case, fear (of the torture, that is to say, not of the initial experiment) seems neither appropriate, nor inappropriate, nor appropriately equivocal. Relatedly, the subject has an incurable difficulty about how he may think about S. If he

---

[3] For a more detailed treatment of issues related to this, see *Imagination and the Self*, British Academy (London, 1966); reprinted in P. F. Strawson (ed.), *Studies in Thought and Action* (Oxford, 1968).

engages in projective imaginative thinking (about how it will be for him), he implicitly answers the necessarily unanswerable question; if he thinks that he cannot engage in such thinking, it looks very much as if he also answers it, though in the opposite direction. Perhaps he must just refrain from such thinking; but is he just refraining from it, if it is incurably undecidable whether he can or cannot engage in it?

It may be said that all that these considerations can show is that fear, at any rate, does not get its proper footing in this case; but that there could be some other, more ambivalent, form of concern which would indeed be appropriate to this particular expectation, the expectation of the conceptually undecidable situation. There are, perhaps, analogous feelings that actually occur in actual situations. Thus material objects do occasionally undergo puzzling transformations which leave a conceptual shadow over their identity. Suppose I were sentimentally attached to an object to which this sort of thing then happened; then it might be that I could neither feel about it quite as I did originally, nor be totally indifferent to it, but would have some other and rather ambivalent feeling toward it. Similarly, it may be said, toward the prospective sufferer of pain, my identity relations with whom are conceptually shadowed, I can feel neither as I would if he were certainly me, nor as I would if he were certainly not, but rather some such ambivalent concern.

But this analogy does little to remove the most baffling aspect of the present case—an aspect which has already turned up in what was said about the subject's difficulty in thinking either projectively or non-projectively about the situation. For to regard the prospective pain-sufferer *just* like the transmogrified object of sentiment, and to conceive of my ambivalent distress about his future pain as just like ambivalent distress about some future damage to such an object, is of course to leave him and me clearly distinct from one another, and thus to displace the conceptual shadow from its proper place. I have to get nearer to him than that. But is there any nearer that I can get to him without expecting his pain? If there is, the analogy has not shown us it. We can certainly not get nearer by expecting, as it were, *ambivalent* pain; there is no place at all for that. There seems to be an obstinate bafflement to mirroring in my expectations a situation in which it is conceptually undecidable whether I occur.

The bafflement seems, moreover, to turn to plain absurdity if we move from conceptual undecidability to its close friend and neighbor, conventionalist decision. This comes out if we consider another description, overtly conventionalist, of the series of cases which occasioned the present discussion. This description would reject a point I relied on in an earlier argument—namely, that if we deny that the A-body-person in (*vi*) is A (because the B-body-person is), then we must deny that the A-body-person in (*v*) is A, since they are exactly the same. 'No,' it may be said, 'this is just to assume that we say the same in different sorts of situation. No doubt when we have the very good candidate for being A— namely, the B-body-person—we call him A; but this does not mean that we should not call the A-body-person A in that other situation when we have no better candidate around. Different situations call for different descriptions.' This line of talk is the sort of thing indeed appropriate to lawyers deciding the owner- ship of some property which has undergone some bewildering set of transformations; they just have to decide, and in each situation, let us suppose, it has got to go to somebody, on as reasonable grounds as the facts and the law admit. But as a line to deal with a person's fears or expectations about his own future, it seems to have no sense at all. If A's fears can extend to what will happen to the A-body-person in (*v*), I do not see how they can be rationally diverted from the fate of the exactly similar person in (*vi*) by his being told that someone would have a reason in the latter situation which he would not have in the former for deciding to call another person A.

Thus, to sum up, it looks as though there are two presentations of the imagined experiment and the choice associated with it, each of which carries conviction, and which lead to contrary con- clusions. The idea, moreover, that the situation after the experi- ment is conceptually undecidable in the relevant respect seems not to assist, but rather to increase, the puzzlement; while the idea (so often appealed to in these matters) that it is convention- ally decidable is even worse. Following from all that, I am not in the least clear which option it would be wise to take if one were presented with them before the experiment. I find that rather disturbing.

Whatever the puzzlement, there is one feature of the arguments which have led to it which is worth picking out, since it runs counter to something which is, I think, often rather vaguely supposed. It is often recognized that there are 'first-personal' and 'third-personal' aspects of questions about persons, and that there are difficulties about the relations between them. It is also recognized that 'mentalistic' considerations (as we may vaguely call them) and considerations of bodily continuity are involved in questions of personal identity (which is not to say that there are mentalistic and bodily criteria of personal identity). It is tempting to think that the two distinctions run in parallel: roughly, that a first-personal approach concentrates attention on mentalistic considerations, while a third-personal approach emphasizes considerations of bodily continuity. The present discussion is an illustration of exactly the opposite. The first argument, which led to the 'mentalistic' conclusion that A and B would change bodies and that each person should identify himself with the destination of his memories and character, was an argument entirely conducted in third-personal terms. The second argument, which suggested the bodily continuity identification, concerned itself with the first-personal issue of what A could expect. That this is so seems to me (though I will not discuss it further here) of some significance.

I will end by suggesting one rather shaky way in which one might approach a resolution of the problem, using only the limited materials already available.

The apparently decisive arguments of the first presentation, which suggested that A should identify himself with the B-body-person, turned on the extreme neatness of the situation in satisfying, if any could, the description of 'changing bodies.' But this neatness is basically artificial; it is the product of the will of the experimenter to produce a situation which would naturally elicit, with minimum hesitation, that description. By the sorts of methods he employed, he could easily have left off earlier or gone on further. He could have stopped at situation (v), leaving B as he was; or he could have gone on and produced two persons each with A-like character and memories, as well as one or two with B-like characteristics. If he had done either of those, we should have been in yet greater difficulty about what to say; he just chose to make it as easy as possible for us to find something to say. Now if we had some model of ghostly persons in bodies, which were in some sense actually moved around by certain procedures, we could regard the neat experiment just as the *effective* experiment: the one method that really did result in the ghostly persons' changing places without being destroyed, dispersed, or whatever. But we cannot seriously use such a model. The experimenter has not in the sense of that model *induced* a change of bodies; he has rather produced the one situation out of a range of equally possible situations which we should be most disposed to call a change of bodies. As against this, the principle that one's fears can extend to future pain whatever psychological changes precede it seems positively straightforward. Perhaps, indeed, it is not; but we need to be shown what is wrong with it. Until we are shown what is wrong with it, we should perhaps decide that if we were the person A then, if we were to decide selfishly, we should pass the pain to the B-body-person. It would be risky: that there is room for the notion of a *risk* here is itself a major feature of the problem.

Source: Philosophical Review, 1970.

ARITHMETIC, LOGIC AND PROOF

11 Demonstration and the Science of Number (1843)

J. S. MILL

[. . .] Wherein lies the peculiar certainty always ascribed to the sciences which are entirely, or almost entirely, deductive? Why are they called the Exact Sciences? Why are mathematical certainty, and the evidence of demonstration, common phrases to express the very highest degree of assurance attainable by reason? Why are mathematics by almost all philosophers and (by some) even those branches of natural philosophy which, through the medium of mathematics, have been converted into deductive sciences, considered to be independent of the evidence of experience and observation, and characterised as systems of Necessary Truth?

The answer I conceive to be, that this character of necessity ascribed to the truths of mathematics, and even (with some reservations to be hereafter made) the peculiar certainty attributed to them, is an illusion; in order to sustain which, it is necessary to suppose that those truths relate to, and express the properties of purely imaginary objects. It is acknowledged that the conclusions of geometry are deduced, partly at least, from the so-called Definitions, and that those definitions are assumed to be correct representations, as far as they go, of the objects with which geometry is conversant. Now we have pointed out that, from a definition as such, no proposition, unless it be one concerning the meaning of a word, can ever follow; and that what apparently follows from a definition, follows in reality from an implied assumption that there exists a real thing conformable thereto.

This assumption in the case of the definitions of geometry, is not strictly true: there exist no real things exactly conformable to the definitions. There exist no points without magnitude; no lines without breadth, nor perfectly straight; no circles with all their radii exactly equal, nor squares with all their angles perfectly right. It will perhaps be said that the assumption does not extend to the actual, but only to the possible existence of such things. I answer that, according to any test we have of possibility, they are not even possible. Their existence, so far as we can form any judgment, would seem to be inconsistent with the physical constitution of our planet at least, if not of the universe. To get rid of this difficulty, and at the same time to save the credit of the supposed system of necessary truth, it is customary to say that the points, lines, circles, and squares which are the subject of geometry, exist in our conceptions merely, and are part of our minds; which minds, by working on their own materials, construct an *a priori* science, the evidence of which is purely mental, and has nothing whatever to do with outward experience. By howsoever high authorities this doctrine may have been sanctioned, it appears to me psychologically incorrect. The points, lines, circles, and squares which any one has in his mind, are (I apprehend) simply copies of the points, lines, circles, and squares which he has known in his experience. Our idea of a point I apprehend to be simply our idea of the *minimum visible*, the smallest portion of surface which we can see. A line as defined by geometers is wholly inconceivable. We can reason about a line as if it had no breadth; because we have a power, which is the foundation of all the control we can exercise over the operations of our minds; the power, when a perception is present to our senses or a conception to our intellects, of *attending* to a part only of that perception or conception, instead of the whole. But we cannot *conceive* a line without breadth; we can form no mental picture of such a line; all the lines which we have in our minds are lines possessing breadth. If any one doubts this, we may refer him to his own experience. I much question if any one who fancies that he can conceive what is called a mathematical line, thinks so from the evidence of his consciousness: I suspect it is rather because he supposes that unless such a conception were possible, mathematics could not exist as a science: a supposition which there will be no difficulty in showing to be entirely groundless.

Since, then, neither in nature, nor in the human mind, do there exist any objects exactly corresponding to the definitions of geometry, while yet that science cannot be supposed to be conversant about non-entities; nothing remains but to consider geometry as conversant with such lines, angles, and figures as really exist; and the definitions, as they are called, must be regarded as some of our first and most obvious generalisations concerning those natural objects. The correctness of those generalisations, *as* generalisations, is without a flaw: the equality of all the radii of a circle is true of all circles, so far as it is true of any one: but it is not exactly true of any circle; it is only nearly true; so nearly that no error of any importance in practice will be incurred by feigning it to be exactly true. When we have occasion to extend these inductions, or their consequences, to cases in which the error would be appreciable—to lines of perceptible breadth or thickness, parallels which deviate sensibly from equidistance, and the like— we correct our conclusions by combining with them a fresh set of propositions relating to the aberration; just as we also take in propositions relating to the physical or chemical properties of the material, if those properties happen to introduce any modification into the result; which they easily may, even with respect to figure and magnitude, as in the case, for instance, of expansion by heat. So long, however, as there exists no practical necessity for attending to any of the properties of the object except its geometrical properties, or to any of the natural irregularities in those, it is convenient to neglect the consideration of the other properties and of the irregularities, and to reason as if these did not exist: accordingly, we formally announce in the definitions, that we intend to proceed on this plan. But it is an error to suppose, because we resolve to confine our attention to a certain number of the properties of an object, that we therefore conceive, or have an idea of, the object denuded of its other properties. We are thinking, all the time, of precisely such objects as we have seen and touched, and with all the properties which naturally belong to them; but, for scientific convenience, we feign them to be divested of all properties, except those which are material to our purpose, and in regard to which we design to consider them.

The peculiar accuracy, supposed to be characteristic of the first principles of geometry thus appears to be fictitious. The assertions on which the reasonings of the science are founded do not, any more than in other sciences, exactly correspond with the fact, but we suppose that they do so for the sake of tracing the consequences which follow from the supposition. The opinion of Dugald Steward respecting the foundations of geometry, is, I conceive, substantially correct; that it is built on hypotheses; that it owes to this alone the peculiar certainty supposed to distinguish it; and that in any science whatever, by reasoning from a set of hypotheses, we may obtain a body of conclusions as certain as those of geometry, that is as strictly in accordance with the hypotheses, and as irresistibly compelling assent, *on condition* that those hypotheses are true.

When, therefore, it is affirmed that the conclusions of geometry are necessary truths, the necessity consists in reality only in this, that they correctly follow from the suppositions from which they are deduced. Those suppositions are so far from being necessary, that they are not even true; they purposely depart, more or less widely, from the truth. The only sense in which necessity can be ascribed to the conclusions of any scientific investigation, is that of legitimately following from some assumption, which, by the conditions of the inquiry, is not to be questioned. In this relation, of course, the derivative truths of every deductive science must stand to the inductions, or assumptions, on which the science is founded, and which, whether true or untrue, certain or doubtful in themselves, are always supposed certain for the purposes of the particular science. And therefore the conclusions of all deductive sciences were said by the ancients to be necessary propositions. We have observed already that to be predicated necessarily was characteristic of the predicable Proprium, and that a proprium was any property of a thing which could be deduced from its essence, that is, from the properties included in its definition. [. . .]

I

In our examination . . . into the nature of the evidence of those deductive sciences which are commonly represented to be systems of necessary truth, we have been led to the following conclusions. The results of those sciences are indeed necessary, in the sense of necessarily following from certain first principles, commonly called axioms and definitions; that is, of being certainly true if those axioms and definitions are so; for the word necessity, even in this acceptation of it, means no more than certainty. But their claim to the character of necessity in any sense beyond this, as implying an evidence independent of and superior to observation and experience, must depend on the previous establishment of such a claim in favour of the definitions and axioms themselves. With regard to axioms, we found that, considered as experimental truths, they rest on superabundant and obvious evidence. We inquired whether, since this is the case, it be imperative to suppose any other evidence of those truths than experimental evidence, any other origin for our belief of them than an experimental origin. We decided that the burden of proof lies with those who maintain the affirmative, and we examined, at considerable length, such arguments as they have produced. The examination having led to the rejection of those arguments, we have thought ourselves warranted in concluding that axioms are but a class, the most universal class, of inductions from experience; the simplest and easiest cases of generalisation from the facts furnished to us by our senses or by our internal consciousness.

While the axioms of demonstrative sciences thus appeared to be experimental truths, the definitions, as they are incorrectly called, in those sciences, were found by us to be generalisations from experience which are not even, accurately speaking, truths; being propositions in which, while we assert of some kind of object some property or properties which observation shows to belong to it, we at the same time deny that it possesses any other properties, though in truth other properties do in every individual instance accompany, and in almost all instances modify, the property thus exclusively predicated. The denial, therefore, is a mere fiction or supposition, made for the purpose of excluding the consideration of those modifying circumstances, when their influence is of too trifling amount to be worth considering, or adjourning it, when important, to a more convenient moment.

From these considerations it would appear that Deductive or Demonstrative Sciences are all without exception, Inductive Sciences; that their evidence is that of experience; but that they are also, in virtue of the peculiar character of one indispensable portion of the general formulae according to which their inductions are made, Hypothetical Sciences. Their conclusions are only true on certain suppositions, which are, or ought to be, approximations to the truth, but are seldom, if ever, exactly true; and to this hypothetical character is to be ascribed the peculiar certainty which is supposed to be inherent in demonstration.

What we have now asserted, however, cannot be received as universally true of Deductive or Demonstrative Sciences, until verified by being applied to the most remarkable of all those sciences, that of Numbers; the theory of the Calculus; Arithmetic and Algebra. It is harder to believe of the doctrines of this science than of any other, either that they are not truths *a priori*, but experimental truths, or that their peculiar certainty is owing to their being not absolute, but only conditional truths. This, therefore, is a case which merits examination apart; and the more so, because on this subject we have a double set of doctrines to contend with; that of the *a priori* philosophers on one side; and on the other, a theory the most opposite to theirs, which was at one time very generally received, and is still far from being altogether exploded among metaphysicians.

II

This theory attempts to solve the difficulty apparently inherent in the case, by representing the propositions of the science of numbers as merely verbal, and its processes as simple transformations of language, substitutions of one expression for another. The proposition, Two and one is equal to three, according to these writers, is not a truth, is not the assertion of a really existing fact, but a definition of the word three; a statement that mankind have agreed to use the name three as a sign exactly equivalent to two and one; to call by the former name whatever is called by the other more clumsy phrase. According to this doctrine the longest process in algebra is but a succession of changes in terminology, by which equivalent expressions are substituted one for another; a series of translations of the same fact, from one into another language; though how, after such a series of translations, the fact itself comes out changed, (as when we demonstrate a new geometrical theorem by algebra,) they have not explained; and it is a difficulty which is fatal to their theory.

It must be acknowledged that there are peculiarities in the processes of arithmetic and algebra which render the theory in question very plausible, and have not unnaturally made those sciences the stronghold of Nominalism. The doctrine that we can discover facts, detect the hidden processes of nature, by an artful manipulation of language, is so contrary to common sense, that a person must have made some advances in philosophy to believe it; men fly to so paradoxical a belief to avoid, as they think, some even greater difficulty, which the vulgar do not see. What has led many to believe that reasoning is a mere verbal process is, that no other theory seemed reconcilable with the nature of the Science of Numbers. For we do not carry any ideas along with us when we use the symbols of arithmetic or of algebra. In a geometrical demonstration we have a mental diagram, if not one on paper; AB, AC, are present to our imagination as lines, intersecting other lines, forming an angle with one another, and the like; but not so *a* and *b*. These may represent lines or any other magnitudes, but those magnitudes are never thought of; nothing is realised in our imagination but *a* and *m*. The ideas which, on the particular occasion, they happen to represent, are banished from the mind during every intermediate part of the process, between the beginning, when the premises are translated from things into signs, and the end, when the conclusion is translated back from signs into things. Nothing, then, being in the reasoner's mind but the symbols, what can seem more inadmissible than to contend that the reasoning process has to do with anything more? We seem to have come to one of Bacon's Prerogative Instances; an *experimentum crucis* on the nature of reasoning itself.

Nevertheless it will appear on consideration, that this apparently so decisive instance is no instance at all; that there is in every step of an arithmetical or algebraical calculation a real induction, a real inference of facts from facts; and that what disguises the induction is simply its comprehensive nature and the consequent extreme generality of the language. All numbers must be numbers of something; there are no such things as numbers in the abstract. *Ten* must mean ten bodies, or ten sounds, or ten beatings of the pulse. But though numbers must be numbers of something, they may be numbers of anything. Propositions, therefore, concerning numbers have the remarkable peculiarity that they are propositions concerning all things whatever; all objects, all existences of every kind, known to our experience. All things possess quantity; consist of parts which can be numbered; and in that character possess all the properties which are called properties of numbers. That half of four is two, must be true whatever the word four represents, whether four hours, four miles, or four pounds weight. We need only conceive a thing divided into four equal parts (and all things may be conceived as so divided) to be able to predicate of it every property of the number four, that is, every arithmetical proposition in which the number four stands on one side of the equation. Algebra extends the generalisation still farther: every number represents that particular number of all things without distinction, but every algebraical symbol does more, it represents all numbers without distinction. As soon as we conceive a thing divided into equal parts, without knowing into what number of parts, we may call it *a* or *x*, and apply to it, without danger of error, every algebraical formula in the books. The proposition, $2(a+b)=2a+2b$, is a truth co-extensive with all nature. Since then algebraical truths are true of all things whatever, and not, like those of geometry, true of lines only or of angles only, it is no wonder that the symbols should not excite in our minds ideas of any things in particular. When we demonstrate the forty-seventh proposition of Euclid, it is not necessary that the words should raise in us an image of all right-angled triangles, but only of some one right-angled triangle; so in algebra we need not under the symbol *a*, picture to ourselves all things whatever, but only some one thing; why not, then, the letter itself? The mere written characters, *a*, *b*, *x*, *y*, *z*, serve as well for representatives of Things in general, as any more complex and apparently more concrete conception. That we are conscious of them, however, in their character of things, and not of mere signs, is evident from the fact that our whole process of reasoning is carried on by predicating of them the properties of things. In resolving an algebraic equation, by what rules do we proceed? By applying at each step to *a*, *b*, and *x*, the proposition that equals added to equals make equals; that equals taken from equals leave equals; and other propositions founded on these two. These are not properties of language, or of signs as such, but of magnitudes, which is as much as to say, of all things. The inferences, therefore, which are successively drawn, are inferences concerning things, not symbols; though as any Things whatever will serve the turn, there is no necessity for keeping the idea of the Thing at all distinct, and consequently the process of thought may, in this case, be allowed without danger to do what all processes of thought, when they have been performed often, will do if permitted, namely, to become entirely mechanical. Hence the general language of algebra comes to be used familiarly without exciting ideas, as all other general language is prone to do from mere habit, though in no other case than this can it be done with complete safety. But when we look back to see from whence the probative force of the process is derived, we find that at every single step, unless we suppose ourselves to be thinking and talking of the things, and not the mere symbols, the evidence fails.

There is another circumstance, which, still more than that which we have now mentioned, gives plausibility to the notion that the propositions of arithmetic and algebra are merely verbal. That is, that when considered as propositions respecting Things, they all have the appearance of being identical propositions. The assertion, Two and one is equal to three, considered as an assertion respecting objects, as for instance 'Two pebbles and one pebble are equal to three pebbles,' does not affirm equality between two collections of pebbles, but absolute identity. It affirms that if we put one pebble to two pebbles, those very pebbles are three. The objects, therefore, being the very same, and the mere assertion that 'objects are themselves' being insignificant, it seems but natural to consider the proposition Two and one is equal to three, as asserting mere identity of signification between the two names.

This, however, though it looks so plausible, will not bear examination. The expression 'two pebbles and one pebble,' and the expression 'three pebbles,' stand indeed for the same aggregation of objects, but they by no means stand for the same physical fact. They are names of the same objects, but of those objects in two different states: though they *de*note the same things, their *con*notation is different. Three pebbles in two separate parcels, and three pebbles in one parcel, do not make the same impression on our senses; and the assertion that the very same pebbles may by an alteration of place and arrangement be made to produce either the one set of sensations or the other, though a very familiar proposition, is not an identical one. It is a truth known to us by early and constant experience—an inductive truth: and such truths are the foundation of the science of Numbers. The fundamental truths of that science all rest on the evidence of sense; they are proved by showing to our eyes and our fingers that any given number of objects, ten balls, for example, may by separation and rearrangement exhibit to our senses all the different sets of numbers the sum of which is equal to ten. All the improved methods of teaching arithmetic to children proceed on a knowledge of this fact. All who wish to carry the child's *mind* along with them in learning arithmetic; all who wish to teach numbers and not mere ciphers—now teach it through the evidence of the senses, in the manner we have described.

We may, if we please, call the proposition, 'Three is two and one,' a definition of the number three, and assert that arithmetic, as it has been asserted that geometry, is a science founded on definitions. But they are definitions in the geometrical sense, not the logical; asserting not the meaning of a term only, but along with it an observed matter of fact. The proposition, 'A circle is a figure bounded by a line which has all its points equally distant from a point within it,' is called the definition of a circle; but the proposition from which so many consequences follow, and which is really a first principle in geometry, is, that figures answering to this description exist. And thus we may call 'Three is two and one' a definition of three; but the calculations which depend on that proposition do not follow from the definition itself, but from an arithmetical theorem presupposed in it, namely, that collections of objects exist, which while they impress the senses thus, $^0_0{}^0$, may be separated into two parts, thus, $_{00}$ $_0$. This proposition being granted, we term all such parcels Threes, after which the enunciation of the above-mentioned physical fact will serve also for a definition of the word Three.

The Science of Numbers is thus no exception to the conclusion we previously arrived at, that the processes even of deductive sciences are altogether inductive, and that their first principles are generalisations from experience. It remains to be examined whether this science resembles geometry in the further circumstance that some of its inductions are not exactly true; and that the peculiar certainty ascribed to it, on account of which its propositions are called necessary truths, is fictitious and hypothetical, being true in no other sense than that those propositions legitimately follow from the hypothesis of the truth of premises which are avowedly mere approximations to truth.

III

The inductions of arithmetic are of two sorts: first, those which we have just expounded, such as One and one are two, Two and one are three, etc., which may be called the definitions of the various numbers, in the improper or geometrical sense of the word Definition; and secondly, the two following axioms: The sums of equals are equal, The differences of equals are equal. These two are sufficient; for the corresponding propositions respecting unequals may be proved from these by a *reductio ad absurdum*.

These axioms, and likewise the so-called definitions, are, as has already been said, results of induction; true of all objects whatever, and, as it may seem, exactly true, without the hypothetical assumption of unqualified truth where an approximation to it is all that exists. The conclusions, therefore, it will naturally be inferred, are exactly true, and the science of numbers is an exception to other demonstrative sciences in this, that the categorical certainty which is predicable of its demonstrations is independent of all hypothesis.

On more accurate investigation, however, it will be found that, even in this case, there is one hypothetical element in the ratiocination. In all propositions concerning numbers, a condition is implied, without which none of them would be true: and that condition is an assumption which may be false. The condition is, that $1 = 1$; that all the numbers are numbers of the same or of equal units. Let this be doubtful and not one of the propositions of arithmetic will hold true. How can we know that one pound and one pound make two pounds if one of the pounds may be troy, and the other avoirdupois? They may not make two pounds of either, or of any weight. How can we know that a forty-horse-power is always equal to itself, unless we assume that all horses are of equal strength? It is certain that 1 is always equal in *number* to 1; and where the mere number of objects, or of the parts of an object, without supposing them to be equivalent in any other respect, is all that is material, the conclusions of arithmetic, so far as they go to that alone, are true without mixture of hypothesis. There are such cases in statistics; as, for instance, an inquiry into the amount of the population of any country. It is indifferent to that inquiry whether they are grown people or children, strong or weak, tall or short; the only thing we want to ascertain is their number. But whenever, from equality or inequality of number, equality or inequality in any other respect is to be inferred, arithmetic carried into such inquiries becomes as hypothetical a science as geometry. All units must be assumed to be equal in that other respect; and this is never accurately true, for one actual pound weight is not exactly equal to another, nor one measured mile's length to another; a nicer balance, or more accurate measuring instruments, would always detect some difference.

What is commonly called mathematical certainty, therefore, which comprises the twofold conception of unconditional truth and perfect accuracy, is not an attribute of all mathematical truths, but of those only which relate to pure Number, as distinguished from Quantity in the more enlarged sense; and only so long as we abstain from supposing that the numbers are a precise index to actual quantities. The certainty usually ascribed to the conclusions of geometry, and even to those of mechanics, is nothing whatever but certainty of inference. We can have full assurance of particular results under particular suppositions, but we cannot have the same assurance that these suppositions are accurately true, nor that they include all the data which may exercise an influence over the result in any given instance.

IV

It appears, therefore, that the method of all Deductive Sciences is hypothetical. They proceed by tracing the consequences of certain assumptions; leaving for separate consideration whether the assumptions are true or not, and if not exactly true, whether they are a sufficiently near approximation to the truth. The reason is obvious. Since it is only in questions of pure number that the assumptions are exactly true, and even there, only so long as no conclusions except purely numerical ones are to be founded on them; it must, in all other cases of deductive investigation, form a part of the inquiry to determine how much the assumptions want of being exactly true in the case in hand. This is generally a matter of observation, to be repeated in every fresh case; or if it has to be settled by argument instead of observation, may require in every different case different evidence, and present every degree of difficulty, from the lowest to the highest. But the other part of the process—namely, to determine what else may be concluded if we find, and in proportion as we find, the assumptions to be true—may be performed once for all, and the results held ready to be employed as the occasions turn up for use. We thus do all beforehand that can be so done, and leave the least possible work to be performed when cases arise and press for a decision. This inquiry into the inferences which can be drawn from assumptions is what properly constitutes Demonstrative Science.

It is of course quite as practicable to arrive at new conclusions from facts assumed, as from facts observed; from fictitious, as from real, inductions. Deduction, as we have seen, consists of a series of inferences in this form—*a* is a mark of *b*, *b* of *c*, *c* of *d*, therefore *a* is a mark of *d*, which last may be a truth inaccessible to direct observation. In like manner it is allowable to say, *suppose* that *a* were a mark of *b*, *b* of *c*, and *c* of *d*, *a* would be a mark of *d*, which last conclusion was not thought of by those who laid down the premises. A system of propositions as complicated as geometry might be deduced from assumptions which are false; as was done by Ptolemy, Descartes, and others, in their attempts to explain synthetically the phenomena of the solar system on the supposition that the apparent motions of the heavenly bodies were the real motions, or were produced in some way more or less different from the true one. Sometimes the same thing is knowingly done for the purpose of showing the falsity of the assumption; which is called a *reductio ad absurdum*. In such cases the reasoning is as follows: *a* is a mark of *b*, and *b* of *c*; now if *c* were also a mark of *d*, *a* would be a mark of *d*; but *d* is known to be a mark of the absence of *a*; consequently *a* would be a mark of its own absence, which is a contradiction; therefore *c* is not a mark of *d*.

Source: *A System of Logic* (Longmans), Bk. II, Ch. V, sec. 1, and Ch. VI, secs. 1–4. (Extracts.)

12 The Foundations of Arithmetic: Introduction (1884)

G. FREGE

When we ask someone what the number one is, or what the symbol 1 means,* we get as a rule the answer 'Why, a thing'. And if we go on to point out that the proposition
        'the number one is a thing'
is not a definition, because it has the definite article on one side and the indefinite on the other, or that it only assigns the number one to the class of things, without stating which thing it is, then we shall very likely be invited to select something for ourselves— anything we please—to call one. Yet if everyone had the right to understand by this name whatever he pleased, then the same proposition about one would mean different things for different people,—such propositions would have no common content. Some, perhaps, will decline to answer the question, pointing out that it is impossible to state, either, what is meant by the letter *a*, as it is used in arithmetic; and that if we were to say '*a* means a

---

* [I have tried throughout to translate *Bedeutung* and its cognates by 'meaning' and *Sinn* and its cognates by 'sense', in view of the importance Frege later attached to the distinction. But it is quite evident that he attached no special significance to the words at this period.—Transl.]

number,' this would be open to the same objection as the definition
'one is a thing.' Now in the case of a it is quite right to decline to
answer: a does not mean some one definite number which can be
specified, but serves to express the generality of general propositions. If, in $a + a - a = a$, we put for a some number, any we
please but the same throughout, we get always a true identity.*
This is the sense in which the letter a is used. With one, however,
the position is essentially different. Can we, in the identity
$1 + 1 = 2$, put for 1 in both places some one and the same
object, say the Moon? On the contrary, it looks as though, whatever we put for the first 1, we must put something different for
the second. Why is it that we have to do here precisely what
would have been wrong in the other case? Again, arithmetic
cannot get along with a alone, but has to use further letters
besides (b, c and so on), in order to express in general form
relations between different numbers. It would therefore be
natural to suppose that the symbol 1 too, if it served in some
similar way to confer generality on propositions, could not be
enough by itself. Yet surely the number one looks like a definite
particular object, with properties that can be specified, for
example that of remaining unchanged when multiplied by itself?
In this sense, a has no properties that can be specified, since
whatever can be asserted of a is a common property of all numbers, whereas $1^1 = 1$ asserts nothing of the Moon, nothing of the
Sun, nothing of the Sahara, nothing of the Peak of Teneriffe; for
what could be the sense of any such assertion?

Questions like these catch even mathematicians for that matter,
or most of them, unprepared with any satisfactory answer. Yet is
it not a scandal that our science should be so unclear about the
first and foremost among its objects, and one which is apparently
so simple? Small hope, then, that we shall be able to say what
number is. If a concept fundamental to a mighty science gives rise
to difficulties, then it is surely an imperative task to investigate it
more closely until those difficulties are overcome; especially as we
shall hardly succeed in finally clearing up negative numbers, or
fractional or complex numbers, so long as our insight into the
foundation of the whole structure of arithmetic is still defective.

---

* [*Gleichung*. This also means, and would often be more naturally translated, 'equation'. But I have generally retained 'identity', because this is
sometimes essential and because Frege does understand equations as identities. For similar reasons I have translated *gleich* 'identical', though it can
mean 'equal' or even merely 'similar'.—Transl.]

Many people will be sure to think this not worth the trouble. Naturally, they suppose, this concept is adequately dealt with in the elementary textbooks, where the subject is settled once and for all. Who can believe that he has anything still to learn on so simple a matter? So free from all difficulty is the concept of positive whole number held to be, that an account of it fit for children can be both scientific and exhaustive; and that every schoolboy, without any further reflexion or acquaintance with what others have thought, knows all there is to know about it. The first prerequisite for learning anything is thus utterly lacking —I mean, the knowledge that we do not know. The result is that we still rest content with the crudest of views, even though since Herbart's[1] day a better doctrine has been available. It is sad and discouraging to observe how discoveries once made are always threatening to be lost again in this way, and how much work promises to have been done in vain, because we fancy ourselves so well off that we need not bother to assimilate its results. My work too, as I am well aware, is exposed to this risk. A typical crudity confronts me, when I find calculation described as 'aggregative mechanical thought'.[2] I doubt whether there exists any thought whatsoever answering to this description. An aggregative imagination, even, might sooner be let pass; but that has no relevance to calculation. Thought is in essentials the same everywhere: it is not true that there are different kinds of laws of thought to suit the different kinds of objects thought about. Such differences as there are consist only in this, that the thought is more pure or less pure, less dependent or more upon psychological influences and on external aids such as words or numerals, and further to some extent too in the finer or coarser structure of the concepts involved; but it is precisely in this respect that mathematics aspires to surpass all other sciences, even philosophy.

The present work will make it clear that even an inference like that from n to $n + 1$, which on the face of it is peculiar to mathematics, is based on the general laws of logic, and that there is no need of special laws for aggregative thought. It is possible, of course, to operate with figures mechanically, just as it is possible to speak like a parrot: but that hardly deserves the name of thought. It only becomes possible at all after the mathematical

---

[1] Collected Works, ed. Hartenstein, Vol. X, part i, *Umriss pädagogischer Vorlesungen*, § 252, n. 2: 'Two does not mean two things, but doubling' etc.

[2] K. Fischer, *System der Logik und Metaphysik oder Wissenschaftslehre*, 2nd edn.

notation has, as a result of genuine thought, been so developed that it does the thinking for us, so to speak. This does not prove that numbers are formed in some peculiarly mechanical way, as sand, say, is formed out of quartz granules. In their own interests mathematicians should, I consider, combat any view of this kind, since it is calculated to lead to the disparagement of a principal object of their study, and of their science itself along with it. Yet even in the works of mathematicians are to be found expressions of exactly the same sort. The truth is quite the other way: the concept of number, as we shall be forced to recognize, has a finer structure than most of the concepts of the other sciences, even although it is still one of the simplest in arithmetic.

In order, then, to dispel this illusion that the positive whole numbers really present no difficulties at all, but that universal concord reigns about them, I have adopted the plan of criticizing some of the views put forward by mathematicians and philosophers on the questions involved. It will be seen how small is the extent of their agreement—so small, that we find one dictum precisely contradicting another. For example, some hold that 'units are identical with one another,' others that they are different, and each side supports its assertion with arguments that cannot be rejected out of hand. My object in this is to awaken a desire for a stricter enquiry. At the same time this preliminary examination of the views others have put forward should clear the ground for my own account, by convincing my readers in advance that these other paths do not lead to the goal, and that my opinion is not just one among many all equally tenable; and in this way I hope to settle the question finally, at least in essentials.

I realize that, as a result, I have been led to pursue arguments more philosophical than many mathematicians may approve; but any thorough investigation of the concept of number is bound always to turn out rather philosophical. It is a task which is common to mathematics and philosophy.

It may well be that the co-operation between these two sciences, in spite of many démarches from both sides, is not so flourishing as could be wished and would, for that matter, be possible. And if so, this is due in my opinion to the predominance in philosophy of psychological methods of argument, which have penetrated even into the field of logic. With this tendency mathematics is completely out of sympathy, and this easily accounts for the aversion to philosophical arguments felt by many mathematicians. When Stricker,[8] for instance, calls our ideas* of numbers motor phenomena and makes them dependent on muscular sensations, no mathematician can recognize his numbers in such stuff or knows where to begin to tackle such a proposition. An arithmetic founded on muscular sensations would certainly turn out sensational enough, but also every bit as vague as its foundation. No, sensations are absolutely no concern of arithmetic. No more are mental pictures, formed from the amalgamated traces of earlier sense-impressions. All these phases of consciousness are characteristically fluctuating and indefinite, in strong contrast to the definiteness and fixity of the concepts and objects of mathematics. It may, of course, serve some purpose to investigate the ideas and changes of ideas which occur during the course of mathematical thinking; but psychology should not imagine that it can contribute anything whatever to the foundation of arithmetic. To the mathematician as such these mental pictures, with their origins and their transformations, are immaterial. Stricker himself states that the only idea he associates with the word 'hundred' is the symbol 100. Others may have the idea of the letter C or something else; does it not follow, therefore, that these mental pictures are, so far as concerns us and the essentials of our problem, completely immaterial and incidental— as incidental as chalk and blackboard, and indeed that they do not deserve to be called ideas of the number a hundred at all? Never, then, let us suppose that the essence of the matter lies in such ideas. Never let us take a description of the origin of an idea for a definition, or an account of the mental and physical conditions on which we become conscious of a proposition for a proof of it. A proposition may be thought, and again it may be true; let us never confuse these two things. We must remind ourselves, it seems, that a proposition no more ceases to be true when I cease to think of it than the sun ceases to exist when I shut my eyes. Otherwise, in proving Pythagoras' theorem we should be reduced to allowing for the phosphorous content of the human brain; and astronomers would hesitate to draw any conclusions about the distant past, for fear of being charged with anachronism,—with reckoning twice two as four regardless of the fact that our idea of number is a product of evolution and has a history behind it. It

---

[8] *Studien über Association der Vorstellungen*, Vienna 1883.

* [*Vorstellungen*. I have translated this word consistently by 'idea', and cognate words by 'imagination', etc. For Frege it is a psychological term.—Transl.]

might be doubted whether by that time it had progressed so far. How could they profess to know that the proposition $2 \times 2 = 4$ was already in existence in that remote epoch? Might not the creatures then extant have held the proposition $2 \times 2 = 5$, from which the proposition $2 \times 2 = 4$ was only evolved later through a process of natural selection in the struggle for existence? Why, it might even be that $2 \times 2 = 4$ itself is destined in the same way to develop into $2 \times 2 = 3$! *Est modus in rebus, sunt certi denique fines!* * The historical approach, with its aim of detecting how things begin and of arriving from these origins at a knowledge of their nature, is certainly perfectly legitimate; but it has also its limitations. If everything were in continual flux, and nothing maintained itself fixed for all time, there would no longer be any possibility of getting to know anything about the world and everything would be plunged in confusion. We suppose, it would seem, that concepts sprout in the individual mind like leaves on a tree, and we think to discover their nature by studying their birth: we seek to define them psychologically, in terms of the nature of the human mind. But this account makes everything subjective, and if we follow it through to the end, does away with truth. What is known as the history of concepts is really a history either of our knowledge of concepts or of the meanings of words. Often it is only after immense intellectual effort, which may have continued over centuries, that humanity at last succeeds in achieving knowledge of a concept in its pure form, in stripping off the irrelevant accretions which veil it from the eyes of the mind. What, then, are we to say of those who, instead of advancing this work where it is not yet completed, despise it, and betake themselves to the nursery, or bury themselves in the remotest conceivable periods of human evolution, there to discover, like John Stuart Mill, some gingerbread or pebble arithmetic!† It remains only to ascribe to the flavour of the bread some special meaning for the concept of number. A procedure like this is surely the very reverse of rational, and as unmathematical, at any rate, as it could well be. No wonder the mathematicians turn their backs on it. Do the concepts, as we approach their supposed sources, reveal themselves in peculiar purity? Not at all; we see everything as through a fog, blurred and undifferentiated. It is as though everyone who wished to know about America were to try

* A quotation from Horace. 'There is moderation in things: certain boundaries are fixed'.—Ed.

† See the Reading from Mill, p. 97.—Ed.

to put himself back in the position of Columbus, at the time when he caught the first dubious glimpse of his supposed India. Of course, a comparison like this proves nothing; but it should, I hope, make my point clear. It may well be that in many cases the history of earlier discoveries is a useful study, as a preparation for further researches; but it should not set up to usurp their place.

So far as mathematicians are concerned, an attack on such views would indeed scarcely have been necessary; but my treatment was designed to bring each dispute to an issue for the philosophers as well, as far as possible, so that I found myself forced to enter a little into psychology, if only to repel its invasion of mathematics.

Besides, even mathematical textbooks do at times lapse into psychology. When the author feels himself obliged to give a definition, yet cannot, then he tends to give at least a description of the way in which we arrive at the object or concept concerned. These cases can easily be recognized by the fact that such explanations are never referred to again in the course of the subsequent exposition. For teaching purposes, introductory devices are certainly quite legitimate; only they should always be clearly distinguished from definitions. A delightful example of the way in which even mathematicians can confuse the grounds of proof with the mental or physical conditions to be satisfied if the proof is to be given is to be found in E. Schröder.[4] Under the heading 'Special Axiom' he produces the following: 'The principle I have in mind might well be called the Axiom of Symbolic Stability. It guarantees us that throughout all our arguments and deductions the symbols remain constant in our memory—or preferably on paper,' and so on.

No less essential for mathematics than the refusal of all assistance from the direction of psychology, is the recognition of its close connexion with logic. I go so far as to agree with those who hold that it is impossible to effect any sharp separation of the two. This much everyone would allow, that any enquiry into the cogency of a proof or the justification of a definition must be a matter of logic. But such enquiries simply cannot be eliminated from mathematics, for it is only through answering them that we can attain to the necessary certainty.

In this direction too I go, certainly, further than is usual. Most mathematicians rest content, in enquiries of this kind, when they have satisfied their immediate needs. If a definition shows itself

[4] *Lehrbuch der Arithmetik und Algebra* [Leipzig 1873].

tractable when used in proofs, if no contradictions are anywhere encountered, and if connexions are revealed between matters apparently remote from one another, this leading to an advance in order and regularity, it is usual to regard the definition as sufficiently established, and few questions are asked as to its logical justification. This procedure has at least the advantage that it makes it difficult to miss the mark altogether. Even I agree that definitions must show their worth by their fruitfulness: it must be possible to use them for constructing proofs. Yet it must still be borne in mind that the rigour of the proof remains an illusion, even though no link be missing in the chain of our deductions, so long as the definitions are justified only as an after-thought, by our failing to come across any contradiction. By these methods we shall, at bottom, never have achieved more than an empirical certainty, and we must really face the possibility that we may still in the end encounter a contradiction which brings the whole edifice down in ruins. For this reason I have felt bound to go back rather further into the general logical foundations of our science than perhaps most mathematicians will consider necessary.

In the enquiry that follows, I have kept to three fundamental principles:

always to separate sharply the psychological from the logical, the subjective from the objective;

never to ask for the meaning of a word in isolation, but only in the context of a proposition;

never to lose sight of the distinction between concept and object.

In compliance with the first principle, I have used the word 'idea' always in the psychological sense, and have distinguished ideas from concepts and from objects. If the second principle is not observed, one is almost forced to take as the meanings of words mental pictures or acts of the individual mind, and so to offend against the first principle as well. As to the third point, it is a mere illusion to suppose that a concept can be made an object without altering it. From this it follows that a widely-held formalist theory of fractional, negative, etc., numbers is untenable. How I propose to improve upon it can be no more than indicated in the present work. With numbers of all these types, as with the positive whole numbers, it is a matter of fixing the sense of an identity.

My results will, I think, at least in essentials, win the adherence of those mathematicians who take the trouble to attend to my arguments. They seem to me to be in the air, and it may be that every one of them singly, or at least something very like it, has been already put forward; though perhaps, presented as they are here in connexion with each other, they may still be novel. I have often been astonished at the way in which writers who on one point approach my view so closely, on others depart from it so violently.

Their reception by philosophers will be varied, depending on each philosopher's own position; but presumably those empiricists who recognize induction as the sole original process of inference (and even that as a process not actually of inference but of habituation) will like them least. Some one or another, perhaps, will take this opportunity to examine afresh the principles of his theory of knowledge. To those who feel inclined to criticize my definitions as unnatural, I would suggest that the point here is not whether they are natural, but whether they go to the root of the matter and are logically beyond criticism.

I permit myself the hope that even the philosophers, if they examine what I have written without prejudice, will find in it something of use to them.

Source: Introduction to *The Foundations of Arithmetic*, trans. J. L. Austin (Blackwell).

13 On the Foundations of Logic and Arithmetic (1904)

D. HILBERT

[...] While we are essentially in agreement today as to the paths to be taken and the goals to be sought when we are engaged in research into the foundations of geometry, the situation is quite different with regard to the inquiry into the foundations of arithmetic; here investigators still hold a wide variety of sharply conflicting opinions.

In fact, some of the difficulties in the foundations of arithmetic are different in nature from those that had to be overcome when the foundations of geometry were established. In examining the foundations of geometry it was possible for us to leave aside certain difficulties of a purely arithmetic nature; but recourse to another fundamental discipline does not seem to be allowed when the foundations of arithmetic are at issue. The principal difficulties that we encounter when providing a foundation for arithmetic will be brought out most clearly if I submit the points of view of several investigators to a brief critical discussion.

L. Kronecker, as is well known, saw in the notion of the integer the real foundation of arithmetic; he came up with the idea that the integer—and, in fact, the integer as a general notion (parameter value)—is directly and immediately given; this prevented him from recognizing that the notion of integer must and can have a foundation. I would call him a *dogmatist*, to the extent that he accepts the integer with its essential properties as a dogma and does not look further back.

H. Helmholtz represents the standpoint of the *empiricist*; the standpoint of pure experience, however, seems to me to be refuted by the objection that the existence, possible or actual, of an arbitrarily large number can never be derived from experience, that is, through experiment. For even though the number of things that are objects of our experience is large, it still lies below a finite bound.

E. B. Christoffel and all those opponents of Kronecker's who, guided by the correct feeling that without the notion of irrational number the whole of analysis would be condemned to sterility, attempt to save the existence of the irrational number by discovering 'positive' properties of this notion or by similar means, I would call *opportunists*. In my opinion they have not succeeded in giving a pertinent refutation of Kronecker's conception.

Among the scholars who have probed more deeply into the essence of the integer I mention the following.

G. Frege sets himself the task of founding the laws of arithmetic by the devices of *logic*, taken in the traditional sense. He has the merit of having correctly recognized the essential properties of the notion of integer as well as the significance of inference by mathematical induction. But, true to his plan, he accepts among other things the fundamental principle that a concept (a set) is defined and immediately usable if only it is determined for every object whether the object is subsumed under the concept or not, and here he imposes no restriction on the notion 'every';

he thus exposes himself to precisely the set-theoretic paradoxes that are contained, for example, in the notion of the set of all sets and that show, it seems to me, that the conceptions and means of investigation prevalent in logic, taken in the traditional sense, do not measure up to the rigorous demands that set theory imposes. *Rather, from the very beginning a major goal of the investigations into the notion of number should be to avoid such contradictions and to clarify these paradoxes.*

R. *Dedekind* clearly recognized the mathematical difficulties encountered when a foundation is sought for the notion of number; for the first time he offered a construction of the theory of integers, and in fact an extremely sagacious one. However, I would call his method *transcendental* insofar as in proving the existence of the infinite he follows a method that, though its fundamental idea is used in a similar way by philosophers, I cannot recognize as practicable or secure because it employs the notion of the totality of all objects, which involves an unavoidable contradiction.

G. *Cantor* sensed the contradictions just mentioned and expressed this awareness by differentiating between 'consistent' and 'inconsistent' sets. But, since in my opinion he does not provide a precise criterion for this distinction, I must characterize his conception on this point as one that still leaves latitude for *subjective* judgment and therefore affords no objective certainty.

It is my opinion that all the difficulties touched upon can be overcome and that we can provide a rigorous and completely satisfying foundation for the notion of number, and in fact by a method that I would call *axiomatic* and whose fundamental idea I wish to develop briefly in what follows.

Arithmetic is often considered to be a part of logic, and the traditional fundamental logical notions are usually presupposed when it is a question of establishing a foundation for arithmetic. If we observe attentively, however, we realize that in the traditional exposition of the laws of logic certain fundamental arithmetic notions are already used, for example, the notion of set and, to some extent, also that of number. Thus we find ourselves turning in a circle, and that is why a partly simultaneous development of the laws of logic and of arithmetic is required if paradoxes are to be avoided.

In the brief space of an address I can merely indicate how I conceive of this common construction. I beg to be excused, therefore, if I succeed only in giving you an approximate idea of the direction my researches are taking. In addition, to make myself more easily understood, I shall make more use of ordinary language 'in words' and of the laws of logic indirectly expressed in it than would be desirable in an exact construction.

Let an object of our thought be called a *thought-object* (*Gedankending*) or, briefly, an *object* (*Ding*) and let it be denoted by a sign.

We take as a basis of our considerations a first thought-object, 1 (one). We call what we obtain by putting together two, three, or more occurrences of this object, for example,

$$11, 111, 1111,$$

combinations (*Kombinationen*) of the object 1 with itself; also, any combinations of these combinations, such as

$$(1)(11), \quad (11)(11)(11), \quad ((11)(11))(11), \quad ((111)(1))(1),$$

are again called combinations of the object 1 with itself. The combinations likewise are just called objects and then, to distinguish it, the basic thought-object 1 is called a *simple* object.

We now add a second simple thought-object and denote it by the sign $=$ (equals). Then we form combinations of these two thought-objects, for example,

$$1=, \; 11=,\ldots, \; (1)(=1)(===), \quad ((11)(1)(=))(==),$$
$$1=1, \quad (11)=(1)(1).$$

We say that the combination a of the simple objects 1 and $=$ *differs* from the combination b of these objects if the combinations deviate in any way from each other with regard to the mode and order of succession in the combinations or the choice and place of the objects 1 and $=$ themselves, that is, if a and b are not *identical* with each other.

Now we think of the combinations of these two simple objects as falling into two classes, the *class of entities* (die *Klasse der Seienden*) and that *of nonentities* (die *der Nichtseienden*): each object belonging to the class of entities differs from each object belonging to the class of nonentities. Every combination of the two simple objects 1 and $=$ belongs to one of these two classes.

If a is a combination of the two objects 1 and $=$ taken as primitive, then we denote also by a the *proposition* that a belongs to the class of entities and by $\bar{a}$ the *proposition* that a belongs to the class of nonentities. We call a a *true* proposition if a belongs to the class of entities; on the other hand, let $\bar{a}$ be called a *true* proposition if a belongs to the class of nonentities. The propositions a and $\bar{a}$ form a *contradiction*.

The composite (Inbegriff) of two propositions A and B, expressed in signs by

$$A|B,$$

and in words by 'from A, B follows' or 'if A is true, so is B', is also called a proposition; here A is called the *supposition* (*Voraussetzung*) and B the *assertion* (*Behauptung*). Supposition and assertion may themselves in turn consist of several propositions A_1, A_2, or B_1, B_2, B_3, and so forth, and we have in signs

$$A_1 \text{ a. } A_2 \mid B_1 \text{ o. } B_2 \text{ o. } B_3,$$

in words 'from A_1 and A_2, B_1 or B_2 or B_3 follows', and so forth.

With the sign o. (or) at our disposal it would be possible to avoid the sign $|$, since negation has already been introduced; I use it in this address merely in order to follow ordinary language as closely as possible.

We shall understand by A_1, A_2, . . . the propositions that, briefly stated, result from a proposition $A(x)$ if we take the thought-objects 1 and = and their combinations in place of the '*arbitrary object*' (der '*Willkürlichen*') x; then we write the propositions $A_1 \text{ o. } A_2 \text{ o. } A_3 \ldots$ and $A_1 \text{ a. } A_2 \text{ a. } A_3 \ldots$ also as follows: $A(x^{(o)})$, in words 'for at least one x', and $A(x^{(a)})$, in words 'for every x', respectively; we regard this merely as an abbreviated way of writing.

From the two objects 1 and = taken as primitive we now form the following propositions:

1. $x = x$,
2. $\{x = y \text{ a. } w(x)\} \mid w(y)$.

Here x (in the sense of $x^{(a)}$) means each of the two thought-objects taken as primitive and every combination of them; in 2, y (in the sense of $y^{(a)}$) likewise can be each of these objects and every combination; further, $w(x)$ is an 'arbitrary' combination containing the 'arbitrary object' x (in the sense of $x^{(a)}$). Proposition 2 reads in words 'from $x = y$ and $w(x)$, $w(y)$ follows'.

Propositions 1 and 2 form the *definition of the notion* = (equals) and accordingly are also called *axioms*.

If we put the simple objects 1 and = or particular combinations of them in place of the arbitrary objects x and y in Axioms 1 and 2, particular propositions result, which may be called *consequences* (*Folgerungen*) of these axioms. We consider a sequence of certain consequences such that the suppositions of the last consequence of the sequence are identical with the assertions of the preceding consequences. If we then take the suppositions of the preceding consequences as supposition, and the assertion of the last consequence as assertion, a new proposition results, which can in turn be called a *consequence* of the axioms. By continuing this deduction process we can obtain further consequences.

We now select from these consequences those that have the simple form of the proposition a (assertion without supposition), and we gather the objects a thus obtained into the class of entities, whereas the objects that differ from these are to belong to the class of nonentities. We recognize that only consequences of the form $\alpha = \alpha$ result from 1 and 2, where α is a combination of the objects 1 and $=$. Axioms 1 and 2 for their part, too, are satisfied with regard to this partition of the objects into the two classes, that is, they are true propositions, and because of this property of Axioms 1 and 2 we say that the notion $=$ (equals) defined by them is a *consistent* notion.

Source: Frege to Gödel (Harvard U.P.), ed. J. van Heijenoort, pp. 131–3.

MORAL PHILOSOPHY

14 Moral Beliefs (1958)

PHILIPPA FOOT

To many people it seems that the most notable advance in moral philosophy during the past fifty years or so has been the refutation of naturalism; and they are a little shocked that at this late date such an issue should be reopened. It is easy to understand their attitude: given certain apparently unquestionable assumptions, it would be about as sensible to try to reintroduce naturalism as to try to square the circle. Those who see it like this have satisfied themselves that they know in advance that any naturalistic theory must have a catch in it somewhere, and are put out at having to waste more time exposing an old fallacy. This paper is an attempt to persuade them to look critically at the premises on which their arguments are based.

It would not be an exaggeration to say that the whole of moral philosophy, as it is now widely taught, rests on a contrast between statements of fact and evaluations, which runs something like this: 'The truth or falsity of statements of fact is shown by means of evidence; and what counts as evidence is laid down in the meaning of the expressions occurring in the statement of fact. (For instance, the meaning of 'round' and 'flat' made Magellan's voyages evidence for the roundness rather than the flatness of the Earth; someone who went on questioning whether the evidence was evidence could eventually be shown to have made some linguistic mistake.) It follows that no two people can make the same statement and count completely different things as evidence; in the end one at least of them could be convicted of linguistic ignorance. It also follows that if a man is given good evidence for a factual conclusion he cannot just refuse to accept the conclusion

115

on the ground that in his scheme of things this evidence is not evidence at all. With evaluations, however, it is different. An evaluation is not connected logically with the factual statements on which it is based. One man may say that a thing is good because of some fact about it, and another may refuse to take that fact as any evidence at all, for nothing is laid down in the meaning of 'good' which connects it with one piece of 'evidence' rather than another. It follows that a moral eccentric could argue to moral conclusions from quite idiosyncratic premises; he could say, for instance, that a man was a good man because he clasped and unclasped his hands, and never turned NNE after turning SSW. He could also reject someone else's evaluation simply by denying that his evidence was evidence at all.

'The fact about "good" which allows the eccentric still to use this term without falling into a morass of meaninglessness, is its "action-guiding" or "practical" function. This it retains; for like everyone else he considers himself bound to choose the things he calls "good" rather than those he calls "bad". Like the rest of the world he uses "good" in connection only with a "pro-attitude"; it is only that he has pro-attitudes to quite different things, and therefore calls them good.'

There are here two assumptions about 'evaluations', which I will call assumption (1) and assumption (2).

Assumption (1) is that some individual may, without logical error, base his beliefs about matters of value entirely on premises which no one else would recognise as giving any evidence at all. Assumption (2) is that, given the kind of statement which other people regard as evidence for an evaluative conclusion, he may refuse to draw the conclusion because *this* does not count as evidence for *him*.

Let us consider assumption (1). We might say that this depends on the possibility of keeping the meaning of 'good' steady through all changes in the facts about anything which are to count in favour of its goodness. (I do not mean, of course, that a man can make changes as fast as he chooses; only that, whatever he has chosen, it will not be possible to rule him out of order.) But there is a better formulation, which cuts out trivial disputes about the meaning which 'good' happens to have in some section of the community. Let us say that the assumption is that the evaluative function of 'good' can remain constant through changes in the evaluative principle; on this ground it could be said that even if no one can call a man *good* because he clasps and unclasps his hands, he can commend him or express his *pro-attitude* towards him, and if necessary can invent a new moral vocabulary to express his unusual moral code.

Those who hold such a theory will naturally add several qualifications. In the first place, most people now agree with Hare, against Stevenson, that such words as 'good' only apply to individual cases through the application of general principles, so that even the extreme moral eccentric must accept principles of commendation. In the second place 'commending', 'having a pro-attitude', and so on, are supposed to be connected with doing and choosing, so that it would be impossible to say, e.g. that a man was a good man only if he lived for a thousand years. The range of evaluation is supposed to be restricted to the range of possible action and choice. I am not here concerned to question these supposed restrictions on the use of evaluative terms, but only to argue that they are not enough.

The crucial question is this. Is it possible to extract from the meaning of words such as 'good' some element called 'evaluative meaning' which we can think of as externally related to its objects? Such an element would be represented, for instance, in the rule that when any action was 'commended' the speaker must hold himself bound to accept an imperative 'let me do these things'. This is externally related to its object because, within the limitation which we noticed earlier, to possible actions, it would make sense to think of anything as the subject of such 'commendation'. On this hypothesis a moral eccentric could be described as commending the clasping of hands as the action of a good man, and we should not have to look for some background to give the supposition sense. That is to say, on this hypothesis the clasping of hands could be commended without any explanation; it could be what those who hold such theories call 'an ultimate moral principle'.

I wish to say that this hypothesis is untenable, and that there is no describing the evaluative meaning of 'good', evaluation, commending, or anything of the sort, without fixing the object to which they are supposed to be attached. Without first laying hands on the proper object of such things as evaluation, we shall catch in our net either something quite different, such as accepting an order or making a resolution, or else nothing at all.

Before I consider this question, I shall first discuss some other mental attitudes and beliefs which have this internal relation to their object. By this I hope to clarify the concept of internal

relation to an object, and incidentally, if my examples arouse
resistance, but are eventually accepted, to show how easy it is to
overlook an internal relation where it exists.

Consider, for instance, pride.

People are often surprised at the suggestion that there are
limits to the things a man can be proud of, about which indeed he
can feel pride. I do not know quite what account they want to
give of pride; perhaps something to do with smiling and walking
with a jaunty air, and holding an object up where other people
can see it; or perhaps they think that pride is a kind of internal
sensation, so that one might naturally beat one's breast and say
'pride is something I feel *here*'. The difficulties of the second
view are well known; the logically private object cannot be what
a name in the public language is the name of.[1] The first view is
the more plausible, and it may seem reasonable to say that given
certain behaviour a man can be described as showing that he is
proud of something, whatever that something may be. In one
sense this is true, and in another sense not. Given any description
of an object, action, personal characteristic, etc., it is not possible
to rule it out as an object of pride. Before we can do so we need
to know what would be said about it by the man who is to be
proud of it, or feels proud of it; but if he does not hold the right
beliefs about it then whatever his attitude is it is not pride. Consider, for instance, the suggestion that someone might be proud
of the sky or the sea: he looks at them and what he feels is *pride,*
or he puffs out his chest and gestures with *pride* in their direction.
This makes sense only if a special assumption is made about his
beliefs, for instance, that he is under some crazy delusion and
believes that he has saved the sky from falling, or the sea from
drying up. The characteristic object of pride is something seen
(*a*) as in some way a man's own, and (*b*) as some sort of achievement or advantage; without this object pride cannot be described.
To see that the second condition is necessary, one should try
supposing that a man happens to feel proud because he has laid
one of his hands on the other, three times in an hour. Here again
the supposition that it is pride that he feels will make perfectly
good sense if a special background is filled in. Perhaps he is ill,
and it is an achievement even to do this; perhaps this gesture has
some religious or political significance, and he is a brave man
who will so defy the gods or the rulers. But with no special back-

---

[1] See L. Wittgenstein, *Philosophical Investigations* (1967), especially sections 243–315.

ground there can be no pride, not because no one could psychologically speaking feel pride in such a case, but because whatever
he did feel could not logically be pride. Of course, people can see
strange things as achievements, though not just anything, and
they can identify themselves with remote ancestors, and relations,
and neighbours, and even on occasions with Mankind. I do not
wish to deny there are many far-fetched and comic examples of
pride.

We could have chosen many other examples of mental attitudes
which are internally related to their object in a similar way. For
instance, fear is not just trembling, and running, and turning pale;
without the thought of some menacing evil no amount of this will
add up to fear. Nor could anyone be said to feel dismay about
something he did not see as bad; if his thoughts about it were
that it was altogether a good thing, he could not say that (oddly
enough) what he felt about it was dismay. 'How odd, I feel dismayed when I ought to be pleased' is the prelude to a hunt for
the adverse aspect of the thing, thought of as lurking behind the
pleasant façade. But someone may object that pride and fear and
dismay are feelings or emotions and therefore not a proper
analogy for 'commendation', and there will be an advantage in
considering a different kind of example. We could discuss, for
instance, the belief that a certain thing is dangerous, and ask
whether this could logically be held about anything whatsoever.
Like 'this is good', 'this is dangerous' is an assertion, which we
should naturally accept or reject by speaking of its truth or
falsity; we seem to support such statements with evidence, and
moreover there may seem to be a 'warning function' connected
with the word 'dangerous' as there is supposed to be a 'commending function' connected with the word 'good'. For suppose that
philosophers, puzzled about the property of dangerousness,
decided that the word did not stand for a property at all, but was
essentially a practical or action-guiding term, used for *warning*.
Unless used in an 'inverted comma sense' the word 'dangerous'
was used to warn, and this meant that anyone using it in such a
sense committed himself to avoiding the things he called dangerous, to preventing other people from going near them, and perhaps
to running in the opposite direction. If the conclusion were not
obviously ridiculous, it would be easy to infer that a man whose
application of the term was different from ours throughout might
say that the oddest things were dangerous without fear of disproof; the idea would be that he could still be described as

'thinking them dangerous', or at least as 'warning', because by his attitude and actions he would have fulfilled the condition for these things. This is nonsense because without its proper object *warning*, like *believing dangerous*, will not be there. It is logically impossible to warn about anything not thought of as threatening evil, and for danger we need a particular kind of serious evil such as injury or death.

There are, however, some differences between thinking a thing dangerous and feeling proud, frightened or dismayed. When a man says that something is dangerous he must support his statement with a special kind of evidence; but when he says that he feels proud or frightened or dismayed the description of the object of his pride or fright or dismay does not have quite this relation to his original statement. If he is shown that the thing he was proud of was not his after all, or was not after all anything very grand, he may have to say that his pride was not justified, but he will not have to take back the statement that he was proud. On the other hand, someone who says that a thing is dangerous, and later sees that he made a mistake in thinking that an injury might result from it, has to go back on his original statement and admit that he was wrong. In neither case, however, is the speaker able to go on as before. A man who discovered that it was not his pumpkin but someone else's which had won the prize could only say that he still felt proud, if he could produce some other ground for pride. It is in this way that even feelings are logically vulnerable to facts.

It will probably be objected against these examples that for part of the way at least they beg the question. It will be said that indeed a man can only be proud of something he thinks a good action, or an achievement, or a sign of noble birth; as he can only feel dismay about something which he sees as bad, frightened at some threatened evil; similarly he can only warn if he is also prepared to speak, for instance, of injury. But this will only limit the range of possible objects of those attitudes and beliefs if the range of these terms is limited in its turn. To meet this objection I shall discuss the meaning of 'injury' because this is the simplest case. Anyone who feels inclined to say that anything could be counted as an achievement, or as the evil of which people were afraid, or about which they felt dismayed, should just try this out. I wish to consider the proposition that anything could be thought of as dangerous, because if it causes injury it is dangerous, and anything could be counted as an injury. I shall consider bodily injury because this is the injury connected with danger; it is not correct to put up a notice by the roadside reading 'Danger!' on account of bushes which might scratch a car. Nor can a substance be labelled 'dangerous' on the ground that it can injure delicate fabrics; although we can speak of the danger that it may do so, that is not the use of the word which I am considering here.

When a body is injured it is changed for the worse in a special way, and we want to know which changes count as injuries. First of all, it matters how an injury comes about; e.g. it cannot be caused by natural decay. Then it seems clear that not just any kind of thing will do, for instance, any unusual mark on the body, however much trouble a man might take to have it removed. By far the most important class of injuries are injuries to a part of the body, counting as injuries because there is interference with the function of that part; injury to a leg, an eye, an ear, a hand, a muscle, the heart, the brain, the spinal cord. An injury to an eye is one that affects, or is likely to affect, its sight; an injury to a hand one which makes it less well able to reach out and grasp, and perform other operations of this kind. A leg can be injured because its movements and supporting power can be affected; a lung because it can become too weak to draw in the proper amount of air. We are most ready to speak of an injury where the function of a part of the body is to perform a characteristic operation, as in these examples. We might hesitate to say that a skull can be injured, and might prefer to speak of damage to it, since although there is indeed a function (a protective function) there is no operation. But thinking of the protective function of the skull we may want to speak of injury here. In so far as the concept of *injury* depends on that of *function* it is narrowly limited, since not even every use to which a part of the body is put will count as its function. Why is it that, even if it is the means by which they earn their living, we would never consider the removal of the dwarf's hump or the bearded lady's beard as a bodily injury? It will be tempting to say that these things are disfigurements, but this is not the point; if we suppose that a man who had some invisible extra muscle made his living as a court jester by waggling his ears, the ear would not have been injured if this were made to disappear. If it were natural to men to communicate by movements of the ear, then ears would have the function of signalling (we have no word for this kind of 'speaking') and an impairment of this function would be an injury; but things are not like this.

This court jester would use his ears to make people laugh, but this is not the function of ears.

No doubt many people will feel impatient when such facts are mentioned, because they think that it is quite unimportant that this or that *happens* to be the case, and it seems to them arbitrary that the loss of the beard, the hump, or the ear muscle would not be called an injury. Isn't the loss of that by which one makes one's living a pretty catastrophic loss? Yet it seems quite natural that these are not counted as injuries if one thinks about the conditions of human life, and contrasts the loss of a special ability to make people gape or laugh with the ability to see, hear, walk, or pick things up. The first is only needed for one very special way of living; the other in any foreseeable future for any man. This restriction seems all the more natural when we observe what other threats besides that of injury can constitute danger: of death, for instance, or mental derangement. A shock which could cause mental instability or impairment of memory would be called dangerous, because a man needs such things as intelligence, memory, and concentration as he needs sight or hearing or the use of hands. Here we do not speak of injury unless it is possible to connect the impairment with some physical change, but we speak of danger because there is the same loss of a capacity which any man needs.

There can be injury outside the range we have been considering; for a man may sometimes be said to have received injuries where no part of his body has had its function interfered with. In general, I think that any blow which disarranged the body in such a way that there was lasting pain would inflict an injury, even if no other ill resulted, but I do not know of any other important extension of the concept.

It seems therefore that since the range of things which can be called injuries is quite narrowly restricted, the word 'dangerous' is restricted in so far as it is connected with injury. We have the right to say that a man cannot decide to call just anything dangerous, however much he puts up fences and shakes his head.

So far I have been arguing that such things as pride, fear, dismay, and the thought that something is dangerous have an internal relation to their object, and hope that what I mean is becoming clear. Now we must consider whether those attitudes or beliefs which are the moral philosopher's study are similar, or whether such things as 'evaluation' and 'thinking something good' and 'commendation' could logically be found in combination with any object whatsoever. All I can do here is to give an example which may make this suggestion seem implausible, and to knock away a few of its supports. The example will come from the range of trivial and pointless actions such as we were considering in speaking of the man who clasped his hands three times an hour, and we can point to the oddity of the suggestion that this can be called a good action. We are bound by the terms of our question to refrain from adding any special background, and it should be stated once more that the question is about what can count in favour of the goodness or badness of a man or an action, and not what could be, or be thought, good or bad with a special background. I believe that the view I am attacking often seems plausible only because the special background is surreptitiously introduced.

Someone who said that clasping the hands three times in an hour was a good action would first have to answer the question 'How do you mean?' For the sentence 'this is a good action' is not one which has a clear meaning. Presumably, since our subject is moral philosophy, it does not here mean 'that was a good thing to do' as this might be said of a man who had done something sensible in the course of any enterprise whatever; we are to confine our attention to 'the moral use of "good"'. I am not clear that it makes sense to speak of a 'moral use of "good"', but we can pick out a number of cases which raise moral issues. It is because these are so diverse and because 'this is a good action' does not pick out any one of them, that we must ask 'How do you mean?' For instance, some things that are done fulfil a duty, such as the duty of parents to children or children to parents. I suppose that when philosophers speak of good actions they would include these. Some come under the heading of a virtue such as charity, and they will be included too. Others again are actions which require the virtues of courage or temperance, and here the moral aspect is due to the fact that they are done in spite of fear or the temptation of pleasure; they must indeed be done for the sake of some real or fancied good, but not necessarily what philosophers would want to call a moral good. Courage is not *particularly* concerned with saving other people's lives, or temperance with leaving them their share of the food and drink, and the goodness of *what is done* may here be all kinds of usefulness. It is because there are these very diverse cases included (I suppose) under the expression 'a good action' that we should refuse to consider applying it without asking what is meant, and we should now ask

what is intended when someone is supposed to say that 'clasping
the hands three times in an hour is a good action'. Is it supposed
that this action fulfils a duty? Then in virtue of what does a man
have this duty, and to whom does he owe it? We have promised
not to slip in a special background, but he cannot possibly have a
duty to clasp his hands unless such a background exists. Nor
could it be an act of charity, for it is not thought to do anyone any
good, nor again a gesture of humility unless a special assumption
turns it into this. The action could be courageous, but only if it
were done both in the face of fear and for the sake of a good; and
we are not allowed to put in special circumstances which could
make this the case.

I am sure that the following objection will now be raised. 'Of
course clasping one's hands three times in an hour cannot be
brought under one of the virtues which we recognise, but that is
only to say that it is not a good action by our current moral code.
It is logically possible that in a quite different moral code quite
different virtues should be recognised, for which we have not even
got a name.' I cannot answer this objection properly, for that
would need a satisfactory account of the concept of a virtue. But
anyone who thinks it would be easy to describe a new virtue
connected with clasping the hands three times in an hour should
just try. I think he will find that he has to cheat, and suppose that
in the community concerned the clasping of hands has been given
some special significance, or is thought to have some special effect.
The difficulty is obviously connected with the fact that without a
special background there is no possibility of answering the question 'What's the point?' It is no good saying that here would be a
point in doing the action because the action was a morally good
action: the question is how it can be given any such description if
we cannot first speak about the point. And it is just as crazy to
suppose that we can call *anything* the point of doing something
without having to say what the point of *that* is. In clasping one's
hands one may make a slight sucking noise, but what is the point
of that? It is surely clear that moral virtues must be connected
with human good and harm, and that it is quite impossible to call
anything you like good or harm. Consider, for instance, the
suggestion that a man might say he had been harmed because a
bucket of water had been taken out of the sea. As usual it would
be possible to think up circumstances in which this remark would
make sense; for instance, when coupled with a belief in magical
influences; but then the harm would consist in what was done by

the evil spirits, not in the taking of the water from the sea. It would be just as odd if someone were supposed to say that harm had been done to him because the hairs of his head had been reduced to an even number.[2]

I conclude that assumption (1) is very dubious indeed, and that no one should be allowed to speak as if we can understand 'evaluation', 'commendation' or 'pro-attitude', whatever the actions concerned.

II

I propose now to consider what was called assumption (2), which said that a man might always refuse to accept the conclusion of an argument about values, because what counted as evidence for other people did not count for him. Assumption (2) could be true even if assumption (1) were false, for it might be that once a particular question of values—say a moral question—had been accepted, any disputant was bound to accept particular pieces of evidence as relevant, the same pieces as everyone else, but that he could always refuse to draw any moral conclusions whatsoever or to discuss any questions which introduced moral terms. Nor do we mean 'he might refuse to draw the conclusion' in the trivial sense in which anyone can perhaps refuse to draw *any* conclusion; the point is that any statement of value always seems to go beyond any statement of fact, so that he might have a reason for accepting the factual premises but refusing to accept the evaluative conclusion. That this is so seems to those who argue in this way to follow from the practical implications of evaluation. When a man uses a word such as 'good' in an 'evaluative' and not an 'inverted comma' sense, he is supposed to commit his will. From this it has seemed to follow inevitably that there is a logical gap between fact and value; for is it not one thing to say that a thing is so, and another to have a particular attitude towards its being so; one thing to see that certain effects will follow from a given action, and another to care? Whatever account was offered of the essential feature of evaluation—whether in terms of feelings, attitudes, the acceptance of imperatives or what not—the fact remained that with an evaluation there was a committal in a new

[2] In face of this sort of example many philosophers take refuge in the thicket of aesthetics. It would be interesting to know if they are willing to let their whole case rest on the possibility that there might be aesthetic objections to what was done.

dimension, and that this was not guaranteed by any acceptance of facts.

I shall argue that this view is mistaken; that the practical impli-cation of the use of moral terms has been put in the wrong place, and that if it is described correctly the logical gap between factual premises and moral conclusion disappears.

In this argument it will be useful to have as a pattern the practical or 'action-guiding' force of the word 'injury', which is in some, though not all, ways similar to that of moral terms. It is clear I think that an injury is necessarily something bad and therefore something which as such anyone always has a reason to avoid, and philosophers will therefore be tempted to say that any-one who uses 'injury' in its full 'action-guiding' sense commits himself to avoiding the things he calls injuries. They will then be in the usual difficulties about the man who says he knows he ought to do something but does not intend to do it; perhaps also about weakness of the will. Suppose that instead we look again at the kinds of things which count as injuries, to see if the connec-tion with the will does not start here. As has been shown, a man is injured whenever some part of his body, in being damaged, has become less well able to fulfil its ordinary function. It follows that he suffers a disability, or is liable to do so; with an injured hand he will be less well able to pick things up, hold on to them, tie them together or chop them up, and so on. With defective eyes there will be a thousand other things he is unable to do, and in both cases we should naturally say that he will often be unable to get what he wants to get or avoid what he wants to avoid.

Philosophers will no doubt seize on the word 'want', and say that if we suppose that a man happens to want the things which an injury to his body prevents him from getting, we have slipped in a supposition about a 'pro-attitude' already; and that anyone who does not happen to have these wants can still refuse to use 'injury' in its prescriptive, or 'action-guiding' sense. And so it may seem that the only way to make a *necessary* connection between 'injury' and the things that are to be avoided, is to say that it is only used in an 'action-guiding sense' when applied to something the speaker intends to avoid. But we should look carefully at the crucial move in that argument, and query the suggestion that someone might happen not to want anything for which he would need the use of hands or eyes. Hands and eyes, like ears and legs, play a part in so many operations that a man could only be said not to need them if he had no wants at all. That such people exist, in asylums, is not to the present purpose at all; the proper use of his limbs is something a man has reason to want if he wants anything.

I do not know just what someone who denies this proposition could have in mind. Perhaps he is thinking of changing the facts of human existence, so that merely wishing, or the sound of the voice, will bring the world to heel? More likely he is proposing to rig the circumstances of some individual's existence within the framework of the ordinary world, by supposing for instance that he is a prince whose servants will sow and reap and fetch and carry for him, and so use their hands and eyes in his service that he will not need the use of his. Let us suppose that such a story could be told about a man's life; it is wildly implausible, but let us pretend that it is not. It is clear that in spite of this we could say that any man had a reason to shun injury; for even if at the end of his life it could be said that by a strange set of circumstances he had never needed the use of his eyes, or his hands, this could not possibly be foreseen. Only by once more changing the facts of human existence, and supposing every vicissitude foreseeable, could such a supposition be made.

This is not to say that an injury might not bring more incidental gain than necessary harm; one has only to think of times when the order has gone out that able-bodied men are to be put to the sword. Such a gain might even, in some peculiar circumstances, be reliably foreseen, so that a man would have even better reason for seeking than for avoiding injury. In this respect the word 'injury' differs from terms such as 'injustice'; the practical force of 'injury' means only that anyone has *a* reason to avoid injuries, not that he has an overriding reason to do so.

It will be noticed that this account of the 'action-guiding' force of 'injury' links it with reasons for acting rather than with actually doing something. I do not think, however, that this makes it a less good pattern for the 'action-guiding' force of moral terms. Philosophers who have supposed that actual action was required if 'good' were to be used in a sincere evaluation have got into difficulties over weakness of will, and they should surely agree that enough has been done if we can show that any man has reason to aim at virtue and avoid vice. But is this impossibly difficult if we consider the kinds of things that count as virtue and vice? Consider, for instance, the cardinal virtues, prudence, temperance, courage and justice. Obviously any man needs prudence, but does he not also need to resist the temptation of pleasure when there is harm involved? And how could it be argued that he would never need to face what was fearful for the sake of some good? It is not obvious what someone would mean if he said that temperance or courage were not good qualities, and this not because of the 'praising' sense of these *words*, but because of the things that courage and temperance are.

I should like to use these examples to show the artificiality of the notions of 'commendation' and of 'pro-attitudes' as these are commonly employed. Philosophers who talk about these things will say that after the facts have been accepted—say that X is the kind of man who will climb a dangerous mountain, beard an irascible employer for a rise in pay, and in general face the fearful for the sake of something he thinks worth while—there remains the question of 'commendation' or 'evaluation'. If the word 'courage' is used they will ask whether or not the man who speaks of another as having courage is supposed to have commended him. If we say 'yes' they will insist that the judgement about courage *goes beyond the facts*, and might therefore be rejected by someone who refused to do so; if we say 'no' they will argue that 'courage' is being used in a purely descriptive or 'inverted comma sense', and that we have not got an example of the evaluative use of language which is the moral philosopher's special study. What sense can be made, however, of the question 'does he commend?'? What is this extra element which is supposed to be present or absent after the facts have been settled? It is not a matter of liking the man who has courage, or of thinking him altogether good, but of 'commending him for his courage'. How are we supposed to do that? The answer that will be given is that we only commend someone else in speaking of him as courageous if we accept the imperative 'let me be courageous' for ourselves. But this is quite unnecessary. I can speak of someone else as having the virtue of courage, and of course recognise it as a virtue in the proper sense, while knowing that I am a complete coward, and making no resolution to reform. I know that I should be better off if I were courageous, and so have a reason to cultivate courage, but I may also know that I will do nothing of the kind.

If someone were to say that courage was not a virtue he would have to say that it was not a quality by which a man came to act well. Perhaps he would be thinking that someone might be worse off for his courage, which is true, but only because an incidental harm might arise. For instance, the courageous man might have under-estimated a risk, and run into some disaster which a cowardly man would have avoided because he was not prepared to take any risk at all. And his courage, like any other virtue, could be the cause of harm to him because possessing it he fell into some disastrous state of pride.[3] Similarly, those who question the virtue of temperance are probably thinking not of the virtue itself but of men whose temperance has consisted in resisting pleasure for the sake of some illusory good, or those who have made this virtue their pride.

But what, it will be asked, of justice? For while prudence, courage and temperance are qualities which benefit the man who has them, justice seems rather to benefit others, and to work to the disadvantage of the just man himself. Justice as it is treated here, as one of the cardinal virtues, covers all those things owed to other people: it is under injustice that murder, theft and lying come, as well as the withholding of what is owed for instance by parents to children and by children to parents, as well as the dealings which would be called unjust in everyday speech. So the man who avoids injustice will find himself in need of things he has returned to their owner, unable to obtain an advantage by cheating and lying; involved in all those difficulties painted by Thrasymachus in the first book of the Republic, in order to show that injustice is more profitable than justice to a man of strength and wit. We will be asked how, on our theory, justice can be a virtue and injustice a vice, since it will surely be difficult to show that any man whatsoever must need to be just as he needs the use of his hands and eyes, or needs prudence, courage and temperance?

Before answering this question I shall argue that if it cannot be answered, then justice can no longer be recommended as a virtue. The point of this is not to show that it must be answerable, since justice is a virtue, but rather to suggest that we should at least consider the possibility that justice is not a virtue. This suggestion was taken seriously by Socrates in the Republic, where it was assumed by everyone that if Thrasymachus could establish his premise—that injustice was more profitable than justice—his conclusion would follow: that a man who had the strength to get away with injustice had reason to follow this as the best way of life. It is a striking fact about modern moral philosophy that no one sees any difficulty in accepting Thrasymachus' premise and rejecting his conclusion, and it is because Nietzsche's position is at

[3] Cf. Aquinas, *Summa Theologica*, I–II, q. 55, Art. 4.

this point much closer to that of Plato that he is remote from academic moralists of the present day.

In the Republic it is assumed that if justice is not a good to the just man, moralists who recommend it as a virtue are perpetrating a fraud. Agreeing with this, I shall be asked where exactly the fraud comes in; where the untruth that justice is profitable to the individual is supposed to be told? As a preliminary answer we might ask how many people are prepared to say frankly that injustice is more profitable than justice? Leaving aside, as elsewhere in this paper, religious beliefs which might complicate the matter, we will suppose that some tough atheistical character has asked 'Why should I be just?' (Those who believe that this question has something wrong with it can employ their favourite device for sieving out 'evaluating meaning', and suppose that the question is 'Why should I be "just"?') Are we prepared to reply 'As far as you are concerned you will be better off if you are unjust, but it matters to the rest of us that you should be just, so we are trying to get you to be just'? He would be likely to enquire into our methods, and then take care not to be found out, and I do not think that many of those who think that it is not necessary to show that justice is profitable to the just man would easily accept that there was nothing more they could say.

The crucial question is: 'Can we give anyone, strong or weak, a reason why he should be just?'—and it is no help at all to say that since 'just' and 'unjust' are 'action-guiding words' no one can even ask 'Why should I be just?' Confronted with that argument the man who wants to do unjust things has only to be careful to avoid the *word*, and he has not been given a reason why he should not do the things which other people call 'unjust'. Probably it will be argued that he has been given a reason so far as anyone can ever be given a reason for doing or not doing anything, for the chain of reasons must always come to an end somewhere, and it may seem that one man may always reject the reason which another man accepts. But this is a mistake; some answers to the question 'why should I?' bring the series to a close and some do not. Hume showed how *one* answer closed the series in the following passage:

'Ask a man *why he uses exercise*; he will answer, *because he desires to keep his health*. If you then enquire, *why he desires health*, he will readily reply, *because sickness is painful*. If you push your enquiries further, and desire a reason *why he hates pain*, it is impossible he can ever give any. This is an ultimate end, and is never referred to any other object.' (*Enquiries*, appendix I, para. v.) Hume might just as well have ended this series with boredom: sickness often brings boredom, and no one is required to give a reason why he does not want to be bored, any more than he has to give a reason why he does want to pursue what interests him. In general, anyone is given a reason for acting when he is shown the way to something he wants; but for some wants the question 'Why do you want that?' will make sense, and for others it will not.[4] It seems clear that in this division justice falls on the opposite side from pleasure and interest and such things. 'Why shouldn't I do that?' is not answered by the words 'because it is unjust' as it is answered by showing that the action will bring boredom, loneliness, pain, discomfort or certain kinds of incapacity, and this is why it is not true to say that 'it's unjust' gives a reason in so far as any reasons can ever be given. 'It's unjust' gives a reason only if the nature of justice can be shown to be such that it is necessarily connected with what a man wants.

This shows why a great deal hangs on the question of whether justice is or is not a good to the just man, and why those who accept Thrasymachus' premise and reject his conclusion are in a dubious position. They recommend justice to each man, as something he has a reason to follow, but when challenged to show why he should do so they will not always be able to reply. This last assertion does not depend on any 'selfish theory of human nature' in the philosophical sense. It is often possible to give a man a reason for acting by showing him that someone else will suffer if he does not; someone else's good may really be more to him than his own. But the affection which mothers feel for children, and lovers for each other, and friends for friends, will not take us far when we are asked for reasons why a man should be just; partly because it will not extend far enough, and partly because the actions dictated by benevolence and justice are not always the same. Suppose that I owe someone money; '. . . what if he be my enemy, and has given me just cause to hate him? What if he be a vicious man, and deserves the hatred of all mankind? What if he be a miser, and can make no use of what I would deprive him of? What if he be a profligate debauchee, and would rather receive harm than benefit from large possessions?'[5] Even if the general practice of justice could be brought under the motive of universal

---

[4] For an excellent discussion of reasons for action, see G. E. M. Anscombe, *Intention* (Oxford 1957) sections 34–40.

[5] Hume, *Treatise*, III. ii. 1.

benevolence—the desire for the greatest happiness of the greatest number—many people certainly do not have any such desire. So that if injustice is only to be recommended on these grounds a thousand tough characters will be able to say that they have been given no reason for practising justice, and many more would say the same if they were not too timid or too stupid to ask questions about the code of behaviour which they have been taught. Thus, given Thrasymachus' premise Thrasymachus' point of view is reasonable; we have no particular reason to admire those who practise justice through timidity or stupidity.

It seems to me, therefore, that if Thrasymachus' thesis is accepted things cannot go on as before; we shall have to admit that the belief on which the status of justice as a virtue was founded is mistaken, and if we still want to get people to be just we must recommend justice to them in a new way. We shall have to admit that injustice is more profitable than justice, at least for the strong, and then do our best to see that hardly anyone can get away with being unjust. We have, of course, the alternative of keeping quiet, hoping that for the most part people will follow convention into a kind of justice, and not ask awkward questions, but this policy might be overtaken by a vague scepticism even on the part of those who do not know just what is lacking; we should also be at the mercy of anyone who was able and willing to expose our fraud.

Is it true, however, to say that justice is not something a man needs in his dealings with his fellows, supposing only that he be strong? Those who think that he can get on perfectly well without being just should be asked to say exactly how such a man is supposed to live. We know that he is to practise injustice whenever the unjust act would bring him advantage; but what is he to say? Does he admit that he does not recognise the rights of other people, or does he pretend? In the first case even those who combine with him will know that on a change of fortune, or a shift of affection, he may turn to plunder them, and he must be as wary of their treachery as they are of his. Presumably the happy unjust man is supposed, as in Book II of the *Republic*, to be a very cunning liar and actor, combining complete injustice with the appearance of justice: he is prepared to treat others ruthlessly, but pretends that nothing is further from his mind. Philosophers often speak as if a man could thus hide himself even from those around him, but the supposition is doubtful, and in any case the price in vigilance would be colossal. If he lets even a few people see his true attitude he must guard himself against them; if he lets no one into the secret he must always be careful in case the least spontaneity betray him. Such facts are important because the need a man has for justice in dealings with other men depends on the fact that they are men and not inanimate objects or animals. If a man only needed other men as he needs household objects, and if men could be manipulated like household objects, or beaten into a reliable submission like donkeys, the case would be different. As things are, the supposition that injustice is more profitable than justice is very dubious, although like cowardice and intemperance it might turn out incidentally to be profitable.

The reason why it seems to some people so impossibly difficult to show that justice is more profitable than injustice is that they consider in isolation particular just acts. It is perfectly true that if a man is just it follows that he will be prepared, in the event of very evil circumstances, even to face death rather than to act unjustly—for instance, in getting an innocent man convicted of a crime of which he has been accused. For him it turns out that his justice brings disaster on him, and yet like anyone else he had good reason to be a just and not an unjust man. He could not have it both ways and while possessing the virtue of justice hold himself ready to be unjust should any great advantage accrue. The man who has the virtue of justice is not ready to do certain things, and if he is too easily tempted we shall say that he was ready after all.

Source: 'Moral Beliefs', *Proceedings of the Aristotelian Society*, 1958–9.

APPENDIX (1967)[1]

In the first half of the article I had argued against the idea of an evaluative element in the meaning of the word 'good' which should be independent of its descriptive meaning, saying that we cannot make sense of the notion that a man is thinking 'this is a good action' if he brings the wrong sort of evidence to show that

[1] Extract from Philippa Foot's introduction to *Theories of Ethics*, ed. Philippa Foot (O.U.P.).

it *is* a good action. Nor will it necessarily help to appeal to feelings that he has, for there are some feelings that cannot be
attributed to a man unless he has the right thoughts. This part of
the article suggested that the expression 'a good action' had a
fixed descriptive meaning, or at least that it was fixed within a
certain range.

Now, this, though it has been in fact rejected by emotivists and
prescriptivists, who think it a contingent matter if *our* evaluative
terms possess a fixed descriptive meaning, is not right at the
centre of the dispute between the two parties. For the anti-
naturalist could agree that an expression such as 'good action'
had a fixed descriptive meaning while still arguing for an extra
'volitional element' in value judgements. Perhaps a man who calls
an action a good action must apply certain descriptions to it but
also have certain feelings or attitudes, or accept particular rules
of conduct? How else is the action-guiding force of the word to
be maintained? In the second part of the article I suggested that
it could perfectly well be given by the particular facts with which
the goodness of a good action is connected. For some facts about
a thing are such as to give *any* man a reason for choosing that
thing. The difficulty was, of course, to show that the actions that
we think of as good actions are actions of this kind. It can indeed
be shown that any man is likely to need the virtues of courage,
temperance and prudence, whatever his particular aims and
desires. But what about justice? To be just is not obviously to
one's own advantage, and may not happen to fit with one's affec-
tions and plans.

I was in this difficulty because I had supposed—with my opponents—that the thought of a good action must be related to the
choices of each individual in a very special way. It had not
occurred to me to question the often repeated dictum that moral
judgements give reasons for acting to each and every man. This
now seems to me to be a mistake. Quite generally the reason why
someone choosing an A may 'be expected' to choose good A's
rather than bad A's is that our criteria of goodness for any class of
things are related to certain interests that someone or other has in
those things. When someone shares these interests he will have
reason to choose the good A's: otherwise not. Since, in the case of
actions, we distinguish good and bad on account of the interest
we take in the common good, someone who does not care a damn
what happens to anyone but himself may truly say that he has no
reason to be just. The rest of us, so long as we continue as we are,

will try to impose good conduct upon such a man, saying 'you
ought to be just', and there is this much truth in the idea that
there are categorical imperatives in morals. There is also this
much truth in the idea that the moral 'ought' has a special action-
guiding force, for we should not say that a word in another
language was a moral term unless it could be used to *urge* conduct
in this way. But this is not to say that when used to do other
things it has a different sense. After saying 'you ought to do X' one
may without impropriety add 'but I hope to God you won't'; and
one may say 'I ought to do it, so what?' without using the word
'ought' in a special 'inverted comma' sense; one means 'I ought
to do it', not 'it's what you other chaps think I ought to do'. Of
course such utterances must be an exception, since if people in
general did not take an interest in the good of other people, and
the establishment of rules of justice in their society, the moral use
of 'ought' would not exist. But this gives one no reason to invent
a special sense of 'ought'. One might as well say that there are
two special senses, one for a man who in general takes account of
moral considerations but is kicking over the traces just here and
another for the amoral man who never takes any notice of what
he ought to do.

15 On Morality's having a Point (1965)

D. Z. PHILLIPS and H. O. MOUNCE

In 1958, moral philosophers were given rather startling advice.
They were told that their subject was not worth pursuing further
until they possessed an adequate philosophy of psychology.[1]
What is needed, they were told, is an enquiry into what type of
characteristic a virtue is, and, furthermore, it was suggested that
this question could be resolved in part by exploring the connection between what a man ought to do and what he *needs*:
perhaps man needs certain things in order to flourish, just as a
plant needs water; and perhaps what men need are the virtues,
courage, honesty, loyalty, etc. Thus, in telling a man that he

[1]'Modern Moral Philosophy' by G. E. M. Anscombe, *Philosophy*, xxx
(1958).

ought to be honest, we should not be using any special (moral) sense of ought: a man ought to be honest just as a plant ought to be watered. The 'ought' is the same; it tells us what a man needs.

Those who agree with the above advice must be pleased at the way things have gone since. Its implications have been worked out in some detail by Philippa Foot in a number of influential papers.[2] The attack on the naturalistic fallacy which it involves has been welcomed by a contemporary defender of Utilitarianism.[3] Strong support for a deductive argument from facts to values has come from a leading American philosopher,[4] while agreement with this general approach in ethics can be found in the work of a recent Gifford lecturer, who, amid all the varieties of goodness, cannot find a peculiar *moral* sense of 'good'.[5] Also, contemporary philosophers have been prompted to explore the connections between morality and prudence,[6] and even to express the hope that past masters will have a salutary influence on the future relationship between philosophy and psychology.[7] It seems fair to say that the advice of 1958 has produced a climate of opinion, a way of doing moral philosophy. For this reason, it is all the more important to expose the radical misunderstanding involved in it.

I

It has come to be thought important once again in ethics to ask for the point of morality. Why does it matter whether one does one thing rather than another? Surely, it is argued, if one wants to show someone why it is his duty to do something, one must be prepared to point out the importance of the proposed action, the harm involved in failing to do it, and the advantage involved in performing it. Such considerations simply cannot be put aside.

[2] 'Moral Beliefs', 'Goodness and Choice'; *Proceedings of the Aristotelian Society* suppl. vol. xxxv (1961). [See Reading 14,—Ed.]

[3] See Mary Warnock's *Introduction to Utilitarianism*, Fontana ed. (1962), p. 31.

[4] 'The gap between "is" and "should"' by Max Black, *Philosophical Review*, LXXIII (1964).

[5] *The Varieties of Goodness* by G. H. von Wright (Routledge, 1963).

[6] See R. S. Peters and A. Phillips Griffiths: 'The Autonomy of Prudence', in *Mind*, LXXI (1962).

[7] See Richard Wollheim's Introduction to Bradley's *Ethical Studies*, O.U.P. paperback ed. (1962), p. xvi.

On the contrary, the point of moral conduct must be elucidated in terms of the reasons for performing it. Such reasons separate moral arguments from persuasion and coercion, and moral judgements from likes and dislikes; they indicate what constitutes human good and harm.

If we take note of the role of reasons in morality, we shall see that not anything can count as a moral belief. After all, why does one regard some rules as moral principles, and yet never regard others as such? Certainly, we *can* see the point of some rules as moral principles, but in the case of other rules we cannot. How is the point seen? There is much in the suggestion that it is to be appreciated in terms of the backgrounds which attend moral beliefs and principles.[8] When rules which claim to be moral rules are devoid of these backgrounds we are puzzled. We do not know what is being said when someone claims that the given rule is a moral rule.

Normally, we do not speak of these backgrounds when we express and discuss moral opinions. It is only when we are asked to imagine their absence that we see how central they must be in any account we try to give of morality. Consider the rules, 'Never walk on the lines of a pavement', and 'Clap your hands every two hours'. If we saw people letting such rules govern their lives in certain ways, taking great care to observe them, feeling upset whenever they or other people infringe the rules, and so on, we should be hard put to understand what they were doing. We fail to see any point in it. On the other hand, if backgrounds are supplied for such rules, if further descriptions of the context in which they operate are given, sometimes, they can begin to look like moral principles. Given the background of a religious community, one can begin to see how the rule, 'Never walk on the lines of a pavement', could have moral significance. Think of, 'Take off thy shoes for thou art on holy ground', and its connections with the notions of reverence and disrespect. It is more difficult, though we do not say it is impossible, to think of a context in which the rule, 'Clap your hands every two hours', could have moral significance. Our first example shows how we can be brought to some understanding of a moral view when it is brought under a concept with which we are familiar. By linking disapproval of walking on the lines of a pavement with lack of reverence and disrespect, even those not familiar with the

[8] See Mrs. Foot's excellent paper, 'When Is A Principle A Moral Principle?', in *Proceedings of the Aristotelian Society*, supp. vol. xxviii (1954).

religious tradition in question may see that a *moral* view is being expressed. Such concepts as sincerity, honesty, courage, loyalty, respect, and, of course, a host of others, provide the kind of background necessary in order to make sense of rules as moral principles. It does not follow that all the possible features of such backgrounds need be present in every case. The important point to stress is that unless the given rule has *some* relation to such backgrounds, we would not know what is meant by calling it a moral principle.

The above conclusion follows from a more extensive one, namely, that commendation is internally related to its object. Mrs. Foot, for example, suggests that there is an analogy between commendation on the one hand, and mental attitudes such as pride and beliefs such as 'This is dangerous' on the other. One cannot feel proud of *anything*, any more than one can say that *anything* is dangerous. Similarly in the case of commendation: how can one say that clapping one's hands every two hours is a good action? The answer is that one cannot, unless the context in which the action is performed, for example, recovery from paralysis, makes its point apparent.

Certainly, those who have insisted on the necessity of a certain conceptual background in order to make sense of moral beliefs and moral judgements have done philosophy a service. They have revealed the artificiality of locating what is characteristically moral in a mental attitude such as a pro-attitude, or in a mental activity such as commending. They have shown the impossibility of making sense of something called 'evaluative meaning' which is thought of as being externally or contingently related to its objects. One could have a pro-attitude towards clapping one's hands every two hours, and one could commend one's never walking on the lines of a pavement, but neither pro-attitude nor commendation would, in themselves, give a point to such activities.

If the point of virtues is not to be expressed in terms of pro-attitudes or commendations, how is it to be brought out? It has been suggested that this could be done by showing the connection between virtues and human good and harm. But this is where the trouble starts, for if we are not careful, we may, in our eagerness to exorcise the spirit of evaluative meaning, fall under the spell of the concept of human good and harm, which is an equally dangerous idea. Unfortunately, this has already happened, and much of the current talk about human good and harm is as artificial as the talk about 'attitudes' in moral philosophy which it set out to criticise.

The point of calling an action (morally) good, it is suggested, is that it leads to human good and avoids harm. Further, what is to count as human good and harm is said to be a *factual* matter. Thus, one must try to show that there is a logical connection between statements of fact and statements of value, and that the logical gap supposed to exist between them can be closed. Men cannot pick and choose which facts are relevant to a moral conclusion, any more than they can pick and choose which facts are relevant in determining a physical ailment. Admittedly, the notion of a fact is a complex one, but this makes it all the more important to exercise care in the use of it. Let us try to appreciate this complexity in terms of an example.

Someone might think that pushing someone roughly is rude, and that anyone who denies this is simply refusing to face the facts. But this example, as it stands, is worthless, since it tells one nothing of the context in which the pushing took place. The reference to the context is all important in giving an account of the action, since not any kind of pushing can count as rudeness. Consider the following examples:

(a) One man pushing another person violently in order to save his life.

(b) A doctor pushing his way through a football-match crowd in response to an urgent appeal.

(c) The general pushing which takes place in a game of rugby.

(d) A violent push as a customary form of greeting between close friends.

In all these cases, pushing someone else is not rude. If someone took offence at being pushed, he might well see in the light of the situation that no offence had been caused. But what of situations where there is general agreement that an offence *has* been caused? Is the offence a fact from which a moral conclusion can be deduced? Clearly not, since what this suggestion ignores is the fact that *standards already prevail* in the context in which the offence is recognised. If one wants to call the offence a fact, one must recognise that it is a fact which already has moral import. The notion of 'offence' is parasitic on the notion of a standard or norm, although these need not be formulated. The person who wishes to say that the offence is a 'pure fact' from which a moral conclusion can be deduced is simply confused. What are the 'pure facts' relating to the pushing and the injury it is supposed to cause? A physiological account of the pushing (which might be regarded as pure enough) would not enable one to say what was going on, any more than a physiological account of the injury would tell us anything about what moral action (if any) is called for as a result. It makes all the difference morally whether the grazed ankle is caused by barging in the line-out or by barging in the bus queue. Any attempt to characterise the fact that an offence has been caused as a non-evaluative fact from which a moral conclusion can be deduced begs the question, since in asserting that a *kind of offence* has been caused, a specific background and the standards inherent in it have already been invoked.

But our opponent is still not beaten. He might give way on the confusion involved in the talk about deducing moral conclusions from 'pure facts', and agree that 'pushing' does not constitute rudeness in all contexts. Nevertheless, he might argue, where the circumstances *are* appropriate, it is possible to determine the rudeness of an action in a way which will settle any disagreement. But, again, this is clearly not the case. Whenever anyone says, 'That action is rude', there is no logical contradiction involved in denying the assertion, since although two people may share a moral concept such as rudeness, they may still differ strongly in its application. This is possible because views about rudeness do not exist *in vacuo*, but are often influenced by *other* moral beliefs. A good example of disagreement over the application of the concept of rudeness can be found in Malcolm's Memoir of Wittgenstein. Wittgenstein had lost his temper in a philosophical discussion with Moore, and would not allow Moore sufficient time to make his point. Moore thought that Wittgenstein's behaviour was rude, holding that good manners should always prevail, even in philosophical discussion. Wittgenstein, on the other hand, thought Moore's view of the matter absurd: philosophy is a serious business, important enough to justify a loss of temper; to think this rudeness is simply to misapply the judgement. Here, one can see how standards of rudeness have been influenced by wider beliefs; in other words, how the judgement, 'That is rude', is not entailed by the facts.

The position we have arrived at does not satisfy a great many contemporary moral philosophers. They are not prepared to recognise the possibility of permanent radical moral disagreement. They want to press on towards ultimate agreement, moral finality, call it what you will. They propose to do this by considering certain non-moral concepts of goodness in the belief that they will throw light on the notion of human good and harm. The non-moral example, 'good knife', has been popular in this respect. The word 'knife' names an object in respect of its function. Furthermore, the function is involved in the meaning of the word, so that if we came across a people who possessed objects which looked exactly like knives, but who never used these objects as we use them, we should refuse to say that they had the concept of a knife. Now when a thing has a function, the main criterion for its goodness will be that it serves that function well. Clearly, then, not anything can count as a good knife. But how does this help our understanding of moral goodness? Moral concepts are not functional. One can see what is to count as a good knife by asking what a knife is *for*, but can one see the point of generosity in the same way? To ask what generosity is *for* is simply to vulgarise the concept; it is like thinking that 'It is more blessed to give than to receive' is some kind of policy!

Yet, although moral concepts are not functional words, they are supposed to resemble them in important respects. The interesting thing, apparently, about many non-functional words, is that when they are linked with 'good' they yield criteria of goodness in much the same way as 'good knife' and other functional words do. For example, it seems as if 'good farmer' might yield criteria of goodness in this way. After all, farming is an activity which has a certain point. To call someone a good farmer will be to indicate that he has fulfilled the point of that activity. What 'the point' amounts to can be spelled out in terms of healthy crops and herds, and a good yield from the soil. The philosophical importance of these examples is that they show that the range of words whose meaning provides criteria of goodness extends beyond that of functional words. But what if the range is even wider than these examples suggest? It is clear what the philosophers who ask this question have in mind: what if the meaning of moral concepts could yield criteria of goodness in the same way? If this were possible, one need not rest content with expounding 'good knife' or 'good farmer'; 'good man' awaits elucidation. The goal is to find out what constitutes human flourishing. Furthermore, once these greater aims are achieved, all moral disputes would be, in principle at least, resolvable. Anyone claiming to have a good moral argument would have to justify it by showing its point in terms of human good and harm. And, once again, not anything could count as human good and harm.

The programme is nothing if not ambitious. Unfortunately, it will not work. The reason why is no minor defect: the whole enterprise is misconceived almost from the start. As far as land farming is concerned, the confusion could have been avoided had one asked why 'farming' yields criteria when joined with 'good'. To say that this type of farming is an activity which has a point, that farming serves some end, and that to call someone a good farmer is to say that he achieves this end, is only to tell part of the story. The most important part is left out, namely, *that the end in question is not in dispute.* That is why it makes sense to talk of experts in farming, and why problems in farming can be solved by technical or scientific means. For example, farmers might disagree over which is the best method of growing good wheat, but there is no disagreement over what is to count as good wheat. On the other hand, the situation is different where animal farming is concerned. Suppose it were established that the milk yield was not affected by keeping the cattle indoors in confined quarters, and by cutting their food supply.[9] Many people would say that no good farmer would be prepared to do this, despite the economic factors involved. Others may disagree and see nothing wrong in treating animals in this way. The point to note is that here one has a *moral* dispute. We recognise it as such because of the issues of cruelty, care, and expediency involved in it. The dispute cannot be settled by reference to the point of farming in this instance, since it is agreed that whichever side one takes, the milk yield remains the same. One must recognise that there are different conceptions of what constitutes good farming. Similarly, we shall find that there is no common agreement on what constitutes human good and harm. We shall argue presently that human good is not independent of the moral beliefs people hold, but is determined by them. In short, what must be recognised is that there are different conceptions of human good and harm.

II

The above argument would not satisfy the philosophers we have in mind. For them, moral views are founded on facts, the facts concerning human good and harm. We shall argue, on the other hand, that moral viewpoints determine what is and what is not to count as a relevant fact in reaching a moral decision. This philosophical disagreement has important consequences, for if we

[9] We owe this example to Dr. H. S. Price.

believe that moral values can be justified by appeal to *the* facts, it is hard to see how one man can reject another man's reasons for his moral beliefs, since these reasons too, presumably, refer to the facts. If, on the other hand, we hold that the notion of factual relevance is parasitic on moral beliefs, it is clear that deadlock in ethics will be a common occurrence, simply because of what some philosophers have unwisely regarded as contingent reasons, namely, the different moral views people hold.

Many philosophers are not convinced that there need be a breakdown in moral argument. It is tempting to think that anyone who has heard *all* the arguments in favour of a moral opinion cannot still ask why he ought to endorse it, any more than anyone who has heard all there is to say about the earth's shape can still ask why he ought to believe that the earth is round. Anyone who has heard *all* the reasons for a moral opinion has, it seems, heard all the facts. Sometimes the facts are difficult to discern, but there is in principle no reason why moral disagreement should persist. Therefore, it is difficult to see how 'x is good' can be a well-founded moral argument when 'x is bad' is said to be equally well founded. So runs the argument.

Certainly, it is difficult for philosophers who argue in this way to account for moral disagreement, since for them, moral judgements are founded on the facts of human good and harm, and the facts are incontrovertible. It is not surprising to find Bentham being praised in this context, since he too alleged that there is a common coinage into which 'rival' moral views could be cashed. The rivalry is only apparent, since the felicific calculus soon discovers the faulty reasoning. On this view, moral opinions are hypotheses whose validity is tested by reference to some common factor which is the sole reason for holding them. Bentham said the common factor was pleasure; nowadays it is called human good and harm. Whether one's moral views are 'valid' depends on whether they lead to human good and harm. But how does one arrive at these facts? One is said to do so by asking the question, 'What is the point?' often enough.

Philosophers are led to argue in this way by misconstruing the implications of the truth that a certain conceptual background is necessary in order for beliefs to have moral significance. Instead of being content to locate the point of such beliefs in their moral goodness, they insist on asking further what the point of *that* is. If one does not give up questioning too soon, one will arrive at the incontrovertible facts of human good and harm which do not invite any further requests for justification. Injury seems to be thought of as one such final halting place. To ask what is the point of calling injury a bad thing is to show that one has not grasped the concept of injury. To say that an action leads to injury is to give *a* reason for avoiding it. Injury may not be an overriding reason for avoiding the action which leads to it, as injustice is, but its being *a* reason is justified because injury is necessarily a bad thing. Even if we grant the distinction between reasons and overriding reasons, which is difficult enough if one asks who is to say which are which, is it clear that injury is always a reason for avoiding the action which leads to it?

The badness of injury, it is argued, is made explicit if one considers what an injury to hands, eyes, or ears, prevents a man from doing and getting; the badness is founded on what all men want. Mrs. Foot, for example, expounds the argument as follows,

> . . . the proper use of his limbs is something a man has reason to want if he wants anything.
>
> I do not know just what someone who denies this proposition could have in mind. Perhaps he is thinking of changing the facts of human existence, so that merely wishing, or the sound of the voice, will bring the world to heel? More likely he is proposing to rig the circumstances of some individual's existence within the framework of the ordinary world, by supposing for instance that he is a prince whose servants will sow and reap and fetch and carry for him, and so use their hands and eyes in his service that he will not need the use of his.[10]

But, Mrs. Foot argues, not even this supposition will do, since the prince cannot foresee that his circumstances will not change. He still has good reason to avoid injury to his hands and eyes, since he may need them some day. But there was no need to have thought up such an extravagant example to find objections to the view that injury is necessarily bad. There are more familiar ones close at hand which are far more difficult to deal with than the case of the fortunate prince. For example, consider the following advice,

> And if thine eye offend thee, pluck it out, and cast it from thee: it is better to enter into life with one eye, rather than having two eyes to be cast into hell fire. (Matt. xviii. 9.)

[10] See 'Moral Beliefs,' p. 127.

Or again, consider how Saint Paul does not think 'the thorn in the flesh' from which he suffered to be a bad thing. At first, he does so regard it, and prays that it be taken away. Later, however, he thanks God for his disability, since it was a constant reminder to him that he was not sufficient unto himself. Another example is worth quoting.[11] Brentano was blind at the end of his life. When friends commiserated with him over the harm that had befallen him, he denied that his loss of sight was a bad thing. He explained that one of his weaknesses had been a tendency to cultivate and concentrate on too many diverse interests. Now, in his blindness, he was able to concentrate on his philosophy in a way which had been impossible for him before. We may not want to argue like Saint Paul or Brentano, but is it true that we have no idea what they have in mind?

A readiness to admit that injury might result in incidental gain will not do as an answer to the above argument. True, there would be a gain in being injured if an order went out to put all able-bodied men to the sword, but are we to regard the examples of Saint Paul and Brentano as being in this category? In some peculiar circumstances where this gain could be foreseen, we might even imagine a person seeking injury rather than trying to avoid it. But is this the way we should account for saints who prayed to be partakers in the sufferings of Christ? Obviously not. It is clear that Paul himself does not regard his ailment as something which happens to be useful in certain circumstances. But in any case, why speak of *incidental* gain in any of these contexts, and why speak of the contexts themselves as *peculiar*? In doing so, is not the thesis that injury is necessarily bad being defended by calling any examples which count against it incidental or peculiar? In so far as moral philosophers argue in this way, they lay themselves open to the serious charge which Sorel has made against them:

The philosophers always have a certain amount of difficulty in seeing clearly into these ethical problems, because they feel the impossibility of harmonising the ideas which are current at a given time in a class, and yet imagine it to be their duty to reduce everything to a unity. To conceal from themselves the fundamental heterogeneity of all this civilised morality, they have recourse to a great number of subterfuges, sometimes

[11] We owe it to Mr. Rush Rhees.

relegating to the rank of exceptions, importations, or survivals, everything which embarrasses them. . . .[12]

Is it not the case that we cannot understand Brentano's attitude to his blindness unless we understand the kind of dedication to intellectual enquiry of which he was an example, and the virtues which such dedication demands in the enquirer? Again, we cannot understand Saint Paul's attitude to his ailment unless we understand something of the Hebrew-Christian conception of man's relationship to God, and the notions of insufficiency, dependence, and divine succour, involved in it. These views of personal injury or physical harm cannot be cashed in terms of what all men want. On the contrary, it is the specific contexts concerned, namely, dedication to enquiry and dedication to God, which determine what is to constitute goodness and badness. We can deny this only by elevating one concept of harm as being paradigmatic in much the same way as Bentham elevated one of the internal sentiments. We can say that injury is necessarily bad at the price of favouring one idea of badness.

In so far as philosophers construct a paradigm in their search for 'the unity of the facts of human good and harm', they are not far removed from the so-called scientific rationalists and their talk of proper functions, primary purpose, etc. One of these, in an argument with a Roman Catholic housewife over birth control, stressed the harm which could result from having too many children. He obviously thought that the reference to physical harm clinched the matter. The housewife, on the other hand, stressed the honour a mother has in bringing children into the world. It seems more likely that the scientific rationalist was blind to what the housewife meant by honour, than that she was blind to what he meant by harm. Are we for that reason to call the honour incidental gain?

How would the scientific rationalist and the housewife reach the agreement which some philosophers seem to think inevitable if all the facts were known? It is hard to see how they could without renouncing what they believe in. Certainly, one cannot regard their respective moral opinions as hypotheses which the facts will either confirm or refute, for what would the evidence be? For the rationalist, the possibility of the mother's death or injury, the economic situation of the family, the provision of good

---

[12] Georges Sorel, *Reflections On Violence*, trans. T. E. Hulme (Collier-Macmillan, 1961), pp. 229–30.

facilities for the children, and so on, would be extremely important. The housewife too agrees about providing the good things
of life for children, but believes that one ought to begin by
allowing them to enter the world. For her, submission to the will
of God, the honour of motherhood, the creation of a new life, and
so on, are of the greatest importance. But there is no settling of
the issue in terms of some supposed common evidence called
human good and harm, since what they differ over is precisely
the question of what constitutes human good and harm. The
same is true of all fundamental moral disagreements, for example,
the disagreement between a pacifist and a militarist. The argument is unlikely to proceed very far before deadlock is reached.

Deadlock in ethics, despite philosophical misgivings which have
been voiced, does not entail liberty to argue as one chooses. The
rationalist, the housewife, the pacifist, or the militarist, cannot
say what they like. Their arguments are rooted in different moral
traditions within which there are rules for what can and what
cannot be said. Because philosophers believe that moral opinions
rest on common evidence, they are forced to locate the cause of
moral disagreement in the evidence's complexity: often, experience and imagination are necessary in assessing it. One can
imagine someone versed in the views we have been attacking,
and sympathetic with them, saying to an opponent in a moral
argument, 'If only you could see how wrong you are. If only you
had the experience and the imagination to appreciate the evidence
for the goodness of the view I am advocating, evidence, which,
unfortunately, is too complex for you to master, you would see
that what I want is good for you too, since really, all men want
it'. Such appeals to 'the common good' or to 'what all men want'
are based on conscious or unconscious deception. It may be
admitted that the majority of mothers nowadays want to plan the
birth of their children, to fit in with the Budget if possible, and
regard the rearing of their children as a pause in their careers.
But this will not make the slightest difference to the housewife of
our previous example. She believes that what the majority wants
is a sign of moral decadence, and wants different things. But she
does not believe because she wants; she wants because she believes.

The view that there are ways of demonstrating goodness by
appeal to evidence which operate *independently* of the various
moral opinions people hold is radically mistaken. Sometimes,
philosophers seem to suggest that despite the moral differences

which separate men, they are really pursuing the same end, namely, what all men want. The notion of what all men want is as artificial as the common evidence which is supposed to support it. There are no theories of goodness.

Source: 'On morality's having a point', *Philosophy*, 1965.

POLITICAL PHILOSOPHY

16 The First Societies (1762)

J. J. ROUSSEAU

I

Man was born free, and he is everywhere in chains. Those who think themselves the masters of others are indeed greater slaves than they. How did this transformation come about? I do not know. How can it be made legitimate? That question I believe I can answer.

If I were to consider only force and the effects of force, I should say: 'So long as a people is constrained to obey, and obeys, it does well; but as soon as it can shake off the yoke, and shakes it off, it does better; for since it regains its freedom by the same right as that which removed it, a people is either justified in taking back its freedom, or there is no justifying those who took it away.' But the social order is a sacred right which serves as a basis for all other rights. And as it is not a natural right, it must be one founded on covenants. The problem is to determine what those covenants are. But before we pass on to that question, I must substantiate what I have so far said.

II

The oldest of all societies, and the only natural one, is that of the family; yet children remain tied to their father by nature only so long as they need him for their preservation. As soon as this need ends, the natural bond is dissolved. Once the children are freed from the obedience they owe their father, and the father is freed from his responsibilities towards them, both parties equally regain

149

their independence. If they continue to remain united, it is no longer nature, but their own choice, which unites them; and the family as such is kept in being only by agreement.

This common liberty is a consequence of man's nature. Man's first law is to watch over his own preservation; his first care he owes to himself; and as soon as he reaches the age of reason, he becomes the only judge of the best means to preserve himself; he becomes his own master.

The family may therefore perhaps be seen as the first model of political societies: the head of the state bears the image of the father, the people the image of his children, and all, being born free and equal, surrender their freedom only when they see advantage in doing so. The only difference is that in the family, a father's love for his children repays him for the care he bestows on them, while in the state, where the ruler can have no such feeling for his people, the pleasure of commanding must take the place of love.

Grotius denies that all human government is established for the benefit of the governed, and he cites the example of slavery. His characteristic method of reasoning is always to offer fact as a proof of right.[1] It is possible to imagine a more logical method, but not one more favourable to tyrants.

According to Grotius, therefore, it is doubtful whether humanity belongs to a hundred men, or whether these hundred men belong to humanity, though he seems throughout his book to lean to the first of these views, which is also that of Hobbes. These authors show us the human race divided into herds of cattle, each with a master who preserves it only in order to devour its members.

Just as a shepherd possesses a nature superior to that of his flock, so do those shepherds of men, their rulers, have a nature superior to that of their people. Or so, we are told by Philo, the Emperor Caligula argued, concluding, reasonably enough on this same analogy, that kings were gods or alternatively that the people were animals.

The reasoning of Caligula coincides with that of Hobbes and Grotius. Indeed Aristotle, before any of them, said that men

---

[1] 'Learned researches on public law are often only the history of ancient abuses, and one is misled when one gives oneself the trouble of studying them too closely.' *Traité manuscrit des intérêts de la France avec ses voisins par M. L. M. d'A.* This is exactly what Grotius does. [Rousseau's quotation is from the Marquis d'Argenson. *Trans.*]

were not at all equal by nature, since some were born for slavery and others born to be masters.

Aristotle was right; but he mistook the effect for the cause. Anyone born in slavery is born for slavery—nothing is more certain. Slaves, in their bondage, lose everything, even the desire to be free. They love their servitude even as the companions of Ulysses loved their life as brutes.[2] But if there are slaves by nature, it is only because there has been slavery against nature. Force made the first slaves; and their cowardice perpetuates their slavery.

I have said nothing of the King Adam or of the Emperor Noah, father of the three great monarchs who shared out the universe among them, like the children of Saturn, with whom some authors have identified them. I hope my readers will be grateful for this moderation, for since I am directly descended from one of those princes, and perhaps in the eldest line, how do I know that if the deeds were checked, I might not find myself the legitimate king of the human race? However that may be, there is no gainsaying that Adam was the king of the world, as was Robinson Crusoe of his island, precisely because he was the sole inhabitant; and the great advantage of such an empire was that the monarch, secure upon his throne, had no occasion to fear rebellions, wars or conspirators.

Source: The Social Contract, trans. M. Cranston (Penguin) Bk. I, Chs. 1 and 2.

17 The Kingdom of Ends (1785)

IMMANUEL KANT

[. . .] Now I say that man, and in general every rational being, *exists* as an end in himself, *not merely as a means* for arbitrary use by this or that will: he must in all his actions, whether they are directed to himself or to other rational beings, always be viewed *at the same time as an end*. All the objects of inclination have only a conditioned value; for if there were not these

[2] See a short treatise of Plutarch entitled: *That Animals use Reason.*

inclinations and the needs grounded on them, their object would be valueless. Inclinations themselves, as sources of needs, are so far from having an absolute value to make them desirable for their own sake that it must rather be the universal wish of every rational being to be wholly free from them. Thus the value of all objects that can *be produced* by our actions is always conditioned. Beings whose existence depends, not on our will, but on nature, have none the less, if they are non-rational beings, only a relative value as means and are consequently called *things*. Rational beings, on the other hand, are called *persons* because their nature already marks them out as ends in themselves—that is, as something which ought not to be used merely as a means—and consequently imposes to that extent a limit on all arbitrary treatment of them (and is an object of reverence). Persons, therefore, are not merely subjective ends whose existence as an object of our actions has a value *for us*: they are *objective ends*—that is, things whose existence is in itself an end, and indeed an end such that in its place we can put no other end to which they should serve *simply* as means; for unless this is so, nothing at all of *absolute* value would be found anywhere. But if all value were conditioned —that is, contingent—then no supreme principle could be found for reason at all.

If then there is to be a supreme practical principle and—so far as the human will is concerned—a categorical imperative, it must be such that from the idea of something which is necessarily an end for every one because it is an *end in itself* it forms an *objective* principle of the will and consequently can serve as a practical law. The ground of this principle is: *Rational nature exists as an end in itself.* This is the way in which a man necessarily conceives his own existence: it is therefore so far a *subjective* principle of human actions. But it is also the way in which every other rational being conceives his existence on the same rational ground which is valid also for me; hence it is at the same time an *objective* principle, from which, as a supreme practical ground, it must be possible to derive all laws for the will. The practical imperative will therefore be as follows: *Act in such a way that you always treat humanity, whether in your own person or in the person of any other, never simply as a means, but always at the same time as an end.* [. . .]

The concept of every rational being as one who must regard himself as making universal law by all the maxims of his will, and must seek to judge himself and his actions from this point of view, leads to a closely connected and very fruitful concept— namely, that of *a kingdom of ends.*

I understand by a *'kingdom'* a systematic union of different rational beings under common laws. Now since laws determine ends as regards their universal validity, we shall be able—if we abstract from the personal differences between rational beings, and also from all the content of their private ends—to conceive a whole of all ends in systematic conjunction (a whole both of rational beings as ends in themselves and also of the personal ends which each may set before himself); that is, we shall be able to conceive a kingdom of ends which is possible in accordance with the above principles.

For rational beings all stand under the *law* that each of them should treat himself and all others, *never merely as a means,* but always *at the same time as an end in himself.* But by so doing there arises a systematic union of rational beings under common objective laws—that is, a 'kingdom'. Since these laws are directed precisely to the relation of such beings to one another as ends and means, this kingdom can be called a kingdom of ends (which is admittedly only an Ideal).

A rational being belongs to the kingdom of ends as a *member,* when, although he makes its universal laws, he is also himself subject to these laws. He belongs to it as its *head,* when as the maker of laws he is himself subject to the will of no other.

A rational being must always regard himself as making laws in a kingdom of ends which is possible through freedom of the will —whether it be as member or as head. The position of the latter he can maintain, not in virtue of the maxim of his will alone, but only if he is a completely independent being, without needs and with an unlimited power adequate to his will.

Thus morality consists in the relation of all action to the making of laws whereby alone a kingdom of ends is possible. This making of laws must be found in every rational being himself and must be able to spring from his will. The principle of his will is therefore never to perform an action except on a maxim such as can also be a universal law, and consequently such *that the will can regard itself as at the same time making universal law by means of its maxim.* Where maxims are not already by their very nature in harmony with this objective principle of rational beings as makers of universal law, the necessity of acting on this principle is practical necessitation—that is, *duty.* Duty does not apply to the head in a kingdom of ends, but it does apply to every member and to all members in equal measure.

The practical necessity of acting on this principle—that is, duty —is in no way based on feelings, impulses, and inclinations, but only on the relation of rational beings to one another, a relation in which the will of a rational being must always be regarded as *making universal law*, because otherwise he could not be conceived as *an end in himself*. Reason thus relates every maxim of the will, considered as making universal law, to every other will and also to every action towards oneself: it does so, not because of any further motive or future advantage, but from the Idea of the *dignity* of a rational being who obeys no law other than that which he at the same time enacts himself.

Source: *The Moral Law*, trans. H. J. Paton (Hutchinson), pp. 90–1
    and 95–6.

18 Justice and Equality (1959)

S. I. BENN and R. S. PETERS

I. Equality and natural rights

The theory of natural rights . . . is related closely to the idea of equality. The state of Nature, declared Locke, is

> 'a state also of equality, wherein all the power and jurisdiction is reciprocal, no one having more than another, there being nothing more evident than that creatures of the same species and rank, promiscuously born to all the same advantages of Nature, and the use of the same faculties, should also be equal one amongst another, without subordination or subjection . . .';

and the law of Nature

> 'teaches all mankind who will but consult it, that being all equal and independent, no one ought to harm another in his life, health, liberty, or possessions . . .'[1]

[1] *Second Treatise of Civil Government*, Chap. II (Everyman edn pp. 118–119).

The American Declaration of Independence proclaimed, as self-evident truths, 'that all men are created equal, that they are endowed by their Creator with certain unalienable Rights'; the Declaration of 1789 echoed: 'Men are born and live free and equal in their rights'; and that of 1948: 'All human beings are born free and equal in dignity and rights'.

We have seen that the universality claimed for natural rights strongly suggests the criterion of impartiality for a moral rule. If, for instance, democratic rights were to be accorded to white men, we decided one must show good cause to deny them to black men. Where there are no relevant differences it would be unfair—or we might say *unjust*—to treat people differently.

In this chapter we shall begin by relating the concepts 'morality' and 'justice' to 'equality' as a social and political idea . . .

II. Analysis of 'equality'

The word 'equality' is used in one of its senses when we make comparisons. Now we can compare things only because they have some quality or attribute in common. We do not compare an elephant with a cabbage; we compare the relative size, weight, or colour of elephants and cabbages. It would, therefore, be as meaningless to say 'All elephants are equal' (in this sense of 'equal') as it would be to say 'Some elephants are more than others'. Neither statement is complete without a reference to some quality common to all elephants. What then of 'All men are equal'? If this were meant in this descriptive-comparative sense, it is difficult to think of a human quality—physical, intellectual, or moral—of which it could be true.

In social and political theory, however, 'equality' is more often prescriptive than descriptive. In this sense, 'All men are equal' would imply not that they possess some attribute or attributes in the same degree, but that they ought to be treated alike. But it is hardly likely that anyone would want to see all men treated alike in every respect. We should not wish rheumatic patients to be treated like diabetics. A poll tax is generally considered less just than an income tax, and a progressive tax fairer than a flat rate. There are clearly some differences that are proper grounds for differences in treatment. Equals (i.e. in the descriptive-comparative sense) ought to be treated alike in the respect in which they are equal; but there may be other respects in which they differ (or, are 'unequal') which justify differences in treatment. Men who make identical tax returns ought to be taxed alike, but if they suffer from different ailments they should be treated with different medicines. Injustice, said Aristotle, arises as much from treating unequals equally as from treating equals unequally. But if we agree to that, could it be right to treat *all* men equally in *any* respect, unless there were *some* attribute that they all possessed in the same degree?

It might well be asked whether there is really any respect in which a serious and responsible demand could be made for treating all men as if they were all equal in the sense of falling into one category. The obvious answer is that there are some demands like that of equality before the law which suggest just this. It might, therefore, be maintained that there must be some positive quality which all men have in common to *justify* them all being put in a universal category such as that of being a legal person. This would commit us to a search for some esoteric 'fundamental' quality in respect of which all are alike. Yet if this quality is so elusive, how can political theorists say with such confidence that all men possess it equally and ought accordingly to be treated as equals?

The difficulties arise, in our view, from putting the question in the wrong way. Consider Hobhouse's treatment of the subject:

> 'As a matter of the interpretation of experience, there is something peculiar to human beings and common to human beings without distinction of class, race or sex, which lies far deeper than all differences between them. Call it what we may, soul, reason, the abysmal capacity for suffering, or just human nature, it is something generic, of which there may be many specific, as well as quantitative differences, but which underlies and embraces them all. If this common nature is what the doctrine of equal rights postulates, it has no reason to fear the test of our ordinary experience of life, or of our study of history and anthropology.'[2]

Hobhouse seems to be making a distinction between all the particular differences between men, which he would treat as accidentals, and some essential or fundamental quality of 'men as men'—something called 'human nature', 'human dignity', 'personality', 'soul', etc.—by virtue of which they must be treated as fundamentally equal. But if we strip away all the qualities in

[2] L. T. Hobhouse, *Elements of Social Justice* (1922), p. 95.

respect of which men might differ, what is left? If from human nature we abstract talents, dispositions, character, intelligence, and all other possible grounds of distinction, we are left with an undifferentiated potentiality. To say that X is a person, or a human being, is to say that though we may not know enough about him to say whether he is wise or foolish, musical or unmusical, extrovert or introvert, we do know that he is the sort of object of which such things might be said. 'Human nature' implies a varying potentiality for a certain limited range of qualities ('limited' because it rules out having, say, the trunk and dimensions of an elephant); it is not another quality that all men possess equally, on account of which they should in some positive way be treated alike. 'The abysmal capacity for suffering' looks, on the face of it, a more promising candidate for universality. But while all human beings are liable to suffer, if some suffer more from a given cause than others, there would seem to be a case for unequal treatment, to protect the more sensitive. Conversely, the human species is not unique in this respect, yet we do not proclaim a fundamental equality between men and dogs.

It might be argued[3] that all men have certain basic needs, for food, clothing, shelters, etc., which must be satisfied if suffering is to be avoided; 'basic', in that, whatever the variety of their needs, these are common to them all: and further, if these are not satisfied, none can be satisfied. But while all men need *some* food, they do not all need the same sort, or even the same amount; and while in cold climates they need elaborate clothing and shelter, in warmer climates they can survive with none at all. Differences in circumstances create differences in needs, and it is no help to say that all men are equal in possessing basic needs, if they are needs for different things.[4]

Equality of consideration

These difficulties arise from treating 'All men are equal' as if it were a positive prescription, i.e. as if it meant 'Treat all men alike (if not in all, at least in certain fundamental respects'). For if it is unjust to treat unequals equally, there would have to be some sort of universal human equality, in the descriptive sense. Yet this is not to be found. The dilemma can be avoided, however,

[3] *Ibid.* p. 109.
[4] Cf. E. F. Carritt, *Ethical and Political Thinking.* (1947), pp. 156–7.

by re-formulating the prescription. What we really demand, when we say that all men are equal, is that *none shall be held to have a claim to better treatment than another, in advance of good grounds being produced.*

The only universal right, it has been said, is the right to equal consideration. This is not a right in the ordinary sense. Its existence cannot be established by referring to law, for it is presupposed by the idea of law, as a rule of *general* application, and by the procedure whereby a judge must consider relevant evidence and apply a rule in order to reach a decision. We cannot show that such a right *ought* to exist in law by pointing to the advantages of recognizing it; for until we admit the principle of equal consideration we cannot know whose advantage would be relevant.

'Equal consideration' is really the 'impartiality', which we examined in Chapter 2,* in a somewhat different guise. And this, we said, was one of the criteria implied in the idea of morality. Similarly, equality of consideration is implicit in the idea of justice. When we ask a judge, or anyone else making a decision between competing claims, 'Why do you treat A differently from B?' we expect him to justify discrimination by showing in what relevant respects they differ. If there is no relevant difference, we consider that he has been unreasonable. If he answered: 'I decided in that way because I felt like it', or 'because I like A better than B', his answer would be unsatisfactory because it is either an explanation of his conduct rather than a justification, or a justification on irrelevant grounds. We are seeking a reason that will satisfy the criterion that differences in treatment must be based on relevant differences of condition: what we have been offered is an explanation or justification in terms of the judge's own feelings or preferences.

When we have to decide between claims, impose burdens or allot benefits, the only rational ground for treating men differently is that they differ in some way that is relevant to the distinction we propose to make. We cannot know whether they do until we have considered their claims impartially. To do otherwise would be to treat a man purely as a means for someone else's satisfaction (one's own, perhaps, or a friend's). If we refuse to consider his claims on their own merits, we presume an inequality without

* Not reprinted in this volume.—Ed.

troubling to establish it. This is very like what Kant meant when he said: 'treat humanity, whether in your own person or in that of any other, in every case as an end, never solely as a means'. He did not mean that when every particular difference between men has been evaluated, there remains something of value in itself, a fundamental 'humanity'.

Understood in this way, the principle of equality does not prescribe positively that all human beings be treated alike; it is a presumption against treating them differently, in any respect, until grounds for distinction have been shown. It does not assume, therefore, a quality which all men have to the same degree, which is the ground of the presumption, for to say that there is a presumption means that no grounds need be shown. The onus of justification rests on whoever would make distinctions.

To act justly, then, is to treat all men alike except where there are relevant differences between them. This is not a formula from which anyone can deduce in particular cases, how he ought to act, or make decisions. For what constitutes a *relevant* difference, and what sort of distinction ought to be made in respect of it? So far we have achieved no more than a definition of 'justice' in terms of equality, and definitions cannot prescribe action, since they merely elucidate the meanings of words. At the most we have arrived at a rule of procedure for taking decisions: Presume equality until there is reason to presume otherwise. But this is a formal, not a substantive rule. [. . .]

Source: Social Principles and the Democratic State (Allen & Unwin) Pt. II, Ch. 5, Sec. I and II. (Extract.)

19 The Idea of Equality (1962)

BERNARD WILLIAMS

The idea of equality is used in political discussion both in statements of fact, or what purport to be statements of fact—that men *are* equal—and in statements of political principles or aims—that men *should be* equal, as at present they are not. The two can be, and often are, combined: the aim is then described as that of securing a state of affairs in which men are treated as the equal

beings which they in fact already are, but are not already treated
as being. In both these uses, the idea of equality notoriously
encounters the same difficulty: that on one kind of interpretation
the statements in which it figures are much too strong, and on
another kind much too weak, and it is hard to find a satisfactory
interpretation that lies between the two.[1]

To take first the supposed statement of fact: it has only too
often been pointed out that to say that all men are equal in all
those characteristics in respect of which it makes sense to say
that men are equal or unequal, is a patent falsehood; and even if
some more restricted selection is made of these characteristics,
the statement does not look much better. Faced with this obvious
objection, the defender of the claim that all men are equal is
likely to offer a weaker interpretation. It is not, he may say, in
their skill, intelligence, strength, or virtue that men are equal,
but merely in their being men: it is their common humanity that
constitutes their equality. On this interpretation, we should not
seek for some special characteristics in respect of which men are
equal, but merely remind ourselves that they are all men. Now to
this it might be objected that being men is not a respect in which
men can strictly speaking be said to be *equal*; but, leaving that
aside, there is the more immediate objection that if all that the
statement does is to remind us that men are men, it does not do
very much, and in particular does less than its proponents in
political arguments have wanted it to do. What looked like a
paradox has turned into a platitude.

I shall suggest in a moment that even in this weak form the
statement is not so vacuous as this objection makes it seem; but it
must be admitted that when the statement of equality ceases to
claim more than is warranted, it rather rapidly reaches the point
where it claims less than is interesting. A similar discomfiture
tends to overcome the practical maxim of equality. It cannot be
the aim of this maxim that all men should be treated alike in all
circumstances, or even that they should be treated alike as much
as possible. Granted that, however, there is no obvious stopping
point before the interpretation which makes the maxim claim
only that men should be treated alike in similar circumstances;
and since 'circumstances' here must clearly include reference to
what a man is, as well as to his purely external situation, this

---

[1] For an illuminating discussion of this and related questions, see
R. Wollheim and I. Berlin, 'Equality', *Proceedings of the Aristotelian
Society*, Vol. LVI (1955–6), p. 281 seq.

comes very much to saying that for every difference in the way men are treated, some general reason or principle of differentiation must be given. This may well be an important principle; some indeed have seen in it, or in something very like it, an essential element of morality itself.[2] But it can hardly be enough to constitute the principle that was advanced in the name of *equality*. It would be in accordance with this principle, for example, to treat black men differently from others just because they were black, or poor men differently just because they were poor, and this cannot accord with anyone's idea of equality.

In what follows I shall try to advance a number of considerations that can help to save the political notion of equality from these extremes of absurdity and of triviality. These considerations are in fact often employed in political argument, but are usually bundled together into an unanalysed notion of equality in a manner confusing to the advocates, and encouraging to the enemies, of that ideal. These considerations will not enable us to define a distinct third interpretation of the statements which use the notion of equality; it is rather that they enable us, starting with the weak interpretations, to build up something that in practice can have something of the solidity aspired to by the strong interpretations. In this discussion, it will not be necessary all the time to treat separately the supposedly factual application of the notion of equality, and its application in the maxim of action. Though it is sometimes important to distinguish them, and there are clear grounds for doing so, similar considerations often apply to both. The two go significantly together: on the one hand, the point of the supposedly factual assertion is to back up social ideals and programmes of political action; on the other hand—a rather less obvious point, perhaps—those political proposals have their force because they are regarded not as gratuitously egalitarian, aiming at equal treatment for reasons, for instance, of simplicity or tidiness, but as affirming an equality which is believed in some sense already to exist, and to be obscured or neglected by actual social arrangements.

1. *Common humanity.* The factual statement of men's equality was seen, when pressed, to retreat in the direction of merely asserting the equality of men as men; and this was thought to be trivial. It is certainly insufficient, but not, after all, trivial. That all men are human is, if a tautology, a useful one, serving as a

[2] For instance, R. M. Hare: see his *Language of Morals* (Oxford: The Clarendon Press, 1952).

reminder that those who belong anatomically to the species *homo sapiens*, and can speak a language, use tools, live in societies, can interbreed despite racial differences, etc., are also alike in certain other respects more likely to be forgotten. These respects are notably the capacity to feel pain, both from immediate physical causes and from various situations represented in perception and in thought; and the capacity to feel affection for others, and the consequences of this, connected with the frustration of this affection, loss of its objects, etc. The assertion that men are alike in the possession of these characteristics is, while indisputable and (it may be) even necessarily true, not trivial. For it is certain that there are political and social arrangements that systematically neglect these characteristics in the case of some groups of men, while being fully aware of them in the case of others; that is to say, they treat certain men as though they did not possess these characteristics, and neglect moral claims that arise from these characteristics and which would be admitted to arise from them.

Here it may be objected that the mere fact that ruling groups in certain societies treat other groups in this way does not mean that they neglect or overlook the characteristics in question. For, it may be suggested, they may well recognize the presence of these characteristics in the worse-treated group, but claim that in the case of that group, the characteristics do not give rise to any moral claim; the group being distinguished from other members of society in virtue of some further characteristic (for instance, by being black), this may be cited as the ground of treating them differently, whether they feel pain, affection, etc., or not.

This objection rests on the assumption, common to much moral philosophy that makes a sharp distinction between fact and value, that the question whether a certain consideration is *relevant* to a moral issue is an evaluative question: to state that a consideration is relevant or irrelevant to a certain moral question is, on this view, itself to commit oneself to a certain kind of moral principle or outlook. Thus, in the case under discussion, to say (as one would naturally say) that the fact that a man is black is, by itself, quite irrelevant to the issue of how he should be treated in respect of welfare, etc., would, on this view, be to commit to oneself to a certain sort of moral principle. This view, taken generally, seems to me quite certainly false. The principle that men should be differentially treated in respect of welfare merely on grounds of their colour is not a special sort of moral principle, but (if anything) a purely arbitrary assertion of will, like that of some Caligulan ruler who decided to execute everyone whose name contained three 'R's'.

This point is in fact conceded by those who practise such things as colour discrimination. Few can be found who will explain their practice merely by saying, 'But they're black: and it is my moral principle to treat black men differently from others'. If any reasons are given at all, they will be reasons that seek to correlate the fact of blackness with certain other considerations which are at least candidates for relevance to the question of how a man should be treated: such as insensitivity, brute stupidity, ineducable irresponsibility, etc. Now these reasons are very often rationalizations, and the correlations claimed are either not really believed, or quite irrationally believed, by those who claim them. But this is a different point; the argument concerns what counts as a moral reason, and the rationalizer broadly agrees with others about what counts as such—the trouble with him is that his reasons are dictated by his policies, and not conversely. The Nazis' 'anthropologists' who tried to construct theories of Aryanism were paying, in very poor coin, the homage of irrationality to reason.

The question of relevance in moral reasons will arise again, in a different connection, in this paper. For the moment its importance is that it gives a force to saying that those who neglect the moral claims of certain men that arise from their human capacity to feel pain, etc., are *overlooking* or *disregarding* those capacities; and are not just operating with a special moral principle, conceding the capacities to these men, but denying the moral claim. Very often, indeed, they have just persuaded themselves that the men in question have those capacities in a lesser degree. Here it is certainly to the point to assert the apparent platitude that these men are also human.

I have discussed this point in connection with very obvious human characteristics of feeling pain and desiring affection. There are, however, other and less easily definable characteristics universal to humanity, which may all the more be neglected in political and social arrangements. For instance, there seems to be a characteristic which might be called 'a desire for self-respect'; this phrase is perhaps not too happy, in suggesting a particular culturally-limited, bourgeois value, but I mean by it a certain human desire to be identified with what one is doing, to be able to realize purposes of one's own, and not to be the instrument of another's will unless one has willingly accepted such a role. This is a very inadequate and in some ways rather empty specification of a human desire; to a better specification, both philosophical reflection and the evidences of psychology and anthropology would be relevant. Such investigations enable us to understand more deeply, in respect of the desire I have gestured towards and of similar characteristics, what it is to be human; and of what it is to be human, the apparently trivial statement of men's equality as men can serve as a reminder.

2. *Moral capacities.* So far we have considered respects in which men can be counted as all alike, which respects are, in a sense, negative: they concern the capacity to suffer, and certain needs that men have, and these involve men in moral relations as the recipients of certain kinds of treatment. It has certainly been a part, however, of the thought of those who asserted that men were equal, that there were more positive respects in which men were alike; that they were equal in certain things that they could do or achieve, as well as in things that they needed and could suffer. In respect of a whole range of abilities, from weight-lifting to the calculus, the assertion is, as was noted at the beginning, not plausible, and has not often been supposed to be. It has been held, however, that there are certain other abilities, both less open to empirical test and more essential in moral connections, for which it is true that men are equal. These are certain sorts of moral ability or capacity, the capacity for virtue or achievement of the highest kind of moral worth.

The difficulty with this notion is that of identifying any purely moral capacities. Some human capacities are more relevant to the achievement of a virtuous life than others: intelligence, a capacity for sympathetic understanding, and a measure of resoluteness would generally be agreed to be so. But these capacities can all be displayed in non-moral connections as well, and in such connections would naturally be thought to differ from man to man like other natural capacities. That this is the fact of the matter has been accepted by many thinkers, notably, for instance, by Aristotle. But against this acceptance, there is a powerful strain of thought that centres on a feeling of ultimate and outrageous absurdity in the idea that the achievement of the highest kind of moral worth should depend on natural capacities, unequally and fortuitously distributed as they are; and this feeling is backed up by the observation that these natural capacities are not themselves the bearers of the moral worth, since those that have them are as gifted for vice as for virtue.

This strain of thought has found many types of religious expression; but in philosophy it is to be found in its purest form in Kant. Kant's view not only carries to the limit the notion that moral worth cannot depend on contingencies, but also emphasizes, in its picture of the Kingdom of Ends, the idea of *respect* which is owed to each man as a rational moral agent—and, since men are equally such agents, is owed equally to all, unlike admiration and similar attitudes, which are commanded unequally by men in proportion to their unequal possession of different kinds of natural excellence. These ideas are intimately connected in Kant, and it is not possible to understand his moral theory unless as much weight is given to what he says about the Kingdom of Ends as is always given to what he says about duty.

The very considerable consistency of Kant's view is bought at what would generally be agreed to be a very high price. The detachment of moral worth from all contingencies is achieved only by making man's characteristic as a moral or rational agent a transcendental characteristic; man's capacity to will freely as a rational agent is not dependent on any empirical capacities he may have—and, in particular, is not dependent on empirical capacities which men may possess unequally—because, in the Kantian view, the capacity to be a rational agent is not itself an empirical capacity at all. Accordingly, the respect owed equally to each man as a member of the Kingdom of Ends is not owed to him in respect of any empirical characteristics that he may possess, but solely in respect of the transcendental characteristic of being a free and rational will. The ground of the respect owed to each man thus emerges in the Kantian theory as a kind of secular analogue of the Christian conception of the respect owed to all men as equally children of God. Though secular, it is equally metaphysical: in neither case is it anything empirical *about* men that constitutes the ground of equal respect.

This transcendental, Kantian conception cannot provide any solid foundation for the notions of equality among men, or of equality of respect owed to them. Apart from the general difficulties of such transcendental conceptions, there is the obstinate fact that the concept of 'moral agent', and the concepts allied to it such as that of responsibility, do and must have an empirical basis. It seems empty to say that all men are equal as moral agents, when the question, for instance, of men's responsibility for their actions is one to which empirical considerations are clearly relevant, and one which moreover receives answers in

terms of different degrees of responsibility and different degrees
of rational control over action. To hold a man responsible for his
actions is presumably the central case of treating him as a moral
agent, and if men are not treated as equally responsible, there is
not much left to their equality as moral agents.

If, without its transcendental basis, there is not much left to
men's equality as moral agents, is there anything left to the
notion of the *respect* owed to all men? This notion of 'respect' is
both complex and unclear, and I think it needs, and would repay,
a good deal of investigation. Some content can, however, be
attached to it; even if it is some way away from the ideas of moral
agency. There certainly is a distinction, for instance, between
regarding a man's life, actions or character from an aesthetic or
technical point of view, and regarding them from a point of view
which is concerned primarily with what it is *for him* to live that
life and do those actions in that character. Thus from the tech-
nological point of view, a man who has spent his life in trying to
make a certain machine which could not possibly work is merely
a failed inventor, and in compiling a catalogue of those whose
efforts have contributed to the sum of technical achievement, one
must 'write him off': the fact that he devoted himself to this useless task with constant effort and so on, is merely irrelevant. But
from a human point of view, it is clearly not irrelevant: we are
concerned with him, not merely as 'a failed inventor', but as a
man who wanted to be a successful inventor. Again, in professional
relations and the world of work, a man operates, and his activities
come up for criticism, under a variety of professional or technical
titles, such as 'miner' or 'agricultural labourer' or 'junior execu-
tive'. The technical or professional attitude is that which regards
the man solely under that title, the human approach that which
regards him as *a man who has* that title (amongst others), willingly,
unwillingly, through lack of alternatives, with pride, etc.

That men should be regarded from the human point of view,
and not merely under these sorts of titles, is part of the content
that might be attached to Kant's celebrated injunction 'treat each
man as an end in himself, and never as a means only'. But I do
not think that this is all that should be seen in this injunction, or
all that is concerned in the notion of 'respect'. What is involved
in the examples just given could be explained by saying that each
man is owed an effort at identification: that he should not be
regarded as the surface to which a certain label can be applied,
but one should try to see the world (including the label) from his

point of view. This injunction will be based on, though not of course fully explained by, the notion that men are conscious beings who necessarily have intentions and purposes and see what they are doing in a certain light. But there seem to be further injunctions connected with the Kantian maxim, and with the notion of 'respect', that go beyond these considerations. There are forms of exploiting men or degrading them which would be thought to be excluded by these notions, but which cannot be excluded merely by considering how the exploited or degraded men see the situation. For it is precisely a mark of extreme exploitation or degradation that those who suffer it do *not* see themselves differently from the way they are seen by the exploiters; either they do not see themselves as anything at all, or they acquiesce passively in the role for which they have been cast. Here we evidently need something more than the precept that one should respect and try to understand another man's consciousness of his own activities; it is also that one may not suppress or destroy that consciousness.

All these I must confess to be vague and inconclusive considerations, but we are dealing with a vague notion: one, however, that we possess, and attach value to. To try to put these matters properly in order would be itself to try to reach conclusions about several fundamental questions of moral philosophy. What we must ask here is what these ideas have to do with equality. We started with the notion of men's equality as moral agents. This notion appeared unsatisfactory, for different reasons, in both an empirical and a transcendental interpretation. We then moved, *via* the idea of 'respect', to the different notion of regarding men not merely under professional, social, or technical titles, but with consideration of their own views and purposes. This notion has at least this much to do with equality: that the titles which it urges us to look behind are the conspicuous bearers of social, political, and technical *inequality*, whether they refer to achievement (as in the example of the inventor), or to social roles (as in the example of work titles). It enjoins us not to let our fundamental attitudes to men be dictated by the criteria of technical success of social position, and not to take them at the value carried by these titles and by the structures in which these titles place them. This does not mean, of course, that the more fundamental view that should be taken of men is in the case of every man the same: on the contrary. But it does mean that each man is owed the effort of understanding, and that in achieving it, each man is to be (as it were) abstracted from certain conspicuous structures of inequality in which we find him.

These injunctions are based on the proposition that men are beings who are necessarily to some extent conscious of themselves and of the world they live in. (I omit here, as throughout the discussion, the clinical cases of people who are mad or mentally defective, who always constitute special exceptions to what is in general true of men.) This proposition does not assert that men are equally conscious of themselves and of their situation. It was precisely one element in the notion of exploitation considered above that such consciousness can be decreased by social action and the environment; we may add that it can similarly be increased. But men are at least potentially conscious, to an indeterminate degree, of their situation and of what I have called their 'titles', are capable of reflectively standing back from the roles and positions in which they are cast; and this reflective consciousness may be enhanced or diminished by their social condition.

It is this last point that gives these considerations a particular relevance to the political aims of egalitarianism. The mere idea of regarding men from 'the human point of view', while it has a good deal to do with politics, and a certain amount to do with equality, has nothing specially to do with political equality. One could, I think, accept this as an ideal, and yet favour, for instance, some kind of hierarchical society, so long as the hierarchy maintained itself without compulsion, and there was human understanding between the orders. In such a society, each man would indeed have a very conspicuous title which related him to the social structure; but it might be that most people were aware of the human beings behind the titles, and found each other for the most part content, or even proud, to have the titles that they had. I do not know whether anything like this has been true of historical hierarchical societies; but I can see no inconsistency in someone's espousing it as an ideal, as some (influenced in many cases by a sentimental picture of the Middle Ages) have done. Such a person would be one who accepted the notion of 'the human view', the view of each man as something more than his title, as a valuable ideal, but rejected the ideals of political equality.

Once, however, one accepts the further notion that the degree of man's consciousness about such things as his role in society is itself in some part the product of social arrangements, and that it can be increased, this ideal of a stable hierarchy must, I think, disappear. For what keeps stable hierarchies together is the idea of necessity, that it is somehow foreordained or inevitable that there should be these orders; and this idea of necessity must be eventually undermined by the growth of people's reflective consciousness about their role, still more when it is combined with the thought that what they and the others have always thought about their roles in the social system was the product of the social system itself.

It might be suggested that a certain man who admitted that people's consciousness of their roles was conditioned in this way might nevertheless believe in the hierarchical ideal: but that in order to preserve the society of his ideal, he would have to make sure that the idea of the conditioning of consciousness did not get around to too many people, and that their consciousness about their roles did not increase too much. But such a view is really a very different thing from its naïve predecessor. Such a man, no longer himself 'immersed' in the system, is beginning to think in terms of compulsion, the deliberate *prevention* of the growth of consciousness, which is a poisonous element absent from the original ideal. Moreover, his attitude (or that of rulers similar to himself) towards the other people in the ideal society must now contain an element of condescension or contempt, since he will be aware that their acceptance of what they suppose to be necessity is a delusion. This is alien to the spirit of human understanding on which the original ideal was based. The hierarchical idealist cannot escape the fact that certain things which can be done decently without self-consciousness can, with self-consciousness, be done only hypocritically. This is why even the rather hazy and very general notions that I have tried to bring together in this section contain some of the grounds of the ideal of political equality.

3. *Equality in unequal circumstances.* The notion of equality is invoked not only in connections where men are claimed in some sense all to be equal, but in connections where they are agreed to be unequal, and the question arises of the distribution of, or access to, certain goods to which their inequalities are relevant. It may be objected that the notion of equality is in fact misapplied in these connections, and that the appropriate ideas are those of fairness or justice, in the sense of what Aristotle called 'distributive justice', where (as Aristotle argued) there is no question of regarding or treating everyone as equal, but solely a

question of distributing certain goods in proportion to men's recognized inequalities.

I think it is reasonable to say against this objection that there is some foothold for the notion of equality even in these cases. It is useful here to make a rough distinction between two different types of inequality, inequality of *need* and inequality of *merit*, with a corresponding distinction between goods—on the one hand, goods demanded by the need, and on the other, goods that can be earned by the merit. In the case of needs, such as the need for medical treatment in case of illness, it can be presumed for practical purposes that the persons who have the need actually desire the goods in question, and so the question can indeed be regarded as one of distribution in a simple sense, the satisfaction of an existing desire. In the case of merit, such as for instance the possession of abilities to profit from a university education, there is not the same presumption that everyone who has the merit has the desire for the goods in question, though it may, of course, be the case. Moreover, the good of a university education may be legitimately, even if hopelessly, desired by those who do not possess the merit; while medical treatment or unemployment benefit are either not desired, or not legitimately desired, by those who are not ill or unemployed, i.e. do not have the appropriate need. Hence the distribution of goods in accordance with merit has a competitive aspect lacking in the case of distribution according to need. For these reasons, it is appropriate to speak, in the case of merit, not only of the distribution of the good, but of the distribution of the opportunity of achieving the good. But this, unlike the good itself, can be said to be distributed equally to everybody, and so one does encounter a notion of *general* equality, much vaunted in our society today, the notion of equality of opportunity.

Before considering this notion further, it is worth noticing certain resemblances and differences between the cases of need and of merit. In both cases, we encounter the matter (mentioned before in this paper) of the relevance of reasons. Leaving aside preventive medicine, the proper ground of distribution of medical care is ill health: this is a necessary truth. Now in very many societies, while ill health may work as a necessary condition of receiving treatment, it does not work as a sufficient condition, since such treatment costs money, and not all who are ill have the money; hence the possession of sufficient money becomes in fact an additional necessary condition of actually receiving treatment. Yet more extravagantly, money may work as a sufficient condition by itself, without any medical need, in which case the reasons that actually operate for the receipt of this good are just totally irrelevant to its nature; however, since only a few hypochondriacs desire treatment when they do not need it, this is, in this case, a marginal phenomenon.

When we have the situation in which, for instance, wealth is a further necessary condition of the receipt of medical treatment, we can once more apply the notions of equality and inequality: not now in connection with the inequality between the well and the ill, but in connection with the inequality between the rich ill and the poor ill, since we have straightforwardly the situation of those whose needs are the same not receiving the same treatment, though the needs are the ground of the treatment. This is an irrational state of affairs.

It may be objected that I have neglected an important distinction here. For, it may be said, I have treated the ill health and the possession of money as though they were regarded on the same level, as 'reasons for receiving medical treatment', and this is a muddle. The ill health is, at most, a ground of the *right* to receive medical treatment; whereas the money is, in certain circumstances, the causally necessary condition of securing the right, which is a different thing. There is something in the distinction that this objection suggests: there is a distinction between a man's rights, the reasons why he should be treated in a certain way, and his power to secure those rights, the reasons why he can in fact get what he deserves. But this objection does not make it inappropriate to call the situation of inequality an 'irrational' situation: it just makes it clearer what is meant by so calling it. What is meant is that it is a situation in which reasons are insufficiently *operative*; it is a situation insufficiently controlled by reasons—and hence by reason itself. The same point arises with another form of equality and equal rights, equality before the law. It may be said that in a certain society, men have equal rights to a fair trial, to seek redress from the law for wrongs committed against them, etc. But if a fair trial or redress from the law can be secured in that society only by moneyed and educated persons, to insist that everyone *has* this right, though only these particular persons can *secure* it, rings hollow to the point of cynicism: we are concerned not with the abstract existence of rights, but with the extent to which those rights govern what actually happens.

Thus when we combine the notions of the *relevance* of reasons, and the *operativeness* of reasons, we have a genuine moral weapon, which can be applied in cases of what is appropriately called unequal treatment, even where one is not concerned with the equality of people as a whole. This represents a strengthening of the very weak principle mentioned at the beginning of this paper, that for every difference in the way men are treated, a reason should be given: when one requires further that the reasons should be relevant, and that they should be socially operative, this really says something.

Similar considerations will apply to cases of merit. There is, however, an important difference between the cases of need and merit, in respect of the relevance of reasons. It is a matter of logic that particular sorts of needs constitute a reason for receiving particular sorts of good. It is, however, in general a much more disputable question whether certain sorts of merit constitute a reason for receiving certain sorts of good. For instance, let it be agreed, for the sake of argument, that the public school system provides a superior type of education, which it is a good thing to receive. It is then objected that access to this type of education is unequally distributed, because of its cost: among boys of equal promise or intelligence, only those from wealthy homes will receive it, and, indeed, boys of little promise or intelligence will receive it, if from wealthy homes; and this, the objection continues, is irrational.

The defender of the public school system might give two quite different sorts of answer to this objection; besides, that is, the obvious type of answer which merely disputes the facts alleged by the objector. One is the sort of answer already discussed in the case of need: that we may agree, perhaps, that boys of promise and intelligence have a right to a superior education, but in actual economic circumstances, this right cannot always be secured, etc. The other is more radical: this would dispute the premise of the objection that intelligence and promise are, at least by themselves, the grounds for receiving this superior type of education. While perhaps not asserting that wealth itself constitutes the ground, the defender of the system may claim that other characteristics significantly correlated with wealth are such grounds; or, again, that it is the purpose of this sort of school to maintain a tradition of leadership, and the best sort of people to maintain this will be people whose fathers were at such schools. We need not try to pursue such arguments here. The important point is that, while there can indeed be genuine disagreements about what constitutes the relevant sort of merit in such cases, such disagreements must also be disagreements about the nature of the good to be distributed. As such, the disagreements do not occur in a vacuum, nor are they logically free from restrictions. There is only a limited number of reasons for which education could be regarded as a good, and a limited number of purposes which education could rationally be said to serve; and to the limitations on this question, there correspond limitations on the sorts of merit or personal characteristic which could be rationally cited as grounds of access to this good. Here again we encounter a genuine strengthening of the very weak principle that, for differences in the way that people are treated, reasons should be given.

We may return now to the notion of equality of opportunity; understanding this in the normal political sense of equality of opportunity for *everyone in society* to secure certain goods. This notion is introduced into political discussion when there is question of the access to certain goods which, first, even if they are not desired by everyone in society, are desired by large numbers of people in all sections of society (either for themselves, or, as in the case of education, for their children), or would be desired by people in all sections of society if they knew about the goods in question and thought it possible for them to attain them; second, are goods which people may be said to earn or achieve; and third, are goods which not all the people who desire them can have. This third condition covers at least three different cases, however, which it is worth distinguishing. Some desired goods, like positions of prestige, management, etc., are *by their very nature* limited: whenever there are some people who are in command or prestigious positions, there are necessarily others who are not. Other goods are *contingently* limited, in the sense that there are certain conditions of access to them which in fact not everyone satisfies, but there is no intrinsic limit to the numbers who might gain access to it by satisfying the conditions: university education is usually regarded in this light nowadays, as something which requires certain conditions of admission to it which in fact not everyone satisfies, but which an indefinite proportion of people might satisfy. Third, there are goods which are *fortuitously* limited, in the sense that although everyone or large numbers of people satisfy the conditions of access to them, there is just not enough of them to go round; so some more stringent conditions or system of rationing have to be imposed, to govern access in an imperfect situation. A good can, of course, be both contingently and fortuitously limited at once: when, due to shortage of supply, not even the people who are qualified to have it, limited in numbers though they are, can in every case have it. It is particularly worth distinguishing those kinds of limitation, as there can be significant differences of view about the way in which a certain good is limited. While most would now agree that high education is contingently limited, a Platonic view would regard it as necessarily limited.

Now the notion of equality of opportunity might be said to be the notion that a limited good shall in fact be allocated on grounds which do not *a priori* exclude any section of those that desire it. But this formulation is not really very clear. For suppose grammar school education (a good perhaps contingently, and certainly fortuitously, limited) is allocated on grounds of ability as tested at the age of 11; this would normally be advanced as an example of equality of opportunity, as opposed to a system of allocation on grounds of parents' wealth. But does not the criterion of ability exclude *a priori* a certain section of people, viz. those that are not able—just as the other excludes *a priori* those who are not wealthy? Here it will obviously be said that this was not what was meant by *a priori* exclusion: the present argument just equates this with exclusion of anybody, i.e. with the mere existence of some condition that has to be satisfied. What then is *a priori* exclusion? It must mean exclusion on grounds *other* than those appropriate or rational for the good in question. But this still will not do as it stands. For it would follow from this that so long as those allocating grammar school education on grounds of wealth thought that such grounds were appropriate or rational (as they might in one of the ways discussed above in connection with public schools), they could sincerely describe their system as one of equality of opportunity—which is absurd.

Hence it seems that the notion of equality of opportunity is more complex than it first appeared. It requires not merely that there should be no exclusion from access on grounds other than those appropriate or rational for the good in question, but that the grounds considered appropriate for the good should themselves be such that people from all sections of society have an equal chance of satisfying them. What now is a 'section of society'? Clearly we cannot include under this term sections of the populace identified just by the characteristics which figure in the grounds for allocating the good—since, once more, any grounds at all must exclude some section of the populace. But what about sections identified by characteristics which are *correlated* with the grounds of exclusion? There are important difficulties here: to illustrate this, it may help first to take an imaginary example.

Suppose that in a certain society great prestige is attached to membership of a warrior class, the duties of which require great physical strength. This class has in the past been recruited from certain wealthy families only; but egalitarian reformers achieve a change in the rules, by which warriors are recruited from all sections of the society, on the results of a suitable competition. The effect of this, however, is that the wealthy families still provide virtually all the warriors, because the rest of the populace is so under-nourished by reason of poverty that their physical strength is inferior to that of the wealthy and well nourished. The reformers protest that equality of opportunity has not really been achieved; the wealthy reply that in fact it has, and that the poor now have the opportunity of becoming warriors—it is just bad luck that their characteristics are such that they do not pass the test. 'We are not,' they might say, 'excluding anyone *for* being poor; we exclude people for being weak, and it is unfortunate that those who are poor are also weak.'

This answer would seem to most people feeble, and even cynical. This is for reasons similar to those discussed before in connection with equality before the law; that the supposed equality of opportunity is quite empty—indeed, one may say that it does not really exist—unless it is made more effective than this. For one knows that it could be made more effective; one knows that there is a causal connection between being poor and being undernourished, and between being undernourished and being physically weak. One supposes further that something could be done—subject to whatever economic conditions obtain in the imagined society—to alter the distribution of wealth. All this being so, the appeal by the wealthy to the 'bad luck' of the poor must appear as disingenuous.

It seems then that a system of allocation will fall short of equality of opportunity if the allocation of the good in question in fact works out unequally or disproportionately between different sections of society, if the unsuccessful sections are under a disadvantage which could be removed by further reform or social action. This was very clear in the imaginary example that was given, because the causal connections involved are simple and well known. In actual fact, however, the situations of this type that arise are more complicated, and it is easier to overlook the causal connections involved. This is particularly so in the case of educational selection, where such slippery concepts as 'intellectual ability' are involved. It is a known fact that the system of selection for grammar schools by the '11 +' examination favours children in direct proportion to their social class, the children of professional homes having proportionately greater success than those from working-class homes. We have every reason to suppose that these results are the product, in good part, of environmental factors; and we further know that imaginative social reform, both of the primary educational system and of living conditions, would favourably effect those environmental factors. In these circumstances, this system of educational selection falls short of equality of opportunity.[3]

This line of thought points to a connection between the idea of equality of opportunity, and the idea of equality of persons, which is stronger than might at first be suspected. We have seen that one is not really offering equality of opportunity to Smith and Jones if one contents oneself with applying the same criteria to Smith and Jones at, say, the age of 11; what one is doing there is to apply the same criteria to Smith as affected by favourable conditions and to Jones as affected by unfavourable but curable conditions. Here there is a necessary pressure to equal up the conditions: to give *Smith* and *Jones* equality of opportunity involves regarding their conditions, where curable, as themselves part of what is done to Smith and Jones, and not part of Smith and Jones themselves. Their identity, for these purposes, does not include their curable environment, which is itself unequal and a contributor of inequality. This abstraction of persons in themselves from unequal environments is a way, if not of regarding them as equal, at least of moving recognizably in that direction; and is itself involved in equality of opportunity.

One might speculate about how far this movement of thought might go. The most conservative user of the notion of equality of opportunity is, if sincere, prepared to abstract the individual from some effects of his environment. We have seen that there is good reason to press this further, and to allow that the individuals whose opportunities are to be equal should be abstracted from

[3] See on this C. A. R. Crosland, 'Public Schools and English Education', *Encounter* (July 1961).

more features of social and family background. Where should this stop? Should it even stop at the boundaries of heredity? Suppose it were discovered that when all curable environmental disadvantages had been dealt with, there was a residual genetic difference in brain constitution, for instance, which was correlated with differences in desired types of ability; but that the brain constitution could in fact be changed by an operation.[4] Suppose further that the wealthier classes could afford such an operation for their children, so that they always came out top of the educational system; would we then think that poorer children did not have equality of opportunity, because they had no opportunity to get rid of their genetic disadvantages?

Here we might think that our notion of personal identity itself was beginning to give way; we might well wonder *who were* the people whose advantages and disadvantages were being discussed in this way. But it would be wrong, I think, to try to solve this problem simply by saying that in the supposed circumstances our notion of personal identity would have collapsed in such a way that we could no longer speak of the individuals involved—in the end, we could still pick out the individuals by spatio-temporal criteria, if no more. Our objections against the system suggested in this fantasy must, I think, be moral rather than metaphysical. They need not concern us here. What is interesting about the fantasy, perhaps, is that if one reached this state of affairs, the individuals would be regarded as in all respects equal in themselves—for in themselves they would be, as it were, pure subjects or bearers of predicates, everything else about them, including their genetic inheritance, being regarded as a fortuitous and changeable characteristic. In these circumstances, where everything about a person is controllable, equality of opportunity and absolute equality seem to coincide; and this itself illustrates something about the notion of equality of opportunity.

I said that we need not discuss here the moral objections to the kind of world suggested in this fantasy. There is, however, one such point that is relevant to the different aspects of equality that have been discussed in this paper as a whole. One objection that we should instinctively feel about the fantasy world is that far too much emphasis was being placed on achieving high ability;

---

[4] A yet more radical situation—but one more likely to come about—would be that in which an individual's characteristics could be *pre-arranged* by interference with the genetic material. The dizzying consequences of this I shall not try to explore.

that the children were just being regarded as locations of abilities. I think we should still feel this even if everybody (with results hard to imagine) was treated in this way; when not everybody was so treated, the able would also be more successful than others, and those very concerned with producing the ability would probably also be over-concerned with success. The moral objections to the excessive concern with such aims are, interestingly, not unconnected with the ideal of equality itself; they are connected with equality in the sense discussed in the earlier sections of this paper, the equality of human beings despite their differences, and in particular with the complex of notions considered in the second section under the heading of 'respect'.

This conflict within the ideals of equality arises even without resort to the fantasy world. It exists today in the feeling that a thorough-going emphasis on equality of opportunity must destroy a certain sense of common humanity which is itself an ideal of equality.[5] The ideals that are felt to be in conflict with equality of opportunity are not necessarily other ideals of equality—there may be an independent appeal to the values of community life, or to the moral worth of a more integrated and less competitive society. Nevertheless, the idea of equality itself is often invoked in this connection, and not, I think, inappropriately.

If the idea of equality ranges as widely as I have suggested, this type of conflict is bound to arise with it. It is an idea which, on the one hand, is invoked in connection with the distribution of certain goods, some at least of which are bound to confer on their possessors some preferred status or prestige. On the other hand, the idea of equality of respect is one which urges us to give less consideration to those structures in which people enjoy status or prestige, and to consider people independently of those goods, on the distribution of which equality of opportunity precisely focuses our, and their, attention. There is perhaps nothing formally incompatible in these two applications of the idea of equality: one might hope for a society in which there existed both a fair, rational, and appropriate distribution of these goods, and no contempt, condescension, or lack of human communication between persons who were more and less successful recipients of the distribution. Yet in actual fact, there are deep psychological and social obstacles to the realization of this hope; as things are, the competitiveness and considerations of prestige that surround

[5] See, for example, Michael Young, *The Rise of the Meritocracy* (London: Thames and Hudson, 1958).

the first application of equality certainly militate against the second. How far this situation is inevitable, and how far in an economically developed and dynamic society, in which certain skills and talents are necessarily at a premium, the obstacles to a wider realization of equality might be overcome, I do not think that we know: these are in good part questions of psychology and sociology, to which we do not have the answers.

When one is faced with the spectacle of the various elements of the idea of equality pulling in these different directions, there is a strong temptation, if one does not abandon the idea altogether, to abandon some of its elements: to claim, for instance, that equality of opportunity is the only ideal that is at all practicable, and equality of respect a vague and perhaps nostalgic illusion; or, alternatively, that equality of respect is genuine equality, and equality of opportunity an inegalitarian betrayal of the ideal—all the more so if it were thoroughly pursued, as now it is not. To succumb to either of these simplifying formulae would, I think, be a mistake. Certainly, a highly rational and efficient application of the ideas of equal opportunity, unmitigated by the other considerations, could lead to a quite inhuman society (if it worked—which, granted a well-known desire of parents to secure a position for their children at least as good as their own, is unlikely). On the other hand, an ideal of equality of respect that made no contact with such things as the economic needs of society for certain skills, and human desire for some sorts of prestige, would be condemned to a futile Utopianism, and to having no rational effect on the distribution of goods, position, and power that would inevitably proceed. If, moreover, as I have suggested, it is not really known how far, by new forms of social structure and of education, these conflicting claims might be reconciled, it is all the more obvious that we should not throw one set of claims out of the window; but should rather seek, in each situation, the best way of eating and having as much cake as possible. It is an uncomfortable situation, but the discomfort is just that of genuine political thought. It is no greater with equality than it is with liberty, or any other noble and substantial political ideal.

Source: Philosophy, Politics and Society (2nd Series), ed. Laslett and Runciman (Blackwell), Ch. XII.

CAUSE AND EFFECT

20 Of the Idea of Necessary Connexion (1748)

DAVID HUME

When we look about us towards external objects, and consider the operation of causes, we are never able, in a single instance, to discover any power or necessary connexion; any quality, which binds the effect to the cause, and renders the one an infallible consequence of the other. We only find, that the one does actually, in fact, follow the other. The impulse of one billiard-ball is attended with motion in the second. This is the whole that appears to the *outward* senses. The mind feels no sentiment or *inward* impression from this succession of objects: Consequently, there is not, in any single, particular instance of cause and effect, any thing which can suggest the idea of power or necessary connexion. [. . .]

It appears, then, that this idea of a necessary connexion among events arises from a number of similar instances which occur of the constant conjunction of these events; nor can that idea ever be suggested by any one of these instances, surveyed in all possible lights and positions. But there is nothing in a number of instances, different from every single instance, which is supposed to be exactly similar; except only, that after a repetition of similar instances, the mind is carried by habit, upon the appearance of one event, to expect its usual attendant, and to believe that it will exist. This connexion, therefore, which we *feel* in the mind, this customary transition of the imagination from one object to its usual attendant, is the sentiment or impression from which we form the idea of power or necessary connexion. Nothing farther is in the case. Contemplate the subject on all sides; you will never

181

find any other origin of that idea. This is the sole difference between one instance, from which we can never receive the idea of connexion, and a number of similar instances, by which it is suggested. The first time a man saw the communication of motion by impulse, as by the shock of two billiard balls, he could not pronounce that the one event was *connected*: but only that it was *conjoined* with the other. After he has observed several instances of this nature, he then pronounces them to be *connected*. What alteration has happened to give rise to this new idea of *connexion*? Nothing but that he now *feels* these events to be *connected* in his imagination, and can readily foretell the existence of one from the appearance of the other. When we say, therefore, that one object is connected with another, we mean only that they have acquired a connexion in our thought, and give rise to this inference, by which they become proofs of each other's existence: A conclusion which is somewhat extraordinary, but which seems founded on sufficient evidence.

Source: An Enquiry Concerning Human Understanding, Sec. VII. (Extract.)

21 Natural Laws and Natural Necessity (1949)

WILLIAM KNEALE

Natural laws are often said to be concerned with necessary connexions, and it is therefore a plausible suggestion that they may be principles of necessitation which for some special reason we cannot hope to establish by intuitive induction. This was apparently Locke's view. In the fourth book of his *Essay on the Human Understanding* he says several times that we cannot have insight into the connexions which we assert in natural science; but he holds nevertheless that they may be necessary in the same sense as connexions which we are able to comprehend, and he implies that a sufficiently powerful mind which was furnished with the appropriate ideas of what he calls the real internal essences of things might see the necessity of natural laws.

According to his doctrine the reason why we cannot establish such laws by intuitive induction is not simply that our intellects are too feeble, but that our experience does not furnish us with the ideas which would be required for an understanding of the connexions we assert.

The chief objection to this view was formulated by Hume.[1] Although he referred only to causal laws, his argument may be applied to laws of other kinds. Take any supposed law you please, he says, and you will find that you can conceive the contradictory. If, for example, it were really a principle of necessitation that salt dissolves in water, it would be impossible that salt should not dissolve in water. For if α-ness necessitates β-ness it is impossible that anything should be α and not β. And what is impossible is inconceivable. For if anyone tried to conceive the impossible, he would not succeed in conceiving anything. Nevertheless, we can quite easily conceive of salt remaining in water without dissolving, although we have not found it to do so, and from this it seems to follow that it is not necessary that salt should dissolve in water. This is an extremely formidable objection, and it is not surprising that many modern philosophers have taken it to be a conclusive refutation of the suggestion that natural laws are principles of necessitation. [. . .]

Hume allows that we often talk of natural laws as though they were principles of necessary connexion, but he holds that the necessity is, as it were, the projection of our feeling of expectation, which itself is due to the constant conjunction of certain items in our experience. To assert a law of nature is, then, only to assert a constant conjunction without restriction to the field of our actual experience. Some modern followers of Hume speak of this as the regularity theory of natural laws; in order to keep as close as possible to Hume's own phraseology I shall call it the *constancy* theory.

It is often objected against this theory that there cannot be facts of unrestricted universality or, to put the matter in another way, that sentences which purport to state such facts are meaningless. The philosophers who maintain such a view do not deny that we can formulate truisms of unrestricted universality such as 'All coloured things are extended', but they hold that no significant universal statement can be at once contingent and unrestricted. In the past the thesis was often put forward without argument by idealist writers who assumed a connexion between

[1] *Treatise*, Book I, Part III, Section vi.

universality and necessity, but in recent times it has been defended by positivists with an argument based on their theory of meaning. It is said that no sentence can express a contingent proposition unless it admits of verification by experience. But an unrestricted universal proposition cannot be verified by experience. Therefore no such proposition can be a contingent truth, and so the constancy theory of laws is refuted. I do not find this argument convincing. It depends on the use of a criterion of significance which I see no reason to accept, and it leads to some very curious consequences. According to the ordinary rules of logic a sentence of the form 'All α things are β' must be supposed equivalent to the negation of a sentence of the form 'There is an α thing, which is not β'. Now a sentence of the second form may very well be verified in experience by the discovery of something which is α and not β, and so it must be supposed to express a contingent proposition. It is surely very strange indeed to say that this sentence has no significant negation, and yet this is the conclusion to which we are led by the argument now commonly urged against the constancy theory. It is true we can never have any good ground for asserting a contingent proposition of unrestricted universality, and there may conceivably be some good argument against the possibility of such propositions, but I have seen none.

The constancy theory of natural laws ought nevertheless to be rejected for another reason. It is impossible to conceive natural laws as facts, whether of restricted or unrestricted universality. In order to make this point clear it will be useful to consider an imaginary example in which the special difficulties connected with unrestricted universality are avoided. Let us suppose for the sake of argument that the term 'dodo' is defined in such a way that nothing can be called a dodo unless it lived on the earth within a certain period of years which ended in the eighteenth century. Then we can say with confidence that the number of dodos is finite. Let us suppose further that it has been established by complete enumeration that every dodo which existed had a white feather in its tail. It is, of course, impossible to establish this proposition now, because most of the evidence has been lost; but we can conceive that there might have been an organization of bird-watchers which kept records of all the dodos from the origin to the extinction of the species. Are we to say that the universal proposition so established is a law of nature which has been proved for certain? Surely not, for laws of nature are normally expressed in the timeless present, and are assumed to be concerned not only with actual instances of some kind, but with anything which might have satisfied a certain description. If on the strength of our records we suggest that there is a law of nature that all dodos have a white feather in their tails, we say in effect that, if there had been any dodos other than those mentioned in our records, they too would have had a white feather in their tails. But an unfulfilled hypothetical proposition of this kind cannot be derived from a proposition which is concerned only with the actual. A contingent universal proposition can always be expressed in the form 'There are in fact no α things which are not β', and from such a proposition it is impossible to deduce that if something which was not in fact α had been α it would also have been β. [. . .]

In any sense of the word 'conceive' which is relevant to the argument, an ability to conceive the contradictory of a supposed law of nature does not disprove the suggestion that the supposed law is a principle of necessitation. This can be seen from consideration of a mathematical analogy. In 1742 Goldbach, an otherwise unknown correspondent of the Swiss mathematician Euler, suggested that every even number greater than two is the sum of two primes. This conjecture has been confirmed for all the even numbers for which it has been tested, but during the past two centuries, no one has succeeded in demonstrating its truth. The attitude of mathematicians towards it can, therefore, be expressed by the statement 'Goldbach's conjecture looks like a theorem, but it may conceivably be false'. There is, of course, a very important difference between this case and the case of natural laws, for we do not think that a natural law might perhaps be demonstrated to-morrow. But this difference only makes my argument stronger. If the conceivability of the contradictory is not to be taken as a disproof of necessity in mathematics, where proof is attainable by *a priori* reasoning, why should it be supposed to furnish such a disproof in natural science? What we call conceiving is often little more in fact than readiness to manipulate symbols according to established rules. In mathematics such manipulation may on occasions enable us to discover principles of modality which were not obvious at first. But in natural science there is no such hope, because the linguistic rules which give meaning to the special symbols of natural science are different in character from those which govern the usage of mathematical symbols.

When the misleading associations of old terminology have been eliminated, the contentions of those who oppose the necessitation theory of natural laws reduce to this: 'Since we cannot say what it would be like to know the necessity of a natural law, it is senseless even to suggest that such a law may be a principle of necessitation.' The hypothesis that something we cannot know *a priori* is nevertheless a truth of principle seems curious, I admit, but I think that it seems so only because we fail to notice the peculiarity of the concepts used in natural science. Having once assumed that there is no important difference between the rules which give meaning to such a word as 'lightning' and those which govern the usage of 'red' in the sensum terminology or 'two' in the language of mathematics, we are naturally led on to say that, if there are any truths of principle concerning lightning, they must be knowable *a priori*. Then, since men undoubtedly speak of necessity in nature, we find ourselves driven to say that the word 'necessity' must have a special meaning in this context and cudgel our brains to give an analysis. In fact, the word 'necessity' is the least troublesome of those with which we have to deal in this part of philosophy. For it has the same sense here as elsewhere. A principle of necessitation is a boundary of possibility.

Source: Probability and Induction (O.U.P.) Pt. II, Secs. 17 and 18. (Extracts.)

22 Laws of Nature and Causality (1953)

R. B. BRAITHWAITE

Scientific hypotheses have been taken to be general empirical propositions whose generality is not restricted to limited regions of space or of time. For the reasons explained . . . scientific laws, corresponding to true scientific hypotheses, have been taken to assert no more than constant conjunctions of properties, so that the scientific law that everything which is *A* is *B* asserts no more than that all the things which are *A* as a matter of fact are also *B*. It is now time to examine this assumption in order to see whether the Humean analysis of scientific laws is adequate, or whether it is necessary to suppose that the sort of necessity of scientific law ('nomic' necessity) requires some extra element of 'necessary connexion' over and above a merely factual uniformity. To express the matter in another way, everyone will agree that everything which is, was or will be *A* is, was or will be *B* is a logical consequence of the scientific law expressed apodeictically as 'Every *A* nomically must be *B*'; the question is whether or not it is justifiable to regard the former proposition, not as a consequence, but as an analysis of the meaning of 'Every *A* nomically must be *B*'.

I have used W. E. Johnson's adjective 'nomic' rather than the more usual 'causal' to express, without prejudging the analysis, the characteristic sort of necessary connexion with which we are here concerned, because the notion of causality might well be held to involve considerations of temporal precedence and of spatio-temporal continuity which are irrelevant to the present issue. For here we are concerned with the nature of the difference, if any, between 'nomic laws' and 'mere generalizations'; in Johnson's language, between 'universals of law' and 'universals of fact'.[1]

David Hume maintained that objectively there is no difference, but that a psychological fact about the way in which our minds work causes us to ascribe necessity to scientific laws, the 'idea of necessary connexion' being derived from our experience of the constant conjunction of properties and not from anything in nature over and above constant conjunction. In common with most of the scientists who have written on the philosophy of science from Ernst Mach and Karl Pearson to Harold Jeffreys, I agree with the principal part of Hume's thesis—the part asserting that universals of law are objectively just universals of fact, and that in nature there is no extra element of necessary connexion. The time has now come to defend this thesis against philosophers who disagree with it. [. . .]

If this book were concerned with attacking rival views, cogent criticisms could be made of attempts to justify induction which build on a nomic necessity distinct from constant conjunction. Those philosophers, for example, who wish to identify nomic necessity with logical necessity lay themselves wide open to the charge that, since all the premises in a valid inference to a logically necessary conclusion must be logically necessary propositions, to treat scientific laws as being logically necessary propositions removes all possibility of basing them upon empirical data. And those philosophers who wish to make nomic necessity

[1] W. E. Johnson, *Logic, Part III* (Cambridge, 1924), Chapter I.

a third ultimate category distinct both from logical necessity and from constant conjunction lay themselves open to the charge that their nomic connexion is, as 'substance' was for Locke, 'something I know not what'; and that a philosopher is shirking his duty who uses Butler's maxim 'Every thing is what it is, and not another thing' to avoid having to consider whether the difference between universals of law and universals of fact may not lie in the different roles which they play in our thinking rather than in any difference in their objective contents.

For it cannot be disputed that we do make a distinction of some sort between those empirical general propositions which we dignify with the name of 'laws of nature' or 'natural laws' and those which we call, sometimes derogatorily, 'mere generalizations'. A Humean philosopher may well deny that this distinction is one of objective fact; but if he denies that there is any distinction whatever, he runs counter to ordinary usages of language.

Subjunctive Conditionals

One of the relevant usages of language to which philosophers have recently given a great deal of attention has been the use of conditional sentences of the form 'If a thing is A, it is B' under circumstances in which nothing is A and the use of hypothetical sentences 'If p then q' under circumstances in which p is false. These sentences have been called conditionals or hypotheticals which were 'contrary to fact', 'counterfactual', or, since the subjunctive mood is one way of expressing them in English, 'subjunctive'. We shall use the term 'subjunctive conditional' for an assertion of the form: Although there are no A's, if there were to be any A's, all of them would be B's, e.g. If there were to be a gas whose molecules had zero extension and did not attract one another (although in fact there are no such gases) its pressure and volume would be related by Boyle's law. We shall use the term 'subjunctive hypothetical' for an assertion of the form: Although p is false, if p were to be true, q would be true, e.g. If the picture-wire had broken (although it didn't), the picture would have fallen to the ground.[2] At present we are concerned

[2] Many contemporary logicians use the terms 'conditional' and 'hypothetical' synonymously, and call what I am calling a 'conditional' a 'general conditional' or 'general hypothetical'. My distinction between the use of 'conditional' and 'hypothetical' was suggested by that made by J. N. Keynes (*Studies and Exercises in Formal Logic*, fourth edition (London, 1906),

with subjunctive conditionals. The problem which they present to a Humean is the following dilemma. The constant-conjunction analysis leaves two choices open for the analysis of «If a thing is *A*, it is *B*». One choice is «Every *A* is *B*» taken, as traditional logic would say, 'existentially', i.e. understood in such a way as to assert the existence of at least one thing which is *A*. The other alternative is «Every *A* is *B*» taken non-existentially, i.e. understood as not to assert the existence of an *A*. On the first interpretation, «Every *A* is *B*» is equivalent to the conjunction of «Nothing is both *A* and non-*B*» with «Something is *A*». A subjunctive conditional would combine this conjunctive assertion with the assertion that there is nothing which is *A*, and would thus be self-contradictory. On the second interpretation «Every *A* is *B*» is equivalent to the single proposition «Nothing is both *A* and non-*B*». A subjunctive conditional would conjoin this assertion with the assertion that there is nothing which is *A*. But since, if nothing is *A*, *a fortiori* nothing is both *A* and non-*B*, the conjunction of these two propositions is logically equivalent to the former one alone. Thus a Humean analysis, it is alleged, makes the assertion of a subjunctive conditional either self-contradictory or one which adds nothing to the assertion that nothing is *A*, which is expressed by the subjunctive mood being used. Each horn of the dilemma is equally uncomfortable, since neither horn will account for the fact that we make subjunctive conditional assertions freely and without consciousness of paradox. The opponents of the constant conjunction view conclude that 'If a thing is *A*, it is *B*', used to express a nomic connexion, must mean more than «Nothing is both *A* and non-*B*» (with or without the conjunction of «Something is *A*») in order to account for the function played in our thinking by subjunctive conditionals.

This criticism can be met without requiring that the proposition expressed by the sentence 'If a thing is *A*, it is *B*', used nomically, should be distinguished from the proposition that nothing is both *A* and non-*B*. What is required is that what is involved in *asserting* the subjunctive conditional expressed by such a sentence as

pp. 249 f.). In the considerable amount of recent literature dealing with subjunctive conditionals and the related question of natural laws solutions resembling the account to be given here have been published by Hans Reichenbach (*Elements of Symbolic Logic* (New York, 1947), Chapter VIII) and by J. R. Weinberg (*Journal of Philosophy*, vol. 48 (1951), pp. 17ff.). F. P. Ramsey (*The Foundations of Mathematics and other logical essays*, pp. 237ff.) and David Pears (*Analysis*, vol. 10 (1950), pp. 49ff.) have also approached the questions along lines similar to mine.

'Although nothing is A, yet, if a thing were to be A, it would be B' is distinct from what is involved in *asserting* a conjunction of «Nothing is A» with «Nothing is both A and non-B». We can make this distinction by taking the assertion of «Nothing is both A and non-B» involved in asserting the subjunctive conditional as being not simply the assertion of «Nothing is both A and non-B» as being a true proposition, but also the assertion of «Nothing is both A and non-B» as being deduced from a higher-level hypothesis in a true and established scientific deductive system. To put the matter metaphorically, the generalization «Nothing is both A and non-B» enters into an assertion of a subjunctive conditional accompanied by a certificate of origin. Though the generalization itself conjoined with the proposition «Nothing is A» is logically equivalent to this latter proposition alone, a belief in the truth of the generalization which is accompanied by a belief about its origin, conjoined with a belief that nothing is A, is by no means equivalent to this latter belief alone.

   Perhaps it is easiest to think of the matter in terms of the temporal order in which beliefs are acquired. Suppose that a person who has never considered whether or not there are any A's has come to accept a scientific deductive system in which the proposition that nothing is both A and non-B is deducible from higher-level hypotheses in the system which have been established by induction from evidence which does not include any instances of the generalization «Every A is B». If the person then makes this deduction in the scientific system, he will have confirmed the proposition «Nothing is both A and non-B» indirectly; if he regards the higher-level hypotheses as established, he will also regard it as established that nothing is both A and non-B, and will add this proposition to his body of rational belief. Now suppose that he subsequently discovers that in fact there are no A's. Had he acquired reasonable belief that there are no A's before he had acquired his reasonable belief that nothing is both A and non-B, he could have deduced this latter proposition from the former, and would not have required to establish it by deducing it from higher-level hypotheses in the scientific deductive system. But he did not do this; he arrived at his reasonable belief in the generalization «Nothing is both A and non-B» quite independently of his subsequently acquired belief that this generalization was 'vacuously' satisfied. The assertion of a subjunctive conditional may be regarded as a summary statement of this whole situation.

   Take, for example, the statement 'Although there are no gases whose molecules have zero extension and do not attract one another, yet if there were to be such gases, all of them would obey Boyle's law, PV=a constant'. The assertion of this statement envisages a situation in which, before it was known that there were no such gases, a functional law had been established relating the pressure and volume of a gas by examining gases with extended molecules which did attract one another, e.g. van der Waals's equation $(P + a/V^2)$ $(V - b)$ = a constant. From this functional law the special law for gases whose molecules have zero extension and do not attract one another can be deduced by putting $a = b = 0$; i.e. from van der Waals's equation deducing Boyle's law. This special law will then have been established quite independently of any knowledge as to whether or not there are any gases whose molecules have zero extension and do not attract one another. To assert the subjunctive conditional is then to refer to the fact that the proposition that no gases whose molecules have zero extension and do not attract one another fail to obey Boyle's law has been established independently of the fact, which the subjunctive conditional also asserts, that there are no such gases.

Since «Nothing is A» is logically equivalent to the conjunction of «Nothing is both A and non-B» with «Nothing is both A and B», to establish «Nothing is A» after «Nothing is both A and non-B» has been established is to establish in addition only «Nothing is both A and B». The evidence for «Nothing is both A and non-B» provided by the evidence, direct or indirect, for «Nothing is A» will, of course, be additional to the evidence for «Nothing is both A and non-B» provided by the evidence for higher-level hypotheses from which this generalization logically follows; but, since this generalization is supposed to have been already established by a deduction from the established higher-level hypotheses, the additional evidence will not serve to establish it. In Freudian language, its establishment is 'over-determined': there are two sets of evidence each sufficient to establish it, and the set which in fact establishes it is the one which gets in first.

Let us now remove the condition that the generalization «Nothing is both A and non-B» has been established by deducing it from established higher-level hypotheses before it has been considered whether or not it is vacuously true. We then have the situation that there are two ways of establishing the generalization: I can choose which of the two I regard as having got in first and as being the genuine establishment. One way is to deduce the generalization from the proposition, supposed to have been established, that nothing is *A*—call this the 'vacuous' establishment; the other way is to deduce the generalization from the supposedly established higher-level hypotheses—call this the 'hypothetico-deductive' establishment. The assertion of the subjunctive conditional «Although there are no *A*'s, yet if there were to be any *A*'s all of them would be *B*'s» asserts that there are no *A*'s, that nothing is both *A* and non-*B*, and that the latter of these propositions is establishable hypothetico-deductively without reference to the establishment of the former. The peculiarity of the subjunctive conditional is that to assert it is not only to assert two propositions, one of which is a logical consequence of the other, but is also to assert that this former proposition, though vacuously establishable by deduction from the latter, is also hypothetico-deductively establishable in an independent way. The assertion of the subjunctive conditional makes a remark about the relation of two of the propositions asserted in regard to the way that they can be established. This analysis, it seems to me, satisfactorily explains the peculiarity of subjunctive conditionals without our having to suppose that the sentence 'Every *A* is *B*', used nomically, need mean any more than that nothing is both *A* and non-*B*. [. . .]

Laws of Nature

Our solution of the problem of how our use of subjunctive conditionals is consistent with a constant conjunction analysis of nomic generalizations will enable us to solve a related problem which is posed to Humeans, namely, that of distinguishing between what are laws of nature (or natural laws) and what anti-Humeans contemptuously call 'mere generalizations'. Surely, they say, this distinction must be admitted: for us it consists in the laws of nature asserting principles of nomically necessary connexion; since you decline to admit such principles how can you make the distinction? The problem is sometimes put in the form that we all distinguish between uniformities due to natural law and those which are merely accidentally true, 'historical accidents on the cosmic scale';[3] if natural laws are just uniformities, how can this distinction be made?

It seems to me foolish to deny (as some Humeans do) that such a distinction is made in common speech; but it also seems per-

[3] William Kneale, in *Analysis*, vol. 10 (1950), p. 123.

fectly sensible to try to give a rationale for this distinction within the ambit of a constant conjunction view. The distinction will then have to depend upon knowledge or belief in the general proposition rather than in anything intrinsic to the general proposition itself; but this is exactly how we have solved the related problem of subjunctive conditionals. Let us try to use this solution to pick out some among true contingent general propositions to be given the honorific title of 'natural law'.

Let us tentatively try the following criterion: A true contingent general proposition «Every *A* is *B*» whose generality is not limited to any particular regions of space or of time will be called by a person *C* a *law of nature* or *natural law* if either the corresponding subjunctive conditional «Although there are no *A*'s, yet if there were any *A*'s they would all be *B*'s» is reasonably believed by *C*, or this subjunctive conditional would be reasonably believed by *C* if he were reasonably to believe that there are no *A*'s. In terms of the notion of *C*'s rational corpus of knowledge and reasonable belief, the criterion requires that the corresponding subjunctive conditional should form part of his rational corpus if this includes a belief that there are no *A*'s, or, if it does not include this belief, would form part of his rational corpus if it did include this belief. In terms of the notion of assertion used in the discussion of subjunctive conditionals, an assertion of a natural law together with an assertion that there are no *A*'s would come to the same thing as an assertion of the corresponding subjunctive conditional.

In addition all true hypotheses containing theoretical concepts will be given the title of natural laws.

The condition for an established hypothesis *h* being *lawlike* (i.e. being, if true, a natural law) will then be that the hypothesis either occurs in an established scientific deductive system as a higher-level hypothesis containing theoretical concepts or that it occurs in an established scientific deductive system as a deduction from higher-level hypotheses which are supported by empirical evidence which is not direct evidence for *h* itself. This condition will exclude a hypothesis for which the only evidence is evidence of instances of it, but it will not exclude a hypothesis which is supported partly directly by evidence of its instances and partly indirectly by evidence of instances of same-level hypotheses which, along with it, are subsumed under a higher-level hypothesis. This account of natural law makes the application of the notion dependent upon the way in which the hypothesis is regarded by a particular person at a particular time as having been established: 'lawlike' may be thought of as a honorific epithet which is employed as a mark of origin. If the hypothesis that all men are mortal is regarded as supported solely by the direct evidence that men have died, then it will not be regarded as a law of nature; but if it is regarded as also being supported by being deduced from the higher-level hypothesis that all animals are mortal, the evidence for this being also that horses have died, dogs have died, etc., then it will be accorded the honorific title of 'law of nature' which will then indicate that there are other reasons for believing it than evidence of its instances alone.

This criterion for lawlikeness has the paradoxical consequence that the hypothesis that all men are mortal will be regarded as a natural law if it occurs in an established scientific deductive system at a lower level than a hypothesis (e.g. All animals are mortal) which has other lower-level hypotheses under it which are directly confirmed by experience; whereas the higher-level hypothesis that all animals are mortal, if it appears as the highest-level hypothesis in the established deductive system, will not be regarded as a natural law, since the ground for its establishment is solely the evidence of its instances. However, it seems to me that this corresponds to the way in which, generally speaking, we use the notion of natural law. A hypothesis to be regarded as a natural law must be a general proposition which can be thought to *explain* its instances; if the reason for believing the general proposition is solely direct knowledge of the truth of its instances, it will be felt to be a poor sort of explanation of these instances. If, however, there is evidence for it which is independent of its instances, such as the indirect evidence provided by instances of a same-level general proposition subsumed along with it under the same higher-level hypothesis, then the general proposition will *explain* its instances in the sense that it will provide grounds for believing in their truth independently of any direct knowledge of such truth. And this connexion with a notion of explanation fits in well with the honorific title of natural law being ascribable to every hypothesis containing theoretical concepts, whether or not such a hypothesis stands at the highest level in the established scientific system. For even if the hypothesis with theoretical concepts is not deducible from an established higher-level hypothesis, yet it will not have been established simply by induction by simple enumeration; it will have been obtained by the hypothetico-deductive method of proposing it as a hypothesis and deducing its testable consequences. The case for accepting any particular higher-level hypothesis containing theoretical concepts is exactly that it serves as an explanation of the lower-level generalizations deducible from it, whereas the case for accepting a particular generalization not containing theoretical concepts and not deducible from any higher-level hypothesis is the fact that it covers its known instances rather than that it explains them.

I do not wish to emphasize unduly this relation between explanation and natural law: the marginal uses of both of these concepts are indefinite, and the boundaries of their uses will certainly not agree. Generally speaking, however, a true scientific hypothesis will be regarded as a law of nature if it has an explanatory function with regard to lower-level hypotheses or its instances; vice versa, to the extent that a scientific hypothesis provides an explanation, to that extent will there be an inclination to endow it with the honourable status of natural law. [...]*

Particular Causal Propositions, Indicative and Subjunctive Hypotheticals

It remains to say a few words upon particular causal propositions of the form «*q* because *p*», where *p* and *q* are particular contingent propositions and the statement '*q* because *p*' is used to assert that *p* is a cause, or part of a cause, of *q*, and is not used either to state that a relation of logical consequence holds between *q* and *p* or merely to state something about belief in *q*, e.g. that knowledge of *p* makes it reasonable to believe *q*. With particular causal propositions of the form «*q* because *p*» (e.g. This picture fell to the floor at noon yesterday because its wire broke then) we may also consider indicative hypotheticals of the form «If *p* then *q*» (e.g. If the wire of this picture breaks at noon tomorrow, the picture will then fall to the floor) and also subjunctive hypotheticals of the form «Although *p* is false, yet if *p* were to be true, *q* would be true» (e.g. Although the wire of this picture did not break at noon yesterday, yet, had it done so, the picture would have then fallen to the floor), *p* and *q* in all these cases being particular contingent propositions and the hypotheticals being used nomically.

Let us start by considering indicative hypotheticals of the form «If *p* then q», the analysis of which has been much discussed

* Several sections, including those on 'Causal Laws' and on 'Cause and Effect' have been omitted.—Ed.

recently by logicians. It seems to be certain that, as used in normal empirical contexts, the *assertion* of «If p then q» involves more than the mere *assertion* of «Not both p and not-q», whether the meaning of the statement 'If p then q' is the same as or comprises more than that of 'Not both p and not-q'. The assertion of «If p then q» asserts, besides the proposition «Not both p and not-q», the proposition that this proposition has been established, or could be established, by deducing it from hypotheses in a scientific deductive system which is both true and established, together, perhaps, with certain other propositions p_1, p_2, etc., which are implicitly assumed to be common property to the asserter and his hearer. To assert, for example, that if the picture wire breaks at noon tomorrow, the picture will then fall to the floor, asserts not only that it is false both that the wire will break tomorrow and that the picture will not fall to the floor, but also that this proposition is deducible from an established scientific law (that unsupported bodies fall) together with certain propositions taken to be common knowledge to both the asserter and the hearer (e.g. that there will be no solid object between the position of the picture just before the wire breaks and the floor, that the picture will not be supported by its standing on a ledge as well as by the picture wire, etc.). The difficulty in saying exactly what are the scientific hypotheses and the additional propositions involved in any particular assertion of a proposition of the form «If p then q» should not lead us to think that there are not definite hypotheses and definite extra particular propositions involved in the assertion of the 'If p then q' statement. These hypotheses and propositions may differ in each case of the same indicative hypothetical. But unless the asserter is prepared to specify, more or less precisely, what are the hypotheses and extra particular propositions involved, he can with doubtful propriety be said to be asserting the indicative hypothetical statement.[4]

The assertion of a subjunctive hypothetical is similar to that of an indicative hypothetical except that the assertion includes an assertion that p is false (indicated by the use of the subjunctive mood or by some other device) and that the assertion that the

[4] The objection to an analysis of the meaning of the statement 'If p then q' into «There are a set of true hypotheses and a set of true propositions which are such that «Not both p and not-q» is a logical consequence of the conjunction of these hypotheses and these propositions» is that, on any occasion of the assertion of «If p then q», something more definite is implied about the hypotheses and the extra propositions than merely that there are such true hypotheses and propositions.

asserted proposition «Not both p and not-q» is deducible in an established deductive system must be qualified by adding that such a deduction must be independent of the falsity of p.

The assertion of a particular causal proposition of the form «q because p» (e.g. This picture fell to the floor at noon yesterday, because its wire broke then) is also similar to that of an indicative hypothetical except that the assertion includes assertions both that p is true and that q is true. (p and q will have to be subject to certain temporal, or spatio-temporal, restrictions in relation to one another in order that p may be the cause-proposition and q the effect-proposition; but this restriction, whatever exactly it may be, is extraneous to the present argument.) Though the conjunction of p with «Not both p and not-q» is logically equivalent to the conjunction of p with q, yet the assertion of «q because p» involves more than the joint assertion of p and of q. The extra element, as in the case of indicative and subjunctive hypotheticals, is the assertion that the proposition «Not both p and not-q» is deducible within a true and established deductive system from hypotheses of that system together, usually, with propositions about cause factors which have not been explicitly mentioned. My example of the assertion that this picture fell to the floor at noon yesterday because its wire then broke omits explicit reference to other cause factors in the absence of which the picture would not have fallen or, if it had fallen, would not have fallen to the floor, the hypotheses in the deductive system concerned remaining unchanged. Many of these cause factors are the 'permanent conditions' of Mill. Why it is usually unnecessary to mention them is because they are, as it were, fixtures; these fixtures may be negative, as in our example (there was no rail upon which the picture rested, there was no sofa under the picture, etc.). Nevertheless for a full account of the logic of the assertion they will have to be mentioned explicitly. It is because of the fact that the relevant causal conditions are hardly ever all explicitly mentioned that it is difficult to hold that a particular causal proposition explicitly mentions the general hypothesis of which it is an instance. But what is certain, I think, is that the *assertion* of a particular causal proposition «q because p» involves the assertion of a general hypothesis in the sense that the asserter must always reply to a demand for the citing of the hypothesis upon which he has based his particular causal proposition—on pain of being accused of doing no more than asserting the conjunction of q with p if he is unable to meet this demand.

Conclusion

The argument of this chapter cannot be regarded as a knock-out blow to those who wish to maintain that nomic necessity is, quite apart from epistemological considerations, objectively something over and above constant conjunction. The thesis which has been maintained is that the genuine differences between assertions of constant conjunction and assertions of natural law arise out of the way in which the propositions concerned in the assertions are related to other propositions in the deductive systems used by the asserter. This thesis makes the notion of natural law an epistemological one and makes the 'naturalness' of each natural law relative to the rational corpus of the thinker.[5] Thus it is impossible to say in general that to assert that «Every A is B» is a law of nature, or that if a thing were to be A, it would also be B, is to assert exactly so-and-so or such-and-such; and the anti-Humean who demands a precise answer to the question as to what exactly is the difference between a specific law of nature and its corresponding 'mere generalization' cannot properly be given one. The imprecise answer which has been given in this chapter . . . is, I suspect, still not subtle enough to do justice to the complexities of the situation. But the complexities are those of the nuances in our use of language to describe, explicitly or implicitly, the scientific deductive systems with which we think about the empirical world: there is no need to suppose that they spring from anything transempirical in the world itself.

Source: Scientific Explanation (C.U.P.), Ch. IX. (Extracts.)

[5] C. D. Broad says that it seems to him 'fairly certain on inspection' that he does not mean by 'causal laws' propositions of the form «A is always accompanied by B» 'limited by conditions about spatio-temporal and qualitative continuity and decked out with psychological frillings' (*Aristotelian Society Supplementary Volume* 14 (1935), p. 93). The 'frillings' with which the constant-conjunction propositions are decked out in this chapter in order to elevate them to higher rank are epistemological, not psychological.

23 The Real Cause of a Phenomenon (1843)

J. S. MILL

[. . .] If a person eats of a particular dish, and dies in consequence, that is, would not have died if he had not eaten of it, people would be apt to say that eating of that dish was the cause of his death. There needs not, however, be any invariable connection between eating of the dish and death; but there certainly is, among the circumstances which took place, some combination or other on which death is invariably consequent: as, for instance, the act of eating of the dish, combined with a particular bodily constitution, a particular state of present health, and perhaps even a certain state of the atmosphere; the whole of which circumstances perhaps constituted in this particular case the *conditions* of the phenomenon, or, in other words, the set of antecedents which determined it, and but for which it would not have happened. The real Cause is the whole of these antecedents; and we have, philosophically speaking, no right to give the name of cause to one of them exclusively of the others. [. . .]

If we do not, when aiming at accuracy, enumerate all the conditions, it is only because some of them will in most cases be understood without being expressed, or because for the purpose in view they may without detriment be overlooked. For example, when we say, the cause of a man's death was that his foot slipped in climbing a ladder, we omit as a thing unnecessary to be stated the circumstance of his weight, though quite as indispensable a condition of the effect which took place. [. . .]

In all these instances the fact which was dignified with the name of cause was the one condition which came last into existence. But it must not be supposed that in the employment of the term this or any other rule is always adhered to. Nothing can better show the absence of any scientific ground for the distinction between the cause of a phenomenon and its conditions, than the capricious manner in which we select from among the conditions that which we choose to denominate the cause. However numerous the conditions may be, there is hardly any of them which may not, according to the purpose of our immediate discourse, obtain that nominal pre-eminence. [. . .]

Thus we see that each and every condition of the phenomenon may be taken in its turn, and, with equal propriety in common parlance, but with equal impropriety in scientific discourse, may be spoken of as if it were the entire cause. And in practice that particular condition is usually styled the cause whose share in the matter is superficially the most conspicuous, or whose requisiteness to the production of the effect we happen to be insisting on at the moment. So great is the force of this last consideration, that it sometimes induces us to give the name of cause even to one of the negative conditions. We say for example, The army was surprised because the sentinel was off his post. But since the sentinel's absence was not what created the enemy or put the soldiers asleep, how did it cause them to be surprised? All that is really meant is, that the event would not have happened if he had been at his duty. His being off his post was no producing cause, but the mere absence of a preventing cause: it was simply equivalent to his non-existence. [. . .]

It now remains to advert to a distinction which is of first-rate importance both for clearing up the notion of cause, and for obviating a very specious objection often made against the view which we have taken of the subject.

When we define the cause of anything (in the only sense in which the present inquiry has any concern with causes) to be 'the antecedent which it invariably follows,' we do not use this phrase as exactly synonymous with 'the antecedent which it invariably *has* followed in our past experience.' Such a mode of conceiving causation would be liable to the objection very plausibly urged by Dr. Reid, namely, that according to this doctrine night must be the cause of day, and day the cause of night; since these phenomena have invariably succeeded one another from the beginning of the world. But it is necessary to our using the word cause that we should believe not only that the antecedent always *has* been followed by the consequent, but that as long as the present constitution of things endures it always *will* be so. [. . .]

Invariable sequence, therefore, is not synonymous with causation, unless the sequence, besides being invariable, is unconditional. There are sequences, as uniform in past experience as any others whatever, which yet we do not regard as cases of causation, but as conjunctions in some sort accidental. Such, to an accurate thinker, is that of day and night. The one might have existed for any length of time, and the other not have followed the sooner for its existence; it follows only if certain other antecedents exist; and where those antecedents existed, it would follow in any case. No one, probably, ever called night the cause of day; mankind must so soon have arrived at the very obvious generalisation, that the state of general illumination which we call day would follow from the presence of a sufficiently luminous body, whether darkness had preceded or not.

We may define, therefore, the cause of a phenomenon to be the antecedent, or the concurrence of antecedents, on which it is invariably and *unconditionally* consequent.

Source: J. S. Mill, *A System of Logic*, Bk. III, Ch. V, Secs. 3 and 6. (Extracts.)

24 Causation and Common Sense (1959)

H. L. A. HART and A. M. HONORÉ

Cause and effect: the central notion

Human beings have learnt, by making appropriate movements of their bodies, to bring about desired alterations in objects, animate or inanimate, in their environment, and to express these simple achievements by transitive verbs like push, pull, bend, twist, break, injure. The process involved here consists of an initial immediate bodily manipulation of the thing affected and often takes little time. Men have, however, learnt to extend the range of their actions and have discovered that by doing these relatively simple actions they can, in favourable circumstances, bring about secondary changes, not only in the objects actually manipulated, but in other objects. Here the process initiated by bodily movements and manipulation may be protracted in space or time, may be difficult to accomplish and involve a series of changes, sometimes of noticeably different kinds. Here we use the correlative terms 'cause' and 'effect' rather than simple transitive verbs: the effect is the desired secondary change and the cause is our action in bringing about the primary change in the things manipulated or those primary changes themselves. So we cause one thing to move by striking it with another, glass to break by throwing stones, injuries by blows, things to get hot by putting them on fires. Here the notions of cause and effect come together with the notion of means to ends and of producing one thing by doing another. Cases of this exceedingly simple type are not only those where the expressions cause and effect have their most obvious application; they are also paradigms for the understanding of the causal language used of very different types of case. This is so for two reasons: first some important point of resemblance, or at least analogy, with these simple cases is traceable in the wider range to which causal language is extended; and, secondly, expressions which have a literal use in the simple cases have come to be used in a metaphorical and sometimes baffling way in cases far outside their scope. [. . .]

In these simple cases, where we speak of a deliberate human intervention or the primary changes initiated by it as the cause of an occurrence, we rely upon general knowledge and commit ourselves to a general proposition of some kind; but this is something very different from causal 'laws' or general propositions asserting invariable sequence which Mill regarded as essential to causal connexion. When we assert that A's blow made B's nose bleed or A's exposure of the wax to the flame caused it to melt, the general knowledge used here is knowledge of the familiar 'way' to produce, by manipulating things, certain types of change which do not normally occur without our intervention. If formulated they are broadly framed generalizations, more like recipes[1] in which we assert that doing one thing will 'under normal conditions' produce another than statements of 'invariable sequence' between a complex set of specified conditions and an event of the given kind. Mill's description of common sense 'selecting' the cause from such a set of conditions is a *suggestio falsi* so far as these simple causal statements are concerned; for, though we may gradually come to know more and more of the conditions required for our interventions to be successful, we do not 'select' from them the one we treat as the cause. Our intervention is regarded as the cause from the start before we learn more than a few of the other necessary conditions. We simply continue to call it the cause when we know more. [. . .]

[1] For this aspect of causation see D. Gasking, 'Causation as Recipes', *Mind* (1955), xciv, 479.

Causal generalizations

What kinds of generalization are involved in ordinary singular causal statements? How are these defended from the objection that the alleged cause did not cause but was merely followed by the effect? So far we have provisionally assumed that Mill's account of this is substantially correct: that the primary meaning of causation is 'invariable and unconditional sequence'[2] of classes of complex events or conditions; and hence that when we identify a single event as a cause of an event we 'select' it from a set known or believed to be 'invariably and unconditionally' followed by an event of that kind. Plainly this account must be qualified, for it is obvious that, though singular causal statements are frequently made not only with confidence but with a confidence not judged improper, very little confidence would either be felt or judged proper in any generalization of this exceptionless kind. In what relevant generalization of 'invariable and unconditional sequence' would or should we feel the same confidence as we do in the singular causal statement that the kettle boiled because it had been put on the fire? Precisely what qualifications are needed to represent the normal standards of everyday life is a question of some difficulty. It is tempting to say that the generalizations involved in ordinary causal statements merely assert that in *most cases* events of one kind are and will be followed by events of the other; we need merely scale down Mill's 'invariably' to 'in the great majority of cases'. The truth unfortunately is not thus simple.[3]

The type of generalization in fact involved in singular causal statements will best be seen if we consider various ways in which Mill's theory is defective as an account of 'The common notion of a cause'. There is first the general objection that Mill's standard of 'invariable and unconditional sequence' cannot be met. Even the scientist can only discover uniformities which he has evidence for believing will hold good over a far wider range of conditions than any that can be discovered by common sense: he does not

[2] We have written hitherto as if Mill had merely said 'invariable' (as he often does). We have done this both for brevity and because the difference between this and 'invariable and unconditional' has not been important: but it needs attention here.

[3] Though this too simple view was previously taken by the authors: see 'Causation in the Law', (1956) 72 *L.Q.R.* 58, 71.

assert or have grounds for asserting that they will hold good under 'all possible conditions' (unconditionally) or 'always' (invariably). This is in fact an absurdity both in practice and principle. To meet such a standard there would have to be evidence that 'everything' (*all* other things, events or states) apart from the set of conditions specified in the generalization was irrelevant, so that the specified conditions would be unconditionally and invariably sufficient.[4] Neither in practice nor in principle is this possible. Even when some persistent feature of the universe is known and identified (e.g. the motion of the planets) it may be impossible to tell whether, if this were to change, any given causal generalization would be affected and so whether a full statement of the generalization should include it; and of course there must be many such persistent features still unidentified, as cosmic radiation was till recently. Apart from these practical difficulties, the supposition that there are in the 'universe' a finite number of things or events or states, which in principle could be examined and found relevant or irrelevant, is chimerical; the 'universe' is not a box with a finite number of objects in it each describable in a finite number of ways.

More important than these general objections is the fact that Mill's view that we 'select' or 'single out' the cause from a complex set of conditions previously identified, and that these are known or believed to be invariably followed by the effect is misleading. It radically misrepresents the character of those actual situations (in and outside law courts) where we ask and succeed in obtaining a satisfactory answer to questions about the cause of some particular past occurrence. For there is in fact no 'selection' or 'singling out' of the cause from a set of jointly sufficient conditions: what is true is that, after causes have been identified, we come in the course of later experience to learn more detail both about the conditions (i.e. other factors without which they would not be followed by their effects) and about the process of change between cause and effect. So we identify a 'blow' as the cause of a child's injury, for example, a broken leg, without knowing or caring what conditions must also be satisfied, if a blow of just that force is always to be followed by such an injury. When we learn later that the blow would be sufficient only if the bone structure

---

4 It would not be enough if those conditions not included in the generalization always in fact coexisted with those included, for then the specified conditions would merely be 'invariably' followed by the effect but not 'unconditionally'.

was, as in the child's case, of less than a certain thickness, nothing is added to our confidence in the initial statement that this blow caused the injury, though we would have been grateful for this information had we been attempting to predict the outcome of the blow.

Mill's account in fact suggests—and this is its main defect—that, in order to answer the question what was the cause of this occurrence, we should ideally be able to *predict* with certainty that it would happen, from detailed and precise knowledge of antecedent conditions. It is, however, vital to see that logically the demands of the situation in which we ask for the cause of what has happened, and that in which we are concerned to predict are very different. In the first case it is an *inquest* that we are conducting. The 'effect' has happened: it is a particular puzzling or unusual occurrence, or divergence from the standard state or performance of something with whose ordinary states or modes of functioning we are familiar; and when we look for the cause of this we are looking for something, usually earlier in time, which is abnormal or an interference in the sense that it is not present when things are as usual. Such abnormalities or interferences we recognize and describe in broad general terms (as 'blows', 'storms', 'heat') which sit loosely to their instances, since they cover a wide range of different occurrences, and we are indifferent to their detailed specification. In identifying some such occurrence, thus broadly described, as the cause of what has happened we must be satisfied that its connexion with the effect is itself unproblematic, not in need of explanation. It is in ordinary life enough for this purpose if we know: first, that contingencies of these broadly described kinds ('blows', 'injuries') commonly go together as a familiar feature of experience the statement of which might often be quite platitudinous; and, secondly, if cases where these general connexions do not hold can be distinguished from the case before us. In all but the simplest cases the causal connexion will be 'indirect', i.e. will have to be traced through a number of successive stages which exemplify a number of different familiar general connexions. The statement that a slate falling from a house top caused the bruises of a passenger in an open car on whom it fell rests, for common sense, on a set of both mechanical and physiological platitudes.

In effect, in the typical case with which the law is concerned, when we ask for the cause, we are asking that some abnormal lapse from routine (some accident, injury, or loss) be rendered intelligible by being exhibited as an instance of certain other normalities, namely, those general connexions which characterize experience and are formulated in broad and general terms. It is therefore not a defect, but an essential feature of the generalizations used in establishing that something was the cause of another, that these should remain formulated in broad terms capable of covering not only the particular case before us (and any exactly like it) but many similar cases differing from it in detail. If the particular case cannot be connected in this way by a broad generalization with a multiplicity of past cases, the minimum explanatory force, which discovery of the cause must have, will be lacking. The abnormality will not have been shown to be some variety of the usual or familiar.

This concern, in giving the cause of a particular occurrence, to link the case in question with others that have happened is not present when we are attempting to predict. What we want then is *certainty* not explanatory force, and a generalization which is as near Mill's prescription as possible will serve us best, even if it is so specific and complex as to apply only to this case. This is a warning: it shows that acceptance of the theory that the only respectable support for a singular causal statement is a Mill-like generalization would drive us into an *impasse*. In our asymptotic approach to the inappropriate ideal of 'invariable sequence' we should have to treat a multiplicity of cases, which at present fall under a single unifying generalization, as instances of separate generalizations, specially adapted to the quantitative and qualitative differences of different cases. These separate generalizations, with their application only to cases falling under such highly specific descriptions, could not possibly guide us to or be our warrant for asserting any singular causal statement; for this must have the link with other cases provided by broad generalizations such as those of common experience. Only when highly specific generalizations are deductions from a single wider theory do these form part of the ground for singular causal statements. In such cases the theory has a unifying and explanatory force comparable to those of the loosely framed generalizations of common sense. This is notably the case when the cause of mechanical failures or the breakdown of scientifically constructed devices, for example, an electrical circuit, are identified by reference to deductions from the theory on which they are constructed.

These considerations explain why it is that we do not regard a singular causal statement, made on the strength of the rough rubrics of common experience, for example, that the cause of a particular fire was the dropping of a lighted cigarette, as strengthened when we learn from science that without the presence of oxygen the fire would not have occurred. Of course this would have to be mentioned if we were really concerned to exhibit the case as an instance of a generalization specifying the conditions in the present case which would be invariably followed by fire. Yet when we come to learn such further necessary conditions we do not treat our past statement of the cause, though made in ignorance of it, as one made without proper justification which has luckily turned out to be correct: indeed it adds nothing to it. For the same reason, there is nothing absurd in combining with the assertion that this was the cause of the fire a refusal to formulate or assent to any given generalization specifying conditions of invariable sequence, though we do not and could not deny the formal claim of (unspecified) *ceteris paribus*, i.e. that there are some factors in the present case which, if they recurred, would always be followed by fire.

At this point, however, a caution is necessary. We must not conclude, from the fact that the generalizations we use in identifying the cause of a particular event are broadly formulated, that it is sufficient to defend a singular causal statement by a simple appeal to 'high probabilities', i.e. generalizations to the effect that the alleged cause is and will be followed by the effect in 'the great majority' of cases. We may be tempted into this belief by a very common form of general causal statement such as 'A short circuit very frequently causes fire' or 'A bent rail will very probably cause an accident'. These may suggest that singular causal statements state merely that a given case is one of the majority or large number of cases to which such statements refer, and are established by simple appeal to these statements of high probabilities. Yet, that this is not so, is perhaps evident from the fact that causal statements of this form also include statements such as 'Diphtheria now very *rarely* causes death'. These causal apophthegms (as they might be called) merely indicate what on particular occasions (numerous in the case of short circuits, few in the case of diphtheria) have been found to be the causes of the events to which they refer; but they are *not* the generalizations used on these particular occasions to establish the cause. They could be paraphrased to read, 'It has been very often or on rare occasions found that X was the cause of Y.' So too general statements (not including the word 'cause') of high probability of sequence, though relevant to establish causal statements, are not sufficient support for them *per se*. The statement that on this occasion X was the cause of Y differs from the conjunctive statement that X was followed by Y on this occasion and X's are followed by Y's in the great majority of cases. The statement that the dropping of the lighted cigarette caused the fire asserts more than that fire followed in this case and there was a high probability that this would be so. The crucial difference is that, if we assert that X was followed by Y in a given case and Y's are highly probable given X's, we are *not* committed to explaining the cases where X's have not been followed by Y's nor to showing that the given case differs from them. On the other hand, if it is asserted that X was the cause of Y, something must be done to anticipate and answer the objection 'Yes: X was here followed by Y as in the majority of cases, but was it the cause in this case?'

This requirement means that counter-examples or exceptions to the generalizations used in support of particular causal statements must be distinguished from the case in hand; till this is done a rival causal explanation must still be sought. Of course the applied sciences represent a vast storehouse of counter-examples with which commonsense judgments about the causes of accidents, injuries, and losses, which typically come before law courts, must be reconciled; and scientific accounts of the fine detail of different causal processes often determines a choice between rival causal explanations. Very often, however, a description in non-scientific terms of the successive stages of, for example, an accident will show that these stages are linked by firm if platitudinous generalizations; and, though there may be many cases where the same injury would not have resulted from the same initiating occurrence, a simple description of the stages would reveal differences. Though a falling tile may rarely kill a passer-by, we may in a particular case easily trace the connexion from fall to impact, and from impact to injury, because there is nothing to suggest that any counter-examples to the simple rough generalizations implicitly used are relevant here. Of course in the face of Cartesian doubt we could marshal scientific theories and measurements of forces and velocities to prove the point, but this would be sensible only if there was a rival explanation to disprove.

Let us use the expression 'causal principles' as a compendious term both for the generalizations by which singular causal statements are defended, and the manner in which they are brought to bear on particular cases. It can be said then that, when it is asserted that something is the cause of a particular occurrence, the case must be shown (if necessary by a description of its component stages) to exemplify generalizations broad enough to cover a variety of different cases; secondly, the case must be distinguishable from counter-examples or cases outside the known limits of any generalization used. There is also a third requirement of particular importance in the law. Though it is true in all cases that the factor we designate as the cause would not be followed by the effect without the co-operation of many others, if we find, on attempting to trace by stages a causal connexion, that these factors include voluntary interferences, or independent abnormal contingencies, this brings into question our right to designate the earlier factor as *the* cause; for this expression is used of something which, with the co-operation only of factors that rank as mere conditions and not themselves as causes, is sufficient to 'produce' the effect. The fact that a fire would not have spread to a neighbouring house without the normal breeze does not inhibit us in treating the lighting of it as the cause of the disaster: it would be different if someone deliberately fanned the embers or, just as they were dying out, a leaking petrol tin fell from the back of a jeep. This displacement of one event from the position of 'the cause' by other events, which have also the characteristics by which common sense distinguishes causes from mere conditions, is of crucial importance, as we show in the next chapter, when causal connexion is the basis of the attribution of responsibility.

There are also intermediate cases where it is natural to speak of each of two contingencies as *a* cause and of neither as *the* cause. This is so where both are abnormal in some degree sufficient to preclude their classification as 'mere conditions' but their abnormality is not of that extreme or coincidental character required for the contingency in question to be regarded as the sole cause.

This account of causal principles, though applicable to the type of case with which the law is usually concerned, does not cover every sort of singular causal statement. As we have said, an account of the way in which deductions from scientific theories are used in the identification of the causes of failures of machines or other artefacts would show that something more nearly approaching Mill's ideal formed part of the reasoning. Indeed any really comprehensive account of the general element implicit in singular causal statements would show that this varied with different types of subject-matter.

Finally, it is to be noted that the account in this section of causal principles is not directly applicable to those cases, especially numerous and important in the law, where an *omission* or failure to act is identified as the cause of some (usually untoward) event. Someone's failure to wrap up is commonly and intelligibly taken to be the cause of his catching cold, and driving in the dark without lights to be the cause of an accident. The background to this use of causal language is that the natural course of events or human activities has been found to be generally harmful and we have learnt from experience how to counteract the harm by certain procedures. Accordingly the generalizations on which such identifications of omissions as causes of harm rest relate primarily to the adequacy, under standard conditions, of the omitted precautions. Then causal principles require that the conditions of the case in hand should be shown not to differ from the standard case; for example, that the temperature was not so low as to make protective clothing useless, or that the victim of the accident was not so drunk as to be incapable of seeing a lighted car. Our concern here is to show that the omitted precaution *would* have averted the harm, not that when it is omitted harm always results.

Source: Causation in the Law (O.U.P.) Ch. II, Secs. II and IV. (Extracts.)

FREEDOM AND DETERMINISM

25 My Opinion about Liberty and Necessity (1652)*

THOMAS HOBBES

First I conceive, that when it cometh into a man's mind to do or not to do some certain action, if he have no time to *deliberate*, the doing it or abstaining *necessarily* follow the *present* thought he hath of the *good* or *evil* consequence thereof to himself. As for example, in sudden *anger*, the *action* shall follow the thought of *revenge*; in sudden *fear*, the thought of *escape*. Also when a man hath time to *deliberate*, but deliberates not, because never anything appeared that could make him doubt of the consequence, the *action* follows his opinion of the *goodness* or *harm* of it. These actions I call VOLUNTARY, my Lord, if I understand him aright that calls them SPONTANEOUS. I call them *voluntary*, because those *actions* that follow immediately the *last* appetite, are *voluntary*, and here where is one only appetite, that one is the last. Besides, I see it is reasonable to punish a *rash* action, which could not be justly done by man to man, unless the same were *voluntary*. For no *action* of a man can be said to be without *deliberation*, though never so sudden, because it is supposed he had time to *deliberate* all the precedent time of his life, whether

* This Reading is an extract from a letter addressed by Hobbes to the Lord Marquis of Newcastle. In his Introduction to *Body, Man, and Citizen* Professor Peters writes: 'In 1645 [Hobbes] had discussed the problem of free will with Bishop Bramhall . . . in Newcastle's presence. At Newcastle's request they both wrote down their views on this matter soon afterwards. But a young disciple of Hobbes (John Davys) had managed to obtain a copy of the discussion, and published Hobbes' contribution in 1654 without Hobbes' consent.'—Ed.

he should do that kind of action or not. And hence it is, that he that killeth in a sudden passion of *anger*, shall nevertheless be justly put to *death*, because all the time, wherein he was able to consider whether to kill were good or evil, shall be held for one continual *deliberation*, and consequently the killing shall be judged to proceed from *election*.

Secondly, I conceive when a man *deliberates* whether he shall do a thing or not do it, that he does nothing else but consider whether it be better for himself to do it or not to do it. And to *consider* an action, is to imagine the *consequences* of it, both *good* and *evil*. From whence is to be inferred that *deliberation* is nothing else but *alternate* imagination of the *good* and *evil* sequels of an *action*, or, which is the same thing, alternate *hope* and *fear*, or alternate *appetite* to do or quit the action of which he *deliberateth*.

Thirdly, I conceive that in all *deliberations*, that is to say, in all alternate *succession* of contrary *appetites*, the last is that which we call the WILL, and is immediately next before the doing of the action, or next before the doing of it become impossible. All other *appetites* to do, and to quit, that come upon a man during his deliberations, are called *intentions* and *inclinations*, but not *wills*, there being but one *will*, which also in this case may be called the *last will*, though the *intentions* change often.

Fourthly, I conceive that those *actions*, which a man is said to do upon *deliberation*, are said to be *voluntary*, and done upon *choice* and *election*, so that *voluntary* action, and action proceeding from *election* is the same thing; and that of a *voluntary agent*, it is all one to say, he is *free*, and to say, he hath not made an end of *deliberating*.

Fifthly, I conceive *liberty* to be rightly defined in this manner: *Liberty is the absence of all the impediments to action that are not contained in the nature and intrinsical quality of the agent.* As for example, the water is said to descend *freely*, or to have *liberty* to descend by the channel of the river, because there is no impediment that way, but not across, because the banks are impediments. And though the water cannot ascend, yet men never say it wants the *liberty* to ascend, but the *faculty* or *power*, because the impediment is in the nature of the water, and intrinsical. So also we say, he that is tied, wants the *liberty* to go, because the impediment is not in him, but in his hands, whereas we say not so of him that is sick or lame, because the impediment is in himself.

Sixthly, I conceive that nothing taketh beginning from *itself*, but from the *action* of some other immediate *agent* without itself. And that therefore, when first a man hath an *appetite* or *will* to something, to which immediately before he had no appetite nor will, the *cause* of his *will*, is not the *will* itself, but *something* else not in his own disposing. So that whereas it is out of controversy, that of *voluntary* actions the *will* is the *necessary* cause, and by this which is said, the *will* is also *caused* by other things whereof it disposeth not, it followeth, that *voluntary* actions have all of them *necessary* causes, and therefore are *necessitated*.

Seventhly, I hold that to be a *sufficient cause*, to which nothing is wanting that is needful to the producing of the *effect*. The same also is a *necessary* cause. For if it be possible that a *sufficient* cause shall not bring forth the *effect*, then there wanteth somewhat which was needful to the producing of it, and so the *cause* was not *sufficient*; but if it be impossible that a *sufficient* cause should not produce the *effect*, then is a *sufficient* cause a *necessary* cause, for that is said to produce an effect *necessarily* that cannot but produce it. Hence it is manifest, that whatsoever is produced, is produced *necessarily*; for whatsoever is produced hath had a *sufficient* cause to produce it, or else it had not been; and therefore also *voluntary* actions are *necessitated*.

Lastly, that ordinary *definition* of a *free agent*, namely, *that a free agent is that, which, when all things are present which are needful to produce the* effect, *can nevertheless not produce it*, implies a contradiction, and is nonsense, being as much as to say, the cause may be *sufficient*, that is to say, *necessary*, and yet the effect shall not follow.

My reasons

For the first five points, wherein it is explicated I, what *spontaneity* is; II, what *deliberation* is; III, what *will*, *propension* and *appetite* are; IV, what a *free agent* is; V, what *liberty* is; there can no other proof be offered but every man's own experience, by reflection on himself, and remembering what he useth in his mind, that is, what he himself meaneth when he saith an action is *spontaneous*, a man *deliberates*; such is his *will*, that *agent* or that *action* is *free*. Now he that reflecteth so on himself, cannot but be satisfied, that *deliberation* is the *consideration of the good and evil sequels of an action to come;* that by *spontaneity* is meant *inconsiderate action*, or else nothing is meant by it; that *will* is the *last act of our deliberation*; that a *free agent* is he *that can do if he will*, and *forbear if he will*; and that *liberty* is *the absence of external impediments*. But to those that out of custom speak not what they conceive, but what they hear, and are not able, or will not take the pains to consider what they think when they hear such words, no argument can be sufficient, because *experience* and *matter of fact* are not verified by other men's arguments, but by every man's own *sense* and *memory*. For example, how can it be proved that to *love* a thing and to think it *good* is all one, to a man that doth not mark his own meaning by those words? Or how can it be proved that *eternity* is not *nunc stans*[*] to a man that says those words by custom, and never considers how he can conceive the thing in his mind?

Also the sixth point, that a man cannot imagine anything to begin *without a cause*, can no other way be made known, but by trying how he can imagine it; but if he try, he shall find as much reason, if there be no cause of the thing, to conceive it should begin at one time as another, that he hath equal reason to think it should begin at all times, which is impossible, and therefore he must think there was some special cause why it began then, rather than sooner or later; or else that it began never, but was *eternal*.

For the seventh point, which is, that all *events* have *necessary* causes, it is there proved, in that they have *sufficient* causes. Further let us in this place also suppose any event never so causal, as the throwing, for example, *ames ace*[†] upon a pair of dice, and see, if it must not have been *necessary* before it was thrown. For seeing it was thrown, it had a *beginning*, and consequently a *sufficient* cause to produce it, consisting partly in the *dice*, partly in outward things, as the posture of the parts of the *hand*, the measure of *force* applied by the caster, the posture of the parts of the *table*, and the like. In sum, there was nothing wanting which was necessarily requisite to the producing of that particular cast, and consequently the cast was necessarily thrown; for if it had not been thrown, there had wanted somewhat requisite to the throwing of it, and so the cause had not been *sufficient*. In the like manner it may be proved that every other accident, how *contingent* soever it seem, or how *voluntary* soever

[*] A permanent 'now'—Ed.
[†] 'Both aces'; i.e. the lowest throw at dice.—Ed.

it be, is produced *necessarily*, which is that that my Lord Bishop disputes against. The same may be proved also in this manner. Let the case be put, for example, of the weather. *It is necessary that tomorrow it shall rain or not rain.* If therefore it be not *necessary* it shall rain, it is *necessary* it shall not rain, otherwise there is no necessity that the proposition, *it shall rain or not rain,* should be true. I know there be some that say, it may necessarily be true that one of the two shall come to pass, but not, singly that it shall rain, or that it shall not rain, which is as much to say, *one* of them is *necessary*, yet neither of them is *necessary*; and therefore to seem to avoid that absurdity, they make a distinction, that neither of them is true *determinate*, but *indeterminate*; which distinction either signifies no more but this, one of them is true, but we know not which, and so the necessity remains, though we know it not; or if the meaning of the distinction be not that, it hath no meaning, and they might as well have said, one of them is true *Titirice*, but neither of them, *Tu patulice*.

The last thing, in which also consisteth the whole controversy, namely that there is no such thing as an agent, *which when all things requisite to action are present, can nevertheless forbear to produce it*; or, which is all one, that there is no such thing as *freedom from necessity*, is easily inferred from that which hath been before alleged. For if it be an *agent*, it can *work*; and if it *work*, there is nothing wanting of what is requisite to produce the *action*, and consequently the cause of the action is *sufficient*; and if *sufficient*, then also *necessary*, as hath been proved before.

And thus you see how the *inconveniences*, which his Lordship objecteth must follow upon the holding of *necessity*, are avoided, and the *necessity* itself *demonstratively* proved. To which I could add, if I thought it good logic, the *inconvenience* of denying *necessity*, as that it destroyeth both the *decrees* and the *prescience* of God Almighty; for whatsoever God hath *purposed* to bring to pass by *man*, as an instrument, or foreseeth shall come to pass; a man, if he have *liberty*, such as his Lordship affirmeth, from *necessitation*, might frustrate, and make not to come to pass, and God should either not *foreknow* it, and not *decree* it, or he should *foreknow* such things shall be, as shall never be, and *decree* that which shall never *come to pass*.

This is all that hath come into my mind touching this question since I last considered it. And I humbly beseech your Lordship to communicate it only to my Lord Bishop. And so praying God

to prosper your Lordship in all your designs, I take leave, and
am,

My most noble and most obliging Lord,
Your most humble servant,
THOMAS HOBBES.

Rouen; August 20, 1652.*

Source: Body, Man and Citizen, ed. R. S. Peters (Collier Macmillan).

26 Of Liberty and Necessity (1748)

DAVID HUME

I have frequently considered, what could possibly be the reason
why all mankind, though they have ever, without hesitation,
acknowledged the doctrine of necessity in their whole practice
and reasoning, have yet discovered such a reluctance to acknowledge it in words, and have rather shown a propensity, in all ages,
to profess the contrary opinion. The matter, I think, may be
accounted for after the following manner. If we examine the
operations of body, and the production of effects from their
causes, we shall find that all our faculties can never carry us
farther in our knowledge of this relation than barely to observe
that particular objects are *constantly conjoined* together, and that
the mind is carried, by a *customary transition,* from the appearance of one to the belief of the other. But though this conclusion
concerning human ignorance be the result of the strictest scrutiny
of this subject, men still entertain a strong propensity to believe
that they penetrate farther into the powers of nature, and perceive something like a necessary connexion between the cause
and the effect. When again they turn their reflections towards the
operations of their own minds, and *feel* no such connexion of the
motive and the action; they are thence apt to suppose, that there
is a difference between the effects which result from material
force, and those which arise from thought and intelligence. But
being once convinced that we know nothing farther of causation
of any kind than merely the *constant conjunction* of objects, and

* In the first edition of 1654 this date is 1646.—Ed.

the consequent *inference* of the mind from one to another, and finding that these two circumstances are universally allowed to have place in voluntary actions; we may be more easily led to own the same necessity common to all causes. And though this reasoning may contradict the systems of many philosophers, in ascribing necessity to the determinations of the will, we shall find, upon reflection, that they dissent from it in words only, not in their real sentiment. Necessity according to the sense in which it is here taken, has never yet been rejected, nor can ever, I think, be rejected by any philosopher. It may only, perhaps, be pretended that the mind can perceive, in the operations of matter, some farther connexion between the cause and effect; and connexion that has not place in voluntary actions of intelligent beings. Now whether it be so or not, can only appear upon examination; and it is incumbent on these philosophers to make good their assertion, by defining or describing that necessity, and pointing it out to us in the operations of material causes.

It would seem, indeed, that men begin at the wrong end of this question concerning liberty and necessity, when they enter upon it by examining the faculties of the soul, the influence of the understanding, and the operations of the will. Let them first discuss a more simple question, namely, the operations of body and of brute unintelligent matter; and try whether they can there form any idea of causation and necessity, except that of a constant conjunction of objects, and subsequent inference of the mind from one to another. If these circumstances form, in reality, the whole of that necessity, which we conceive in matter, and if these circumstances be also universally acknowledged to take place in the operations of the mind, the dispute is at an end; at least, must be owned to be thenceforth merely verbal. But as long as we will rashly suppose, that we have some farther idea of necessity and causation in the operations of external objects; at the same time, that we can find nothing farther in the voluntary actions of the mind; there is no possibility of bringing the question to any determinate issue, while we proceed upon so erroneous a supposition. The only method of undeceiving us is to mount up higher; to examine the narrow extent of science when applied to material causes; and to convince ourselves that all we know of them is the constant conjunction and inference above mentioned. We may, perhaps, find that it is with difficulty we are induced to fix such narrow limits to human understanding: But we can afterwards find no difficulty when we come to apply this doctrine to the actions of the will. For as it is evident that these have a regular conjunction with motives and circumstances and characters, and as we always draw inferences from one to the other, we must be obliged to acknowledge in words that necessity, which we have already avowed, in every deliberation of our lives, and in every step of our conduct and behaviour.

But to proceed in this reconciling project with regard to the question of liberty and necessity; the most contentious question of metaphysics, the most contentious science; it will not require many words to prove, that all mankind have ever agreed in the doctrine of liberty as well as in that of necessity, and that the whole dispute, in this respect also, has been hitherto merely verbal. For what is meant by liberty, when applied to voluntary actions? We cannot surely mean that actions have so little connexion with motives, inclinations, and circumstances, that one does not follow with a certain degree of uniformity from the other, and that one affords no inference by which we can conclude the existence of the other. For these are plain and acknowledged matters of fact. By liberty, then, we can only mean *a power of acting or not acting, according to the determinations of the will;* that is, if we choose to remain at rest, we may; if we choose to move, we also may. Now this hypothetical liberty is universally allowed to belong to every one who is not a prisoner and in chains. Here, then, is no subject of dispute.

Whatever definition we may give of liberty, we should be careful to observe two requisite circumstances; *first,* that it be consistent with plain matter of fact; *secondly,* that it be consistent with itself. If we observe these circumstances, and render our definition intelligible, I am persuaded that all mankind will be found of one opinion with regard to it.

It is universally allowed that nothing exists without a cause of its existence, and that chance, when strictly examined, is a mere negative word, and means not any real power which has anywhere a being in nature. But it is pretended that some causes are necessary, some not necessary. Here then is the advantage of definitions. Let any one *define* a cause, without comprehending, as a part of the definition, a *necessary connexion* with its effect; and let him show distinctly the origin of the idea, expressed by the definition; and I shall readily give up the whole controversy. But if the foregoing explication of the matter be received, this must be absolutely impracticable. Had not objects a regular conjunction with each other, we should never have entertained any notion of cause and effect; and this regular conjunction produces that inference of the understanding, which is the only connexion, that we can have any comprehension of. Whoever attempts a definition of cause, exclusive of these circumstances, will be obliged either to employ unintelligible terms or such as are synonymous to the term which he endeavours to define. And if the definition above mentioned be admitted; liberty, when opposed to necessity, not to constraint, is the same thing with chance; which is universally allowed to have no existence.

Source: An Enquiry Concerning Human Understanding (O.U.P.), Sec. VIII, Pt. I. (Extract.)

27 Ifs and Cans (1956)

J. L. AUSTIN

Are *cans* constitutionally iffy? Whenever, that is, we say that we can do something, or could do something, or could have done something, is there an *if* in the offing—suppressed, it may be, but due nevertheless to appear when we set out our sentence in full or when we give an explanation of its meaning?

Again, if and when there *is* an *if*-clause appended to a main clause which contains a *can* or *could* or *could have*, what sort of an *if* is it? What is the meaning of the *if*, or what is the effect or the point of combining this *if*-clause with the main clause?

These are large questions, to which philosophers, among them some whom I most respect, have given small answers: and it is two such answers, given recently by English philosophers, that I propose to consider. Both, I believe, are mistaken, yet something is to be learned from examining them. In philosophy, there are many mistakes that it is no disgrace to have made: to make a first-water, ground-floor mistake, so far from being easy, takes one (*one*) form of philosophical genius.[1]

Many of you will have read a short but justly admired book written by Professor G. E. Moore of Cambridge, which is called simply *Ethics*. In it, there is a point where Moore, who is engaged

[1] Plato, Descartes, and Leibniz all had this form of genius, besides of course others.

in discussing Right and Wrong, says that if we are to discuss whether any act that has been done was right or wrong then we are bound to discuss what the person concerned *could have* done instead of what he did in fact do. And this, he thinks, may lead to an entanglement in the problem, so-called, of Free Will: because, though few would deny, at least expressly, that a man could have done something other than what he did actually do *if he had chosen*, many people would deny that he *could* (absolutely) have done any such other thing. Hence Moore is led to ask whether it is ever true, and if so in what sense, that a man could have done something other than what he did actually do. And it is with his answer to this question, not with its bearings upon the meanings of *right* and *wrong* or upon the problem of Free Will, that we are concerned.

With his usual shrewdness Moore begins by insisting that there is at least *one* proper sense in which we can say that a man can do something he does not do or could have done something he did not do—even though there may perhaps be *other* senses of *can* and *could have* in which we cannot say such things. This sense he illustrates by the sentence 'I could have walked a mile in 20 minutes this morning, but I certainly could not have run two miles in 5 minutes': we are to take it that in fact the speaker did not do either of the two things mentioned, but this in no way hinders us from drawing the very common and necessary distinction between undone acts that we could have done and undone acts that we could not have done. So it is certain that, at least in *some* sense, we often could have done things that we did not actually do.

Why then, Moore goes on to ask, should anyone try to deny this? And he replies that people do so (we may call them 'determinists') because they hold that everything that happens has a *cause* which precedes it, which is to say that once the cause has occurred the thing itself is *bound* to occur and *nothing* else *could* ever have happened instead.

However, on examining further the 20-minute-mile example, Moore argues that there is much reason to think that 'could have' in such cases simply means 'could have *if I had chosen*', or, as perhaps we had better say in order to avoid a possible complication (these are Moore's words), simply means '*should* have if I had chosen'. And if this *is* all it means, then there is after all no conflict between our conviction that we often could have, in this sense, done things that we did not actually do and the determinist's theory: for he certainly holds himself that I often, and perhaps even always, should have done something different from what I did do *if I had chosen* to do that different thing, since my choosing differently would constitute a change in the causal antecedents of my subsequent act, which would therefore, on his theory, naturally itself be different. If, therefore, the determinist nevertheless asserts that in *some* sense of 'could have' I could *not* ever have done anything different from what I did actually do, this must simply be a second sense[2] of 'could have' different from that which it has in the 20-minute-mile example.

In the remainder of his chapter, Moore argues that quite possibly his first sense of 'could have', in which it simply means 'could or should have if I had chosen', is all we need to satisfy our hankerings after Free Will, or at least is so if conjoined in some way with yet a third sense of 'could have' in which sense 'I could have done something different' means 'I might, for all anyone could know for certain beforehand, have done something different'. This third kind of 'could have' might, I think, be held to be a vulgarism, 'could' being used incorrectly for 'might': but in any case we shall not be concerned with it here.

In the upshot, then, Moore leaves us with only one important sense in which it can be said that I could have done something that I did not do: he is not convinced that any other sense is necessary, nor has he any clear idea what such another sense would be: and he is convinced that, on his interpretation of 'could have', even the determinist can, and indeed must, say that I could very often have done things I did not do. To summarize his suggestions (he does not put them forward with complete conviction) once again:

1. 'Could have' simply means 'could have if I had chosen'.
2. For 'could have if I had chosen' we may substitute 'should have if I had chosen'.
3. The *if*-clauses in these expressions state the causal conditions upon which it would have followed that I could or should have done the thing different from what I did actually do.

Moore does not state this third point expressly himself: but it seems clear, in view of the connexions he alleges between his interpretation of 'could have' and the determinist theory, that he did believe it, presumably taking it as obvious.

[2] About which Moore has no more to tell us.

There are then three questions to be asked:

1. Does 'could have if I had chosen' mean the same, in general or ever, as 'should have if I had chosen?'
2. In either of these expressions, is the *if* the *if* of causal condition?
3. In sentences having *can* or *could have* as main verb, are we required or entitled always to supply an *if*-clause, and in particular the clause 'if I had chosen'?

It appears to me that the answer in each case is No.

1. Anyone, surely, would admit that in general *could* is very different indeed from *should* or *would*.[3] What a man *could* do is not at all the same as what he *would* do: perhaps he could shoot you if you were within range, but that is not in the least to say that he would. And it seems clear to me, in our present example, that 'I could have run a mile if I had chosen' and 'I should have run a mile if I had chosen' mean quite different things, though unfortunately it is not so clear exactly what either of them, especially the latter, does mean. 'I should have run a mile in 20 minutes this morning if I had chosen' seems to me an unusual, not to say queer, specimen of English: but if I had to interpret it, I should take it to mean the same as 'If I had chosen to run a mile in 20 minutes this morning, I should (jolly well) have done so', that is, it would be an assertion of my strength of character, in that I put my decisions into execution (an assertion which is, however, more naturally made, as I have now made it, with the *if*-clause preceding the main clause). I should certainly not myself understand it to mean that if I had made a certain choice my making that choice would have caused me to do something. But in whichever of these ways we understand it, it is quite different from 'I *could* have walked a mile in 20 minutes this morning if I had chosen', which surely says something rather about my opportunities or powers. Moore, unfortunately, does not explain why he thinks we are entitled to make this all-important transition from 'could' to 'should', beyond saying that by doing so we 'avoid a possible complication'. Later I shall make some suggestions which may in part explain why he was tempted to make the transition: but nothing can justify it.

³ Since Moore has couched his example in the first person, he uses 'should' in the apodosis: but of course in the third person, everyone would use 'would'. For brevity, I shall in what follows generally use 'should' to do duty for both persons.

2. Moore, as I pointed out above, did not discuss what sort of *if* it is that we have in 'I can if I choose' or in 'I could have if I had chosen' or in 'I should have if I had chosen'. Generally, philosophers, as also grammarians, have a favourite, if somewhat blurred and diffuse, idea of an *if*-clause as a 'conditional' clause: putting our example schematically as 'If *p*, then *q*', then it will be said that *q* follows from *p*, typically either in the sense that *p* *entails* *q* or in the sense that *p* is a *cause* of *q*, though other important variations are possible. And it seems to be on these lines that Moore is thinking of the *if* in 'I can if I choose'. But now, it is characteristic of this general sort of *if*, that from 'If *p* then *q*' we *can* draw the inference 'If not *q*, then not *p*', whereas we can *not* infer either 'Whether or not *p*, then *q*' or '*q*' simpliciter. For example, from 'If I run, I pant' we *can* infer 'If I do not pant, I do not run' (or, as we should rather say, 'If I am not panting, I am not running'), whereas we can *not* infer either 'I pant, whether I run or not' or 'I pant' (at least in the sense of 'I am panting'). If, to avoid these troubles with the English tenses, which are unfortunately prevalent but are not allowed to matter, we put the example in the past tense, then from 'If I ran, I panted' it *does* follow that 'If I did not pant, I did not run', but it does *not* follow either that 'I panted whether or not I ran' or that 'I panted' period. These possibilities and impossibilities of inference are typical of the *if* of causal condition: but they are precisely reversed in the case of 'I can if I choose' or 'I could have if I had chosen'. For from these we should not draw the curious inferences that 'If I cannot, I do not choose to' or that 'If I could not have, I had not chosen to' (or 'did not choose to'), whatever these sentences may be supposed to mean. But on the contrary, from 'I can if I choose' we certainly should infer that 'I can, whether I choose to or not' and indeed that 'I can' period: and from 'I could have if I had chosen' we should similarly infer that 'I could have, whether I chose to or not' and that anyway 'I could have' period. So that, whatever this *if* means, it is evidently not the *if* of causal condition.

This becomes even clearer when we observe that it is quite common *elsewhere* to find an ordinary causal conditional *if* in connexion with a *can*, and that then there is no doubt about it, as for example in the sentence 'I can squeeze through if I am thin enough', which *does* imply that 'If I cannot squeeze through I am not thin enough', and of course does *not* imply that 'I can squeeze through'. 'I can if I choose' is precisely different from this.

Nor does *can* have to be a very special and peculiar verb for *ifs* which are not causal conditional to be found in connexion with it: all kinds of *ifs* are found with all kinds of verbs. Consider for example the *if* in 'There are biscuits on the sideboard if you want them', where the verb is the highly ordinary *are*, but the *if* is more like that in 'I can if I choose' than that in 'I panted if I ran': for we can certainly infer from it that 'There are biscuits on the sideboard whether you want them or not' and that anyway 'There are biscuits on the sideboard', whereas it would be folly to infer that 'If there are no biscuits on the sideboard you do not want them', or to understand the meaning to be that you have only to want biscuits to cause them to be on the sideboard.

The *if*, then, in 'I can if I choose' is not the causal conditional *if*. What of the *if* in 'I shall if I choose'? At first glance, we see that this is quite different (one more reason for refusing to substitute *shall* for *can* or *should have* for *could have*). For from 'I shall if I choose' we clearly cannot infer that 'I shall whether I choose to or not' or simply that 'I shall'. But on the other hand, can we infer, either, that 'If I shan't I don't choose to'? (Or should it be rather 'If I don't I don't choose to'?) I think not, as we shall see: but even if some such inference can be drawn, it would still be patently wrong to conclude that the meaning of 'I shall if I choose' is that my choosing to do the thing is sufficient to cause me inevitably to do it or has as a consequence that I shall do it, which, unless I am mistaken, is what Moore was supposing it to mean. This may be seen if we compare 'I shall ruin him if I choose' with 'I shall ruin him if I am extravagant'. The latter sentence does indeed obviously state what would be the consequence of the fulfilment of a condition specified in the *if*-clause—but then, the first sentence has clearly different characteristics from the second. In the first, it makes good sense in general to stress the 'shall', but in the second it does not.[4] This is a symptom of the fact that in the first sentence 'I shall' is the present of that mysterious old verb *shall*, whereas in the second 'shall' is simply being used as an auxiliary, without any meaning of its own, to form the future indicative of 'ruin'.

I expect you will be more than ready at this point to hear something a little more positive about the meanings of these curious expressions 'I can if I choose' and 'I shall if I choose'. Let

[4] In general, though of course in some contexts it does: e.g. 'I may very easily ruin him, and I *shall* if I am extravagant', where 'shall' is stressed to point the contrast with 'may'.

us take the former first, and concentrate upon the *if*. The diction-
ary tells us that the words from which our *if* is descended
expressed, or even meant, 'doubt' or 'hesitation' or 'condition' or
'stipulation'. Of these, 'condition' has been given a prodigious
innings by grammarians, lexicographers, and philosophers alike:
it is time for 'doubt' and 'hesitation' to be remembered, and
these do indeed seem to be the notions present in 'I can if I
choose'. We could give, on different occasions and in different
contexts, many different interpretations of this sentence, which is
of a somewhat primitive and *loose-jointed* type. Here are some:

> I can, quaere do I choose to?
> I can, but do I choose to?
> I can, but perhaps I don't choose to
> I can, but then I should have to choose to, and what about *that*?
> I can, but would it really be reasonable to choose to?
> I can, but whether I choose to is another question
> I can, I have only to choose to
> I can, in case I (should) choose to,
> and so on.

These interpretations are not, of course, all the same: which it
is that we mean will usually be clear from the context (otherwise
we should prefer another expression), but sometimes it can be
brought out by stress, on the 'if' or the 'choose' for example.
What is common to them all is simply that the *assertion*, positive
and complete, that 'I can', is linked to the *raising of the question*
whether I choose to, which may be relevant in a variety of ways.[5]

Ifs of the kind I have been trying to describe are common
enough, for example the *if* in our example 'There are biscuits on
the sideboard if you want them'. I do not know whether you want
biscuits or not, but in case you do, I point out that there are some
on the sideboard. It is tempting, I know, to 'expand' our sentence
here to this: 'There are biscuits on the sideboard *which you can*
(*or may*) *take* if you want them': but this, legitimate or not, will
not make much difference, for we are still left with 'can (or may)
if you want', which is (here) just like 'can if you choose' or 'can if

---

[5] If there were space, we should consider other germane expressions: e.g.
'I can do it or not as I choose', 'I can do whichever I choose' (*quidlibet*).
In particular, 'I can whether I choose to or not' means 'I can, but whether
I choose to or not is an open question': it does *not* mean 'I can on condition
that I choose and likewise on condition that I don't', which is absurd.

you like', so that the *if* is still the *if* of doubt or hesitation, not the
if of condition.[6]

I will mention two further points, very briefly, about 'I can if I
choose', important but not so relevant to our discussion here.
Sometimes the *can* will be the *can*, and the choice the choice, of
legal or other *right*, at other times these words will refer to prac-
ticability or feasibility: consequently, we should sometimes interpret our sentence in some such way as 'I am entitled to do it
(if I choose)', and at other times in some such way as 'I am
capable of doing it (if I choose)'. We, of course, are concerned
with interpretations of this second kind. It would be nice if we
always said 'I *may* if I choose' when we wished to refer to our
rights, as perhaps our nannies once told us to: but the interlocking
histories of *can* and *may* are far too chequered for there to be any
such rule in practice.[7] The second point is that *choose* is an
important word in its own right, and needs careful interpretation:
'I can if I like' is not the same, although the 'can' and the 'if' may
be the same in both, as 'I can if I choose'. Choice is always
between alternatives, that is between several courses to be
weighed in the same scale against each other, the one to be
preferred. 'You can vote whichever way you choose' is different
from 'You can vote whichever way you like'.

And now for something about 'I *shall* if I choose'—what sort of
if have we here? The point to notice is, that 'I shall' is not an
assertion of *fact* but an expression of *intention*, verging towards
the giving of some variety of undertaking: and the *if*, consequently, is the *if* not of condition but of *stipulation*. In sentences
like:

> I shall | marry him if I choose
> I intend | to marry him if I choose
> I promise | to marry him if he will have me

the *if*-clause is a part of the object phrase governed by the initial
verb ('shall', 'intend', 'promise'), if this is an allowable way of

---

[6] An account on these lines should probably be given also of an excellent
example given to me by Mr. P. T. Geach: 'I paid you back yesterday, if you
remember.' This is much the same as 'I paid you back yesterday, don't you
remember?' It does not mean that your now remembering that I did so is a
condition, causal or other, of my having paid you back yesterday.

[7] Formerly I believed that the meaning of 'I can if I choose' was something like 'I can, I have the choice', and that the point of the *if*-clause was
to make clear that the 'can' in the main clause was the 'can' of right. This
account, however, does not do justice to the role of the 'if', and also unduly
restricts in general the meaning of 'choice'.

putting it: or again, the *if* qualifies the *content* of the undertaking given, or of the intention announced, it does *not* qualify the giving of the undertaking. Why, we may ask, is it perverse to draw from 'I intend to marry him if I choose' the inference 'If I do not intend to marry him I do not choose to'? Because 'I intend to marry him if I choose' is not like 'I panted if I ran' in this important respect: 'I panted if I ran' does not assert anything 'categorically' about me—it does not assert that I did pant, and hence it is far from surprising to infer something beginning 'If I did not pant': but 'I intend to marry him if I choose' (and the same goes for 'I shall marry him if I choose') *is* a 'categorical' expression of intention, and hence it is paradoxical to make an inference leading off with 'If I do *not* intend'.

3. Our third question was as to when we are entitled or required to supply *if*-clauses with *can* or *could have* as main verb.

Here there is one thing to be clear about at the start. There are *two* quite distinct and incompatible views that may be put forward concerning *ifs* and *cans*, which are fatally easy to confuse with each other. One view is that wherever we have *can* or *could have* as our main verb, an *if*-clause must always be understood or supplied, if it is not actually present, in order to complete the sense of the sentence. The other view is that the meaning of 'can' or 'could have' can be more clearly reproduced by *some other verb* (notably 'shall' or 'should have') with an *if*-clause appended to *it*. The first view is that an *if* is required to *complete* a *can*-sentence: the second view is that an *if* is required in the *analysis* of a *can*-sentence. The suggestion of Moore that 'could have' means 'could have if I had chosen' is a suggestion of the first kind: but the suggestion also made by Moore that it means 'should have if I had chosen' is a suggestion of the second kind. It may be because it is so easy (apparently) to confuse these two kinds of theory that Moore was tempted to talk as though 'should have' could mean the same as 'could have'.

Now we are concerned at this moment solely with the *first* sort of view, namely that *can*-sentences are not complete without an *if*-clause. And if we think, as Moore was for the most part thinking, about 'could have' (rather than 'can'), it is easy to see why it may be tempting to allege that it always requires an *if*-clause with it. For it is natural to construe 'could have' as a past subjunctive or 'conditional', which is practically as much as to say that it needs a *conditional* clause with it. And of course it is quite true that 'could have' *may* be, and very often is, a past conditional:

but it is *also* true that 'could have' may be and often is the *past (definite) indicative* of the verb *can*. Sometimes 'I could have' is equivalent to the Latin 'Potui' and means 'I *was* in a position to': sometimes it is equivalent to the Latin 'Potuissem' and means 'I *should have been* in a position to'. Exactly similar is the double role of 'could', which is sometimes a conditional meaning 'should be able to', but also sometimes a past indicative (indefinite) meaning 'was able to': no one can doubt this if he considers such contrasted examples as 'I could do it 20 years ago' and 'I could do it if I had a thingummy.' It is not so much that 'could' or 'could have' is ambiguous, as rather that two parts of the verb *can* take the same shape.

Once it is realized that 'could have' can be a past indicative, the general temptation to supply *if*-clauses with it vanishes: at least there is no more temptation to supply them with 'could have' than with 'can'. If we ask how a Roman would have said 'I could have ruined you this morning (although I didn't)', it is clear that he would have used 'potui', and that his sentence is complete without any conditional clause. But more than this, if he had wished to add 'if I had chosen', and however he had expressed that in Latin, he would still not have changed his 'potui' to 'potuissem': but this is precisely what he *would* have done if he had been tacking on some other, more 'normal' kind of *if*-clause, such as 'if I had had one more vote'.[8]

That is to say, the 'could have' in 'could have if I had chosen' is a past indicative, *not* a past conditional, despite the fact that there is what would, I suppose, be called a 'conditional' clause, that is an *if*-clause, with it. And this is, of course, why we can make the inferences that, as we saw, we can make from 'I could have if I had chosen', notably the inference to 'I could have' absolutely. Hence we see how mistaken Moore was in contrasting 'I could have if I had chosen' with the 'absolute' sense of 'I could have': we might almost go so far as to say that the addition of the 'conditional' clause 'if I had chosen' makes it certain that (in Moore's language) the sense of 'could have' is the absolute sense,

---

[8] If the *if*-clause is 'if I had chosen', then I *was* able, *was* actually in a position, to ruin you: hence 'potui'. But if the *if*-clause expresses a genuine *unfulfilled condition*, then plainly I was *not* actually in a position to ruin you, hence not 'potui' but 'potuissem'. My colleague Mr. R. M. Nisbet has pointed out to me the interesting discussion of this point in S. A. Handford, *The Latin Subjunctive*, pp. 130ff. It is interesting that although this author well appreciates the Latin usage, he still takes it for granted that in English the 'could have' is universally subjunctive or conditional.

or as I should prefer to put it, that the mood of 'could have' is indicative.

It might at this point be worth considering in general whether it makes sense to suppose that a language could contain any verb such as *can* has been argued or implied to be, namely one that can never occur without an *if*-clause appended to it. At least if the *if* is the normal 'conditional' *if* this would seem very difficult. For let the verb in question be *to X*: then we shall never say simply 'I X', but always 'I X if I Y': but then also, according to the accepted rules, if it is true that 'I X if I Y', and *also* true (which it must surely sometimes be) that 'I do, in fact, Y', it must surely follow that 'I X', simpliciter, without any *if* about it any longer. Perhaps this was the 'possible complication' that led Moore to switch from the suggestion that 'I could have' (in one sense) has always to be *expanded* to 'I could have if' to the suggestion that it has always to be *analysed* as 'I should have if': for of course the argument I have just given does not suffice to show that there could not be some verb which has always to be *analysed* as something containing a conditional *if*-clause: suggestions that this is in fact the case with some verbs are common in philosophy, and I do not propose to argue this point, though I think that doubt might well be felt about it. The only sort of 'verb' I can think of that might always demand a conditional clause with it is an 'auxiliary' verb, if there is one, which is used solely to form subjunctive or conditional moods (whatever exactly they may be) of other verbs: but however this may be, it is quite clear that *can*, and I should be prepared also to add *shall* and *will* and *may*, are not in this position.

To summarize, then, what has been here said in reply to Moore's suggestions in his book:

(*a*) 'I could have if I had chosen' does not mean the same as 'I should have if I had chosen'.

(*b*) In neither of these expressions is the *if*-clause a 'normal conditional' clause, connecting antecedent to consequent as cause to effect.

(*c*) To argue that *can* always requires an *if*-clause with it to complete the sense is totally different from arguing that *can*-sentences are always to be analysed into sentences containing *if*-clauses.

(*d*) Neither *can* nor any other verb always requires a conditional *if*-clause after it: even 'could have', when a past indicative, does not require such a clause: and in 'I could have if I had chosen' the verb is in fact a past indicative, not a past subjunctive or conditional.

Even, however, if all these contentions are true so far, we must recognize that it may nevertheless still be the case that *can*, *could*, and *could have*, even when used as indicatives, are to be analysed as meaning *shall*, *should*, and *should have*, used as auxiliaries of tense or mood with another verb (i.e. so as to make that other verb into a future or subjunctive), followed by a conditional *if*-clause. There is some plausibility,[9] for example, in the suggestion that 'I can do X' means 'I shall succeed in doing X, if I try' and 'I could have done X' means 'I should have succeeded in doing X, if I had tried'.

It is indeed odd that Moore should have plumped so simply, in giving his account whether of the necessary supplementation or of the analysis of 'could have', for the one particular *if*-clause 'if I had chosen', which happens to be particularly exposed to the above objections, without even mentioning the possibility of invoking other *if*-clauses, at least in some cases. Perhaps the reason was that *choose* (a word itself much in need of discussion) presented itself as well fitted to bridge the gulf between determinists and free-willers, which *try* might not so readily do. But as a matter of fact Moore does himself at one point give an analysis of 'I could have done X' which is different in an interesting way from his usual version, although confusible with it. At a crucial point in his argument, he chooses for his example 'The ship could have gone faster', and the suggestion is made that this is

---

[9] Plausibility, but no more. Consider the case where I miss a very short putt and kick myself because I could have holed it. It is not that I should have holed it if I had tried: I did try, and missed. It is not that I should have holed it if conditions had been different: that might of course be so, but I am talking about conditions as they precisely were, and asserting that I could have holed it. There is the rub. Nor does 'I can hole it this time' mean that I shall hole it this time if I try or if anything else: for I may try and miss, and yet not be convinced that I could not have done it; indeed, further experiments may confirm my belief that I could have done it that time although I did not.

But if I tried my hardest, say, and missed, surely there *must* have been *something* that caused me to fail, that made me unable to succeed? So that I *could not* have holed it. Well, a modern belief in science, in there being an explanation of everything, may make us assent to this argument. But such a belief is not in line with the traditional beliefs enshrined in the word *can*: according to *them*, a human ability or power or capacity is inherently liable not to produce success, on occasion, and that for no reason (or are bad luck and bad form sometimes reasons?).

equivalent to 'The ship *would* have gone faster *if her officers had chosen*'. This may well seem plausible, but so far from being in line, as Moore apparently thinks, with his general analysis, it differs from it in two important respects:

(a) the subject of the *if*-clause ('her officers') is different from the subject of the main clause ('the ship'), the subject of the original sentence:

(b) the verb in the *if*-clause following 'chosen' is different from the verb in the main clause, the verb in the original sentence. We do not readily observe this because of the ellipsis after 'chosen': but plainly the verb must be, not 'to go faster', but 'to make her go faster' or, for example, 'to open the throttle'.

These two features are dictated by the fact that a ship is inanimate. We do not wish seriously to ascribe free will to inanimate objects, and the 'could' of the original sentence is perhaps only justifiable (as opposed to 'might') because it is readily realized that some person's free will is in question.

If we follow up the lines of this new type of analysis, we should have to examine the relations between 'I could have won' and 'I could, or should, have won if I had chosen to lob' and 'I could, or should, have won if he had chosen to lob'. I will do no more here than point out that the difference between 'could' and 'should' remains as before, and that the sense of 'I could have won', if it really is one, in which it means something of the sort 'I should have won if he had chosen to lob' or 'to let me win' (the parallel to the ship example), is of little importance—the 'if' here is of course the conditional *if*. [...]

Source: 'Ifs and Cans', *Proceedings of the British Academy*, 1956. (Extract.)

28 Freedom and the Will (1963)

DAVID PEARS

We can trace back to near the beginning of Western Civilization the notion of individual responsibility: the notion that certain states of affairs in the world can be traced to the actions of human beings, for which those human beings can in various ways be called to account. The actions for which we are in the fullest sense responsible are those for which we can be praised or blamed.

This notion of responsibility is to be found already in the moral and legal thought of the Ancient Greeks. The Greeks already worked with the notion which we have today, that the question whether a man is responsible for something that happens is not *just* the question whether what happens is a consequence of movements of the man's body. For instance, suppose a man's arm moves in such a way as to knock over and break a valuable vase, someone else's property. In a limited sense, we know already in these circumstances what the cause of the damage was—the movement of this man's arm; but we do not yet know whether the man himself is in the full sense responsible for this damage, whether he is to blame. For that, we want to know more about the movement of his arm. In particular, we want to know whether he intended this movement of his arm, or whether perhaps it was just some nervous twitch, out of his control. Again, even if the movement was not out of his control, we still want to know, for instance, whether he realized the vase was there: if not, his breaking of the vase will be unintentional, and to that extent free from blame. There are other sorts of situation, too, that relieve people of responsibility for things that they have done, or at least mitigate it; being in certain peculiar states, for instance, such as sleep-walking or under the influence of drugs; or, rather differently, being forced to do things by other persons.

Aristotle, in his *Ethics*, reviews and classifies these sorts of situation that relieve people of responsibility. His account is complex and subtle, but substantially he reduces the type of situation to two classes: those in which the agent is ignorant of relevant matters, and those in which, as he puts it, the originating principle of the action lies outside the agent himself—by which, I think, he principally means cases in which someone is physically forced to do something by someone else.

Aristotle's account is of interest for two reasons in particular. The first is a positive reason: that it is interesting to find a Greek philosopher giving an analysis of responsibility and the conditions that relieve people of it that so remarkably corresponds, in its essentials, to some of the considerations that we still employ today, both in the law and in everyday life. The second reason is a more negative one. Aristotle's account is concerned, as I have said, with the conditions that relieve people of responsibility for what they have done. I mean by this that he considers and classifies certain *special* circumstances that relieve people of responsibility, while taking it for granted that in the usual circumstances people are responsible. He analyses the framework of praise and blame and responsibility as a going concern, as it were. He never, or scarcely ever, considers the notion that we might *never* really be responsible, that the going concern of praise and blame, our ordinary notions on these matters, might as a whole be founded on an illusion. Aristotle, that is to say, is precisely not concerned with that large-scale philosophical problem or set of philosophical problems which in later times has come to be known as the problem of freedom of the will. For the heart of that problem lies in the fundamental and revolutionary suggestion that our ordinary notions of responsibility may be altogether confused, because based on some false or ultimately unintelligible theory about human beings and their actions.

I think we may be able to see, in historical terms, how this fundamental and revolutionary suggestion came to be made, if we ask first why Aristotle does not consider it. One reason is that Aristotle regards it as certain, and indeed makes it a central point of his philosophy, that there is no necessity about human actions —that it is never necessary in any sense that a man should, on a particular occasion, have done this rather than that. For him, necessity is something that applies only to such things as the movements of the heavenly bodies; human actions, on the contrary, are a sort of thing which could always have happened otherwise. Now Aristotle did believe, I think, that *if* it could be shown that it was a matter of necessity that men acted in one way rather than another, then our ordinary thought about action and responsibility would be undermined. If human actions were necessitated, there would indeed be something radically wrong with our notions of human action; but, he thought, it was quite certainly false that human actions were necessitated. If this is a correct account of Aristotle, we can see one reason why he does not confront the freewill problem. It is because he thinks that it cannot seriously be doubted that human actions are free from necessitation.

This is a very important point, because, as we shall see, one reason that the freewill problem did eventually arise was that men did begin to have serious doubts about just this. I shall come back to this point. First, however, it is worth while, for our historical picture, to look briefly at another reason for Aristotle's silence on this subject. This was his lack of belief in any personal god concerned with human affairs. Some earlier Greek writers, in particular the tragedian Aeschylus, do seem to me concerned with problems not far removed from the problem of freewill. Aeschylus's portrayal of Prometheus, or again of Orestes, seems to be in part a dramatic representation of human freedom as against forces set in motion by the gods, or perhaps we should better say, personified in the gods. Plato, nearly a century later, could still, in a poetic passage, write in these terms, and assert human freedom: 'the responsibility is with the soul that chooses its destiny: God is not responsible'. For Aristotle, a little later, there are no such gods, there are no such forces, and the question does not arise.

This is worth mentioning, because the problem of freewill makes its first large-scale appearance in a religious context, when men had come to believe that there was one God, omnipotent, omniscient, and concerned with human action. The problem of freewill was first definitely stated as a problem of Christian theology. The problem arose, in fact, from a number of different roots in Christian belief: Christianity asserts on the one hand that man does freely choose his actions, but also asserts on the other hand statements not evidently compatible with this, for instance that God being omniscient knows from all eternity what actions a man will in fact perform.

I shall not say anything more about the theological forms of the freewill problem. The theological forms are, not surprisingly, bound up with issues that are both special to Christian belief, and wider than the freewill problem itself; thus any theological discussion of the problem must involve the wider theological question of what it means to say that God's knowledge is outside time, and the special dogmatic issue of the operation of Grace, around which much of the Christian controversy about freewill has historically centred. The freewill problem, however, reaches us today in other forms not so theologically encumbered.

I mentioned earlier that men came eventually to doubt Aristotle's principle that human actions were not necessitated. This they did—or at least, the doubt occurred to them—with the rise of a mechanistic view of the universe, according to which the universe was a closed system, every state of which was determined as a consequence of its earlier states in accordance with natural laws—laws which, in the eighteenth and nineteenth centuries, were believed to have been in essence discovered by Newton. The possibility of such a scientific account of the universe had occurred, indeed, to certain of the Greeks, who realized further that such an account would have consequences for human action. The atomist Epicurus, for instance, was apparently aware of these problems. The speculations of the atomists, however, remained speculations; and it was only with the rise of a successful experimental and predictive mechanical science in the seventeenth century that the problems became acute. How, it was asked, could a human agent intervene in the world, be, in Aristotle's terms, an 'originating principle of action', if every event in the universe was at it was merely in virtue of the earlier states of the universe, however remote? Would not every human action be a case of 'the originating principle lying outside the agent himself', so that there would be no action left for which he would be responsible? Descartes, in the first half of the seventeenth century, both held the mechanistic view of the material universe, and saw this problem; he wished further to safeguard responsible action from the realm of natural necessity. This he tried to do by distinguishing two quite separate realms, that of mind and that of matter, to the second of which alone, matter, the natural laws applied. But this was a quite inadequate kind of solution, even in Descartes' terms. Descartes himself realized that a bodily human action is itself, from one point of view, an event in the material world. If all events in the material world are subject to natural law, how does the mind come into it? Descartes' distinction between two realms, designed to insulate responsible human action from mechanical causation, insulated the world of mechanical causation, that is to say, the whole of the external world, from responsible human action. Man would be free only if there was nothing he could do. Once this way of looking at the problem is accepted, there seem to be only two possibilities. Either all physical changes are subject to natural law, in which case those particular physical changes which constitute human actions are subject to it; or human actions are not subject to natural law, so not all physical changes are subject to it. The belief that all physical changes are subject to natural law has attracted, needless to say, a label: the label 'determinism'. So here we have in outline an apparently simple opposition: either determinism is true, in which case there is no genuine human intervention in the world, that is, no freewill; or there is freewill, in which case determinism is false.

The issue has, of course, been endlessly posed in these terms, and in these terms endlessly discussed. But not all thinkers have accepted these terms, either explicitly by rallying to one side or the other, or implicitly by professing ignorance as to which alternative was true. Right from the seventeenth century there have been philosophers who have criticized this opposition itself, and the terms in which the question was posed. Some have claimed, radically, that when the notions involved are properly understood, the alleged opposition dissolves, and the supposed dilemma can be shown to be a set of muddles and misunderstandings. Hobbes, Hume, and in our own time A. J. Ayer and others have taken this view. Others, less ambitious, have held that although there may be one, or probably more than one, genuine opposition here, nevertheless the terms of the discussion are so imprecise and ill understood that, without much further analysis, it is impossible to understand what the oppositions are, if they exist. Such a view is, I think, held by many linguistic philosophers today.

It certainly does seem that a tremendous number of questions have been begged and important distinctions blurred in the simple sort of formulation of the problem that I sketched just now. First of all, the formulation introduced a good deal of metaphor: one spoke of physical changes being 'subject to' natural laws, as though the natural laws exercised some mechanistic tyranny over events. Though an enticing metaphor, it is a very misleading one, and should be eliminated. What then, without benefit of metaphor, will be the formulation of determinism? It would seem to be something like this: that given any total state-description of the universe, it is in principle possible to predict or retrodict correctly any other, however remote, in virtue of a finite set of scientific laws. But there are still difficulties about this formulation. It is still not free from unclarities and ambiguities— great difficulties, for instance, surround that slippery phrase 'in principle'. Under what conditions could we say that we could *in principle* predict every state of the universe? Just when we *thought* that there were laws in virtue of which we could do it, if only we knew them? This would surely not be enough—this would only be a situation of faith in determinism, not a situation in which determinism had been shown to be true. So perhaps we should say that determinism had been shown to be true if we *knew* all the relevant laws, and could predict all the states of the universe if only we took enough trouble. But then what certainty would we have that we did know all the relevant laws, unless we could actually succeed in making these vast predictions—that is, could not only in principle, but in practice predict? And this even the most fervent determinist would surely agree we could not do.

There are other difficulties in the formulation of determinism. What, for instance, are we to make of the phrase 'a total state-description of the universe'? Even if we made more precise—as we should have to—what terms such a description would have to be in, are there not overwhelming reasons for thinking that no such description could ever be completed? In the eighteenth century the astronomer Laplace could perhaps talk glibly in these terms; in the twentieth we certainly cannot.

Here someone may say: Good. We now understand that the conditions specified by the determinist could never be satisfied—that is to say, determinism is a false or incoherent doctrine. So the enemy of freewill is out of business, and freewill is all right. But such a confident answer would be premature, and this just illustrates the obscurities of the simple opposition we originally set up. For while this extremely grandiose enemy, Laplacean determinism, is perhaps out of business, rather humbler but more effective enemies are certainly still in existence.

Here it is worth while to recall the point we started with right at the beginning: the fact that in ordinary life and the law we admit certain conditions as relieving an agent from responsibility for what he has done: conditions such as somnambulism, *force majeure*, etc. Now it is a most conspicuous feature of our present moral thought that this list of conditions is gradually being extended in the light of advancing psychological and other scientific knowledge. For instance, we now recognize in ordinary life, and perhaps even in the law, the existence of certain compulsive conditions—kleptomania is one sort of example. The proof that an agent was in such a state relieves him of responsibility, or at least mitigates it, for actions of the appropriate type.

Now it is not an accident that the discussion of such cases gives rise to constant difficulty and doubt. We feel compelled to admit more and more such conditions into the class of conditions that exonerate, without really being clear on what principle we are doing it. Moreover, there is the lurking feeling that the principle on which we are doing it might be one that eventually might extend to swallow up wide ranges of action now regarded as normal and responsible. For instance, are we to say that a man is not responsible if there is a psychological explanation of what he did? This by itself is too weak, since the phrase 'psychological explanation' can cover practically anything, including for instance 'he freely chose'. But perhaps some sorts of psychological explanation. . . ? Here we do not know, not just *where* to draw the line, but *how* to, and in this ignorance we can feel no *a priori* confidence how much of our ordinary sphere of action will be left intact by the line when properly drawn. Here we feel the presence perhaps of another type of determinism less grandiose but more pressing than the total physical determinism of Laplace.

In this situation, looking for a criterion, we may turn to the other side of the field. We may ask, not what are the general conditions of non-responsibility, but what are the general conditions of responsibility: perhaps there is some sign that an action is, in the appropriate sense, really ours. Here we meet for the first time a concept that has been absent from the discussion so far—the concept of the will itself. It is in virtue of the operation of the will that some philosophers have tried to distinguish this class of responsible actions. But what is the operation of the will, and what are its signs? We indeed speak in ordinary life of 'efforts of will', and it is in the occurrence of these that in reflective moments we perhaps feel most conscious in some sense of our freedom. But here there are many difficulties. First, it is certain that only a very few of the actions for which people are normally held responsible are accompanied by efforts of will, in this psychological sense; and the same goes for any other conscious process that might be suggested here instead, such as explicit decision, formulated intention and so on. Often we just act, without such processes, nor would we regard such actions as any the less responsible or free for that reason. Again, there is a deep difficulty about what an effort of will really is. There is indeed some kind of psychological process in connection with which the term is used—but might it not be *just* a psychological process which accompanied some actions (perhaps peculiarly difficult ones) and not others? Contrary to what some philosophers have supposed, efforts of will do not wear their metaphysical significance on their face. It may even be that they have none.

Source: Freedom and the Will, ed. David Pears (Macmillan).
    (Extract.)

TRUTH

29 Propositions, Facts and Truth (1910-11)
G. E. MOORE

Propositions

The fact is that absolutely all the contents of the Universe, absolutely everything that *is* at all, may be divided into two classes— namely into *propositions*, on the one hand, and into things which are not propositions on the other hand. There certainly are in the Universe such things as propositions: the sort of thing that I mean by a proposition is certainly one of the things that *is*: and no less certainly there are in the Universe some things which are *not* propositions: and also quite certainly absolutely everything in the Universe either is a proposition or is *not*, if we confine the word 'proposition' to some one, quite definite, sense: for nothing whatever can both have a quite definite property and also *not* have that very same property. This classification, therefore, of all the things in the Universe into those which are and those which are not propositions, is certainly correct and exhaustive. But it may seem, at first sight, as if it were a very unequal classification: as if the number of things in the Universe, which are *not* propositions, was very much greater than that of those which are. Even this, as we shall presently see, may be doubted. And, whether this be so or not, the classification is, I think, by no means unequal, if, instead of considering all that *is* in the Universe, we consider all those things in the Universe which we *know*. For, however it may be with the Universe itself, it is, I think, certain that a very large and important part of *our knowledge* of the Universe consists in the knowledge with regard to propositions that they are true.

Now the new class of facts which I want to call your attention to, are certain facts about propositions and about our knowledge of them.

And, first of all, I want to make it as plain as I can exactly what

239

I mean by a proposition. The sort of thing, which I mean by a proposition is, as I said, something which certainly is. There certainly are things in the Universe, which have the properties which I shall mean to ascribe to a thing when I call it a proposition. And when I call a thing a proposition I shall mean to ascribe to it absolutely no properties, except certain definite ones which some things certainly have. There may be doubt and dispute as to whether these things have or have *not* certain *other* properties besides those which I ascribe to them; and also as to whether what I mean by a proposition is quite the same as what is usually meant. But as to the fact that some things *are* propositions, in the sense in which I intend to use the word, I think there is no doubt.

First of all, then, I do *not* mean by a proposition any of those collections of *words*, which are one of the things that are commonly called propositions. What I mean by a proposition is rather the sort of thing which these collections of words *express*. No collection of words can possibly be a proposition, in the sense in which I intend to use the term. Whenever I speak of a proposition, I shall always be speaking, *not* of a mere sentence—a mere collection of words, but of what these words *mean*.

I do not then mean by a proposition any collection of words. And what I do mean can, I think, be best explained as follows. I will utter now certain words which form a sentence: these words, for instance: Twice two are four. Now, when I say these words, you not only hear *them*—the words—you *also* understand what they mean. That is to say, something happens in your minds—some act of consciousness—*over and above* the hearing of the words, some act of consciousness which may be called the understanding of their meaning. But now I will utter another set of words which also form a sentence: I utter the words: Twice four are eight. Here again you not only hear the words, but also perform some other act of consciousness which may be called the understanding of *their* meaning. Here then we have an instance of two acts of consciousness, each of which may be called an apprehension of the meaning of certain words. The one of them was an apprehension of the meaning of the words: Twice two are four; the other an apprehension of the meaning of the words: Twice four are eight. Both of these two acts of consciousness are alike in respect of the fact that each of them is an act of apprehension, and that each of them is the apprehension of the meaning of a certain set of words which form a sentence. Each of them is

an apprehending of the meaning of a sentence: and each of them
is an *apprehending* in exactly the same sense: they are obviously
exactly alike in *this* respect. But no less obviously they differ in
respect of the fact that *what* is apprehended in the one case, is
different from what is apprehended in the other case. In the one
case *what* is apprehended is the meaning of the words: Twice
two are four; in the other case *what* is apprehended is the meaning of the words: Twice four are eight. And the meaning of the
first set of words is obviously different from that of the second.
In this case, then, we have two acts of apprehension, which are
exactly alike in respect of the fact that they are acts of apprehension, and acts of apprehension, too, of exactly the same kind;
but which differ in respect of the fact that *what* is apprehended in
the one, is different from *what* is apprehended in the other. Now
by a proposition, I mean the sort of thing which *is apprehended*
in these two cases. The two acts of consciousness differ in respect
of the fact that *what* is apprehended in the one, is different from
what is apprehended in the other. And *what* is apprehended in
each case is what I mean by a proposition. We might say, then,
that the two acts of apprehension differ in respect of the fact that
one is an apprehension of one proposition, and the other the
apprehension of a different proposition. And we might say also
that *the* proposition apprehended in the one is the proposition
that twice two are four—*not* the *words*, twice two are four, but
the *meaning* of these words; and that *the* proposition apprehended
in the other is the different proposition that twice four are eight—
again *not* the words, twice four are eight, but the meaning of
these words.

   This, then, is the sort of thing that I mean by a proposition.
And whether you agree or not that it is a proper use of the word,
I hope it is plain that there certainly *are* things which are proposi-
tions in this sense. [. . .]

   But now, if we use the word 'proposition' in this sense, it is
plain, I think, that we can say several other things about propositions and about the apprehension of them.

   In the first place, it is, I think, plain that we apprehend a
proposition in exactly the same sense in three different cases.
When we hear certain words spoken and understand their meaning, we may do three different things: we may *believe* the
proposition which they express, we may *disbelieve* it, or we may
simply *understand* what the words mean, without either believing
or disbelieving it. In all these three cases, we do I think obviously

apprehend the proposition in question in exactly the same sense: namely, we understand the meaning of the words. The difference between the three cases merely consists in the fact, that when we believe or disbelieve, we *also* do something else *beside* merely apprehending the proposition. [. . .]

One point then with regard to propositions and our apprehension of them, is that there is a definite sort of apprehension of them, which occurs equally, whenever we either believe, disbelieve, or merely understand a proposition on actually hearing spoken words which express it.

And a second point is this. It is, I think, also plain that we often apprehend propositions in exactly the same sense, when instead of *hearing* words which express them, we *see* written or printed words which express them—provided, of course, that we are able to read and understand the language to which the words belong. This understanding of the meaning of written or printed sentences, which occurs when we actually read them, is, I think, obviously an apprehension of propositions in exactly the same sense as is the understanding of sentences, which we hear spoken. But just as we apprehend propositions in exactly the same sense in both these two cases—whether we hear spoken sentences which express them, or *see* these sentences written or printed—so also, obviously, we very often apprehend propositions in exactly the same sense, when we *neither* hear nor see any words which express them. We constantly think of and believe or disbelieve, or merely consider, propositions, at moments when we are neither hearing nor seeing any words which express them; and in doing so, we are *very often* apprehending them in exactly the same sense in which we apprehend them when we do understand the meaning of written or spoken sentences. [. . .]

Our second point, then, with regard to propositions and our apprehension of them is this: namely, that in exactly the same sense in which we apprehend them, when we hear certain words spoken of which we understand the meaning, we also often apprehend them, when we neither see nor hear any words which express them, and probably often without even having before our minds any *images* of words which would express them. [. . .]

Whenever we utter a complete sentence, which the whole sentence does, as a rule, express a proposition, some of the words or sets of words of which it is composed express something which is *not* a proposition. For instance, consider again the sentence:

Twice two are four. This whole sentence, as we saw, does express a proposition. But, if we take some one of the words of which it is composed, for instance the word 'two', this word by itself does not make a complete sentence and does not express a proposition. But it *does* express *something*. What we mean by the word 'two' is certainly something. This something, therefore, *is*—is something, and yet is not a proposition. In fact, whenever we do apprehend a proposition we always also apprehend things which are *not* propositions; namely, things which would be expressed by *some* of the words, of which the whole sentence, which would express the proposition, is composed.

A third point, then, with regard to propositions and our apprehension of them, is that propositions are by no means the only kind of things which we apprehend; but that whenever we do apprehend a proposition, we always *also* apprehend something else, which is *not* a proposition.

Beliefs and propositions

And a fourth point with regard to propositions is this. Namely, that propositions, in the sense in which I have been using the term, are obviously a sort of thing which can properly be said to be *true* or *false*. Some propositions are true propositions and other propositions are false propositions. And I mention this point, because some philosophers seem inclined to say that nothing can be properly said to be true or false, *except* an act of belief: that, therefore, *propositions*, not being acts of belief, cannot properly be said to be so. And I do not here wish to deny that an act of belief may be properly said to be true or false; though I think it may be doubted. We do undoubtedly speak of true and false beliefs; so that *beliefs*, at all events, may be properly said to be true or false. But the fact is, I think, that, as with so many other words, we use the word 'belief' in two different senses: sometimes, no doubt, we mean by a belief an *act* of belief, but very often, I think, we mean by it simply the proposition which is believed. For instance, we often say of two different people that they entertain *the same belief*. And here, I think, we certainly do not mean to say that any act of belief performed by the one is the *same act* as an act of belief performed by the other. The two acts of belief are certainly different—numerically different: the one act is the act of one person, and the other is the act of a different person; and we certainly do not mean to assert that these two acts are identical—that they are not *two* acts, but one and the same act. What we do, I think, mean, when we say that both persons have the same belief, is that *what* is believed in both of the two different acts is the same: we mean by a belief, in fact, *not* the act of belief, but *what* is believed; and what is believed is just nothing else than what I mean by a proposition. But let us grant that acts of belief may be properly said to be true and false. Even if this be so, it seems to me we must allow that propositions, in the sense I have given to the term, can be properly said to be true and false *also*, though in a different sense. For what I mean by a proposition is simply *that* in respect of which an act of belief, which is a *true* act, differs from another, which is a false one; or that in respect of which two qualitatively different acts of belief, which are both false or both true, differ from one another. And obviously the quality in virtue of which one act of belief is true, and another false, cannot be the quality which they both have in common: it cannot be the fact that they are both of them acts of belief: we cannot say that the one is true, simply because it is an act of belief, and the other false, for the same reason—namely, simply because it is an act of belief. What makes the one true and the other false must be that in respect of which they differ; and that in respect of which they differ—whatever it may be—is just that which I mean by the proposition which is apprehended in each of them. Even, therefore, if we admit that nothing but an act of belief can be properly said to be true or false, in *one* sense of these words, we must, I think, admit that there is another corresponding sense in which propositions are true and false. Every true act of belief partly consists in the apprehension of a proposition; and every false act of belief also partly consists in the apprehension of a proposition. And any proposition apprehended in a true act of belief must be different from any proposition apprehended in a false act of belief. Consequently all the propositions apprehended in true acts of belief must have some common property which is not possessed by any of those which are apprehended in false acts of belief. And there is no reason why we should not call *this* property 'truth'; and similarly the property possessed in common by all propositions apprehended in false acts of belief 'falsity'.

Propositions are, then, a sort of thing which may be properly said to be true or false. And this gives us one way of distinguishing what is a proposition from what is *not* a proposition; since nothing that is *not* a proposition can be true or false in exactly the same sense in which a proposition is true or false. There are, indeed, we may say, two other senses of the words 'true' and 'false', which are closely allied to those in which propositions are true or false. There is, to begin with, *if* acts of belief can be properly said to be true or false at all, the sense in which an act of belief is true or false. An act of belief is true, if and only if the proposition believed in it is true; and it is false, if and only if the proposition believed in it is false. Or, putting the matter the other way, we may say: A proposition is true, if and only if any act of belief, which was a belief in it, would be a true act of belief; and a proposition is false, if and only if any act of belief, which was a belief in it, would be false. I do not pretend to say here which of these two ways of putting the matter is the better way. Whether, that is to say, the sense in which acts of belief are true and false, should be defined by reference to that in which propositions are true and false; or whether the sense in which propositions are true and false should be defined by reference to that in which acts of belief are true and false. I do not pretend to say which of these two senses is the more fundamental; and it does not seem to me to matter much which is. What is quite certain is that they are two different senses, but *also* that each *can* be defined by reference to the other. One sense, then, of the words true and false, *beside* that in which propositions are true and false, is the sense in which acts of belief are true and false. And there is obviously, also, another sense of the words, which, though different from these two, is equally closely related to both of them. Namely, the sense in which any set of words—any sentence, for instance—which *expresses* a true proposition is true; and any set of words which *expresses* a false proposition is false. Or here again, putting the matter the other way, we may say: Any proposition which is such that any verbal statement which expressed it *would* be a true statement, is true; and any proposition which is such that a verbal statement which expressed it *would* be a false statement, is false. We may, therefore, say that another sense of the words true and false is that in which anything that *expresses* a true proposition is true; and anything which *expresses* a false proposition is false. And obviously in this sense not only words, but also other things, gestures, for instance, may be true or false. If, for instance, somebody asks you: 'Where are my scissors?' and you point to a particular place by way of answer, your gesture—the gesture of pointing—expresses a proposition. By pointing you obviously express the same proposition as if you had used the words 'Your scissors are there', or had named the particular place where they were. And just as any words you might have used would have been true or false, according as the proposition they expressed was true or false, so your gesture might be said to be true or false, according as the scissors really are in the place you point to or not. There are, therefore, these three senses of the words true and false: The sense in which propositions are true or false; the sense in which acts of belief are true or false, according as the propositions believed in them are true or false; and the sense in which anything that *expresses* a proposition is true or false, according as the proposition expressed is true or false. And obviously these three senses are not *the same*, though each can be defined by reference to the others. That is to say, neither an act of belief nor the *expression* of a proposition, can be true or false in exactly the same sense in which a proposition is true or false. And the same, I think, is true universally: nothing but a proposition can be true or false in exactly the same sense in which propositions are so. And why I particularly wanted to call your attention to this, is for the following reason. Some people seem to think that, if you have before your mind an image of an object, which is *like* the object—a copy of it—in certain respects, you may be said, merely because you have this image before your mind, to have a *true* idea of the object—an idea which is *true*, in so far as the image really is like the object. And they seem to think that when this happens, you have a *true* idea of the object, in exactly the same sense as if you believed a true proposition about the object. And this is, I think, at first sight a very natural view to take. It is natural, for instance, to think that if, after looking at this envelope, I have before my mind (as I have) an image, which is like, in certain respects, to the patch of colour which I just now saw, I have, *merely* because I directly apprehend this image, a true *idea* of the patch of colour which I just now saw. It is natural, I say, to think that merely to apprehend this image *is* to have a true idea (true, in certain particulars) of the patch of colour which I saw; and that, in apprehending this image, I have a true idea of the patch of colour, in exactly the same sense as if I had a true belief *about* the patch of colour. But it is, I think, easy to see that this view, however natural, is wholly mistaken. The fact is that if *all* that happened to me were *merely* that I directly apprehended an image, which was in fact like some other object, I could not be properly said to have *any* idea of this other object *at all*—any idea, either true or false. Merely to apprehend something, which is *in fact* like something else, is obviously not the same thing as having an idea *of* the something else. In order to have an idea *of* the something else, I must *not only* apprehend an image, which is *in fact* like the something else: I must also either know or think *that* the image *is* like the something else. In other words, I must apprehend some *proposition about* the relation of the image to the object: only so can I be properly said to have an *idea* of the object at all. If I do apprehend some proposition about the relation of the image to the object, then, indeed, I may be said to have an *idea* of the object: and if I think that the image is like the object in respects in which it is *not* like it, then I shall have a *false* idea of the object, whereas if I think that it is like it in respects in which it is in fact like it, then I shall have, so far, a *true* idea of the object. But if I apprehend *no proposition at all* about the relation of the image to the object, then obviously, however like the image may *in fact* be to the object, I cannot be said to have any idea of the object at all. I might, for instance, all my life through, be directly apprehending images and sense-data, which were *in fact* singularly accurate copies of other things. But suppose I never for a moment even suspected that there were these other things, *of* which my images and sense-data were copies? Suppose it never occurred to me for a moment that there were any other things at all beside my sense-data and images? Obviously I could not be said to have any idea at all about these other things—any idea at all, either true or false; and this in spite of the fact that my sense-data and images were, *in fact*, copies of these other things. We must, therefore, say that merely to apprehend an image (or anything else), which is, in fact, like some other object, but without even thinking that the two are like, is *not* to have a true idea of the object in the same sense as when we apprehend a true proposition about the object. No mere image or sense-datum can possibly *be* either a true idea or a false idea *of* anything else, however like or unlike it may be to the something else. Or, if you choose to say that it is, *in a sense*, a true idea of an object, if it be like it, and an untrue one, if it be unlike it, you must at least admit that it is a *true* idea in quite a different sense from that in which a proposition about the object, if true, *is* a true idea of it. Nothing, in short, can be true or false in the same sense in which propositions are true or false. So that, if we never apprehended any propositions we should not be capable of ever making any mistakes—a mistake, an *error*, would be impossible. Error always consists in believing some proposition which is false. So that if a man merely apprehended something, which was *in fact* unlike something else, but without believing either that it was like or unlike, or anything else at all about it, he could not possibly be said to make any mistake at all: he would never hold any mistaken or false opinions, because he would never hold any *opinions* at all. [. . .]

Truth and facts

The question which I begin with now is the question what truth *is*, or what is the difference between true beliefs and false ones. And this is a question about which it seems to me to be extremely difficult either to think clearly or to speak clearly—far more difficult than in the case of any question I have yet discussed. It is, in the first place, extremely difficult to distinguish clearly and to avoid confusing the different views which may be held about it; and, in the second place, even if you do succeed in doing this, it is extremely difficult to *express* the distinctions clearly. I am afraid I shall not have succeeded in doing either—either in avoiding confusion, or in expressing myself clearly. But I must do the best I can. [. . .]

You all of you know quite well the sort of sounds—the actual sense-data which you would be hearing now if a brass-band were playing loud in this room. This kind of fact, the kind of fact which consists in the actual experience of such striking sense-data as the noise of a brass-band playing quite near you, seems to me to be a kind of fact with regard to which there is the least possibility of mistake as to their nature. And also there is no kind of fact of which each of us can be more certain than that we are or are not, at a given moment, experiencing particular sense-data of this violent nature. There is nothing of which I am more certain than that I am *not* at this moment experiencing those extremely striking and unmistakable sense-data, which I can only describe as those which I should be experiencing if a brass-band were playing loudly in this room. And you all of you, I think, know as well as I do what kind of sense-data I mean—what the noise of a brass-band is like—and that *you* are *not* now hearing these sense-data. Well, suppose that somebody somewhere were believing now that some one of us *is* now hearing the noise of a brass-band. As I say, I suppose it is not at all likely that anybody anywhere is actually making this mistake at the present moment with regard to anyone. But it is a sort of mistake which we certainly do quite often make. [. . .]

Well, if anyone were believing this now, he certainly would be making a mistake. There is no doubt that his belief would be false. And it seems to me that in this case there is as little doubt as possible as to what the essence of his mistake would consist in.

Surely the whole essence of the mistake would lie simply in this, that whereas, on the one hand, he would be believing that we are hearing the noise of a brass-band, the *fact* is on the other hand that we are *not* hearing it. And similarly it is quite plain what would be necessary to make this belief of his a true one. All that would be necessary would be simply that we *should* be hearing the noise in question. If we *were* hearing it, and he believed that we were, then his belief would be true. This surely does state correctly the difference between truth and falsehood in the case of this particular belief; and what I want to ask is: Supposing that it is a correct statement of the difference, what exactly is the difference that has been stated? What does this statement mean, if we try to put it more exactly?

Well, one point seems to me plain, to begin with, and this is a point on which I wish particularly to insist. The difference between truth and falsehood, in the case of this particular belief, does we have said, depend on whether in fact we are or are *not* now hearing the noise of a brass-band. Unless, therefore we can understand the difference between these two alternatives—between our being now hearing that noise, and our *not* being now hearing it, we certainly cannot understand the difference between the truth and falsehood of this belief. This is one essential point, though it is only one. And it seems to me that as to this point there really is no doubt at all. We are *not* now hearing the noise of a brass-band; and we all, I think, can understand quite clearly in one respect the nature of the fact which I express by saying that we are not. What these words imply is that there simply is no such thing in the Universe as our being now hearing that particular kind of noise. The combination of us at this moment with the hearing of that particular kind of noise is a combination which simply has no being. There *is* no such combination. And we all do, I think, understand quite clearly what is meant by saying that there *is* no such thing. If you don't understand this, I'm afraid I can't make it any clearer. This distinction between there being such a thing as our now hearing that particular kind of noise and there being no such thing seems to me to be absolutely fundamental. And I want you to concentrate your attention upon this particular sense of the word 'being'—the sense in which there certainly *is* no such thing as our being hearing now the noise of a brass-band. In one sense, at all events, there certainly *isn't*; and we all know that there *isn't*. And we can recognise the sense in which there *isn't*. And it is this particular sense of the word 'being' that I want to get fixed. Using this sense of the word 'being' we can at once say two things about the difference between the truth and falsehood of this particular belief—the belief that we *are* now hearing the noise of a brass-band. We can say, in the first place that since the belief is false, there simply *is* not in the Universe one thing which would be in it, if the belief were true. And we can say, in the second place, that this thing, which is simply absent from the Universe since the belief is false, and which would be present, if it were true, *is* that fact, whose nature is so unmistakable—the fact which would *be*, if we were now hearing the noise of a brass-band—the fact which would consist in our actually being now hearing it.

But now these two points by themselves don't suffice to give us a perfectly satisfactory *definition* of truth and falsehood. They don't suffice to tell us absolutely definitely what property it is that we should be attributing to this belief, if we were to say that it was true, nor yet what property it is that we are attributing to it now, when we say that it is false. They don't suffice to do this for a reason which I find it very difficult to explain clearly, but which I must do my best to indicate. They do *suggest* a definition; and the definition which they suggest is as follows: To say of this belief that it is true would be to say of it that the fact to which it refers *is*—that there is such a fact in the Universe as the fact to which it refers; while to say of it that it is false is to say of it that *the fact to which it refers* simply is not—that there is no such fact in the Universe. Here we have a definition of what is meant by the truth and falsehood of this belief and a definition which I believe to be the right one; and it is a definition which *might* apply not only to this belief, but to all beliefs which we ever say are true or false. We might say quite generally: To say that a belief is true is to say always that *the fact to which it refers is* or has being, while to say of a belief that it is false is to say always, that the fact to which it refers, is not or has *no* being. But this definition is not perfectly satisfactory and definite because it leaves one point obscure: it leaves obscure what is meant by *the* fact to which a belief refers. In our particular case we happen to know what the fact to which the belief refers *is*: it is our being now hearing the noise of a brass-band, but when we say of this belief that it is false, we don't mean merely to say that we are not in fact hearing the noise of a brass-band. In merely saying this we are not attributing any property to the *belief* at all; whereas when we say that it is false, we certainly do mean to attribute to the belief itself some definite property, and that a property which it shares with other false beliefs. And it won't do to say either, that, when we say that it is false, all that we mean is simply that some fact or other is absent from the Universe. For every *different* false belief a *different* fact is absent from the Universe. And what we mean to say of each, when we say that it is false, is not merely that some *fact or other* is absent from the Universe, but that *the* fact to which it refers is so absent. But then the question is what is meant by *the* fact to which *it* refers? What *is* this relation which we call *referring to* a fact? In saying that there is such a relation, we imply that every true belief has some peculiar relation to one fact, and one fact only—every *different* true belief having the relation in question to a *different* fact. And we need to say what this relation is, in order to define perfectly satisfactorily what we mean by the fact to which a belief refers. *Can* we say what this relation is?

Well, it seems to me the only relation which quite obviously, at first sight, satisfies the requirement is as follows. Every true belief has to one fact and one fact only, *this* peculiar relation namely that we do use and have to use the *name* of the fact, in *naming* the belief. So that we might say: *The* fact to which a belief refers is always *the* fact which has the *same name* as that which we have to use in naming the belief. This, I think, is true; and I want to insist upon it, because I think this partial identity between the name of a belief and the name of the fact to which it refers often leads to confusion, and often serves to conceal the true nature of the problem which we have to face. If we want to give a name to any belief—to point out what belief it is that we are talking about, and to distinguish it from other different beliefs, we always have to do it in the following way. We can only refer to it as *the* belief *that* so and so. One belief for instance is *the* belief that 'lions exist', another is *the* belief that 'bears exist,' another is *the* belief that 'my scissors are lying on my table' and so on. The only way we have of referring to these beliefs and pointing out *which* belief it is that we are talking of is by means of one of these expressions beginning with 'that', or else by the equivalent verbal noun. [...] But, curiously enough, if we want to name *the fact to which belief refers*—the fact which *is*, if the belief be true, and *is not* if it be false—we can only do it by means of exactly the same expressions. If the belief that lions exist be true, then there is in the Universe, some fact which would not be at all if the belief were false. But what is this fact? What is its name? Surely this fact is the fact *that lions exist.* [...] And these words you see are the very same words which we are obliged also to use in naming the belief. The belief *is* the belief *that lions exist*, and the fact, to which the belief refers, is the fact *that lions exist.* [...]

It is, therefore, I think, true that *the* fact to which a belief refers is always the fact which *has the very same name* which we have to use in naming the belief. But obviously the fact that this is the case won't do as a *definition* of what we mean by the fact to which belief refers. It cannot possibly be the case that what we mean by saying that a belief is true, is merely that there is in the Universe the fact which *has the same name*. If this were so, no belief could possibly be true, until it had a name. It must be the case therefore that there is always some *other* relation between a true belief and the fact to which it refers—some *other* relation which is *expressed* by this identity of name.

The question, therefore, which we have to face is: What *is* the relation which always holds between a true belief and the fact to which it refers? The relation which we mean by calling the fact *the* fact to which the belief refers? The relation which we express by saying that the belief does refer to the fact?

Let us try to answer this question by considering again our particular instance of a belief. In this instance, we have the advantage of knowing very clearly what the *fact* would be like, which would *be*, if the belief were true. We all know what it would be like, if we *were* now hearing the noise of a brass-band. And this fact, which certainly *isn't*, is what would *be*, if the particular belief in question were true. In order, therefore, to discover how this fact, if there were such a fact, *would* be related to the belief, we have, it might seem, only to discover what the belief itself is like. And this is where the difficulty would seem to lie. *If* some person were believing now that we are hearing the noise of a brass-band, in what would this belief of his consist? What is the correct analysis of the event that would be happening in his mind? [...]

Possibly some positive analysis of a belief *can* be given, which would enable us to answer this question; but I know of none which seems to be perfectly clear and satisfactory. I propose, therefore, to give up the attempt to analyse beliefs. I think it must be admitted that there is a difficulty and a great difficulty in the analysis of them; and I do not know that any one would say they had a theory about the matter which was quite certainly true.

But if we thus admit that we don't know precisely what the analysis of a belief is, does it follow that we must also admit that we don't know what truth is, and what is the difference between truth and falsehood? It might seem as if it did; for how we were led into this discussion as to the nature of beliefs, was because we found an obscurity in our proposed definition of truth, which it seemed impossible we could entirely clear up except by discovering exactly what sort of a thing a belief is. And I think it is true that the failure to analyse belief, does mean a corresponding failure to give a complete analysis of the property we mean by 'truth'. But the point I want to insist on is that nevertheless we may know perfectly clearly and definitely, in one respect, what truth is; and that this thing which we may know about it is by far the most important and essential thing to know. In short, it seems to me that these questions as to the analysis of belief are quite irrelevant to *the* most important question as to the nature of truth. And I want to insist on this, because I think it is very easy not to distinguish clearly the different questions; and to suppose that because, in one respect, we must admit a doubt as to the nature of truth, this doubt should also throw doubt on other more important matters, which are really quite independent of it.

Let me try to state the matter quite precisely, and to explain what I think is quite certain about truth, and how this much can be certain in spite of the doubt as to the nature of belief. What I proposed to give as the definition of truth was as follows. To say that a belief is true is to say that the *fact to which it refers is* or has being; while to say that a belief is false is to say that the fact to which it refers is not—that there is no such fact. Or, to put it another way, we might say: Every belief has the property of *referring to* some particular fact, every different belief to a different fact; and *the* property which a belief has, when it is true— *the* property which we name when we call it true, is the property which can be expressed by saying that *the* fact to which it refers *is.* This is precisely what I propose to submit as the fundamental definition of truth. And the difficulty we found about it was that of defining exactly what is meant by '*referring to*', by talking of *the* fact to which a belief refers. Obviously this expression 'referring to' stands for some relation which each true belief has to one fact and to one only; and which each false belief has to no fact at all; and the difficulty was to define this relation. Well, I admit I can't define it, in the sense of analysing it completely: I don't think this can be done, without analysing belief. But obviously from the fact that we can't analyse it, it doesn't follow that we may not know perfectly well *what* the relation is; we may be perfectly well *acquainted* with it; it may be perfectly familiar to us; and we may know both that there is such a relation, and that this relation is essential to the definition of truth. And what I want to point out is that we do in this sense *know* this relation; that we are perfectly familiar with it; and that we can, therefore, perfectly well understand this definition of *truth*, though we may not be able to analyse it down to its simplest terms. Take any belief you like; it is, I think, quite plain that there is just one fact, and only one, which would have being—would be in the Universe, if the belief were true; and which would have no being—would simply *not be*, if the being were false. And as soon as we know what the belief is, we know just as well and as certainly what the fact is which in this sense corresponds with it. Any doubt as to the nature of the fact is at the same time a doubt as to the nature of the belief. If we don't know exactly what the nature of the belief is, to that extent we don't know the nature of the corresponding fact; but exactly in proportion as we *do* know the nature of the belief, we also know the nature of the corresponding fact. Take, for instance, the belief that lions exist. You may say you don't know exactly what is meant by the existence of lions—what the fact is, which would *be*, if the belief were true and would not be if it were false. But, if you don't know this, then to exactly the same extent you don't know either what the belief is—you don't know what it is to *believe* that lions exist. Or take a much more difficult instance: take a belief in a hypothetical proposition such as 'If it rains tomorrow we shan't be able to have our picnic'. It is, I admit, very difficult to be sure exactly what sort of a fact is expressed by a hypothetical sentence. Many people might say that it oughtn't to be called a fact at all. But nevertheless it is quite natural to say: It *is* a fact that *if* such and such a thing were to happen, such and such a result would follow; we use this expression as exactly equivalent to 'It is true that, if such and such a thing were to happen, such and such a result would follow', and we may be right or wrong in believing that the consequence would follow from the hypothesis, just as much as we may about anything else. And it is I think quite plain that any doubt as to the nature of the fact expressed by a hypothetical sentence, is equally a doubt as to the nature of the corresponding belief. If you don't know what fact it is that *is* when you believe truly that 'If it rains tomorrow, we shan't have our picnic' you also, and precisely to the same extent, don't know what it is to *believe* this. It is, then, I think, quite obvious that for every different belief, there is one fact and one fact only, which would *be*, if the belief were true, and would *not be*, if it were false; and that in every case we know what the fact in question is just as well or as badly as we know what the belief is. We know that this is so; and of course we could not know it, unless we were *acquainted* with the relation between the fact and the belief, in virtue of which just the one fact and one fact only corresponds to each different belief. I admit that the analysis of this relation is difficult. But any attempt to analyse it, of course, presupposes that there is such a relation and that we are acquainted with it. If we weren't acquainted with it, we couldn't even try to analyse it; and if we didn't already know that this relation is *the* relation that is essential to the defining of truth, of course our analysis, however successful, wouldn't get us any nearer to a definition of truth.

I think, therefore, that the most essential point to establish about truth is merely that every belief *does* refer, in a sense which we are perfectly familiar with, though we may not be able to define it, to *one* fact and one fact only, and that to say of a belief that it is true is merely to say that *the* fact to which it refers *is*; while to say of it that it is false is merely to say that the fact to which it refers, *is not*—that there is no such fact. Of course, this may be disputed; but what I want to insist on is that merely in saying this we are stating a clear view, and a view which may be discussed and settled, *without* entering into any questions as to the analysis of belief. And as for the reasons for believing that this is the right definition of truth, they can I think be seen as clearly as anywhere by considering our original instance. Suppose a man were believing now that we *are* hearing the noise of a brass-band. We know quite well what the fact is which *would* be if the belief were true. We also know quite well what the belief is, and that it is something utterly different from the fact, since the belief might certainly *be* at this moment, although the *fact* most certainly *is not*. And we know quite well that this belief, if it did now exist in anybody's mind, would be false. What *is* the property then which this belief (if it existed) would share with other false beliefs, and which we should mean to ascribe to it by saying that it was false? Surely this property simply consists in the fact that *the fact to which it refers*—namely our being now hearing the noise of a brass-band—has no being; and surely we do know quite well, though we may not be able to define, the exact relation between the belief and the fact, which we thus express by saying that this particular fact is *the* fact to which that particular belief *refers*?

The correspondence theory of truth

[. . .] Suppose that my friend believes that I have gone away for my holidays. There is, I think, no doubt whatever that there is at least *one* ordinary sense of the words 'true' and 'false', such that the following statements hold. We should, I think, certainly say, in the first place, that if this belief of his is *true* then I *must* have gone away for my holidays; his belief that I have gone away can't be true unless I actually have gone away: and, conversely, we should also say that *if* I *have* gone away, then this belief of his certainly *is* true; *if* I have gone away, and he believes that I have, then his belief can't be other than true. In other words, my having actually gone away for my holidays is both a *necessary* and a *sufficient* condition for the truth of this belief: the belief can't be true unless this condition is fulfilled, and it *must* be true, *if* this condition is fulfilled. Surely it is quite plain that at least one sense, in which we commonly use the word 'truth', is of such a nature that these statements are correct. And similarly we may, I think, make the following statements as to the conditions which are necessary and sufficient, if this belief is to be false. We can say: That if this belief is *false*, then I *can't* have gone away for my holidays; the belief that I have gone away can't possibly be false, *if* I *have* gone away: and, conversely, *if* I have not gone away, then the belief that I *have* gone away certainly *must* be false; if I have *not* gone away, and he believes that I *have*, his belief certainly is false. In other words, my *not* having actually gone away is both a necessary and a sufficient condition for the falsehood of this belief. The belief can't be false, unless this condition is fulfilled, and it *must* be false, *if* this condition is fulfilled. It is surely quite plain that one sense at least, in which we use the word 'false', is, of such a nature, that these statements are correct. I don't know that anyone would dispute this much, and I don't well see how it can be disputed.

We have, therefore, found a condition which is both necessary and sufficient for the truth of this belief, in at least one sense of the word 'truth', and also a condition which is both necessary and sufficient for its falsehood, in at least one sense of the word false'. If, therefore, we are to find a correct definition of these senses of the words 'true' and 'false' it must be a definition which does not conflict with the statement that these conditions are necessary and sufficient conditions. But the statement that these conditions are necessary and sufficient does not in itself *constitute* a definition. And I think that part of the trouble about the definition of truth and falsehood arises from the fact that people are apt to suppose that they do. We may be easily tempted to make the following assertion. We may assert: 'To say that the belief that I have gone away is *true*, is *the same thing* as to say that I have gone away: this is the very definition of what we *mean* by saying that the belief is true.' We should, in fact, in ordinary language, say that the two statements do *come to the same thing*; that the one amounts to exactly the same thing as the other. And what we *mean* by this is, of course true. The two statements do really come to the same thing, in the sense we mean. That is to say, they are strictly equivalent: provided that my friend's belief exists at all, neither can be true, unless the other is true too; neither of the facts expressed, can be a fact, unless the other is a fact also. But nevertheless it is, I think, quite plain that the two facts in question are not strictly speaking the same fact; and that to assert the one is not, strictly speaking, the same thing as to assert the other. When we assert: 'The belief that I have gone away is true', we mean to assert that this belief has some property, which it shares with other true beliefs: the possession by it of this property is the fact asserted. But in merely asserting 'I have gone away', we are not attributing any property at all to this belief— far less a property which it shares with other true beliefs. We are merely asserting a fact, which might quite well be a fact, even if no one believed it at all. Plainly I might have gone away, without my friend believing that I had; and if so, his belief would not be true, simply because it would not exist. In asserting, then, that his belief is true, I am asserting a different fact from that which I assert when I merely say that I have gone away. To say that his belief is true is *not*, therefore, strictly speaking, the same thing as to say that I have gone away.

What property is there, then, which this belief, if true, really does share with other true beliefs? Well, it seems to me we can see quite plainly that this belief, if true, has to the fact that I have gone away a certain relation, which that particular belief has to no other fact. This relation, as I admitted and tried to shew last time, is difficult to define, in the sense of analysing it: I didn't profess to be able to analyse it. But we do, I think, see this relation; we are all perfectly familiar with it; and we can, therefore, define it in the sense of pointing out what relation it is, by simply pointing out that it is *the* relation which does hold between this belief, if true, and this fact, and does not hold between this belief and any other fact. Surely you are aware of a relation which would hold between the belief that I had gone away, if true, and the fact that I had gone away—a relation which would hold, between that belief, if true, and that particular fact, and would not hold between that belief and any other fact—a relation which is expressed as I pointed out last time by the partial identity of name between the belief and the fact in question. *The* relation I mean is the relation which the belief '*that I have gone away*', if true, has to the fact '*that I have gone away*', and to no other fact; and which is expressed by the circumstance that the name of the belief is 'The belief that I have gone away' while the name of the fact is 'That I have gone away'. We may take different views as to what the exact nature of this relation is—as to how it is to be analysed, and as to how it resembles or differs from other relations; but in merely attempting to answer these questions, we do, I think, presuppose that we are already acquainted with it—that we have it before our minds; for you cannot try to determine the nature of, or to compare with other things, a thing which you have not got before your mind. Well, it seems to me that the difficulty of *defining* truth and falsehood arises chiefly from the fact that this relation, though we are all acquainted with it, has no unambiguous name; it has no *name* which is just appropriated to it alone, and which may not also be used for other relations, which are perhaps quite different from it. The moment we do give it a name, it becomes, I think, quite easy to define truth and falsehood. Let us give it a name and see how the definition turns out. I propose to call it the relation of 'correspondence'. Only, in giving it this name it must be remembered that I mean by 'correspondence' merely this particular relation which does hold between this particular belief, if true, and the fact that I have gone away, and which does not hold between that precise belief and any other fact. The name 'correspondence' is perhaps used also on other occasions for other relations quite different from this; and I don't mean for a moment to suggest that this relation for which I am using it now either resembles or is different from these other relations in any respect whatever. It must be clearly understood that I mean to use the name 'correspondence' *merely* as a name for *this* particular relation. Well then, using the name 'correspondence' *merely* as a name for this relation, we can at once assert 'To say that this belief is true is to say that there is in the Universe *a* fact to which it corresponds; and that to say that it is false is to say that there is *not* in the Universe any fact to which it corresponds'. And this statement I think, fulfils all the requirements of a definition—a definition of what we actually mean by saying that the belief is true or false. For the properties which we have now identified with truth and 'falsehood' respectively *are* properties which this belief may *share* with other true and false beliefs. We have said that to say it is true is merely to say that it does correspond to a fact; and obviously this *is* a property which may be common to it and other beliefs. The shopman's belief, for instance, that the parcel we ordered this morning has been sent off, may have the property of corresponding to a fact, just as well as this belief that I have gone away may have it. And the same is true of the property which we have now identified with the falsehood of the belief. The property which we have identified with its falsehood is merely that of not corresponding to any fact; and obviously this is a property which may belong to any number of other beliefs just as well as to this one. Moreover it follows from these definitions that the conditions which we saw to be necessary and sufficient for the truth or falsehood of this belief *are* necessary and sufficient for it: there is not only no conflict between these definitions and the statement that these conditions are necessary and sufficient, but it actually follows from the definitions that they are so. For as we have seen the relation which we are calling 'correspondence', is a relation which *does* hold between the belief 'that I have gone away', if true, and the fact that I have gone away, and which does not hold between this belief and any other fact whatever. And hence it follows that if this belief does correspond to a fact at all, then it must *be a fact* that I have gone away: that is to say, if the belief does correspond to a fact, then I *must* have gone away; the belief can't correspond to a fact, unless I have. And conversely it also follows, that *if* I have gone away, then the belief does correspond to a fact: if

I have gone away, the belief *must* correspond to a fact; it can't be the case that I have gone away, and that yet the belief corresponds to no fact. It follows actually therefore, from this definition of truth, that the condition which we saw to be both necessary and sufficient for the truth of this belief is necessary and sufficient for it. And in the same way it follows from our definition of falsehood that the condition which we saw to be necessary and sufficient for its falsehood *is* necessary and sufficient for it. The only point as to which I can see any room for doubt whether these definitions do fulfil all the requirements of a definition of the words 'true' and 'false' as we should apply them to this particular belief, is that it may be doubted whether when we say that the belief is 'true' or 'false', these properties of 'corresponding to a fact' and 'not corresponding to a fact' are the properties which we actually *have before our minds* and express by those words. This is a question which can only be settled by actual inspection; and I admit that it is difficult to be quite sure what result the inspection yields. But I see no reason for answering it in the negative. I see no reason why when we say: The belief that I have gone away is true, the thought which we actually have before our minds and express by these words should *not* be the thought that: The belief in question does correspond to a fact—similarly I see no reason why when we say 'The belief that I have gone away is false' the thought which we actually have before our minds and express by these words should *not* be the thought that the belief in question does *not* correspond to any fact. However, whether *this* is so or not—whether to say that this belief is true is or is not quite strictly the *same* thing as to say that it does correspond to a fact; it is, I think, quite certain that the two expressions are strictly equivalent. When the belief is true, it certainly does correspond to a fact; and when it corresponds to a fact it certainly is true. And similarly when it is false, it certainly does not correspond to any fact; and when it does not correspond to any fact, then certainly it is false.

I want to suggest, therefore, that these definitions really are correct definitions at least of *one* common sense of the words 'true' and 'false': of the sense in which we use the words when we apply them to beliefs such as the one I have taken as an instance. And the only thing that is new about these definitions, so far as I know, is that they assign a perfectly strict and definite sense to the word 'correspondence'; they define this word by pointing out *the* relation for which it stands; namely *the* relation which certainly does hold between the belief that 'I have gone away', if that belief is true, and the *fact* that I have gone away, and which does *not* hold between that precise belief and any other fact. That there *is* such a relation, seems to me clear; and all that is new about my definitions is that they concentrate attention upon just *that* relation, and make *it* the essential point in the definitions of truth and falsehood. The use of the word 'correspondence' as a name for this relation may perhaps be misleading; and so may the word I used instead last time—the word 'referring to'. Both these words may lead you to think that the relation in question is similar to or identical with other relations that are called by the same names on other occasions. And I am particularly anxious not to suggest either that this relation is identical with or similar to any other relation or that it is not: I don't want to pronounce upon that point at all. I don't want, therefore, to insist upon the word 'correspondence'. The essential point is to concentrate attention upon the relation *itself*: to hold it before your mind, in the sense in which when I name the colour 'vermilion', you can hold before your mind the colour that I mean. If you are not acquainted with this relation in the same sort of way as you are acquainted with the colour vermilion, no amount of words will serve to explain what it is, any more than they could explain what vermilion is like to a man born blind. But, if I am right then we are all acquainted with the relation in question; and, if so, then the important point is that it is this relation itself, and not any words by which we may try to name it or to point it out, that is essential to the definition of truth and falsehood.

Source: Some Main Problems of Philosophy (Allen & Unwin), Chs. 3, 14, 15. (Extracts.)

30 Truth and Proof (1969)

ALFRED TARSKI

The subject of this article is an old one. It has been frequently discussed in modern logical and philosophical literature, and it would not be easy to contribute anything original to the discussion. To many readers, I am afraid, none of the ideas put forward in the article will appear essentially novel; nonetheless, I hope they may find some interest in the way the material has been arranged and knitted together.

As the title indicates, I wish to discuss here two different though related notions: the notion of truth and the notion of proof. Actually the article is divided into three sections. The first section is concerned exclusively with the notion of truth, the second deals primarily with the notion of proof, and the third is a discussion of the relationship between these two notions.

The Notion of Truth

The task of explaining the meaning of the term 'true' will be interpreted here in a restricted way. The notion of truth occurs in many different contexts, and there are several distinct categories of objects to which the term 'true' is applied. In a psychological discussion one might speak of true emotions as well as true beliefs; in a discourse from the domain of esthetics the inner truth of an object of art might be analyzed. In this article, however, we are interested only in what might be called the logical notion of truth. More specifically, we concern ourselves exclusively with the meaning of the term 'true' when this term is used to refer to sentences. Presumably this was the original use of the term 'true' in human language. Sentences are treated here as linguistic objects, as certain strings of sounds or written signs. (Of course, not every such string is a sentence.) Moreover, when speaking of sentences, we shall always have in mind what are called in grammar declarative sentences, and not interrogative or imperative sentences.

Whenever one explains the meaning of any term drawn from everyday language, he should bear in mind that the goal and the logical status of such an explanation may vary from one case to another. For instance, the explanation may be intended as an account of the actual use of the term involved, and is thus subject to questioning whether the account is indeed correct. At some other time an explanation may be of a normative nature, that is, it may be offered as a suggestion that the term be used in some definite way, without claiming that the suggestion conforms to the way in which the term is actually used; such an explanation can be evaluated, for instance, from the point of view of its usefulness but not of its correctness. Some further alternatives could also be listed.

The explanation we wish to give in the present case is, to an extent, of mixed character. What will be offered can be treated in principle as a suggestion for a definite way of using the term 'true', but the offering will be accompanied by the belief that it is in agreement with the prevailing usage of this term in everyday language.

Our understanding of the notion of truth seems to agree essentially with various explanations of this notion that have been given in philosophical literature. What may be the earliest explanation can be found in Aristotle's *Metaphysics*:

> To say of what is that it is not, or of what is not that it is, is false, while to say of what is that it is, or of what is not that it is not, is true.

Here and in the subsequent discussion the word 'false' means the same as the expression 'not true' and can be replaced by the latter.

The intuitive content of Aristotle's formulation appears to be rather clear. Nevertheless, the formulation leaves much to be desired from the point of view of precision and formal correctness. For one thing, it is not general enough; it refers only to sentences that 'say' about something 'that it is' or 'that it is not'; in most cases it would hardly be possible to cast a sentence in this mold without slanting the sense of the sentence and forcing the spirit of the language. This is perhaps one of the reasons why in modern philosophy various substitutes for the Aristotelian formulation have been offered. As examples we quote the following:

> A sentence is true if it denotes the existing state of affairs.

> The truth of a sentence consists in its conformity with (or correspondence to) the reality.

Due to the use of technical philosophical terms these formulations have undoubtedly a very 'scholarly' sound. Nonetheless, it is my feeling that the new formulations, when analyzed more closely, prove to be less clear and unequivocal than the one put forward by Aristotle.

The conception of truth that found its expression in the Aristotelian formulation (and in related formulations of more recent origin) is usually referred to as the *classical*, or *semantic conception of truth*. By semantics we mean the part of logic that, loosely speaking, discusses the relations between linguistic objects (such as sentences) and what is expressed by these objects. The semantic character of the term 'true' is clearly revealed by the explanation offered by Aristotle and by some formulations that will be given later in this article. One speaks sometimes of the correspondence theory of truth as the theory based on the classical conception.

(In modern philosophical literature some other conceptions and theories of truth are also discussed, such as the pragmatic conception and the coherence theory. These conceptions seem to be of an exclusively normative character and have little connection with the actual usage of the term 'true'; none of them has been formulated so far with any degree of clarity and precision. They will not be discussed in the present article.)

We shall attempt to obtain here a more precise explanation of the classical conception of truth, one that could supersede the Aristotelian formulation while preserving its basic intentions. To this end we shall have to resort to some techniques of contemporary logic. We shall also have to specify the language whose sentences we are concerned with; this is necessary if only for the reason that a string of sounds or signs, which is a true or a false sentence but at any rate a meaningful sentence in one language, may be a meaningless expression in another. For the time being let us assume that the language with which we are concerned is the common English language.

We begin with a simple problem. Consider a sentence in English whose meaning does not raise any doubts, say the sentence 'snow is white'. For brevity we denote this sentence by 'S', so that 'S' becomes the name of the sentence. We ask ourselves the question: What do we mean by saying that S is true or that it is false? The answer to this question is simple: in the spirit of Aristotelian explanation, by saying that S is true we mean simply that snow is white, and by saying that S is false we mean that snow is not white. By eliminating the symbol 'S' we arrive at the following formulations:

(1) 'snow is white' is true if and only if snow is white.
(1′) 'snow is white' is false if and only if snow is not white.

Thus (1) and (1′) provide satisfactory explanations of the meaning of the terms 'true' and 'false' when these terms are referred to the sentence 'snow is white'. We can regard (1) and (1') as partial definitions of the terms 'true' and 'false', in fact, as definitions of these terms with respect to a particular sentence. Notice that (1), as well as (1'), has the form prescribed for definitions by the rules of logic, namely the form of logical equivalence. It consists of two parts, the left and the right side of the equivalence, combined by the connective 'if and only if'. The left side is the definiendum, the phrase whose meaning is explained by the definition; the right side is the definiens, the phrase that provides the explanation. In the present case the definiendum is the following expression:

'snow is white' is true;

the definiens has the form:

snow is white.

It might seem at first sight that (1), when regarded as a definition, exhibits an essential flaw widely discussed in traditional logic as a vicious circle. The reason is that certain words, for example 'snow', occur in both the definiens and the definiendum. Actually, however, these occurrences have an entirely different character. The word 'snow' is a syntactical, or organic, part of the definiens; in fact the definiens is a sentence, and the word 'snow' is its subject. The definiendum is also a sentence; it expresses the fact that the definiens is a true sentence. Its subject is a name of the definiens formed by putting the definiens in quotes. (When saying something of an object, one always uses a name of this object and not the object itself, even when dealing with linguistic objects.) For several reasons an expression enclosed in quotes must be treated grammatically as a single word having no syntactical parts. Hence the word 'snow', which undoubtedly occurs in the definiendum as a part, does not occur there as a syntactical part. A medieval logician would say that 'snow' occurs in the definiens *in suppositione formalis* and in the definiendum *in suppositione materialis*. However, words which are not syntactical parts of the definiendum cannot create a vicious circle, and the danger of a vicious circle vanishes.

The preceding remarks touch on some questions which are rather subtle and not quite simple from the logical point of view. Instead of elaborating on them, I shall indicate another manner in which any fears of a vicious circle can be dispelled. In formulating (1) we have applied a common method of forming a name of a sentence, or of any other expression, which consists in putting the expression in quotes. The method has many virtues, but it is also the source of the difficulties discussed above. To remove these difficulties let us try another method of forming names of expressions, in fact a method that can be characterized as a letter-by-letter description of an expression. Using this method we obtain instead of (1) the following lengthy formulations:

(2) The string of three words, the first of which is the string of the letters Es, En, O and Double-U, the second is the string of letters I and Es, and the third is the string of the letters Double-U, Aitch, I, Te, and E, is a true sentence if and only if snow is white.

Formulation (2) does not differ from (1) in its meaning; (1) can simply be regarded as an abbreviated form of (2). The new formulation is certainly much less perspicuous than the old one, but it has the advantage that it creates no appearance of a vicious circle.

Partial definitions of truth analogous to (1) (or (2)) can be constructed for other sentences as well. Each of these definitions has the form:

(3) '*p*' is true if and only if *p*,

where '*p*' is to be replaced on both sides of (3) by the sentence for which the definition is constructed. Special attention should be paid, however, to those situations in which the sentence put in place of '*p*' happens to contain the word 'true' as a syntactical part. The corresponding equivalence (3) cannot then be viewed as a partial definition of truth since, when treated as such, it would obviously exhibit a vicious circle. Even in this case, however, (3) is a meaningful sentence, and it is actually a true sentence from the point of view of the classical conception of truth. For illustration, imagine that in a review of a book one finds the following sentence:

(4) Not every sentence in this book is true.

By applying to (4) the Aristotelian criterion, we see that the sentence (4) is true if, in fact, not every sentence in the book concerned is true, and that (4) is false otherwise; in other words, we can assert the equivalence obtained from (3) by taking (4) for '*p*'. Of course, this equivalence states merely the conditions under which the sentence (4) is true or is not true, but by itself the equivalence does not enable us to decide which is actually the case. To verify the judgment expressed in (4) one would have to read attentively the book reviewed and analyze the truth of the sentences contained in it.

In the light of the preceding discussion we can now reformulate our main problem. We stipulate that the use of the term 'true' in its reference to sentences in English then and only then conforms with the classical conception of truth if it enables us to ascertain every equivalence of the form (3) in which 'p' is replaced on both sides by an arbitrary English sentence. If this condition is satisfied, we shall say simply that the use of the term 'true' is adequate. Thus our main problem is: can we establish an adequate use of the term 'true' for sentences in English and, if so, then by what methods? We can, of course, raise an analogous question for sentences in any other language.

The problem will be solved completely if we manage to construct a general definition of truth that will be adequate in the sense that it will carry with it as logical consequences all the equivalences of form (3). If such a definition is accepted by English-speaking people, it will obviously establish an adequate use of the term 'true'.

Under certain special assumptions the construction of a general definition of truth is easy. Assume, in fact, that we are interested, not in the whole common English language, but only in a fragment of it, and that we wish to define the term 'true' exclusively in reference to sentences of the fragmentary language; we shall refer to this fragmentary language as the language L. Assume further that L is provided with precise syntactical rules which enable us, in each particular case, to distinguish a sentence from an expression which is not a sentence, and that the number of all sentences in the language L is finite (though possibly very large). Assume, finally, that the word 'true' does not occur in L and that the meaning of all words in L is sufficiently clear, so that we have no objection to using them in defining truth. Under these assumptions proceed as follows. First, prepare a complete list of all sentences in L; suppose, for example, that there are exactly 1,000 sentences in L, and agree to use the symbols 's_1', 's_2', . . . , '$s_{1,000}$' as abbreviations for consecutive sentences on the list. Next, for each of the sentences 's_1', 's_2', . . . , '$s_{1,000}$' construct a partial definition of truth by substituting successively these sentences for 'p' on both sides of the schema (3). Finally, form the logical conjunction of all these partial definitions; in other words, combine them in one statement by putting the connective 'and' between any two consecutive partial definitions. The only thing that remains to be done is to give the resulting conjunction a different, but logically equivalent, form, so as to satisfy formal requirements imposed on definitions by rules of logic:

(5) For every sentence x (in the language L), x is true if and only if either
s_1, and x is identical to 's_1',
or
s_2, and x is identical to 's_2',
....
....
or finally,
$s_{1,000}$, and x is identical to
'$s_{1,000}$'.

We have thus arrived at a statement which can indeed be accepted as the desired general definition of truth: it is formally correct and is adequate in the sense that it implies all the equivalences of the form (3) in which 'p' has been replaced by any sentence of the language L. We notice in passing that (5) is a sentence in English but obviously not in the language L; since (5) contains all sentences in L as proper parts, it cannot coincide with any of them. Further discussion will throw more light on this point.

For obvious reasons the procedure just outlined cannot be followed if we are interested in the whole of the English language and not merely in a fragment of it. When trying to prepare a complete list of English sentences, we meet from the start the difficulty that the rules of English grammar do not determine precisely the form of expressions (strings of words) which should be regarded as sentences: a particular expression, say an exclamation, may function as a sentence in some given context, whereas an expression of the same form will not function so in some other context. Furthermore, the set of all sentences in English is, potentially at least, infinite. Although it is certainly true that only a finite number of sentences have been formulated in speech and writing by human beings up to the present moment, probably nobody would agree that the list of all these sentences comprehends all sentences in English. On the contrary, it seems likely that on seeing such a list each of us could easily produce an English sentence which is not on the list. Finally, the fact that the word 'true' does occur in English prevents by itself an application of the procedure previously described.

From these remarks it does not follow that the desired definition of truth for arbitrary sentences in English cannot be obtained in some other way, possibly by using a different idea. There is, however, a more serious and fundamental reason that seems to preclude this possibility. More than that, the mere supposition that an adequate use of the term 'true' (in its reference to arbitrary sentences in English) has been secured by any method whatsoever appears to lead to a contradiction. The simplest argument that provides such a contradiction is known as the *antinomy of the liar*; it will be carried through in the next few lines.

Consider the following sentence:

(6) The sentence numbered (6) on page 269 of *Fundamental Problems in Philosophy* is false.*

Let us agree to use '*s*' as an abbreviation for this sentence. Looking at the title of this book, and the number of this page, we easily check that '*s*' is just the only sentence numbered (6) on page 269 of *Fundamental Problems in Philosophy*. Hence it follows, in particular, that

(7) '*s*' is false if and only if the sentence numbered (6) on page 269 of *Fundamental Problems in Philosophy* is false.

On the other hand, '*s*' is undoubtedly a sentence in English. Therefore, assuming that our use of the term 'true' is adequate, we can assert the equivalence (3) in which '*p*' is replaced by '*s*'. Thus we can state:

(8) '*s*' is true if and only if *s*.

We now recall that '*s*' stands for the whole sentence (6). Hence we can replace '*s*' by (6) on the right side of (8); we then obtain

(9) '*s*' is true if and only if the sentence numbered (6) on page 269 of *Fundamental Problems in Philosophy* is false.

By now comparing (8) and (9), we conclude:

(10) '*s*' is false if and only if '*s*' is true.

This leads to an obvious contradiction: '*s*' proves to be both true and false. Thus we are confronted with an antinomy. The above

* Tarski's original example was: 'The sentence printed in red on page 65 of the June 1969 issue of *Scientific American* is false.'—Ed.

formulation of the antinomy of the liar is due to the Polish logician Jan Łukasiewicz.

Some more involved formulations of this antinomy are also known. Imagine, for instance, a book of 100 pages, with just one sentence printed on each page. On page 1 we read:

The sentence printed on page 2 of this book is true.

On page 2 we read:

The sentence printed on page 3 of this book is true.

And so it goes on up to page 99. However, on page 100, the last page of the book, we find:

The sentence printed on page 1 of this book is false.

Assume that the sentence printed on page 1 is indeed false. By means of an argument which is not difficult but is very long and requires leafing through the entire book, we conclude that our assumption is wrong. Consequently we assume now that the sentence printed on page 1 is true—and, by an argument which is as easy and as long as the original one, we convince ourselves that the new assumption is wrong as well. Thus we are again confronted with an antinomy.

It turns out to be an easy matter to compose many other 'antinomial books' that are variants of the one just described. Each of them has 100 pages. Every page contains just one sentence, and in fact a sentence of the form:

The sentence printed on page *00* of this book is *XX*.

In each particular case '*XX*' is replaced by one of the words '*true*' or '*false*', while '*00*' is replaced by one of the numerals '1', '2', . . . , '100'; the same numeral may occur on many pages. Not every variant of the original book composed according to these rules actually yields an antinomy. The reader who is fond of logical puzzles will hardly find it difficult to describe all those variants that do the job. The following warning may prove useful in this connection. Imagine that somewhere in the book, say on page 1, it is said that the sentence on page 3 is true, while somewhere else, say on page 2, it is claimed that the same sentence is false. From this information it does not follow at all that our book is 'antinomial'; we can only draw the conclusion that either the sentence on page 1 or the sentence on page 2 must be false. An antinomy does arise, however, whenever we are able to show that one of the sentences in the book is both true and false, independent of any assumptions concerning the truth or falsity of the remaining sentences.

The antinomy of the liar is of very old origin. It is usually ascribed to the Greek logician Eubulides; it tormented many ancient logicians and caused the premature death of at least one of them, Philetas of Cos. A number of other antinomies and paradoxes were found in antiquity, in the Middle Ages, and in modern times. Although many of them are now entirely forgotten, the antinomy of the liar is still analyzed and discussed in contemporary writings. Together with some recent antinomies discovered around the turn of the century (in particular, the antinomy of Russell), it has had a great impact on the development of modern logic.

Two diametrically opposed approaches to antinomies can be found in the literature of the subject. One approach is to disregard them, to treat them as sophistries, as jokes that are not serious but malicious, and that aim mainly at showing the cleverness of the man who formulates them. The opposite approach is characteristic of certain thinkers of the nineteenth century and is still represented, or was so a short while ago, in certain parts of our globe. According to this approach antinomies constitute a very essential element of human thought; they must appear again and again in intellectual activities, and their presence is the basic source of real progress. As often happens, the truth is probably somewhere in between. Personally, as a logician, I could not reconcile myself with antinomies as a permanent element of our system of knowledge. However, I am not the least inclined to treat antinomies lightly. The appearance of an antinomy is for me a symptom of disease. Starting with premises that seem intuitively obvious, using forms of reasoning that seem intuitively certain, an antinomy leads us to nonsense, a contradiction. Whenever this happens, we have to submit our ways of thinking to a thorough revision, to reject some premises in which we believed or to improve some forms of argument which we used. We do this with the hope not only that the old antinomy will be disposed of but also that no new one will appear. To this end we test our reformed system of thinking by all available means, and, first of all, we try to reconstruct the old antinomy in the new setting; this testing is a very important activity in the realm of speculative thought, akin to carrying out crucial experiments in empirical science.

From this point of view consider now specifically the antinomy of the liar. The antinomy involves the notion of truth in reference to arbitrary sentences of common English; it could easily be reformulated so as to apply to other natural languages. We are confronted with a serious problem: how can we avoid the contradictions induced by this antinomy? A radical solution of the problem which may readily occur to us would be simply to remove the word 'true' from the English vocabulary or at least to abstain from using it in any serious discussion.

Those people to whom such an amputation of English seems highly unsatisfactory and illegitimate may be inclined to accept a somewhat more compromising solution, which consists in adopting what could be called (following the contemporary Polish philosopher Tadeusz Kotarbiński) 'the nihilistic approach to the theory of truth'. According to this approach, the word 'true' has no independent meaning but can be used as a component of the two meaningful expressions 'it is true that' and 'it is not true that'. These expressions are thus treated as if they were single words with no organic parts. The meaning ascribed to them is such that they can be immediately eliminated from any sentence in which they occur. For instance, instead of saying

> it is true that all cats are black

we can simply say

> all cats are black,

and instead of

> it is not true that all cats are black

we can say

> not all cats are black.

In other contexts the word 'true' is meaningless. In particular, it cannot be used as a real predicate qualifying names of sentences. Employing the terminology of medieval logic, we can say that the word 'true' can be used syncategorematically in some special situations, but it cannot ever be used categorematically.

To realize the implications of this approach, consider the sentence which was the starting point for the antinomy of the liar; that is, the sentence numbered (6) on page 269 of this book. From the 'nihilistic' point of view it is not a meaningful sentence, and the antinomy simply vanishes. Unfortunately, many uses of the word 'true', which otherwise seem quite legitimate and reasonable, are similarly affected by this approach. Imagine, for instance, that a certain term occurring repeatedly in the works of an ancient mathematician admits of several interpretations. A historian of science who studies the works arrives at the conclusion that under one of these interpretations all the theorems stated by the mathematician prove to be true; this leads him naturally to the conjecture that the same will apply to any work of this mathematician that is not known at present but may be discovered in the future. If, however, the historian of science shares the 'nihilistic' approach to the notion of truth, he lacks the possibility of expressing his conjecture in words. One could say that truth-theoretical 'nihilism' pays lip service to some popular forms of human speech, while actually removing the notion of truth from the conceptual stock of the human mind.

We shall look, therefore, for another way out of our predicament. We shall try to find a solution that will keep the classical concept of truth essentially intact. The applicability of the notion of truth will have to undergo some restrictions, but the notion will remain available at least for the purpose of scholarly discourse.

To this end we have to analyze those features of the common language that are the real source of the antinomy of the liar. When carrying through this analysis, we notice at once an outstanding feature of this language—its all-comprehensive, universal character. The common language is universal and is intended to be so. It is supposed to provide adequate facilities for expressing everything that can be expressed at all, in any language whatsoever; it is continually expanding to satisfy this requirement. In particular, it is semantically universal in the following sense. Together with the linguistic objects, such as sentences and terms, which are components of this language, names of these objects are also included in the language (as we know, names of expressions can be obtained by putting the expressions in quotes); in addition, the language contains semantic terms such as 'truth', 'name', 'designation', which directly or indirectly refer to the relationship between linguistic objects and what is expressed by them. Consequently, for every sentence formulated in the common language, we can form in the same language another sentence to the effect that the first sentence is true or that it is false. Using an additional 'trick' we can even construct in the language what is sometimes called a self-referential sentence, that is, a sentence S which asserts the fact that S itself is true or that it is false. In case S asserts its own falsity we can show by means of a simple argument that S is both true and false—and we are confronted again with the antinomy of the liar.

There is, however, no need to use universal languages in all possible situations. In particular, such languages are in general not needed for the purposes of science (and by science I mean here the whole realm of intellectual inquiry). In a particular branch of science, say in chemistry, one discusses certain special objects, such as elements, molecules, and so on, but not for instance linguistic objects such as sentences or terms. The language that is well adapted to this discussion is a restricted language with a limited vocabulary; it must contain names of chemical objects, terms such as 'element' and 'molecule', but not names of linguistic objects; hence it does not have to be semantically universal. The same applies to most of the other branches of science. The situation becomes somewhat confused when we turn to linguistics. This is a science in which we study languages; thus the language of linguistics must certainly be provided with names of linguistic objects. However, we do not have to identify the language of linguistics with the universal language or any of the languages that are objects of linguistic discussion, and we are not bound to assume that we use in linguistics one and the same language for all discussions. The language of linguistics has to contain the names of linguistic components of the languages discussed but not the names of its own components; thus, again, it does not have to be semantically universal. The same applies to the language of logic, or rather of that part of logic known as metalogic and metamathematics; here we again concern ourselves with certain languages, primarily with languages of logical and mathematical theories (although we discuss these languages from a different point of view than in the case of linguistics).

The question now arises whether the notion of truth can be precisely defined, and thus a consistent and adequate usage of this notion can be established at least for the semantically restricted languages of scientific discourse. Under certain conditions the answer to this question proves to be affirmative. The main conditions imposed on the language are that its full vocabulary should be available and its syntactical rules concerning the formation of sentences and other meaningful expressions from words listed in the vocabulary should be precisely formulated. Furthermore, the syntactical rules should be purely formal, that is, they should refer exclusively to the form (the shape) of expressions; the function and the meaning of an expression should depend exclusively on its form. In particular, looking at an expression, one should be able in each case to decide whether or not the expression is a sentence. It should never happen that an expression functions as a sentence at one place while an expression of the same form does not function so at some other place, or that a sentence can be asserted in one context while a sentence of the same form can be denied in another. (Hence it follows, in particular, that demonstrative pronouns and adverbs such as 'this' and 'here' should not occur in the vocabulary of the language.) Languages that satisfy these conditions are referred to as formalized languages. When discussing a formalized language there is no need to distinguish between expressions of the same form which have been written or uttered in different places; one often speaks of them as if they were one and the same expression. The reader may have noticed we sometimes use this way of speaking even when discussing a natural language, that is, one which is not formalized; we do so for the sake of simplicity, and only in those cases in which there seems to be no danger of confusion.

Formalized languages are fully adequate for the presentation of logical and mathematical theories; I see no essential reasons why they cannot be adapted for use in other scientific disciplines and in particular to the development of theoretical parts of empirical sciences. I should like to emphasize that, when using the term 'formalized languages', I do not refer exclusively to linguistic systems that are formulated entirely in symbols, and I do not have in mind anything essentially opposed to natural languages. On the contrary, the only formalized languages that seem to be of real interest are those which are fragments of natural languages (fragments provided with complete vocabularies and precise syntactical rules) or those which can at least be adequately translated into natural languages.

There are some further conditions on which the realization of our program depends. We should make a strict distinction between the language which is the object of our discussion and for which in particular we intend to construct the definition of truth, and the language in which the definition is to be formulated and its implications are to be studied. The latter is referred to as the metalanguage and the former as the object-language. The metalanguage must be sufficiently rich; in particular, it must include the object-language as a part. In fact, according to our stipulations, an adequate definition of truth will imply as consequences all partial definitions of this notion, that is, all equivalences of form (3):

'*p*' is true if and only if *p*,

where '*p*' is to be replaced (on both sides of the equivalence) by an arbitrary sentence of the object-language. Since all these consequences are formulated in the metalanguage, we conclude that every sentence of the object-language must also be a sentence of the metalanguage. Furthermore, the metalanguage must contain names for sentences (and other expressions) of the object-language, since these names occur on the left sides of the above equivalences. It must also contain some further terms that are needed for the discussion of the object-language, in fact terms denoting certain special sets of expressions, relations between expressions, and operations on expressions; for instance, we must be able to speak of the set of all sentences or of the operation of juxtaposition, by means of which, putting one of two given expressions immediately after the other, we form a new expression. Finally, by defining truth, we show that semantic terms (expressing relations between sentences of the object-language and objects referred to by these sentences) can be introduced in the metalanguage by means of definitions. Hence we conclude that the metalanguage which provides sufficient means for defining truth must be essentially richer than the object-language; it cannot coincide with or be translatable into the latter, since otherwise both languages would turn out to be semantically universal, and the antinomy of the liar could be reconstructed in both of them. We shall return to this question in the last section of this article.

If all the above conditions are satisfied, the construction of the desired definition of truth presents no essential difficulties. Technically, however, it is too involved to be explained here in detail. For any given sentence of the object-language one can easily formulate the corresponding partial definition of form (3). Since, however, the set of all sentences in the object-language is as a rule infinite, whereas every sentence of the metalanguage is a finite string of signs, we cannot arrive at a general definition simply by forming the logical conjunction of all partial definitions. Nevertheless, what we eventually obtain is in some intuitive sense equivalent to the imaginary infinite conjunction. Very roughly speaking, we proceed as follows. First, we consider the simplest sentences, which do not include any other sentences as parts; for these simplest sentences we manage to define truth directly (using the same idea that leads to partial definitions). Then, making use of syntactical rules which concern the formation of more complicated sentences from simpler ones, we extend the definition to arbitrary compound sentences; we apply here the method known in mathematics as definition by recursion. (This is merely a rough approximation of the actual procedure. For some technical reasons the method of recursion is actually applied to define, not the notion of truth, but the related semantic notion of satisfaction. Truth is then easily defined in terms of satisfaction.)

On the basis of the definition thus constructed we can develop the entire theory of truth. In particular, we can derive from it, in addition to all equivalences of form (3), some consequences of a general nature, such as the famous laws of contradiction and of excluded middle. By the first of these laws, no two sentences one of which is the negation of the other can both be true; by the second law, no two such sentences can both be false.

The Notion of Proof

Whatever may be achieved by constructing an adequate definition of truth for a scientific language, one fact seems to be certain: the definition does not carry with it a workable criterion for deciding whether particular sentences in this language are true or false (and indeed it is not designed at all for this purpose). Consider, for example, a sentence in the language of elementary high school geometry, say 'the three bisectors of every triangle meet in one point'. If we are interested in the question whether this sentence is true and we turn to the definition of truth for an answer, we are in for a disappointment. The only bit of information we get is that the sentence is true if the three bisectors of a triangle always meet in one point, and is false if they do not always meet; but only a geometrical inquiry may enable us to decide which is actually the case. Analogous remarks apply to sentences from the domain of any other particular science: to decide whether or not any such sentence is true is a task of the science itself, and not of logic or the theory of truth.

Some philosophers and methodologists of science are inclined to reject every definition that does not provide a criterion for deciding whether any given particular object falls under the notion defined or not. In the methodology of empirical sciences such a tendency is represented by the doctrine of operationalism; philosophers of mathematics who belong to the constructivist school seem to exhibit a similar tendency. In both cases, however, the people who hold this opinion appear to be in a small minority. A consistent attempt to carry out the program in practice (that is, to develop a science without using undesirable definitions) has hardly ever been made. It seems clear that under this program much of contemporary mathematics would disappear, and theoretical parts of physics, chemistry, biology, and other empirical sciences would be severely mutilated. The definitions of such notions as atom or gene as well as most definitions in mathematics do not carry with them any criteria for deciding whether or not an object falls under the term that has been defined.

Since the definition of truth does not provide us with any such criterion and at the same time the search for truth is rightly considered the essence of scientific activities, it appears as an important problem to find at least partial criteria of truth and to develop procedures that may enable us to ascertain or negate the truth (or at least the likelihood of truth) of as many sentences as possible. Such procedures are known indeed; some of them are used exclusively in empirical science and some primarily in deductive science. The notion of proof—the second notion to be discussed in this paper—refers just to a procedure of ascertaining the truth of sentences which is employed primarily in deductive science. This procedure is an essential element of what is known as the axiomatic method, the only method now used to develop mathematical disciplines.

The axiomatic method and the notion of proof within its framework are products of a long historical development. Some rough knowledge of this development is probably essential for the understanding of the contemporary notion of proof.

Originally a mathematical discipline was an aggregate of sentences that concerned a certain class of objects or phenomena, were formulated by means of a certain stock of terms, and were accepted as true. This aggregate of sentences lacked any structural order. A sentence was accepted as true either because it seemed intuitively evident, or else because it was proved on the basis of some intuitively evident sentences, and thus was shown, by means of an intuitively certain argument, to be a consequence of these other sentences. The criterion of intuitive evidence (and intuitive certainty of arguments) was applied without any restrictions; every sentence recognized as true by means of this criterion was automatically included in the discipline. This description seems to fit, for instance, the science of geometry as it was known to ancient Egyptians and Greeks in its early, pre-Euclidean stage.

It was realized rather soon, however, that the criterion of intuitive evidence is far from being infallible, has no objective character, and often leads to serious errors. The entire subsequent development of the axiomatic method can be viewed as an expression of the tendency to restrict the recourse to intuitive evidence.

This tendency first revealed itself in the effort to prove as many sentences as possible, and hence to restrict as much as possible the number of sentences accepted as true merely on the basis of intuitive evidence. The ideal from this point of view would be to prove every sentence that is to be accepted as true. For obvious reasons this ideal cannot be realized. Indeed, we prove each sentence on the basis of other sentences, we prove these other sentences on the basis of some further sentences, and so on: if we are to avoid both a vicious circle and an infinite regress, the procedure must be discontinued somewhere. As a compromise between that unattainable ideal and the realizable possibilities, two principles emerged and were subsequently applied in constructing mathematical disciplines. By the first of these principles every discipline begins with a list of a small number of sentences, called axioms or primitive sentences, which seem to be intuitively evident and which are recognized as true without any further justification. According to the second principle, no other sentence is accepted in the discipline as true unless we are able to prove it with the exclusive help of axioms and those sentences that were previously proved. All the sentences that can be recognized as true by virtue of these two principles are called theorems, or provable sentences, of the given discipline. Two analogous principles concern the use of terms in constructing the discipline. By the first of them we list at the beginning a few terms, called undefined or primitive terms, which appear to be directly understandable and which we decide to use (in formulating and proving theorems) without explaining their meanings; by the second principle we agree not to use any further term unless we are able to explain its meaning by defining it with the help of undefined terms and terms previously defined. These four principles are cornerstones of the axiomatic method; theories developed in accordance with these principles are called axiomatic theories.

As is well known, the axiomatic method was applied to the development of geometry in the *Elements* of Euclid about 300 B.C. Thereafter it was used for over 2,000 years with practically no change in its main principles (which, by the way, were not even explicitly formulated for a long period of time) nor in the general approach to the subject. However, in the nineteenth and twentieth centuries the concept of the axiomatic method did undergo a profound evolution. Those features of the evolution which concern the notion of proof are particularly significant for our discussion.

Until the last years of the nineteenth century the notion of proof was primarily of a psychological character. A proof was an intellectual activity that aimed at convincing oneself and others of the truth of a sentence discussed; more specifically, in developing a mathematical theory proofs were used to convince ourselves and others that a sentence discussed had to be accepted as true once some other sentences had been previously accepted as such. No restrictions were put on arguments used in proofs, except that they had to be intuitively convincing. At a certain period, however, a need began to be felt for submitting the notion of proof to a deeper analysis that would result in restricting the recourse to intuitive evidence in this context as well. This was probably related to some specific developments in mathematics, in particular to the discovery of non-Euclidean geometries. The analysis was carried out by logicians, beginning with the German logician Gottlob Frege; it led to the introduction of a new notion, that of a *formal proof*, which turned out to be an adequate substitute and an essential improvement over the old psychological notion.

The first step toward supplying a mathematical theory with the notion of a formal proof is the formalization of the language of the theory, in the sense discussed previously in connection with the definition of truth. Thus formal syntactical rules are provided which in particular enable us simply by looking at shapes of expressions, to distinguish a sentence from an expression that is not a sentence. The next step consists in formulating a few rules of a different nature, the so-called rules of proof (or of inference). By these rules a sentence is regarded as directly derivable from given sentences if, generally speaking, its shape is related in a prescribed manner to the shapes of given sentences. The number of rules of proof is small, and their content is simple. Just like the syntactical rules, they all have a formal character, that is, they refer exclusively to shapes of sentences involved. Intuitively all the rules of derivation appear to be infallible, in the sense that a sentence which is directly derivable from true sentences by any of these rules must be true itself. Actually the infallibility of the rules of proof can be established on the basis of an adequate definition of truth. The best-known and most important example of a rule of proof is the rule of detachment known also as *modus ponens*. By this rule (which in some theories serves as the only rule of proof) a sentence 'q' is directly derivable from two given sentences if one of them is the conditional sentence 'if p, then q' while the other is 'p'; here 'p' and 'q' are, as usual, abbreviations of any two sentences of our formalized language. We can now explain in what a formal proof of a given sentence consists. First, we apply the rules of proof to axioms and obtain new sentences that are directly derivable from axioms; next, we apply the same rules to new sentences, or jointly to new sentences and axioms, and obtain further sentences; and we continue this process. If after a finite number of steps we arrive at a given sentence, we say that the sentence has been formally proved. This can also be expressed more precisely in the following way: a formal proof of a given sentence consists in constructing a finite sequence of sentences such that (1) the first sentence in the sequence is an axiom, (2) each of the following sentences either is an axiom or is directly derivable from some of the sentences that precede it in the sequence, by virtue of one of the rules of proof, and (3) the last sentence in the sequence is the sentence to be proved. Changing somewhat the use of the term 'proof', we can even say that a formal proof of a sentence is simply any finite sequence of sentences with the three properties just listed.

An axiomatic theory whose language has been formalized and for which the notion of a formal proof has been supplied is called a formalized theory. We stipulate that the only proofs which can be used in a formalized theory are formal proofs; no sentence can be accepted as a theorem unless it appears on the list of axioms or a formal proof can be found for it. The method of presenting a formalized theory at each stage of its development is in principle very elementary. We list first the axioms and then all the known theorems in such an order that every sentence on the list which is not an axiom can be directly recognized as a theorem, simply by comparing its shape with the shapes of sentences that precede it on the list; no complex processes of reasoning and convincing are involved. (I am not speaking here of psychological processes by means of which the theorems have actually been discovered.) The recourse to intuitive evidence has been indeed considerably re-stricted; doubts concerning the truth of theorems have not been entirely eliminated but have been reduced to possible doubts concerning the truth of the few sentences listed as axioms and the infallibility of the few simple rules of proof. It may be added that the process of introducing new terms in the language of a theory can also be formalized by supplying special formal rules of definitions.

It is now known that all the existing mathematical disciplines can be presented as formalized theories. Formal proofs can be provided for the deepest and most complicated mathematical theorems, which were originally established by intuitive argu-ments.

The Relationship of Truth and Proof

It was undoubtedly a great achievement of modern logic to have replaced the old psychological notion of proof, which could hardly ever be made clear and precise, by a new simple notion of a purely formal character. But the triumph of the formal method carried with it the germ of a future setback. As we shall see, the very simplicity of the new notion turned out to be its Achilles heel.

To assess the notion of formal proof we have to clarify its relation to the notion of truth. After all, the formal proof, just like the old intuitive proof, is a procedure aimed at acquiring new true sentences. Such a procedure will be adequate only if all sentences acquired with its help prove to be true and all true sentences can be acquired with its help. Hence the problem naturally arises: is the formal proof actually an adequate pro-cedure for acquiring truth? In other words: does the set of all (formally) provable sentences coincide with the set of all true sentences?

To be specific, we refer this problem to a particular, very elementary mathematical discipline, namely to the arithmetic of natural numbers (the elementary number theory). We assume that this discipline has been presented as a formalized theory. The vocabulary of the theory is meager. It consists, in fact, of variables such as 'm', 'n', 'p', . . . representing arbitrary natural numbers; of numerals '0', '1', '2', . . . denoting particular num-bers; of symbols denoting some familiar relations between numbers and operations on numbers such as '=', '<', '+', '−'; and, finally, of certain logical terms, namely sentential connectives ('and', 'or', 'if', 'not') and quantifiers (expressions of the form 'for every number m' and 'for some number m'). The syntactical rules and the rules of proof are simple. When speaking of sentences in the subsequent discussion, we always have in mind sentences of the formalized language of arithmetic.

We know from the discussion of truth in the first section that, taking this language as the object-language, we can construct an appropriate metalanguage and formulate in it an adequate definition of truth. It proves convenient in this context to say that what we have thus defined is the set of true sentences; in fact, the definition of truth states that a certain condition formulated in the metalanguage is satisfied by all elements of this set (that is, all true sentences) and only by these elements. Even more readily we can define in the metalanguage the set of provable sentences; the definition conforms entirely with the explanation of the notion of formal proof that was given in the second section. Strictly speaking, the definitions of both truth and provability belong to a new theory formulated in the metalanguage and specifically designed for the study of our formalized arithmetic and its language. The new theory is called the metatheory or, more specifically, the meta-arithmetic. We shall not elaborate here on the way in which the metatheory is constructed—on its axioms, undefined terms, and so on. We only point out that it is within the framework of this metatheory that we formulate and solve the problem of whether the set of provable sentences coincides with that of true sentences.

The solution of the problem proves to be negative. We shall give here a very rough account of the method by which the solution has been reached. The main idea is closely related to the one used by the contemporary American logician (of Austrian origin) Kurt Gödel in his famous paper on the incompleteness of arithmetic.

It was pointed out in the first section that the metalanguage which enables us to define and discuss the notion of truth must be rich. It contains the entire object-language as a part, and therefore we can speak in it of natural numbers, sets of numbers, relations among numbers, and so forth. But it also contains terms needed for the discussion of the object-language and its components; consequently we can speak in the metalanguage of expressions and in particular of sentences, of sets of sentences, of relations among sentences, and so forth. Hence in the metatheory we can study properties of these various kinds of objects and establish connections between them.

In particular, using the description of sentences provided by the syntactical rules of the object-language, it is easy to arrange all sentences (from the simplest ones through the more and more complex) in an infinite sequence and to number them consecutively. We thus correlate with every sentence a natural number in such a way that two numbers correlated with two different sentences are always different; in other words, we establish a one-to-one correspondence between sentences and numbers. This in turn leads to a similar correspondence between sets of sentences and sets of numbers, or relations among sentences and relations among numbers. In particular, we can consider numbers of provable sentences and numbers of true sentences; we call them briefly provable* numbers and true* numbers. Our main problem is reduced then to the question: are the set of provable* numbers and the set of true* numbers identical?

To answer this question negatively, it suffices, of course, to indicate a single property that applies to one set but not to the other. The property we shall actually exhibit may seem rather unexpected, a kind of *deus ex machina.*

The intrinsic simplicity of the notions of formal proof and formal provability will play a basic role here. We have seen in the second section that the meaning of these notions is explained essentially in terms of certain simple relations among sentences prescribed by a few rules of proof; the reader may recall here the rule of *modus ponens.* The corresponding relations among numbers of sentences are equally simple; it turns out that they can be characterized in terms of the simplest arithmetical operations and relations, such as addition, multiplication, and equality—thus in terms occurring in our arithmetical theory. As a consequence the set of provable* numbers can also be characterized in such terms. One can describe briefly what has been achieved by saying that the definition of provability has been translated from the metalanguage into the object-language.

On the other hand, the discussion of the notion of truth in common languages strongly suggests the conjecture that no such translation can be obtained for the definition of truth, otherwise the object-language would prove to be in a sense semantically universal, and a reappearance of the antinomy of the liar would be imminent. We confirm this conjecture by showing that, if the

set of true* numbers could be defined in the language of arithmetic, the antinomy of the liar could actually be reconstructed in
this language. Since, however, we are dealing now with a restricted formalized language, the antinomy would assume a more
involved and sophisticated form. In particular, no expressions
with an empirical content such as 'the sentence printed in such-
and-such place', which played an essential part in the original
formulation of the antinomy, would occur in the new formulation.
We shall not go into any further details here.

Thus the set of provable* numbers does not coincide with the
set of true* numbers, since the former is definable in the language
of arithmetic while the latter is not. Consequently the sets of
provable sentences and true sentences do not coincide either. On
the other hand, using the definition of truth we easily show that
all the axioms of arithmetic are true and all the rules of proof are
infallible. Hence all the provable sentences are true; therefore
the converse cannot hold. Thus our final conclusion is: there are
sentences formulated in the language of arithmetic that are true
but cannot be proved on the basis of the axioms and rules of
proof accepted in arithmetic.

One might think that the conclusion essentially depends on
specific axioms and rules of inference, chosen for our arithmetical
theory, and that the final outcome of the discussion could be
different if we appropriately enriched the theory by adjoining
new axioms or new rules of inference. A closer analysis shows,
however, that the argument depends very little on specific
properties of the theory discussed, and that it actually extends to
most other formalized theories. Assuming that a theory includes
the arithmetic of natural numbers as a part (or that, at least,
arithmetic can be reconstructed in it), we can repeat the essential
portion of our argument in a practically unchanged form; we thus
conclude again that the set of provable sentences of the theory is
different from the set of its true sentences. If, moreover, we can
show (as is frequently the case) that all the axioms of the theory
are true and all the rules of inference are infallible, we further
conclude that there are true sentences of the theory which are not
provable. Apart from some fragmentary theories with restricted
means of expression, the assumption concerning the relation of
the theory to the arithmetic of natural numbers is generally
satisfied, and hence our conclusions have a nearly universal
character. (Regarding those fragmentary theories which do not
include the arithmetic of natural numbers, their languages may

not be provided with sufficient means for defining the notion of provability, and their provable sentences may in fact coincide with their true sentences. Elementary geometry and elementary algebra of real numbers are the best known, and perhaps most important, examples of theories in which these notions coincide.)

The dominant part played in the whole argument by the antinomy of the liar throws some interesting light on our earlier remarks concerning the role of antinomies in the history of human thought. The antinomy of the liar first appeared in our discussion as a kind of evil force with a great destructive power. It compelled us to abandon all attempts at clarifying the notion of truth for natural languages. We had to restrict our endeavours to formalized languages of scientific discourse. As a safeguard against a possible reappearance of the antinomy, we had to complicate considerably the discussion by distinguishing between a language and its metalanguage. Subsequently, however, in the new, restricted setting, we have managed to tame the destructive energy and harness it to peaceful, constructive purposes. The antinomy has not reappeared, but its basic idea has been used to establish a significant metalogical result with far-reaching implications.

Nothing is detracted from the significance of this result by the fact that its philosophical implications are essentially negative in character. The result shows indeed that in no domain of mathematics is the notion of provability a perfect substitute for the notion of truth. The belief that formal proof can serve as an adequate instrument for establishing truth of all mathematical statements has proved to be unfounded. The original triumph of formal methods has been followed by a serious setback.

Whatever can be said to conclude this discussion is bound to be an anticlimax. The notion of truth for formalized theories can now be introduced by means of a precise and adequate definition. It can therefore be used without any restrictions and reservations in metalogical discussion. It has actually become a basic metalogical notion involved in important problems and results. On the other hand, the notion of proof has not lost its significance either. Proof is still the only method used to ascertain the truth of sentences within any specific mathematical theory. We are now aware of the fact, however, that there are sentences formulated in the language of the theory which are true but not provable, and we cannot discount the possibility that some such sentences occur among those in which we are interested and which we attempt to prove. Hence in some situations we may wish to explore the possibility of widening the set of provable sentences. To this end we enrich the given theory by including new sentences in its axiom system or by providing it with new rules of proof. In doing so we use the notion of truth as a guide; for we do not wish to add a new axiom or a new rule of proof if we have reason to believe that the new axiom is not a true sentence, or that the new rule of proof when applied to true sentences may yield a false sentence. The process of extending a theory may of course be repeated arbitrarily many times. The notion of a true sentence functions thus as an ideal limit which can never be reached but which we try to approximate by gradually widening the set of provable sentences. (It seems likely, although for different reasons, that the notion of truth plays an analogous role in the realm of empirical knowledge.) There is no conflict between the notions of truth and proof in the development of mathematics; the two notions are not at war but live in peaceful co-existence.

Source: 'Truth and Proof', *Scientific American*, June 1969.

31 Meaning and Truth (1970)

W. V. QUINE

Objection to propositions

When someone speaks truly, what makes his statement true? We tend to feel that there are two factors: meaning and fact.

A German utters a declarative sentence: 'Der Schnee ist weiss.' In so doing he speaks truly, thanks to the happy concurrence of two circumstances: his sentence means that snow is white, and in point of fact snow *is* white. If meanings had been different, if 'weiss' had meant green, then in uttering what he did he would not have spoken truly. If the facts had been different, if snow had been red, then again he would not have spoken truly.

What I have just said has a reassuring air of platitude about it, and at the same time it shows disturbing signs of philosophical extravagance. The German utters his declarative sentence; also there is this white snow all around; so far so good. But must we go on and appeal also to intangible intervening elements, a meaning and a fact? The *meaning* of the *sentence* is that snow is white, and the *fact* of the *matter* is that snow is white. The meaning of the sentence and the fact of the matter here are apparently identical, or at any rate they have the same name: that snow is white. And it is apparently because of this identity, or homonymy, that the German may be said to have spoken truly. His meaning matches the fact.

This has the ring of a correspondence theory of truth, but as a theory it is a hollow mockery. The correspondence holds only between two intangibles that we have invoked as intervening elements between the German sentence and the white snow.

Someone may protest that I am being too severely literalistic about this seeming invocation of intervening elements. He may protest that when we speak of meaning as a factor in the truth of what the German said, we are merely saying, somewhat figuratively, what nobody can deny; namely, that if, for instance, the word 'weiss' were applied in German to green things instead of white ones, then what the German said about snow would have been false. He may protest likewise that the seeming reference to a fact, as something over and above the snow and its color, is only a manner of speaking.

Very well; as long as we can view matters thus, I have no complaint. But there has long been a strong trend in the philosophy of logic that cannot be thus excused. It is on meanings of sentences, rather than on facts, that this trend has offended most. Meanings of sentences are exalted as abstract entities in their own right, under the name of *propositions*. These, not the sentences themselves, are seen as the things that are true or false. These are the things also that stand in the logical relation of implication. These are the things also that are known or believed or disbelieved and are found obvious or surprising.

Philosophers' tolerance toward propositions has been encouraged partly by ambiguity in the term 'proposition'. The term often is used simply for the sentences themselves, declarative sentences; and then some writers who do use the term for meanings of sentences are careless about the distinction between sentences and their meanings. In inveighing against propositions in ensuing pages, I shall of course be inveighing against them always in the sense of sentence meanings.

Some philosophers, commendably diffident about positing

propositions in this bold sense, have taken refuge in the word 'statement'. The opening question of this chapter illustrates this evasive use. My inveterate use of 'statement' in earlier books does not; I there used the word merely to refer to declarative sentences, and said so. Later I gave up the word in the face of the growing tendency at Oxford to use the word for acts that we perform in uttering declarative sentences. Now by appealing to statements in such a sense, instead of to propositions, certainly no clarity is gained. I shall say no more about statements, but will go on about propositions.

Once a philosopher, whether through inattention to ambiguity or simply through an excess of hospitality, has admitted propositions to his ontology, he invariably proceeds to view propositions rather than sentences as the things that are true and false. He feels he thereby gains directness, saving a step. Thus let us recall the German. He spoke truly, we saw, inasmuch as (1) 'Der Schnee ist weiss' means that the snow is white and (2) snow *is* white. Now our propositionalist saves step (1). The proposition, that snow is white, is true simply inasmuch as (2) snow *is* white. The propositionalist by-passes differences between languages; also differences of formulation within a language.

My objection to recognizing propositions does not arise primarily from philosophical parsimony—from a desire to dream of no more things in heaven and earth than need be. Nor does it arise, more specifically, from particularism—from a disapproval of intangible or abstract entities. My objection is more urgent. If there were propositions, they would induce a certain relation of synonymy or equivalence between sentences themselves: those sentences would be equivalent that expressed the same proposition. Now my objection is going to be that the appropriate equivalence relation makes no objective sense at the level of sentences. This, if I succeed in making it plain, should spike the hypothesis of propositions.

Propositions as information

It is commonplace to speak of sentences as alike or unlike in meaning. This is such everyday, unphilosophical usage that it is apt to seem clearer than it really is. In fact it is vague, and the force of it varies excessively with the special needs of the moment. Thus suppose we are reporting a man's remark in indirect quotation. We are supposed to supply a sentence that is like his in meaning. In such a case we may be counted guilty of distorting his meaning when we so much as substitute a derogatory word for a neutral word having the same reference. Our substitution misrepresents his attitude and, therewith, his meaning. Yet on another occasion, where the interest is in relaying objective information without regard to attitudes, our substitution of the derogatory word for the neutral one will not be counted as distorting the man's meaning. Similar shifting of standards of likeness of meaning is evident in literary translation, according as our interest is in the poetic qualities of the passage or in the objective information conveyed.

The kind of likeness of meaning that is relevant to our present concerns, namely sameness of proposition, is the second of the alternatives mentioned in each of these examples. It is sameness of objective information, without regard to attitudes or to poetic qualities. If the notion of objective information were itself acceptably clear, there would be no quarrel with propositions.

The notion of information is indeed clear enough, nowadays, when properly relativized. It is central to the theory of communication. It makes sense relative to one or another preassigned matrix of alternatives—one or another checklist. You have to say in advance what features are going to count. Thus consider the familiar halftone method of photographic illustration. There is a screen, say six by six inches, containing a square array of regularly spaced positions, say a hundred to the inch in rows and columns. A halftone picture is completely determined by settling which of these 360,000 points are black. Relative to this screen as the matrix of alternatives, information consists in saying which places are black. Two paintings give the same information, relative to this matrix, when they determine the same points as black. Differences in color are, so to speak, purely stylistic relative to this matrix; they convey no information. The case is similar even for differences in shape or position, when these are too slight to be registered in the dots of the halftone. Relative to this matrix, furthermore, a verbal specification of the dots gives the same information as did the painting. (This is the principle of transmitting pictures by telegraph.) And of course two verbal accounts can give the information in very different phrasing; one of them might give the information by saying which positions are white instead of black.

Sameness of information thus stands forth clear against a preassigned matrix of black and white alternatives. But a trouble with trying to equate sentences in real life, in respect of the information they convey, is that no matrix of alternatives is given; we do not know what to count. There is no evident rule for separating the information from stylistic or other immaterial features of the sentences. The question when to say that two sentences mean the same proposition is consequently not adequately answered by alluding to sameness of objective information. This only rephrases the problem.

Ideally, a particle physics does offer a matrix of alternatives and therewith an absolute concept of objective information. Two sentences agree in objective information, and so express the same proposition, when every cosmic distribution of particles that would make either sentence true would make the other true as well. Each distribution of elementary particles of specified kinds over total space-time may be called a possible world; and then two sentences mean the same proposition when they are true in all the same possible worlds. The truths of pure mathematics and logic stand at an extreme, true in *all* possible worlds. The class of possible worlds in which a sentence comes out true is, we might say, the sentence's objective information—indeed, its proposition. But still this idea affords us no general way of equating sentences in real life. For surely we can never hope to arrive at a technique for so analyzing our ordinary sentences as to reveal their implications in respect of the distribution of particles.

A different way of reckoning objective information is suggested by the empiricist tradition in epistemology. Say what difference the truth or falsity of a sentence would make to possible experience, and you have said all there is to say about the meaning of the sentence; such, in substantially the words of C. S. Peirce, is the verification theory of meaning. This theory can be seen still as identifying the proposition or meaning of a sentence with the information conveyed; but the matrix of alternatives to be used in defining information is now the totality of possible distinctions and combinations of sensory input. Some epistemologists would catalog these alternatives by introspection of sense data. Others, more naturalistically inclined, would look to neural stimulation; the organism's triggered nerve endings are the analogues of the halftone's black dots. Either way, however, a doctrine of propositions as empirical meanings runs into trouble. The trouble comes, as we shall now see, in trying to distribute the sensory evidence over separate sentences.

Diffuseness of empirical meaning

Suppose an experiment has yielded a result contrary to a theory currently held in some natural science. The theory comprises a whole bundle of conjoint hypotheses, or is resoluble into such a bundle. The most that the experiment shows is that at least one of those hypotheses is false; it does not show which. It is only the theory as a whole, and not any one of the hypotheses, that admits of evidence or counter-evidence in observation and experiment.

And how wide is a theory? No part of science is quite isolated from the rest. Parts as disparate as you please may be expected to share laws of logic and arithmetic, anyway, and to share various common-sense generalities about bodies in motion. Legalistically, one could claim that evidence counts always for or against the total system, however loose-knit, of science. Evidence against the system is not evidence against any one sentence rather than another, but can be acted on rather by any of various adjustments.

An important exception suggests itself: surely an observation is evidence for the sentence that reports that very observation, and against the sentence that predicted the contrary. Our legalist can stand his ground even here, pointing out that in an extreme case, where beliefs that have been supported overwhelmingly from time immemorial are suddenly challenged by a single contrary observation, the observation will be dismissed as illusion. What is more important, however, is that usually observation sentences are indeed individually responsive to observation. This is what distinguishes observation sentences from theoretical sentences. It is only through the responsiveness of observation sentences individually to observation, and through the connections in turn of theoretical sentences to observation sentences, that a scientific theory admits of evidence at all.

Why certain sentences are thus individually responsive to observations becomes evident when we think about how we learn language. Many expressions, including most of our earliest, are learned *ostensively;* they are learned in the situation that they describe, or in the presence of the things that they describe. They are conditioned, in short, to observations; and to publicly shared observations, since both teacher and learner have to see the appropriateness of the occasion. Now if an expression is learned in this way by everyone, everyone will tend uniformly to apply it in the presence of the same stimulations. This uniformity affords, indeed, a behavioral criterion of what to count as an observation sentence. It is because of this uniformity, also, that scientists who are checking one another's evidence gravitate to observation sentences as a point where concurrence is assured.

We learn further expressions contextually in ways that generate a fabric of sentences, complexly interconnected. The connections are such as to incline us to affirm or deny some of these sentences when inclined to affirm or deny others. These are the connections through which a theory of nature imbibes its empirical substance from the observation sentences. They are also the connections whereby, in an extremity, our theory of nature may tempt us to ignore or disavow an observation, though it would be regrettable to yield often to this temptation.

The hopelessness of distributing empirical information generally over separate sentences, or even over fairly large bundles of sentences, is in some sense widely recognized, if only by implication. For, look at it this way. It will be widely agreed that our theory of nature is under-determined by our data; and not only by the observations we actually have made and will make, but even by all the unobserved events that are of an observable kind. Briefly, our theory of nature is under-determined by all 'possible' observations. This means that there can be a set H of hypotheses, and an alternative set H' incompatible with H, and it can happen that when our total theory T is changed to the extent of putting H' for H in it, the resulting theory T' still fits all possible observations just as well as T did. Evidently then H and H' convey the same empirical information, as far as empirical information can be apportioned to H and H' at all; but still they are incompatible. This reflection should scotch any general notion of propositions as empirical meanings of sentences.

Why then is the notion so stubborn? Partly because the separate sentences of science and common sense do in practice seem after all to carry their separate empirical meanings. This is misleading, and explicable. Thus suppose that from a combined dozen of our theoretical beliefs a scientist derives a prediction in molecular biology, and the prediction fails. He is apt to scrutinize for possible revision only the half dozen beliefs that belonged to molecular biology rather than tamper with the more general half dozen having to do with logic and arithmetic and the gross behavior of bodies. This is a reasonable strategy—a maxim of minimum mutilation. But an effect of it is that the portion of theory to which the discovered failure of prediction is relevant seems narrower than it otherwise might.

Probably, moreover, he will not even confront the six beliefs from molecular biology impartially with the failure of prediction; he will concentrate on one of the six, which was more suspect than the rest. Scientists are indeed forever devising experiments for the express purpose of testing single hypotheses; and this is reasonable, insofar as one hypothesis has been fixed upon as more tentative and suspect than other parts of the theory.

It would be a mistake, however, to see the scientist's move as one of questioning a single hypothesis while keeping *all* else fixed. His experiment is prompted by suspicion of one hypothesis, yes; and if the test proves negative he is resolved to reject that hypothesis, but not quite it alone. Along with it he will reject also any which, as he says, imply it. I must not myself now lean on a notion of implication, for I am challenging that notion (or the associated notion of equivalence, which is simply mutual implication). But we do have to recognize that sentences are interconnected by means of associations entrenched in behavior. There are the complex interconnections lately remarked upon: connections of varying strengths that incline us to affirm or deny some sentences when affirming or denying others. Whoever rejects one hypothesis will be led by these habit patterns to reject other sentences with it.

The scientist's strategy of dividing and conquering serves science well, but it does not show how to allocate separate empirical evidence to separate sentences. We can allocate separate evidence to each observation sentence, but that is about the end of it.

Propositions dismissed

The uncritical acceptance of propositions as meanings of sentences is one manifestation of a widespread myth of meaning. It is as if there were a gallery of ideas, and each idea were tagged with the expression that means it; each proposition, in particular, with an appropriate sentence. In criticism of this attitude I have been airing the problem of individuation of propositions. In this connection a passing attraction of an empirical theory of meaning was the fairly clear individuation enjoyed by the domain of sensory evidence. However, we have since been finding reason to despair of this line.

The question how to individuate propositions is the question how to define equivalence of sentences—if not empirical equivalence, at any rate 'cognitive' equivalence geared somehow to truth conditions. It may be well now to note and reject another inviting idea in this direction, an idea other than empirical equivalence, just to enhance our appreciation of the problem. We can define, it would seem, a strong synonymy relation for single words simply by requiring that they be interchangeable *salva veritate*. That is, putting the one word for the other always preserves the truth value of the context, turning truths into truths and falsehoods into falsehoods. More generally a word and a phrase, for example, 'bachelor' and 'unmarried man', may be called synonymous when always interchangeable *salva veritate*. Afterward we can turn about and call two sentences equivalent, in a strong sense, when they are built up of corresponding parts which are pairwise synonymous in the above sense.

Here, evidently, is a tricky way of promoting a weak relation, mere sameness of truth value, into a strong equivalence relation by sheer force of numbers. The equivalent sentences are parallel structures whose corresponding parts are related each to each by the strong relation of being interchangeable *salva veritate* in *all* sentences. The equivalence relation thus obtained has the drawback of requiring parallel structure; but this limitation can be eased somewhat by listing also some allowable grammatical transformations.

Let us now think critically about the synonymy of words to words and phrases. Consider the terms 'creature with a heart', briefly 'cordate',[1] and 'creature with kidneys', briefly 'renate'. All four terms are true of just the same creatures, but still of course we should not like to call them synonymous. They invite the title of synonymy only in pairs, 'cordate' with 'creature with a heart' and 'renate' with 'creature with kidneys'. Now how, in these cases, does our contemplated definition of synonymy fare—namely, interchangeability *salva veritate*? Can we show interchangeability of 'cordate' with 'creature with a heart', and yet failure of interchangeability of 'cordate' with 'renate'?

Perhaps we can, perhaps not; it all depends on what resources of contextual material we suppose to be available elsewhere in our language. If, for instance, the context:

[1] Not to be confused with 'chordate'.

(1) Necessarily all cordates are cordates

is available in the language, then the desired contrast seems to work out. Interchangeability of 'cordate' with 'renate' fails, as desired; for, putting 'renates' for the second occurrence of 'cordates' in the true sentence (1), we get a falsehood. At the same time, as desired, 'cordate' remains interchangeable with 'creature with a heart', at least in the example (1); for necessarily all cordates, by definition, have hearts.

But this successful contrast depends oddly on the resources of the language. If the adverb 'necessarily' had not been available, and in such a sense as to fail for 'all cordates are renates' and hold for 'all cordates have hearts', then this particular contrast between synonymy and failure of synonymy would have been denied us. And the unsatisfactory thing about this dependence is that the adverb 'necessarily', in the needed sense, is exactly as obscure as the notions of synonymy and equivalence that we are trying in the end to justify. If we had been content with this adverb, we could have defined equivalence in a moment: sentences are equivalent if, necessarily, they are either both true or both false.

True, other examples could be cited. The example:

(2) Tom thinks all cordates are cordates

serves as well as (1), since Tom might well not think that all cordates are renates, while still recognizing that all cordates have hearts. And (2) has the advantage of being couched in more innocent language than (1) with its cooked-up sense of necessity. However, innocence is one thing, clarity another. The 'thinks' idiom in (2), for all its ordinariness, is heir to all the obscurities of the notions of synonymy and equivalence and more.

Anyway, the 'thinks' idiom can scarcely be said to be more ordinary than the notion of equivalence. It is not as though equivalence were a new and technical notion, needing still to be paraphrased into ordinary language. On the contrary, the term is itself ordinary, for all its obscurity. The idea of equivalence, 'cognitive' equivalence, seems to make sense as it stands, until scrutinized. It is only mutual implication, after all, and implication is only deducibility. The complaint against these notions is not lack of familiarity, but lack of clarity.

Are all these notions to be dispensed with in serious science? In large part I think they are . . . there are relativized usages that account for much of the everyday utility of these terms; we speak of equivalence or deducibility relative to one or another tacitly accepted corpus of background information. But none of those uses, of which fair sense can be made, is of any evident avail in individuating propositions.

The doctrine of propositions seems in a way futile on the face of it, even if we imagine the individuation problem solved. For, that solution would consist in some suitable definition of equivalence of sentences; why not then just talk of sentences and equivalence and let the propositions go? The long and short of it is that propositions have been projected as shadows of sentences, if I may transplant a figure of Wittgenstein's. At best they will give us nothing the sentences will not give. Their promise of more is mainly due to our uncritically assuming for them an individuation which matches no equivalence between sentences that we see how to define. The shadows have favored wishful thinking.

Truth and semantic accent

Philosophers who favor propositions have said that propositions are needed because truth only of propositions, not of sentences, is intelligible. An unsympathetic answer is that we can explain truth of sentences to the propositionalist in his own terms: sentences are true whose meanings are true propositions. Any failure of intelligibility here is already his own fault.

But there is a deeper and vaguer reason for his feeling that truth is intelligible primarily for propositions. It is that truth should hinge on reality, not language; sentences are language. His way of producing a reality for truth to hinge on is shabby, certainly: an imaginary projection from sentences. But he is right that truth should hinge on reality, and it does. No sentence is true but reality makes it so. The sentence 'Snow is white' is true, as Tarski has taught us, if and only if real snow is really white. The same can be said of the sentence 'Der Schnee ist weiss'; language is not the point. In speaking of the truth of a given sentence there is only indirection; we do better simply to say the sentence and so speak not about language but about the world. So long as we are speaking only of the truth of singly given sentences, the perfect theory of truth is what Wilfrid Sellars has called the disappearance theory of truth.

Truth hinges on reality; but to object, on this score, to calling sentences true, is a confusion. Where the truth predicate has its utility is in just those places where, though still concerned with reality, we are impelled by certain technical complications to mention sentences. Here the truth predicate serves, as it were, to point through the sentence to the reality; it serves as a reminder that though sentences are mentioned, reality is still the whole point.

What, then, are the places where, though still concerned with unlinguistic reality, we are moved to proceed indirectly and talk of sentences? The important places of this kind are places where we are seeking generality, and seeking it along certain oblique planes that we cannot sweep out by generalizing over objects.

We can generalize on 'Tom is mortal', 'Dick is mortal', and so on, without talking of truth or of sentences; we can say 'All men are mortal'. We can generalize similarly on 'Tom is Tom', 'Dick is Dick', '0 is 0', and so on, saying 'Everything is itself'. When on the other hand we want to generalize on 'Tom is mortal or Tom is not mortal', 'Snow is white or snow is not white', and so on, we ascend to talk of truth and of sentences, saying 'Every sentence of the form "p or not p" is true', or 'Every alternation of a sentence with its negation is true'. What prompts this semantic ascent is not that 'Tom is mortal or Tom is not mortal' is somehow about sentences while 'Tom is mortal' and 'Tom is Tom' are about Tom. All three are about Tom. We ascend only because of the oblique way in which the instances over which we are generalizing are related to one another.

We were able to phrase our generalization 'Everything is itself' without such ascent just because the changes that were rung in passing from instance to instance—'Tom is Tom', 'Dick is Dick', '0 is 0'—were changes in names. Similarly for 'All men are mortal'. This generalization may be read 'x is mortal for all *men x*' —all things x of the sort that 'Tom' is a name of. But what would be a parallel reading of the generalization of 'Tom is mortal or Tom is not mortal'? It would read 'p or not p for all things p of the sort that sentences are names of'. But sentences are not names, and this reading is simply incoherent; it uses 'p' both in positions that call for sentence clauses and in a position that calls for a noun substantive. So, to gain our desired generality, we go up one step and talk about sentences: 'Every *sentence* of the *form* "p or not p" is *true*'.

The incoherent alternative reading might of course be expressly accorded meaning, if there were anything to gain by so doing. One could cause sentences to double as names, by specifying what they were to be names of. One might declare them to be names of propositions. In earlier pages, when propositions were still under advisement, I represented propositions as the meanings of sentences rather than as things named by sentences; still one could declare them to be named by sentences, and some there are who have done so. Until such a line is adopted, the letter 'p' is no variable ranging over objects; it is only a schematic letter for sentences, only a dummy to mark a position appropriate to a component sentence in some logical form or grammatical construction. Once the sentences are taken as names of propositions, on the other hand, the letter 'p' comes to double as a variable ranging over objects which are propositions. Thereafter we can coherently say 'p or not p for all propositions p'.

However, this move has the drawback of reinstating propositions, which we saw reason not to welcome. Moreover, the move brings no visible benefit; for we already saw how to express generalizations of the desired sort without appeal to propositions, by just going up a step and attributing truth to sentences. This ascent to a linguistic plane of reference is only a momentary retreat from the world, for the utility of the truth predicate is precisely the cancellation of linguistic reference. The truth predicate is a reminder that, despite a technical ascent to talk of sentences, our eye is on the world. This cancellatory force of the truth predicate is explicit in Tarski's paradigm:

'Snow is white' is true if and only if snow is white.

Quotation marks make all the difference between talking about words and talking about snow. The quotation is a name of a sentence that contains a name, namely 'snow', of snow. By calling the sentence true, we call snow white. The truth predicate is a device of disquotation. We may affirm the single sentence by just uttering it, unaided by quotation or by the truth predicate; but if we want to affirm some infinite lot of sentences that we can demarcate only by talking about the sentences, then the truth predicate has its use. We need it to restore the effect of objective reference when for the sake of some generalization we have resorted to semantic ascent.

Tarski's paradigm cannot be generalized to read:

'p' is true if and only if p,

since quoting the schematic sentence letter 'p' produces a name only of the sixteenth letter of the alphabet, and no generality over sentences. The truth predicate in its general use, attachable to a quantifiable variable in the fashion 'x is true', is eliminable by no facile paradigm. It can be defined, Tarski shows, in a devious way, but only if some powerful apparatus is available. [. . .]

Tokens and eternal sentences

Having now recognized in a general way that what are true are sentences, we must turn to certain refinements. What are best seen as primarily true or false are not sentences but events of utterance. If a man utters the words 'It is raining' in the rain, or the words 'I am hungry' while hungry, his verbal performance counts as true. Obviously one utterance of a sentence may be true and another utterance of the same sentence be false.

Derivatively, we often speak also of inscriptions as true or false. Just as a sentence may admit of both a true and a false utterance, so also it may admit of both a true and a false inscription. An inscription of the sentence 'You owe me ten dollars' may be true or false depending on who writes it, whom he addresses it to, and when.

We speak yet more derivatively when we speak of sentences outright as true or false. This usage works all right for *eternal* sentences: sentences that stay forever true, or forever false, independently of any special circumstances under which they happen to be uttered or written. Under the head of eternal sentences one thinks first of the sentences of arithmetic, since time and place are so conspicuously irrelevant to the subject matter of arithmetic. One thinks next of the laws of physics; for these, though occupied with the material world in a way that the laws of pure number are not, are meant to hold for all times and places. The general run of eternal sentences, however, are not so august as their name and these examples suggest. Any casual statement of inconsequential fact can be filled out into an eternal sentence by supplying names and dates and cancelling the tenses of verbs. Corresponding to 'It is raining' and 'You owe me ten dollars' we have the eternal sentence. 'It rains in Boston, Mass., on July 15, 1968' and 'Bernard J. Ortcutt owes W. V. Quine ten dollars on July 15, 1968', where 'rains' and 'owes' are to be thought of now as tenseless.

In Peirce's terminology, utterances and inscriptions are *tokens* of the sentence of other linguistic expression concerned; and this linguistic expression is the *type* of those utterances and inscriptions. In Frege's terminology, truth and falsity are the two *truth values*. Succinctly, then, an eternal sentence is a sentence whose tokens all have the same truth value.

Conceivably, by an extraordinary coincidence, one and the same string of sounds or characters could serve for '2 < 5' in one language and '2 > 5' in another. When we speak of '2 < 5' as an eternal sentence, then, we must understand that we are considering it exclusively as a sentence in our language, and claiming the truth only of those of its tokens that are utterances or inscriptions produced in our linguistic community. By a less extraordinary coincidence, for that matter, an eternal sentence that was true could become false because of some semantic change occurring in the continuing evolution of our own language. Here again we must view the discrepancy as a difference between two languages: English as of one date and English as of another. The string of sounds or characters in question is, and remains, an eternal sentence of earlier English, and a true one; it just happens to do double duty as a falsehood in another language, later English.

When we call a sentence eternal, therefore, we are calling it eternal relative only to a particular language at a particular time.[2] Because of this awkward relativity there remains a theoretical advantage in assigning truth values to tokens, since in that quarter there is normally no question of choosing among languages and language stages; we are concerned simply with the language of the speaker or writer as of the time of speaking or writing. But in practice it can be convenient to talk simply of truth values of eternal sentences, tacitly understanding these as relativized to our present-day English language habits.

Let us now sum up our main conclusions. What are best regarded as true and false are not propositions but sentence tokens, or sentences if they are eternal. The desire for a non-linguistic truth vehicle comes of not appreciating that the truth predicate has precisely the purpose of reconciling the mention of linguistic forms with an interest in the objective world. This need of mentioning sentences, when interested rather in things, is merely a technical need that arises when we seek to generalize along a direction that cannot be swept out by a variable.

Source: Philosophy of Logic (Prentice-Hall), Ch. 1.

[2] This point worried L. J. Cohen, *The Diversity of Meaning* (London: Methuen, 1962), p. 19.

KNOWLEDGE AND BELIEF

32 The Sun, the Line and the Cave (427-347 B.C.)

PLATO

[. . .] And what is the organ with which we see the visible things? 507c
The sight, he said.

And with the hearing, I said, we hear, and with the other senses perceive the other objects of sense?

True.

But have you remarked that sight is by far the most costly and complex piece of workmanship which the artificer of the senses ever contrived?

Not exactly, he said.

Then reflect: have the ear and voice need of any third or additional nature in order that the one may be able to hear and the other to be heard? d

Nothing of the sort.

No, indeed, I replied; and the same is true of most, if not all, the other senses—you would not say that any of them requires such an addition?

Certainly not.

But you see that without the addition of some other nature there is no seeing or being seen?

How do you mean?

Sight being, as I conceive, in the eyes, and he who has eyes wanting to see; colour being also present in the objects, still unless there be a third nature specially adapted to the purpose, sight, as you know, will see nothing and the colours will be invisible.

303

e   Of what nature are you speaking?

Of that which you term light, I replied.

True, he said.

508   Then the bond which links together the sense of sight and the
power of being seen, is of an evidently nobler nature than other
such bonds—unless sight is an ignoble thing?

Nay, he said, the reverse of ignoble.

And which, I said, of the gods in heaven would you say was the
lord of this element? Whose is that light which makes the eye to
see perfectly and the visible to appear?

I should answer, as all men would, and as you plainly expect—
the sun.

May not the relation of sight to this deity be described as
follows?

How?

Neither sight nor the organ in which it resides, which we call
the eye, is the sun?

b   No.

Yet of all the organs of sense the eye is the most like the sun?

By far the most like.

And the power which the eye possesses is a sort of effluence
which is dispensed from the sun?

Exactly.

Then the sun is not sight, but the author of sight who is recognized by sight?

True, he said.

And this, you must understand, is he whom I call the child of
the good, whom the good begat in his own likeness, to be in the
visible world, in relation to sight and the things of sight, what

c   the good is in the intellectual world in relation to mind and the
things of mind:

Will you be a little more explicit? he said.

Why, you know, I said, that the eyes, when a person directs
them towards objects on which the light of day is no longer
shining, but the moon and stars only, see dimly, and are nearly

d   blind; they seem to have no clearness of vision in them?

Very true.

But when they are directed towards objects on which the sun
shines, they see clearly and there is sight in them?

Certainly.

And the soul is like the eye: when resting upon that on which
truth and being shine, the soul perceives and understands, and is

radiant with intelligence; but when turned towards the twilight and to those things which come into being and perish, then she has opinion only, and goes blinking about, and is first of one opinion and then of another, and seems to have no intelligence?

Just so.

Now, that which imparts truth to the known and the power of knowing to the knower is, as I would have you say, the Idea of c good, and this Idea, which is the cause of science and of truth, you are to conceive as being apprehended by knowledge, and yet, fair as both truth and knowledge are, you will be right to esteem it as different from these and even fairer; and as in the 509 previous instance light and sight may be truly said to be like the sun and yet not to be the sun, so in this other sphere science and truth may be deemed to be like the good, but it is wrong to think that they are the good; the good has a place of honour yet higher.

What a wonder of beauty that must be, he said, which is the author of science and truth, and yet surpasses them in beauty; for you surely cannot mean to say that pleasure is the good?

God forbid, I replied; but may I ask you to consider the image in another point of view?

In what point of view?   b

You would say, would you not, that the sun is not only the author of visibility in all visible things, but of generation and nourishment and growth, though he himself is not generation?

Certainly.

In like manner you must say that the good not only infuses the power of being known into all things known, but also bestows upon them their being and existence, and yet the good is not existence, but lies far beyond it in dignity and power.

Glaucon said, with a ludicrous earnestness: By the light of c heaven, that is far beyond indeed!

Yes, I said, and the exaggeration may be set down to you; for you made me utter my fancies.

And pray continue to utter them; at any rate let us hear if there is anything more to be said about the similitude of the sun.

Yes, I said, there is a great deal more.

Then omit nothing, however slight.

I expect that I shall omit a great deal, I said, but shall not do so deliberately, as far as present circumstances permit.

I hope not, he said.

You have to imagine, then, that there are two ruling powers, d and that one of them is set over the intellectual world, the other over the visible. I do not say heaven, lest you should fancy that I am playing upon the name (οὐρανός, ὁρατός). May I suppose that you have this distinction of the visible and intelligible fixed in your mind?

I have.

Now take a line which has been cut into two unequal parts, and divide each of them again in the same proportion, and suppose the two main divisions to answer, one to the visible and
e the other to the intelligible, and then compare the subdivisions in respect of their clearness and want of clearness, and you will find that the first section in the sphere of the visible consists of images.
510 And by images I mean, in the first place, shadows, and in the second place, reflections in water and in solid, smooth and polished bodies and the like: Do you understand?

Yes, I understand.

Imagine, now, the other section, of which this is only the resemblance, to include the animals which we see, and every thing that grows or is made.

Very good.

Would you not admit that both the sections of this division have different degrees of truth, and that the copy is to the original as the sphere of opinion is to the sphere of knowledge?

Most undoubtedly.
b   Next proceed to consider the manner in which the sphere of the intellectual is to be divided.

In what manner?

Thus: There are two subdivisions, in the lower of which the soul, using as images those things which themselves were reflected in the former division, is forced to base its enquiry upon hypotheses, proceeding not towards a principle but towards a conclusion; in the higher of the two, the soul proceeds *from* hypotheses, and goes up to a principle which is above hypotheses, making no use of images[1] as in the former case, but proceeding only in and through the Ideas themselves.

I do not quite understand your meaning, he said.
c   Then I will try again; you will understand me better when I have made some preliminary remarks. You are aware that students of geometry, arithmetic, and the kindred sciences assume the odd and the even and the figures and three kinds of angles and the like in their several branches of science; these are their hypotheses, which they and everybody are supposed to know, and

---

[1] Reading ὧνπερ ἐκεῖνο εἰκόνων.

therefore they do not deign to give any account of them either to themselves or others; but they begin with them, and go on until they arrive at last, and in a consistent manner, at the solution d which they set out to find?

Yes, he said, I know.

And do you not know also that although they make use of the visible forms and reason about them, they are thinking not of these, but of the ideals which they resemble; not of the figures which they draw, but of the absolute square and the absolute diameter, and so on—the forms which they draw or make, and which themselves have shadows and reflections in water, are in e turn converted by them into images; for they are really seeking to behold the things themselves, which can only be seen with the eye of the mind?

That is true.

511

And this was what I meant by a subdivision of the intelligible, in the search after which the soul is compelled to use hypotheses; not ascending to a first principle, because she is unable to rise above the region of hypothesis, but employing now as images those objects from which the shadows below were derived, even these being deemed clear and distinct by comparison with the shadows.

I understand, he said, that you are speaking of the province of b geometry and the sister arts.

And when I speak of the other division of the intelligible, you will understand me to speak of that other sort of knowledge which reason herself attains by the power of dialectic, using the hypotheses not as first principles, but literally as hypotheses— that is to say, as steps and points of departure into a world which is above hypotheses, in order that she may soar beyond them to the first principle of the whole; and clinging to this and then to that which depends on this, by successive steps she descends again without the aid of any sensible object, from Ideas, through c Ideas, and in Ideas she ends.

I understand you, he replied; not perfectly, for you seem to me to be describing a task which is really tremendous; but, at any rate, I understand you to say that that part of intelligible Being, which the science of dialectic contemplates, is clearer than that which falls under the arts, as they are termed, which take hypotheses as their principles; and though the objects are of such a kind that they must be viewed by the understanding, and not by the senses, yet, because they start from hypotheses and do not d ascend to a principle, those who contemplate them appear to you not to exercise the higher reason upon them, although when a first principle is added to them they are cognizable by the higher reason. And the habit which is concerned with geometry and the cognate sciences I suppose that you would term understanding and not reason, as being intermediate between opinion and reason.

You have quite conceived my meaning, I said; and now, corresponding to these four divisions, let there be four faculties in the soul—reason answering to the highest, understanding to the second, faith (or conviction) to the third, and perception of shadows to the last—and let there be a scale of them, and let us suppose that the several faculties have clearness in the same degree that their objects have truth.

I understand, he replied, and give my assent, and accept your arrangement. [. . .]

514   And now, I said, let me show in a figure how far our nature is enlightened or unenlightened: Behold! human beings housed in an underground cave, which has a long entrance open towards the light and as wide as the interior of the cave; here they have
b been from their childhood, and have their legs and necks chained, so that they cannot move and can only see before them, being prevented by the chains from turning round their heads. Above and behind them a fire is blazing at a distance, and between the fire and the prisoners there is a raised way; and you will see, if you look, a low wall built along the way, like the screen which marionette players have in front of them, over which they show the puppets.

I see.

And do you see, I said, men passing along the wall carrying all
c sorts of vessels, and statues and figures of animals made of wood
515 and stone and various materials, which appear over the wall? While carrying their burdens, some of them, as you would expect, are talking, others silent.

You have shown me a strange image, and they are strange prisoners.

Like ourselves, I replied; for in the first place do you think they have seen anything of themselves, and of one another, except the shadows which the fire throws on the opposite wall of the cave?
b   How could they do so, he asked, if throughout their lives they were never allowed to move their heads?

And of the objects which are being carried in like manner they would only see the shadows?

Yes, he said.

And if they were able to converse with one another, would they not suppose that the things they saw were the real things?[2]

Very true.

And suppose further that the prison had an echo which came from the other side, would they not be sure to fancy when one of the passers-by spoke that the voice which they heard came from the passing shadow?

No question, he replied.

To them, I said, the truth would be literally nothing but the c shadows of the images.

That is certain.

And now look again, and see in what manner they would be released from their bonds, and cured of their error, whether the process would naturally be as follows. At first, when any of them is liberated and compelled suddenly to stand up and turn his neck round and walk and look towards the light, he will suffer sharp pains; the glare will distress him, and he will be unable to see the realities of which in his former state he had seen the shadows; and then conceive someone saying to him that what he saw before was an illusion, but that now, when he is approaching d nearer to being and his eye is turned towards more real existence, he has a clearer vision,—what will be his reply? And you may further imagine that his instructor is pointing to the objects as they pass and requiring him to name them,—will he not be perplexed? Will he not fancy that the shadows which he formerly saw are truer than the objects which are now shown to him?

Far truer.

And if he is compelled to look straight at the light, will he not e have a pain in his eyes which will make him turn away to take refuge in the objects of vision which he can see, and which he will conceive to be in reality clearer than the things which are now being shown to him?

True, he said.

And suppose once more, that he is reluctantly dragged up that steep and rugged ascent, and held fast until he is forced into the presence of the sun himself, is he not likely to be pained and irritated? When he approaches the light his eyes will be dazzled, 516 and he will not be able to see anything at all of what are now called realities.

[2] [Text uncertain: perhaps 'that they would apply the name *real* to the things which they saw'.]

Not all in a moment, he said.

He will require to grow accustomed to the sight of the upper world. And first he will see the shadows best, next the reflections of men and other objects in the water, and then the objects themselves; and, when he turned to the heavenly bodies and the heaven itself, he would find it easier to gaze upon the light of the
b moon and the stars at night than to see the sun or the light of the sun by day?

Certainly.

Last of all he will be able to see the sun, not turning aside to the illusory reflections of him in the water, but gazing directly at him in his own proper place, and contemplating him as he is.

Certainly.

He will then proceed to argue that this is he who gives the seasons and the years, and is the guardian of all that is in the visible world, and in a certain way the cause of all things which
c he and his fellows have been accustomed to behold?

Clearly, he said, he would arrive at this conclusion after what he had seen.

And when he remembered his old habitation, and the wisdom of the cave and his fellow-prisoners, do you not suppose that he would felicitate himself on the change, and pity them?

Certainly, he would.

And if they were in the habit of conferring honours among themselves on those who were quickest to observe the passing shadows and to remark which of them went before and which
d followed after and which were together, and who were best able from these observations to divine the future, do you think that he would be eager for such honours and glories, or envy those who attained honour and sovereignty among those men? Would he not say with Homer,

'Better to be a serf, labouring for a landless master',

and to endure anything, rather than think as they do and live after their manner?
e   Yes, he said, I think that he would consent to suffer anything rather than live in this miserable manner.

Imagine once more, I said, such a one coming down suddenly out of the sunlight, and being replaced in his old seat; would he not be certain to have his eyes full of darkness?

To be sure, he said.

And if there were a contest, and he had to compete in

measuring the shadows with the prisoners who had never moved out of the cave, while his sight was still weak, and before his eyes 517 had become steady (and the time which would be needed to acquire this new habit of sight might be very considerable), would he not make himself ridiculous? Men would say of him that he had returned from the place above with his eyes ruined; and that it was better not even to think of ascending; and if anyone tried to loose another and lead him up to the light, let them only catch the offender, and they would put him to death.

No question, he said.

This entire allegory, I said, you may now append, dear Glaucon, to the previous argument; the prison-house is the world b of sight, the light of the fire is the power of the sun, and you will not misapprehend me if you interpret the journey upwards to be the ascent of the soul into the intellectual world according to my surmise, which, at your desire, I have expressed—whether rightly or wrongly God knows. But, whether true or false, my opinion is that in the world of knowledge the Idea of good appears last of all, and is seen only with an effort; although, when seen, it is inferred to be the universal author of all things beautiful and c right, parent of light and of the lord of light in the visible world, and the immediate and supreme source of reason and truth in the intellectual; and that this is the power upon which he who would act rationally either in public or private life must have his eye fixed.

I agree, he said, as far as I am able to understand you. [. . .]

Glaucon, I said, we have at last arrived at the hymn of dialectic. 532 This is that strain which is of the intellect only, but which the faculty of sight will nevertheless be found to imitate; for sight, as you may remember, was imagined by us after a while to behold the real animals and stars, and last of all the sun himself. And so with dialectic; when a person starts on the discovery of the real by the light of reason only, and without any assistance of sense, and perseveres until by pure intelligence he arrives at the perception of the absolute good, he at last finds himself at the end of b the intellectual world, as in the case of sight at the end of the visible.

Exactly, he said.

Then this is the progress which you call dialectic?
True.

But the release of the prisoners from chains, and their turning from the shadows to the images and to the light, and the ascent

from the underground cave to the sun, while in his presence they
are vainly trying to look on animals and plants and the light of
the sun, but are able to perceive even with their weak eyes
c images in the water which are divine;[3] and are the shadows of
true existence (not shadows of images cast by a light of fire, which
compared with the sun is only an image)—this power of elevating
the highest principle in the soul to the contemplation of that
which is best in existence, with which we may compare the raising of that faculty which is the very light of the body to the sight
of that which is brightest in the material and visible world—this
power is given, as I was saying, by all that study and pursuit of
d the arts which has been described.

I agree in what you are saying, he replied, which may be hard
to believe, yet from another point of view is harder still to deny.
However, since this is not a theme to be treated of in passing
only, but will have to be discussed again and again, let us assume
that the present statement is true, and proceed at once from the
prelude or preamble to the chief strain[4] and describe that in like
e manner. Say, then, what is the nature and what are the divisions
of the power of dialectic, and what are the paths which lead to
our destination, where we can rest from the journey.

533   Dear Glaucon, I said, you will no longer be able to follow me
here, though I would do my best, and would endeavour to show
you not an image[5] only but the absolute truth, according to my
notion. Whether that notion is or is not correct, it would not be
right for me to affirm. But that it is something like this that you
must see, of that I am confident.[6]

Doubtless, he replied.

But I must also remind you, that the power of dialectic alone
can reveal this, and only to one who is a disciple of the previous
sciences.

Of that assertion you may be as confident as of the last.

b   And assuredly no one will argue that there is any other method
of comprehending by any regular process all true existence or of
ascertaining what each thing is in its own nature; for the arts in
general are concerned with the desires or opinions of men, or
with processes of growth and construction; or they have been

[3] [As opposed to the images of artificial things reflected on the wall of the
cave; for the terminology, compare *Sophist*, 266 b–d.]

[4] A play upon the word νόμος, which means both 'law' and 'strain'.

[5] [Because no image of the most abstract Forms is possible. See *Statesman*
285 d e.]

[6] [Reading, in 533 a 5, ὅτι μὲν δεῖ.]

cultivated in order to care for things grown and constructed; and as to the mathematical sciences which, as we were saying, have some apprehension of true being—geometry and the like—they only dream about being, but never can they behold the waking c reality so long as they leave unmoved the hypotheses which they use, and are unable to give an account of them. For when a man knows not his own first principle, and when the conclusion and intermediate steps are also constructed out of he knows not what, how can he imagine that such a fabric of convention can ever become science?

Impossible, he said.

Then dialectic, and dialectic alone, goes directly to the first principle and is the only science which does away with hypotheses in order to make her ground secure; the eye of the soul, d which is really buried in an outlandish slough, is by her gentle aid lifted upwards; and in this work she uses as handmaids and helpers the sciences which we have been discussing. We have often used the customary name sciences, but they ought to have some other name, implying greater clearness than opinion and less clearness than science: and this, in our previous sketch, was called understanding. But why should we dispute about names when we have realities of such importance to consider?

Why indeed, he said, when any name will do which expresses the thought of the mind with clearness?[7]

At any rate, we are satisfied, as before, to have four divisions; two for intellect and two for opinion, and to call the first division science, the second understanding, the third belief, and the fourth perception of shadows, opinion being concerned with becoming, and intellect with being; and so to make a proportion: 534

As being is to becoming, so is pure intellect to opinion.
And as intellect is to opinion, so is science to belief, and understanding to the perception of shadows.

But let us defer the further correlation and subdivision of the *objects* of opinion and of intellect, for it will be a long inquiry, many times longer than this has been. b

Apart from that, then, he said, as far as I understand, I agree.

And do you also agree, I said, in describing the dialectician as

[7] Text uncertain. As emended in the Oxford text, the passage should run: 'Why indeed? he said.—Then any name will do, which somehow shows what degree of clearness is attributed to the state of mind?—Yes.—At any rate, it will be enough, as before, &c.']

one who attains a conception of the essence of each thing? And he who does not possess and is therefore unable to impart this conception, in whatever degree he fails, may in that degree also be said to fail in intelligence? Will you admit so much?

Yes, he said; how can I deny it?

And you would say the same of the conception of the good? Unless the person is able to abstract from all else and define c rationally the Idea of good, and unless he can run the gauntlet of all objections, and is keen to disprove them by appeals not to opinion but to absolute truth, never faltering at any step of the argument—unless he can do all this, you would say that he knows neither the Idea of good nor any other good; he apprehends only a shadow, if anything at all, which is given by opinion and not by science;—dreaming and slumbering in this life, before he is well awake here, he arrives at the world below, and has his final quietus.

Source: The Republic, trans. F. M. Cornford (O.U.P.), Bks. VI and VII. (Extracts.)

33 Knowledge, Error and Opinion (384–322 B.C.)

ARISTOTLE

I

By a knowledge of the universal then we see the particulars, but we do not know them by the kind of knowledge which is proper to them; consequently it is possible that we may make mistakes about them, but not that we should have the knowledge and error that are contrary to one another: rather we have the knowledge of the universal but make a mistake in apprehending the particular. [...]

Nothing then prevents a man both knowing and being mistaken about the same thing, provided that his knowledge and his error are not contrary. And this happens also to the man whose knowledge is limited to each of the premisses and who has not previously considered the particular question. For when he thinks that the mule is with foal he has not the knowledge in the sense of its actual exercise, nor on the other hand has his thought caused an error contrary to his knowledge: for the error contrary to the knowledge of the universal would be a syllogism.

But he who thinks the essence of good is the essence of bad will think the same thing to be the essence of good and the essence of bad. Let *A* stand for the essence of good and *B* for the essence of bad, and again *C* for the essence of good. Since then he thinks *B* and *C* identical, he will think that *C* is *B*, and similarly that *B* is *A*, consequently that *C* is *A*. For just as we saw that if *B* is *true* of all of which *C* is *true*, and *A* is true of all of which *B* is true, *A* is true of *C*, similarly with the word 'think'. Similarly also with the word 'is'; for we saw that if *C* is the same as *B*, and *B* as *A*, *C* is the same as *A*. Similarly therefore with 'opine'. Perhaps then this[1] is necessary if a man will grant the first point.[2] But presumably that is false, that any one could suppose the essence of good to be the essence of bad, save incidentally. For it is possible to think this in many different ways. But we must consider this matter better.[3] [. . .]

II

All instruction given or received by way of argument proceeds from pre-existent knowledge. This becomes evident upon a survey of all the species of such instruction. The mathematical sciences and all other speculative disciplines are acquired in this way, and so are the two forms of dialectical reasoning, syllogistic and in-ductive; for each of these latter makes use of old knowledge to impart new, the syllogism assuming an audience that accepts its premisses, induction[4] exhibiting the universal as implicit in the clearly known particular. Again, the persuasion exerted by rhetorical arguments is in principle the same, since they use either example, a kind of induction, or enthymeme, a form of syllogism.

The pre-existent knowledge required is of two kinds. In some

---

[1] That a man should think the same thing to be the essence of good and to be the essence of bad.

[2] That the essence of good is the essence of bad.

[3] The reference may be to *Met.* Γ. 4.

[4] The sense of ἐπάγειν implied in the use of ἐπαγωγή by Aristotle is probably that of 'leading the pupil on' from the particular to the universal by making him recognize the latter as implicit in the former.

cases admission of the fact must be assumed, in others comprehension of the meaning of the term used, and sometimes both assumptions are essential. Thus, we assume that every predicate can be either truly affirmed or truly denied of any subject,[5] and that 'triangle'[6] means so and so; as regards 'unit' we have to make the double assumption of the meaning of the word and the existence of the thing. The reason is that these several objects are not equally obvious to us. Recognition of a truth may in some cases contain as factors both previous knowledge and also knowledge acquired simultaneously with that recognition—knowledge, this latter, of the particulars actually falling under the universal and therein already virtually known. For example, the student knew beforehand that the angles of every triangle are equal to two right angles; but it was only at the actual moment at which he was being led on to recognize this as true in the instance before him that he came to know 'this figure inscribed in the semicircle' to be a triangle.[7] For some things (viz. the singulars finally reached which are not predicable of anything else as subject) are only learnt in this way, i.e. there is here no recognition through a middle of a minor term as subject to a major. Before he was led on to recognition or before he actually drew a conclusion, we should perhaps say that in a manner he knew, in a manner not.

If he did not in an unqualified sense of the term *know* the existence of this triangle, how could he *know* without qualification that its angles were equal to two right angles? No: clearly he *knows* not without qualification but only in the sense that he *knows* universally. If this distinction is not drawn, we are faced with the dilemma in the *Meno*:[8] either a man will learn nothing or what he already knows; for we cannot accept the solution

[5] i.e. the law of excluded middle.

[6] Elsewhere τρίγωνον as a rule appears as one of the subjects of which the geometer assumes the meaning and being and demonstrates properties: here it seems to be instanced as a property, of which only the meaning is assumed.

[7] Though he uses syllogistic terms, Aristotle is hardly describing syllogism, but rather the conversion of a universal known ἕξει into actual knowledge. The 'major premiss' here is a previously known universal (in Aristotle's example 'the angles of all triangles are together equal to two right angles'), the 'minor' is the recognition of a singular (in the example, 'this is a triangle'), and the 'conclusion', with which the minor is simultaneous, is the recognition of this singular as an instance embodying the universal ('the angles of this triangle in the semi-circle are equal to two right angles').

[8] Plato, *Meno*, 80 E.

which some people offer. A man is asked, 'Do you, or do you not, know that every pair is even?' He says he does know it. The questioner then produces a particular pair, of the existence, and so *a fortiori* of the evenness, of which he was unaware. The solution which some people offer is to assert that they do not know that every pair is even, but only that everything which they know to be a pair is even: yet what they know to be even is that of which they have demonstrated evenness, i.e. what they made the subject of their premiss, viz. not merely every triangle or number which they know to be such, but any and every number or triangle without reservation. For no premiss is ever couched in the form 'every number which you know to be such', or 'every rectilinear figure which you know to be such': the predicate is always construed as applicable to any and every instance of the thing. On the other hand, I imagine there is nothing to prevent a man in one sense knowing what he is learning, in another not knowing it. The strange thing would be, not if in some sense he knew what he was learning, but if he were to know it in that precise sense and manner in which he was learning it. [. . .]

III

Scientific knowledge and its object differ from opinion and the object of opinion in that scientific knowledge is commensurately universal and proceeds by necessary connexions, and that which is necessary cannot be otherwise. So though there are things which are true and real and yet can be otherwise, *scientific knowledge* clearly does not concern them: if it did, things which can be otherwise would be incapable of being otherwise. Nor are they any concern of *rational intuition*—by rational intuition I mean an originative source of scientific knowledge—nor of indemonstrable knowledge,[9] which is the grasping of the immediate premiss. Since then rational intuition, science, and opinion, and what is revealed by these terms, are the only things that can be 'true', it follows that it is *opinion* that is concerned with that which may be true or false, and can be otherwise: opinion in fact is the grasp of a premiss which is immediate but not necessary. This view also fits the observed facts, for opinion is unstable, and so is the kind of being we have described as its object. Besides, when a man thinks a truth incapable of being otherwise he always

[9] νοῦς grasps the individual nature, τὸ τί ἦν εἶναι or the definition, as a unity; ἐπιστήμη ἀναπόδεικτος gives this as a premiss.

thinks that he knows it, never that he opines it. He thinks that he opines when he thinks that a connexion, though actually so, may quite easily be otherwise; for he believes that such is the proper object of opinion, while the necessary is the object of knowledge.

In what sense, then, can the same thing be the object of both opinion and knowledge? And if any one chooses to maintain that all he knows he can also opine, why should not[10] opinion be knowledge? For he that knows and he that opines will follow the same train of thought through the same middle terms until the immediate premisses are reached; because it is possible to opine not only the fact but also the reasoned fact, and the reason is the middle term; so that, since the former knows, he that opines also has knowledge.

The truth perhaps is that if a man grasp truths that cannot be other than they are, in the way in which he grasps[11] the definitions through which demonstrations take place, he will have not opinion but knowledge: if on the other hand he apprehends these attributes as inhering in their subjects, but not in virtue of the subjects' substance and essential nature, he possesses opinion and not genuine knowledge; and his opinion, if obtained through immediate premisses, will be both of the fact and of the reasoned fact; if not so obtained, of the fact alone. The object of opinion and knowledge is not quite identical; it is only in a sense identical, just as the object of true and false opinion is in a sense identical. The sense in which some maintain that true and false opinion can have the same object leads them to embrace many strange doctrines, particularly the doctrine that what a man opines falsely he does not opine at all. There are really many senses of 'identical', and in one sense the object of true and false opinion can be the same, in another it cannot. Thus, to have a true opinion that the diagonal is commensurate with the side would be absurd: but because the diagonal with which they are both concerned is the same, the two opinions have objects so far the same: on the other hand, as regards their essential definable nature these objects differ. The identity of the objects of knowledge and opinion is similar. Knowledge is the apprehension of, e.g., the attribute 'animal' as incapable of being otherwise, opinion the apprehension of 'animal' as capable of being otherwise—e.g. the apprehension that animal is an element in the essential nature of man is knowledge; the apprehension of animal as predicable of man but not

---

10 Reading ἔσται for ἔστιν with A, B, C, and Waitz.
11 Reading ἔχει with MSS.

as an element in man's essential nature is opinion: man is the subject in both judgments, but the mode of inherence differs.

This also shows that one cannot opine and know the same thing simultaneously; for then one would apprehend the same thing as both capable and incapable of being otherwise—an impossibility. Knowledge and opinion of the same thing can co-exist in two different people in the sense we have explained, but not simultaneously in the same person. That would involve a man's simultaneously apprehending, e.g., (1) that man is essentially animal—i.e. cannot be other than animal—and (2) that man is not essentially animal, that is, we may assume,[12] may be other than animal.

Further consideration of modes of thinking and their distribution under the heads of discursive thought, intuition, science, art, practical wisdom, and metaphysical thinking, belongs rather partly to natural science, partly to moral philosophy.

Source: *Prior Analytics*, II/21 (extracts) and *Posterior Analytics* I/1 and I/33 (extracts), ed. W. D. Ross (O.U.P.).

34 Knowledge, Experience and Understanding (384–322 B.C.)

ARISTOTLE

All men by nature desire to know. An indication of this is the delight we take in our senses; for even apart from their usefulness they are loved for themselves; and above all others the sense of sight. For not only with a view to action, but even when we are not going to do anything, we prefer seeing (one might say) to everything else. The reason is that this, most of all the senses, makes us know and brings to light many differences between things.

By nature animals are born with the faculty of sensation, and from sensation memory is produced in some of them, though not in others. And therefore the former are more intelligent and apt at learning than those which cannot remember; those which are

[12] Reading ἔστω with B, C, and Waitz.

incapable of hearing sounds are intelligent though they cannot be taught, e.g. the bee, and any other race of animals that may be like it; and those which besides memory have this sense of hearing can be taught.

The animals other than man live by appearances and memories, and have but little of connected experience; but the human race lives also by art and reasonings. Now from memory experience is produced in men; for the several memories of the same thing produce finally the capacity for a single experience. And experience seems pretty much like science and art, but really science and art come to men *through* experience; for 'experience made art', as Polus says,[1] 'but inexperience luck'. Now art arises when from many notions gained by experience one universal judgement about a class of objects is produced. For to have a judgement that when Callias was ill of this disease this did him good, and similarly in the case of Socrates and in many individual cases, is a matter of experience; but to judge that it has done good to all persons of a certain constitution, marked off in one class, when they were ill of this disease, e.g. to phlegmatic or bilious people when burning with fever,—this is a matter of art.

With a view to action experience seems in no respect inferior to art, and men of experience succeed even better than those who have theory without experience. (The reason is that experience is knowledge of individuals, art of universals, and actions and productions are all concerned with the individual; for the physician does not cure *man*, except in an incidental way, but Callias or Socrates or some other called by some such individual name, who happens to be a man. If, then, a man has the theory without the experience, and recognizes the universal but does not know the individual included in this, he will often fail to cure; for it is the individual that is to be cured.) But yet we think that *knowledge* and *understanding* belong to art rather than to experience, and we suppose artists to be wiser than men of experience (which implies that Wisdom depends in all cases rather on knowledge); and this because the former know the cause, but the latter do not. For men of experience know that the thing is so, but do not know why, while the others know the 'why' and the cause. Hence we think also that the master-workers in each craft are more honourable and know in a truer sense and are wiser than the manual workers, because they know the causes of the things that are done (we think the manual workers are like certain

[1] Cf. Pl. *Gorg.* 448 c, 462 BC.

lifeless things which act indeed, but act without knowing what they do, as fire burns,—but while the lifeless things perform each of their functions by a natural tendency, the labourers perform them through habit);[2] thus we view them as being wiser not in virtue of being able to act, but of having the theory for themselves and knowing the causes. And in general it is a sign of the man who knows and of the man who does not know, that the former can teach, and therefore we think art more truly knowledge than experience is; for artists can teach, and men of mere experience cannot.

Again, we do not regard any of the senses as Wisdom; yet surely these give the most authoritative knowledge of particulars. But they do not tell us the 'why' of anything—e.g. why fire is hot; they only say *that* it is hot. [...]

Source: Metaphysics ed. W. D. Ross (O.U.P.), A.i: 980a, 21–981b, 13.

35 Knowing How and Knowing That (1949)
GILBERT RYLE

I

When a person is described by one or other of the intelligence-epithets such as 'shrewd' or 'silly', 'prudent' or 'imprudent', the description imputes to him not the knowledge, or ignorance, of this or that truth, but the ability, or inability, to do certain sorts of things. Theorists have been so preoccupied with the task of investigating the nature, the source, and the credentials of the theories that we adopt that they have for the most part ignored the question what it is for someone to know how to perform tasks. In ordinary life, on the contrary, as well as in the special business of teaching, we are much more concerned with people's competences than with their cognitive repertoires, with the operations than with the truths that they learn. Indeed even when we are concerned with their intellectual excellences and deficiencies, we are interested less in the stocks of truths that they

[2] 981[b] 2 τοὺς . . . 5 ἔθος may be a later addition.

acquire and retain than in their capacities to find out truths for themselves and their ability to organize and exploit them, when discovered. Often we deplore a person's ignorance of some fact only because we deplore the stupidity of which his ignorance is a consequence.

There are certain parallelisms between knowing *how* and knowing *that*, as well as certain divergences. We speak of learning how to play an instrument as well as of learning that something is the case; of finding out how to prune trees as well as of finding out that the Romans had a camp in a certain place; of forgetting how to tie a reef-knot as well as of forgetting that the German for 'knife' is '*Messer*'. We can wonder *how* as well as wonder *whether*.

On the other hand we never speak of a person believing or opining *how*, and though it is proper to ask for the grounds or reasons for someone's acceptance of a proposition, this question cannot be asked of someone's skill at cards or prudence in investments.

What is involved in our descriptions of people as knowing how to make and appreciate jokes, to talk grammatically, to play chess, to fish, or to argue? Part of what is meant is that, when they perform these operations, they tend to perform them well, i.e. correctly or efficiently or successfully. Their performances come up to certain standards, or satisfy certain criteria. But this is not enough. The well-regulated clock keeps good time and the well-drilled circus seal performs its tricks flawlessly, yet we do not call them 'intelligent'. We reserve this title for the persons responsible for their performances. To be intelligent is not merely to satisfy criteria, but to apply them; to regulate one's actions and not merely to be well-regulated. A person's performance is described as careful or skilful, if in his operations he is ready to detect and correct lapses, to repeat and improve upon successes, to profit from the examples of others and so forth. He applies criteria in performing critically, that is, in trying to get things right.

This point is commonly expressed in the vernacular by saying that an action exhibits intelligence, if, and only if, the agent is thinking what he is doing while he is doing it, and thinking what he is doing in such a manner that he would not do the action so well if he were not thinking what he is doing. This popular idiom is sometimes appealed to as evidence in favour of the intellectualist legend. Champions of this legend are apt to try to reassimilate knowing *how* to knowing *that* by arguing that intelligent performance involves the observance of rules, or the application of criteria. It follows that the operation which is characterized as intelligent must be preceded by an intellectual acknowledgement of these rules or criteria; that is, the agent must first go through the internal process of avowing to himself certain propositions about what is to be done ('maxims', 'imperatives', or 'regulative propositions' as they are sometimes called); only then can he execute his performance in accordance with those dictates. He must preach to himself before he can practise. The chef must recite his recipes to himself before he can cook according to them; the hero must lend his inner ear to some appropriate moral imperative before swimming out to save the drowning man; the chess-player must run over in his head all the relevant rules and tactical maxims of the game before he can make correct, and skilful moves. To do something thinking what one is doing is, according to this legend, always to do two things; namely, to consider certain appropriate propositions, or prescriptions, and to put into practice what these propositions or prescriptions enjoin. It is to do a bit of theory and then to do a bit of practice.

Certainly we often do not only reflect before we act but reflect in order to act properly. The chess-player may require some time in which to plan his moves before he makes them. Yet the general assertion that all intelligent performance requires to be prefaced by the consideration of appropriate propositions rings unplausibly, even when it is apologetically conceded that the required consideration is often very swift and may go quite unmarked by the agent. I shall argue that the intellectualist legend is false and that when we describe a performance as intelligent, this does not entail the double operation of considering and executing. [. . .]

The crucial objection to the intellectualist legend is this. The consideration of propositions is itself an operation the execution of which can be more or less intelligent, less or more stupid. But if, for any operation to be intelligently executed, a prior theoretical operation had first to be performed and performed intelligently, it would be a logical impossibility for anyone ever to break into the circle.

Let us consider some salient points at which this regress would arise. According to the legend, whenever an agent does anything intelligently, his act is preceded and steered by another internal act of considering a regulative proposition appropriate to his practical problem. But what makes him consider the one maxim which is appropriate rather than any of the thousands which are not? Why does the hero not find himself calling to mind a cooking-recipe, or a rule of Formal Logic? Perhaps he does, but then his intellectual process is silly and not sensible. Intelligently reflecting how to act is, among other things, considering what is pertinent and disregarding what is inappropriate. Must we then say that for the hero's reflections how to act to be intelligent he must first reflect how best to reflect how to act? The endlessness of this implied regress shows that the application of the criterion of appropriateness does not entail the occurrence of a process of considering this criterion.

Next, supposing still that to act reasonably I must first perpend the reason for so acting, how am I led to make a suitable application of the reason to the particular situation which my action is to meet? For the reason, or maxim, is inevitably a proposition of some generality. It cannot embody specifications to fit every detail of the particular state of affairs. Clearly, once more, I must be sensible and not stupid, and this good sense cannot itself be a product of the intellectual acknowledgements of any general principle. A soldier does not become a shrewd general merely by endorsing the strategic principles of Clausewitz; he must also be competent to apply them. Knowing how to apply maxims cannot be reduced to, or derived from, the acceptance of those or any other maxims.

To put it quite generally, the absurd assumptions made by the intellectualist legend is this, that a performance of any sort inherits all its title to intelligence from some anterior internal operation of planning what to do. Now very often we do go through such a process of planning what to do, and, if we are silly, our planning is silly, if shrewd, our planning is shrewd. It is also notoriously possible for us to plan shrewdly and perform stupidly, i.e. to flout our precepts in our practice. By the original argument, therefore, our intellectual planning process must inherit its title to shrewdness from yet another interior process of planning to plan, and this process could in its turn be silly or shrewd. The regress is infinite, and this reduces to absurdity the theory that for an operation to be intelligent it must be steered by a prior intellectual operation. What distinguishes sensible from silly operations is not their parentage but their procedure, and this holds no less for intellectual than for practical performances. 'Intelligent' cannot be defined in terms of 'intellectual' or 'knowing how' in terms of 'knowing *that*'; 'thinking what I am doing' does not connote 'both thinking what to do and doing it'. When

I do something intelligently, i.e. thinking what I am doing, I am doing one thing and not two. My performance has a special procedure or manner, not special antecedents. [. . .]

II

When we describe glass as brittle, or sugar as soluble, we are using dispositional concepts, the logical force of which is this. The brittleness of glass does not consist in the fact that it is at a given moment actually being shivered. It may be brittle without ever being shivered. To say that it is brittle is to say that if it ever is, or ever had been, struck or strained, it would fly, or have flown, into fragments. To say that sugar is soluble is to say that it would dissolve, or would have dissolved, if immersed in water.

A statement ascribing a dispositional property to a thing has much, though not everything, in common with a statement subsuming the thing under a law. To possess a dispositional property is not to be in a particular state, or to undergo a particular change; it is to be bound or liable to be in a particular state, or to undergo a particular change, when a particular condition is realized. The same is true about specifically human dispositions such as qualities of character. My being an habitual smoker does not entail that I am at this or that moment smoking; it is my permanent proneness to smoke when I am not eating, sleeping, lecturing or attending funerals, and have not quite recently been smoking.

In discussing dispositions it is initially helpful to fasten on the simplest models, such as the brittleness of glass or the smoking habit of a man. For in describing these dispositions it is easy to unpack the hypothetical proposition implicitly conveyed in the ascription of the dispositional properties. To be brittle is just to be bound or likely to fly into fragments in such and such conditions; to be a smoker is just to be bound or likely to fill, light and draw on a pipe in such and such conditions. These are simple, single-track dispositions, the actualizations of which are nearly uniform.

But the practice of considering such simple models of dispositions, though initially helpful, leads at a later stage to erroneous assumptions. There are many dispositions the actualizations of which can take a wide and perhaps unlimited variety of shapes; many disposition-concepts are determinable concepts. When an object is described as hard, we do not mean only that it would resist deformation; we mean also that it would, for example, give out a sharp sound if struck, that it would cause us pain if we came into sharp contact with it, that resilient objects would bounce off it, and so on indefinitely. If we wished to unpack all that is conveyed in describing an animal as gregarious, we should similarly have to produce an infinite series of different hypothetical propositions.

Now the higher-grade dispositions of people with which this inquiry is largely concerned are, in general, not single-track dispositions, but dispositions the exercises of which are indefinitely heterogeneous. When Jane Austen wished to show the specific kind of pride which characterized the heroine of *Pride and Prejudice*, she had to represent her actions, words, thoughts, and feelings in a thousand different situations. There is no one standard type of action or reaction such that Jane Austen could say 'My heroine's kind of pride was just the tendency to do this, whenever a situation of that sort arose.'

Epistemologists, among others, often fall into the trap of expecting dispositions to have uniform exercises. For instance, when they recognize that the verbs 'know' and 'believe' are ordinarily used dispositionally, they assume that there must therefore exist one-pattern intellectual processes in which these cognitive dispositions are actualized. Flouting the testimony of experience, they postulate that, for example, a man who believes that the earth is round must from time to time be going through some unique proceeding or cognizing, 'judging', or internally re-asserting, with a feeling of confidence, 'The earth is round'. In fact, of course, people do not harp on statements in this way, and even if they did so and even if we knew that they did, we still should not be satisfied that they believed that the earth was round, unless we also found them inferring, imagining, saying and doing a great number of other things as well. If we found them inferring, imagining, saying and doing these other things, we should be satisfied that they believed the earth to be round, even if we had the best reasons for thinking that they never internally harped on the original statement at all. However often and stoutly a skater avers to us or to himself, that the ice will bear, he shows that he has his qualms, if he keeps to the edge of the pond, calls his children away from the middle, keeps his eye on the life-belts or continually speculates what would happen if the ice broke.

III

It is being maintained throughout that when we characterize people by mental predicates, we are not making untestable inferences to any ghostly processes occurring in streams of consciousness which we are debarred from visiting; we are describing the ways in which those people conduct parts of their predominantly public behaviour. True, we go beyond what we see them do and hear them say, but this going beyond is not a going behind, in the sense of making inferences to occult causes; it is going beyond in the sense of considering, in the first instance, the powers and propensities of which their actions are exercises. [...]

Understanding a person's deeds and words is not, therefore, any kind of problematic divination of occult processes. For this divination does not and cannot occur, whereas understanding does occur. Of course it is part of my general thesis that the supposed occult processes are themselves mythical; there exists nothing to be the object of the postulated diagnoses. But for the present purpose it is enough to prove that, if there were such inner states and operations, one person would not be able to make probable inferences to their occurrence in the inner life of another.

If understanding does not consist in inferring, or guessing, the alleged inner-life precursors of overt actions, what is it? If it does not require mastery of psychological theory together with the ability to apply it, what knowledge does it require? We saw that a spectator who cannot play chess also cannot follow the play of others; a person who cannot read or speak Swedish cannot understand what is spoken or written in Swedish; and a person whose reasoning powers are weak is bad at following and retaining the arguments of others. Understanding is a part of knowing *how*. The knowledge that is required for understanding intelligent performances of a specific kind is some degree of competence in performances of that kind. The competent critic of prose-style, experimental technique, or embroidery, must at least know how to write, experiment or sew. Whether or not he has also learned some psychology matters about as much as whether he has learned any chemistry, neurology or economics. These studies may in certain circumstances assist his appreciation of what he is criticizing; but the one necessary condition is that he has some mastery of the art or procedure, examples of which he is to appraise. For one person to see the jokes that another makes, the one thing he must have is a sense of humour and even that special brand of sense of humour of which those jokes are exercises.

Of course, to execute an operation intelligently is not exactly the same thing as to follow its execution intelligently. The agent is originating, the spectator is only contemplating. But the rules which the agent observes and the criteria which he applies are one with those which govern the spectator's applause and jeers. The commentator on Plato's philosophy need not possess much philosophic originality, but if he cannot, as too many commentators cannot, appreciate the force, drift or motive of a philosophical argument, his comments will be worthless. If he can appreciate them, then he knows how to do part of what Plato knew how to do. [. . .]

Before we conclude this inquiry into understanding, something must be said about partial understanding and misunderstanding.

Attention has already been drawn to certain parallelisms and certain non-parallelisms between the concept of knowing *that* and the concept of knowing *how*. A further non-parallelism must now be noticed. We never speak of a person having partial knowledge of a fact or truth, save in the special sense of his having knowledge of a part of a body of facts or truths. A boy can be said to have partial knowledge of the counties of England, if he knows some of them and does not know others. But he could not be said to have incomplete knowledge of Sussex being an English county. Either he knows this fact or he does not know it. On the other hand, it is proper and normal to speak of a person knowing in part how to do something, i.e. of his having a particular capacity in a limited degree. An ordinary chess-player knows the game pretty well but a champion knows it better, and even the champion has still much to learn.

This holds too, as we should now expect, of understanding. An ordinary chess-player can partly follow the tactics and strategy of a champion; perhaps after much study he will completely understand the methods used by the champion in certain particular matches. But he can never wholly anticipate how the champion will fight his next contest and he is never as quick or sure in his interpretations of the champion's moves as the champion is in making, or perhaps, in explaining them.

Learning *how* or improving in ability is not like learning *that* or acquiring information. Truths can be imparted, procedures can only be inculcated, and while inculcation is a gradual process, imparting is relatively sudden. It makes sense to ask at what

moment someone became apprised of a truth, but not to ask at
what moment someone acquired a skill. 'Part-trained' is a significant phrase, 'part-informed' is not. Training is the art of setting
tasks which the pupils have not yet accomplished but are not any
longer quite incapable of accomplishing.

The notion of misunderstanding raises no general theoretical
difficulties. When the card-player's tactics are misconstrued by his
opponents, the manoeuvre they think they discern is indeed a
possible manoeuvre of the game, though it happens not to be his
manoeuvre. Only someone who knew the game could interpret
the play as part of the execution of the supposed manoeuvre.
Misunderstanding is a by-product of knowing *how*. Only a person
who is at least a partial master of the Russian tongue can make
the wrong sense of a Russian expression. Mistakes are exercises of
competences. [. . .]

Source: *The Concept of Mind* (Hutchinson), Ch. II. (Extracts.)

36 Knowledge, Opinion and Probability (1949)

WILLIAM KNEALE

The extent of our knowledge is less than we could wish. It may
perhaps be wider than some philosophers have supposed, but it is
clearly not wide enough to enable us to answer with certainty all
the questions that arise in the practical affairs of everyday life
and the still more numerous questions that puzzle us when we
study history or science. Probability may be described as the
substitute with which we try to make good the shortcomings of
our knowledge. It does not fill the gap entirely, for there are
many questions about which we cannot even form opinions; but
it often enables us to act rationally when without it we should be
reduced to helplessness, and it gives at least some satisfaction to
our intellectual curiosity. This was perhaps the meaning of Bishop
Butler's famous remark, 'To us, probability is the very guide
of life.'[1] He was contrasting our state with that of an infinite

[1] *Analogy of Religion*, Introduction, § 4.

intelligence which could discern 'each possible object of knowledge, whether past, present or future, . . . absolutely as it is in
itself'; and he wished to argue that, as in the common pursuits of
life we rely on a kind of reasoning which can provide only
probable conclusions, so too in theology we should be prepared
to make tentative arguments from experience. I do not know
whether his method is in favour now among theologians, but
there can be no doubt of the importance which empirical scientists attach to it.

The variety of the situations in which we use the notion of
probability is illustrated by the following sentences, each of
which contains the word 'probable' or one of its derivatives:

(a) It is probable that there will be rain before the day is over.
(b) It is very improbable that a man with testimonials as good
    as these will fall into dishonesty.
(c) Stonehenge was probably built for use as a temple.
(d) If Hannibal had marched on Rome, he would probably
    have taken it.
(e) We know now that the stories which Marco Polo told on
    his return to Venice were true, however improbable they
    may have been for his contemporaries.
(f) The probability of throwing a number greater than four
    with a true die is 1:3.
(g) Statistics indicate that if a wounded man is treated im-
    mediately with penicillin the probability of his escaping
    sepsis is more than 9:10.
(h) We cannot assign high probabilities to the generalizations
    made in sociology, because the number of cases in which
    we are able to confirm them is not very large.
(i) The probability of the atomic theory of matter has been
    greatly increased by the evidence which physicists and
    chemists have collected during the past century.

In ordinary life we often have occasion to make remarks like (a)
and (b), and we often meet statements such as (c), (d), and (e)
when we read works on history. Example (e) is worth special
notice, because it shows that what is improbable may nevertheless be true. Although as plain men we do not often try to make
precise numerical estimates of probability, we all recognize that
statements like (f) and (g) are needed in various branches of
science and in certain specialisms such as actuarial work.
Examples (h) and (i) are interesting as specimens of the way in

which we pass judgement on scientific generalizations and explanatory hypotheses.

Our dependence on the notion of probability is not confined, however, to those cases in which we employ the word 'probable' or one of its derivatives to state our views, for there are other ways of expressing the same thought. Sometimes we speak of the balance of chances. At other times such words as 'likely', 'reliable', 'trustworthy' seem more appropriate. And we must admit on reflection that in many cases in which we do not ordinarily use the word 'probable' or any equivalent expression it would be wiser to do so if there were any danger of misunderstanding. I may, for example, assert without qualification that Julius Caesar landed on the south coast of England and even count this as an item of my knowledge, but if I am pressed to say whether I know it for certain, I can only reply that I have it on good authority and consider it extremely probable or almost certain. It is clear, therefore, that the realm of probability is very large indeed and covers even much of what we loosely call our knowledge. [. . .]

Subjectivist theories of probability: Meanings of 'Belief'

If, as seems natural, we start by contrasting probability statements with statements in which we express knowledge, the question immediately arises: 'What then do we express by probability statements?'

One of the commonest ways of introducing the notion of probability into discourse is by means of an adverb. We may say, for example, 'It is probably raining in the Hebrides.' In late antiquity any statement which included an adverb of this kind or any similar expression (e.g. 'it is probable that . . .' or 'it is possible that . . .') was classified as *modal*, and it is now the custom for logicians to use the name 'modality' for that division of their study in which they treat of necessity, possibility, and probability. This terminology is not illuminating, and may even be misleading. In what sense does the adverb 'probably' signify a mode or manner? Clearly it is not used in the same way as ordinary adverbs, which qualify verbs much as adjectives qualify nouns. When I say that it is raining heavily, I mean that it is raining in a special way, but when I say that it is probably raining, I certainly do not want to suggest that there is a special mode or manner of raining which I call 'probably raining'. Such an interpretation is so obviously absurd that it has never been seriously defended. On the contrary most persons who give any thought to the matter are inclined to jump immediately to the opposite extreme and say that probability must be subjective.

One subjectivist theory which has found its way into many of the older text-books of logic is presented as a doctrine about different modes or manners of assertion. It is argued that a man who utters the sentence 'It is probably raining' is asserting the proposition that it is raining but doing so in a special fashion or with a special qualification, much as a man who says 'Unfortunately it is raining' may be held to assert the proposition that it is raining but with an additional comment about his own state of mind in making the assertion. It is difficult to attach any precise meaning to the phrase 'mode or manner of assertion' as it is used in this theory; but we need not trouble ourselves about the matter, for the doctrine seems to be founded on the mistaken assumption that any sentence which contains one of the modal adverbs must be taken as an assertion of the proposition which would ordinarily be asserted by the use of the sentence without the adverb. This assumption is only plausible when we are dealing with modal statements which contain the adverb 'necessarily'.[2] If I say 'It is necessarily raining', I am indeed committed to the assertion that it is raining. But if I say 'It is probably raining', I am not asserting in any way that it is raining, and the discovery that no rain was falling would not refute my statement, although it might render it useless. The mistake seems to be due to overmuch concentration on the adverbial expression of modality. In order to escape from it we need only remember that 'It is probably raining' is equivalent to 'It is probable that it is raining'. In the second formulation we have no excuse for assuming an assertion that it is raining, since the words 'it is raining' occur here only as they do in 'It is false that it is raining', i.e. as a subordinate clause. In short, the view that probability is a mode of assertion is derived from the same source as the view that probability is a mode of being, namely, from a failure to see that modal adverbs function in a quite peculiar way.

The most common subjectivist theory of probability is based on the very different assumption that a probability statement is really an assertion about the speaker's own state of mind. According to this doctrine probability is neither a mode of being nor a

2 Or 'actually', if that is allowed to be modal.

mode of assertion. It belongs to propositions (i.e. thinkables or assertable contents), but not as an intrinsic property, for it is simply the degree of belief which we attach to them. James Bernoulli, who made great contributions to the mathematical theory of probability, appears to have held some such view, and he has been followed by a number of other distinguished persons. We must therefore examine the suggestion carefully.

Having started with an antithesis between probability and knowledge, it is natural that we should go on to connect probability with belief, since the word 'belief' is commonly supposed to stand for a mental attitude by which we supplement our meagre knowledge. We must be cautious, however, for the word appears to have two very different senses. These can be distinguished most easily by means of examples.

If I say of a man in a lunatic asylum 'The poor fellow believes he is Napoleon', I mean that the man is wholly convinced he is Napoleon and would when questioned say he knew he was Napoleon. This kind of belief may be said to ape knowledge, since it is expressed in precisely the same way as knowledge and is for the believer indistinguishable at the moment from knowledge. It is most striking in lunatics, who maintain their beliefs against all evidence, but it occurs in normal men whenever they fall into error. Anyone who unthinkingly mistakes a stranger for a friend or makes a false step in a calculation is in this condition, although, unlike the lunatic, he can be brought without much difficulty to change his mind. It is not even essential to this use of the word 'belief' that what is believed should be false. Most of us when doing simple calculations in arithmetic speak without apprehending the truth of what we say. No doubt a man who says 'Seven and five make twelve' can, if he chooses, either see the necessity of his statement or at least reflect that he has been well trained and is probably giving the right answer like a well-made calculating machine. But in practice we rarely do either the one or the other; and it is fortunate that we do not, because life is too short for us to be rational all the time. The state of mind which I have described has been variously called 'being under an impression', 'thinking without question', and 'taking for granted'.[3] I shall use the last of these names because such belief is a kind of behaviour rather than a kind of thought in the

[3] J. Cook Wilson, *Statement and Inference*, p. 109, and H. H. Price, 'Some Considerations about Belief', in the *Proceedings of the Aristotelian Society*, 1934–5.

strictest sense of that word. It consists in behaving as though one knew something which one does not in fact know. Here 'behaviour' must be understood to include not only overt bodily movements, but also the use of symbols for making assertions to oneself.

If, on the other hand, I say of myself 'I do not know whether it is raining in the Hebrides, but I believe it is', the situation which I describe is very different. No one would say of himself that at the time of speaking he was behaving in all respects as though he knew something which he did not in fact know. Furthermore, when I contrast my present believing with knowledge, I am prepared to admit, in principle at least, that what I believe may not be the case. Sometimes this situation is distinguished from taking for granted by an antithesis between partial and complete belief; but this terminology is unsatisfactory for technical use in philosophy, because it suggests that we have to do only with a difference of degree whereas in fact there is a difference of kind. It seems desirable, therefore, to drop the use of the word 'belief' in this connexion, whenever there is any possible danger of misunderstanding, and to speak instead of opinion, which can scarcely be confused with taking for granted. What I suggest involves admittedly a small modification of ordinary usage, since we do not commonly apply the word 'opinion' in cases where we claim very high probability for our views. It may also be objected that the verb 'opine' is an unpleasant archaism. These disadvantages are, however, a comparatively small price to pay for clarity about a fundamental distinction.

Corresponding to the difference between taking for granted and opinion there is a difference to be noticed between two senses in which we may speak of the degree of a belief. A man who takes something for granted may be said to believe it more or less firmly, according to the difficulty which there would be in bringing him to change his mind. Normally a man who takes something for granted can easily be brought to realize his situation; but it is well known that emotional prejudice may render a man blind to evidence. In the extreme case of lunacy irrational convictions may become unshakable. What the upholders of the subjectivist theory of probability mean when they speak of degree of belief is clearly not this, but rather the strength of opinion in the mind of a man who admits that what he opines may not be the case. Some philosophers and psychologists speak in this connexion of the degree of confidence which a man feels while

opining, and I think this phrase would be
supporters of the subjectivist theory as a desc
reference to which they try to define probability.

According to this interpretation, the subject.
probability is open to the same objections as hav
urged against subjectivist theories in moral philosc
probability of a proposition for any man were simply
of confidence which he felt in it, every man would be   .ot
judge of the probability of a proposition for himself, an... there
could be no useful argument about probabilities, since every
probability statement would be a report of the speaker's feelings
and nothing more. There would be no incompatibility between a
statement by one man that it was probably raining and a statement by another that rain was unlikely at that time. We do not in
practice admit this. On the contrary, we think it possible to argue
about probabilities and maintain that some men's judgements are
better than those of others. If an expert says that a picture is
probably the work of Rembrandt, we pay more attention to his
view than we should to a similar pronouncement from an ignorant
man. When a man sees a black cat on his way to a casino and
says 'I shall probably win today: give me your money to place on
your behalf', we decline the invitation if we are prudent, even
although we believe the man to be honest.

These considerations have led some philosophers to put forward a revised version of the subjectivist theory according to
which the probability of a proposition *A* is the strength of a
rational opinion that *A*. This new version is much more plausible
than the old and has many supporters, but it cannot be regarded
as satisfactory without some explanation of the meaning of the
word 'rational' in this context.

If the act of opining *A* is to be called rational the proposition *A*
which is opined must be self-consistent. This much is obvious,
but there is also another sense, not so obvious, in which consistency or coherence is required for rationality in opinions. This can
be explained most easily by consideration of betting, in which
men are said to express the strength of their opinions. Let us
suppose that a bookmaker offers odds of two to one against each
of four exhaustive and mutually exclusive alternatives. If a client
lays bets on each of the alternatives at these odds, he is behaving
irrationally. Any one of the four opinions to which he gives expression by his bets may be rational, but they cannot all be
rational. Since the alternatives are related in the way described,

strengths of rational opinions concerning them cannot be independent. We have, so to say, a limited fund of confidence to distribute between the four alternatives, and if we give more than a quarter to one we must give less to some of the others. The man in the example is over-generous somewhere in his distribution and ends with an overdraft on his confidence account. This shows itself in the fact that he is bound to lose by his bets, whatever happens. Indeed, the whole art of the bookmaker consists in so adjusting the odds which he offers that the body of his clients considered as a whole must lose, whatever happens; and this is not difficult, because the opinions expressed by the clients are for the most part not co-ordinated one with another.

These considerations are important (we shall see later that they form the basis of the whole mathematical theory of probability), but they do not provide an explanation of the sense in which the supporters of the revised subjectivist theory speak of rational opinions. For we have shown only that rational opinions must be coherent in so far as they are concerned with related propositions, and we cannot say that coherence is enough to guarantee the rationality of any opinions which cohere. There must, then, it seems, be some sense in which a single opinion can be rational without reference to other opinions. Now the persons who introduce the revised subjectivist theory apparently consider that an act of opining is rational if, and only if, the person who opines has the degree of confidence which he ought to have in what he opines. How are we to interpret the word 'ought' in this context? There is no question of moral obligation here, nor yet of aesthetic fitness, and the only possible explanation seems to be that a man has the degree of confidence which he ought to have in a certain proposition when he has that degree which is logically justified. But in what sense can a certain degree of confidence be logically justified?

It may perhaps be suggested that a certain degree of confidence is justified by the intrinsic character of the proposition opined, and that rational opinion is simply the appropriate attitude to that proposition; but I do not think that anyone would wish seriously to defend such a view. No proposition (unless it is either a truism or an absurdity) contains in itself anything to indicate that we ought to have a certain degree of confidence in it. On the contrary, if we are to do justice to common usage, we must allow that the same proposition may have different probabilities at different times, and this is plainly inconsistent with any attempt to make the probability of a proposition depend on its intrinsic character. There is only one possible account of the matter which makes the revised subjectivist theory at all plausible, and that is to say that the degree of confidence which a man ought to have in what he opines is the degree justified by the evidence at his disposal. When, however, this account is properly developed, it shows that the subjectivist project of defining probability by reference to our feelings of confidence is useless and misguided. [. . .]

The nature of opinion

So far we have spoken of opinion as though it were a mental activity distinct from knowledge and involving or accompanied by a feeling of greater or less confidence. This treatment is suggested by the ordinary linguistic usage according to which opining *A* is contrasted with knowing *A*. If, however, the arguments put forward in the two previous sections are correct, it is possible to simplify our account and to explain more clearly how opinion is related to knowledge.

A man who opines *A* cannot, it seems, be said to have a rational opinion unless the degree of his confidence in *A* is justified by the evidence before his mind. But it is not sufficient for rationality that the evidence should in fact justify the degree of confidence which he has. The man must also know that it does so. Otherwise his condition is like that of a schoolboy who gives the right answer to a mathematical question without knowing why it is right. Even machines may sometimes give right answers to questions, but we do not call them rational, because they do not know the reasons for the answers which they give. Now a man who knows that the evidence at his disposal justifies a certain degree of confidence in proposition *A* must know that the evidence probabilifies *A* to a certain degree; for it is only so that the evidence can justify any degree of confidence. But if a man who has a rational opinion knows all this (even although he may not have the terminology in which to state it explicitly), why need we say in addition that he has a certain degree of confidence in *A* which somehow corresponds with the degree to which the evidence probabilifies *A*? Can we not content ourselves with the assertion that rational opinion is the knowledge that the available evidence probabilifies a proposition to a certain degree?

One possible objection to this simple account of the matter is that, since we began by contrasting opinion with knowledge, we must not end by defining opinion as a kind of knowledge. There is, however, a confusion of thought in this argument. A man who opines A is certainly not knowing A. Indeed, in order to opine A he must know that he does not know A; for we form opinions on questions only when we have realized that we cannot answer those questions with knowledge. But, according to the definition which I have suggested, a man who rationally opines A is knowing not A but a relation between A and some facts which we call the available evidence. It is convenient to state the whole situation by saying that the man opines A, but we must not therefore assume that opining is a simple attitude towards a proposition and excludes knowledge of any kind. We have already seen that, if it is to be rational, opinion must involve knowledge that the available evidence probabilifies a proposition to a certain degree, and there should therefore be no objection on this score to saying that rational opinion is just such knowledge. We may, of course, continue to contrast opinion with knowledge in the ordinary way; for when we do so, we mean by 'opinion' what is opined and we distinguish this from what is known.

A more formidable objection to the proposed definition of rational opinion is based on an appeal to introspection. It is said that, if we examine our state of mind when we are rationally opining, we can discover a certain feeling of confidence in addition to the knowledge which has been mentioned as essential for rational opinion. For my own part, I can discover no such feeling, although I admit that, like other people, I often use such phrases as 'I am confident that . . .'. It is unprofitable, however, in such a matter as this to set one report of introspection against another. If the issue were to be decided in this way, we might conceivably have to conclude that some people have the feeling and others do not, just as some people can hear shrill noises when others can hear nothing. We none of us believe that this is a satisfactory end to the dispute, and I shall therefore try to show that those who maintain there is a specific feeling of confidence must be misreporting their observations.

The degree of confidence felt by a man while he is in the state of rational opinion is supposed to correspond with the degree to which the evidence at his disposal probabilifies the proposition he is entertaining. I have spoken in an earlier section of the distribution of a fund of confidence between various alternatives, and there may be some persons who are disposed to take such metaphors seriously, but on reflection we must surely recognize that there cannot be any feeling of which these things can be said with literal significance.

In the first place, degrees of probability are sometimes measured by fractions between 0 and 1. Are we to maintain that for every conceivable fraction there is some appropriate degree of confidence? Feelings have only intensive magnitude. They may be graded as more or less intense, and we may, if we choose, assign proper fractions to them, so that more intense feelings are co-ordinated with larger fractions. But it is absurd to say of one feeling that it is just twice as intense as another of the same kind, because feelings of great intensity do not have parts which are themselves feelings of less intensity. There can therefore be no measurement of feelings in any strict sense of the word 'measurement', and feelings of confidence cannot correspond in any *necessary* way with probabilities which are measured by fractions. It seems fantastic, indeed, to maintain that there are infinitely many distinguishable degrees of confidence from zero to some maximum intensity, but, even if there were, we could only say that between any two degrees it was possible to find a third, and this would not suffice to connect each necessarily with a particular fraction.

Secondly, even if those who believe in feelings of confidence are content to say that the feelings do not correspond exactly and necessarily with different degrees of probability, they have to face a serious difficulty about the existence of a maximum intensity of confidence. Their account of the matter seems to require that there should be such an upper limit to which feelings of confidence approach asymptotically with increasing probability. I say 'approach asymptotically' because all probability falls short of the certainty which we have in knowledge and it is obvious that knowledge itself is not accompanied by confidence. When we realize that $2 + 2 = 4$, we do not sweat with any feeling of supreme intensity. But there is something absurd in the suggestion that any kind of feeling should have an upper limit of the sort required by this theory. There may in fact be a maximum intensity for feelings such as joy and sorrow, but we do not suppose that the limit is imposed in these cases by logical necessity, or that it is a limit in the sense of something to which actual feelings approach asymptotically. If, however, there are feelings of confidence, they must all, it seems, lie within a range of which the unattainable upper limit is perfect or complete confidence, and this implies that lesser feelings of confidence must be in some way imperfect or incomplete, which is impossible if they are simple feelings such as the upholders of the theory seem to postulate.

When we speak, as we admittedly do, of feeling confident, we are referring, I think, to the absence of serious doubt or questioning from our minds, much as when we speak of feeling tranquil we are referring to the absence of uneasiness. I do not mean to suggest by this that doubt is a simple feeling which can correspond exactly in degree with the interval by which the probability of a proposition falls short of certainty, for such a suggestion would lead us back into difficulties of the same kind as those which beset the doctrine about confidence we have been examining. Doubt appears rather to be a complex state involving (a) a wish to find the answer to some question, (b) a realization that one cannot answer the question with knowledge, and (c) a feeling of frustration and restlessness. Whether pleasure or displeasure predominates in the experience seems to depend on such factors as the relevance of the question at issue to the emotional interests of the doubter, the nature of his mood at the time, and the duration of the doubt; but in general the tone is unpleasant. Anyone who opines feels some doubt about what he opines, but it is undesirable to include a reference to doubt in our definition of opinion, because the emotional element in doubt (i.e. the feeling of frustration and restlessness) is not part of what we have in mind when we use the word 'opinion'. Our attention is directed then to the estimation of probabilities, and doubt is connected with this only in a causal fashion. For it is doubt which provides our motive for seeking fresh evidence and trying to reach rational opinions.

When an opinion has been formed, a disposition to doubt may, and indeed should, persist, since the question at issue has not been answered with certainty; but a wise man tries to prevent the emotional element from disturbing him unduly at this time. If we know that we cannot get more evidence, and that in relation to what we have the probability of a proposition is very high, we may even decide to dismiss all further doubt about the proposition as unprofitable. Such a decision is not a voluntary transition to a state of taking for granted, for we cannot will ourselves into a blind acceptance of anything. It is rather a resolution to treat the question as though it were settled and to take no more steps, whether practical or intellectual, to cope with the contingency of the proposition's being false. We say to ourselves that we have more important things to occupy our minds. No historian, for instance, thinks it worth while to try to work out an historical hypothesis based on the supposition that Julius Caesar did not land in Britain or to look for more evidence in favour of the commonly accepted view. Sometimes, as in the example just cited, no effort is required to reach a state of equanimity, but at other times, when strong emotional interests are concerned and there is a natural disposition to optimism or pessimism, it may be very difficult indeed to dismiss unprofitable doubt. A man who knows that there is only one chance in a thousand of his surviving a serious injury may continue to think of that possibility when he would be better employed in preparing to die; and a man who knows that there is only one chance in a thousand of his being killed in an air-raid may continue to worry about that contingency when he would be better employed in composing himself for sleep by reading a novel.

If anyone maintains in spite of all these arguments that he can still detect by introspection a positive feeling of confidence, with various degrees on various occasions, he must, I think, be confusing confidence with a somewhat vague memory impression of the number of past cases on which his estimate of probability is based. Such memory impressions play a very important part in some of our thought about probabilities, and it will be necessary to consider their use in a later section.

If rational opinion is to be defined as the knowledge that some proposition is probabilified to a certain degree by the available evidence, irrational opinion may be defined as taking the probability of a proposition for granted. There are, however, two ways in which opinion may fall short of rationality. Some proposition which is treated as evidence (in the sense in which evidence must be known) may be merely taken for granted, or the probability relation itself may be taken for granted. These two possible defects are analogous to, although not identical with, defects which may occur in a deductive argument. A man who argues that because *A* therefore *B* may be taking *A* for granted or may be taking for granted that if *A* then *B*. The fault of treating something as evidence which is not known calls for no special comment in a discussion of probability, but some of the ways in which we may depart from rationality when thinking about the probability relation itself will have to be considered in due course. It is perhaps worth repeating here that taking for granted need not necessarily involve error, and that no man can be wholly rational in every minute of his life.

The result of our analysis is a very simple account of the relations between knowledge and belief. In the past some philosophers have grouped these together as kinds of judgement, and then sought vainly for differentiae by which to distinguish them. Others, protesting against this confusion, have assumed that there are two or more faculties (loosely called cognitive) whose exercise may lead to the affirmation of a proposition. According to the view presented here, knowledge is *sui generis* and the two varieties of belief are to be defined by reference to it. The belief we call taking for granted is behaving as though one knew when one does not in fact know, and the belief we identify with opinion is either knowing or taking for granted probability relations. Each of the terms 'knowledge', 'taking for granted', and 'opinion' can, of course, be used either in an actual or in a dispositional sense, but the dispositional sense must always be defined by reference to the actual sense. Actual knowledge, that is to say, noticing or realizing, is therefore the fundamental notion in the study called theory of knowledge.[4]

Source: Probability and Induction (O.U.P.), Secs. 1, 2 and 4.

[4] The dispositional use of 'know' is much commoner than the actual in ordinary speech, but it is not, as some philosophers have maintained, the only permissible usage. Consider, for example, the sentence 'When a bomb fell in the next street, he knew that it was time to take shelter'. Here 'knew' is equivalent to 'realized'.

PERCEPTION

37 The Falsity of the Accepted Notion of Heat (1623)

GALILEO

I want to propose some examination of that which we call heat, whose generally accepted notion comes very far from the truth if my serious doubts be correct, inasmuch as it is supposed to be a true accident, affection, and quality really residing in the thing which we perceive to be heated. Nevertheless I say, that indeed I feel myself impelled by the necessity, as soon as I conceive a piece of matter or corporeal substance, of conceiving that in its own nature it is bounded and figured in such and such a figure, that in relation to others it is large or small, that it is in this or that place, in this or that time, that it is in motion or remains at rest, that it touches or does not touch another body, that it is single, few, or many; in short by no imagination can a body be separated from such conditions; but that it must be white or red, bitter or sweet, sounding or mute, of a pleasant or unpleasant odour, I do not perceive my mind forced to acknowledge it necessarily accompanied by such conditions; so if the senses were not the escorts, perhaps the reason or the imagination by itself would never have arrived at them. Hence I think that these tastes, odours, colours, etc., on the side of the object in which they seem to exist, are nothing else than mere names, but hold their residence solely in the sensitive body; so that if the animal were removed, every such quality would be abolished and annihilated.

Source: Il Saggiatore trans. E. A. Burtt in *The Metaphysical Foundations of Modern Physical Science* (Routledge).

38 (i) Knowledge of Corporeal Objects (1642)

RENÉ DESCARTES

[. . .] I have a passive power of sensation—of getting and recognising the ideas of sensible objects. But I could never have the use of it if there were not also in existence an active power, either in myself or in something else, to produce or make the ideas. This power certainly cannot exist in me; for it presupposes no action of my intellect, and the ideas are produced without my co-operation, and often against my will. The only remaining possibility is that it inheres in some substance other than myself. This must contain all the reality that exists representatively in the ideas produced by this active power; and it must contain it (as I remarked previously) either just as it is represented, or in some higher form. So either this substance is a body—is of corporeal nature—and contains actually whatever is contained representatively in the ideas; or else it is God, or some creature nobler than bodies, and contains the same reality in a higher form. But since God is not deceitful, it is quite obvious that he neither implants the ideas in me by his own direct action, nor yet by means of some creature that contains the representative reality of the ideas not precisely as they represent it, but only in some higher form. For God has given me no faculty at all to discern their origin; on the other hand, he has given me a strong inclination to believe that these ideas proceed from corporeal objects; so I do not see how it would make sense to say God is not deceitful, if in fact they proceed from elsewhere, not from corporeal objects. Therefore corporeal objects must exist. It may be that not all bodies are such as my senses apprehend them, for this sensory apprehension is in many ways obscure and confused; but at any rate their nature must comprise whatever I clearly and distinctly understand—that is, whatever, generally considered, falls within the subject-matter of pure mathematics.

There remain some highly doubtful and uncertain points; either mere details, like the sun's having a certain size or shape, or things unclearly understood, like light, sound, pain, and so on. But since God is not deceitful, there cannot possibly occur any error in my opinions but I can correct by means of some faculty God has given me to that end; and this gives me some hope of arriving at the truth even on such matters. Indeed, all nature's lessons undoubtedly contain some truth; for by nature, as a general term, I now mean nothing other than either God himself, or the order of created things established by God; and by *my* nature in particular I mean the complex of all that God has given *me*. [. . .]

It is a lesson of my 'nature', in this sense, to avoid what gives me a sensation of pain, and pursue what gives me a sensation of pleasure, and so on. But it does not seem to be also a lesson of nature to draw any conclusion from sense-perception as regards external objects without a previous examination by the under-standing; for knowledge of the truth about them seems to belong to the mind alone, not to the composite whole.

Thus a star has no more effect on my eye than the flame of a small candle; but from this fact I have no real, positive inclination to believe it is no bigger; this is just an irrational judgment that I made in my earliest years. Again, I have a sensation of heat as I approach the fire; but when I approach the same fire too closely, I have a sensation of pain; so there is nothing to convince me that something in the fire resembles heat, any more than the pain; it is just that there must be something in it (whatever this may turn out to be) that produces the sensations of heat or pain. Again, even if in some region there is nothing to affect the senses, it does not follow that there is no body in it. I can see that on these and many other questions I habitually pervert the order of nature. My sense-perceptions were given me by nature properly for the sole purpose of indicating to the mind what is good or bad for the whole of which the mind is a part; and to this extent they are clear and distinct enough. But I use them as if they were sure criteria for a direct judgment as to the essence of external bodies; and here they give only very obscure and confused indications.

Source: Sixth Meditation, trans. Anscombe and Geach (Nelson). (Extract.)

(ii) The Three Grades of Perception (1642)

In order rightly to see what amount of certainty belongs to sense we must distinguish three grades as falling within it. To the first belongs the immediate affection of the bodily organ by external objects; and this can be nothing else than the motion of the particles of the sensory organs and the change of figure and position due to that motion. The second comprises the immediate mental result, due to the mind's union with the corporeal organ affected; such are the perceptions of pain, of pleasurable stimulation, of thirst, of hunger, of colours, of sound, savour, odour, cold, heat, and the like, which in my Sixth Meditation are stated to arise from the union and, as it were, the intermixture of mind and body. Finally the third contains all those judgments which, on the occasion of motions occurring in the corporeal organ, we have from our earliest years been accustomed to pass about things external to us.

For example, when I see a staff, it is not to be thought that *intentional species*[1] fly off from it and reach the eye, but merely that rays of light reflected from the staff excite certain motions in the optic nerve and, by its mediation, in the brain as well, as I have explained at sufficient length in the Dioptrics. It is in this cerebral motion, which is common to us and to the brutes, that the first grade of perception consists. But from this the second grade of perception results; and that merely extends to the perception of the colour or light reflected from the stick, and is due to the fact that the mind is so intimately conjoined with the brain as to be affected by the motions arising in it. Nothing more than this should be assigned to sense, if we wish to distinguish it accurately from the intellect. For though my judgment that there is a staff situated without me, which judgment results from the sensation of colour by which I am affected, and likewise my reasoning from the extension of that colour, its boundaries, and its position relatively to the parts of my brain, to the size, the shape, and the distance of the said staff, are vulgarly assigned to

[1] F.V. minute images flying through the air commonly called intentional species.

sense, and are consequently here referred to the third grade of sensation, they clearly depend upon the understanding alone. That magnitude, distance and figure can be perceived by reasoning alone, which deduces them one from another, I have proved in the Dioptrics. The difference lies in this alone, that those judgments which now for the first time arise on account of some new apprehension, are assigned to the understanding; but those which have been made from our earliest years in exactly the same manner as at present, about the things that have been wont to affect our senses, as similarly the conclusions of our reasonings, are referred by us to sense. And the reason for this is just that in these matters custom makes us reason and judge so quickly, or rather we recall the judgments previously made about similar things; and thus we fail to distinguish the difference between these operations and a simple sense perception.

Source: Reply to Objections VI, trans. Haldane and Ross (Cambridge University Press). (Extract.)

(iii) The Representative Theory of Perception (1637)

[DISCOURSE I]. It has doubtless some time happened that you were walking across difficult country by night without a torch and had to use a stick to guide yourself; and you may then have noticed that you felt, by means of the stick, the objects in your neighbourhood, and that you could even distinguish the presence of trees, stones, sand, water, grass, mud, etc. True, without long practice this kind of sensation is rather confused and dim; but if you take men born blind, who have made use of such sensations all their life, you will find they feel things with such perfect exactness that one might almost say that they see with their hands, or that their stick is the organ of a sixth sense, given to them to make up for the lack of sight.

We may use this as an analogy. I would have you conceive of the light in a 'luminous' body as being simply a certain very rapid and lively movement or activity, transmitted to our eyes through air and other transparent bodies, just as the movement or resistance of the bodies a blind man encounters is transmitted to his hand through his stick. This may prevent your finding it strange . . . that in this way we can see all sorts of colours; you may even be prepared to believe that in so-called coloured bodies the colours are simply the different ways in which the bodies receive light and send it on to our eyes; for you have only to consider that by means of his stick a blind man observes differences between trees, stones, water, and so on, apparently just as great as those between red, yellow, green and other colours, and that there is nothing in these various bodies to make these differences except their different ways of moving the stick or resisting its movements.

You will thus be in a position to decide that it is not necessary to assume the transmission of something material from the object to our eyes in order that we may see colours and light, nor even the occurrence in the object of anything resembling our ideas or sensations of it. For in just the same way, when a blind man is feeling bodies, nothing has to issue from them and be transmitted along his stick to his hand; and the resistance or movement of the bodies, which is the sole cause of his sensations of them, is nothing like the ideas he forms of them. [. . .]

[DISCOURSE IV]. In order to facilitate the explanation of the special sense of sight, I must at this point say something about the nature of the senses in general. First, we know for certain that it is to the soul that sense belongs, not to the body; for we observe that when the soul is distracted by ecstasy or deep contemplation, the whole body remains devoid of sensation, in spite of being in contact with various objects. Again, we know that sensation occurs, properly speaking, not in view of the soul's presence in the parts that serve as external sense-organs, but only in view of its presence in the brain, where it employs the faculty called *sensus communis*;[1] for we observe injuries and diseases which attack the brain alone, and yet stop all sensation whatsoever; and this does not mean that the rest of the body ceases to be animated [by the soul]. Finally, we know that it is through the nerves that the impressions made by objects upon the external organs are transmitted to the soul in the brain; for we observe various accidents which, without injuring anything but some nerve, destroy sensibility in all parts of the body to which this nerve sends branches, but do not even diminish it elsewhere.

---

1 [Descartes here writes *sens commun*; but this is a French version of the scholastic term given above, which means a central co-ordinating sensory faculty, as opposed to the special senses of sight, hearing, etc.—Tr.]

So that you may know in more detail how the soul, seated in the brain, is able to receive through the nerves impressions of external objects, . . . I would have you conceive [nerves as] tiny fibres . . . stretching from the brain to the extremities of all parts capable of sensation. Thus the slightest touch that sets in motion a point of attachment of a nerve in these parts also simultaneously sets in motion the point of origin of the nerve in the brain; just as pulling one end of a taut string instantly sets the other end in motion. [. . .]

Further, you must beware of assuming, as philosophers ordinarily do, that it is necessary for sensation that the soul should contemplate certain images transmitted by objects to the brain; or at any rate you must conceive the nature of these images quite differently from their way of thinking. For since they have no notion of the images except that they must be like the objects they represent, they cannot possibly explain how they can be produced by these objects, and received by the external sense-organs, and transmitted by the nerves to the brain. Their sole reason for the assumption is that they have noticed that a picture readily induces us to think of the object depicted, and have thus thought we must be led to conceive of the objects that affect our senses by tiny pictures formed within our head. But we have to consider that thought may be induced by many things besides pictures—e.g. by signs and words, which in no way resemble the things signified.

Even if we think it best, in order to depart as little as possible from received opinions, to admit that the objects of sensation actually do transmit images of themselves to the interior of the brain, we must at least observe that no images have to resemble the objects they represent in all respects (otherwise there would be no distinction between the object and its image); resemblance in a few features is enough, and very often the perfection of an image depends on its not resembling the object as much as it might. For instance, engravings, which consist merely of a little ink spread over paper, represent to us forests, towns, men and even battles and tempests. And yet, out of an unlimited number of different qualities that they lead us to conceive the objects, there is not one in respect of which they actually resemble them, except shape. Even this is a very imperfect resemblance; on a flat surface, they represent objects variously convex or concave; and again, according to the rules of perspective, they often represent circles by ovals rather than by other circles, and squares by diamonds rather than by other squares. Thus very often, in order to be more perfect *qua* images, and to represent the object better, it is necessary for the engravings not to resemble it.

Now we must hold a quite similar view of the images produced on our brain; we must observe that the problem is to know how they can enable the soul to have sensations of all the various qualities in the objects to which the images refer; not, how they can resemble the objects. When our blind man touches bodies with his stick, they certainly transmit nothing to him; they merely set his stick in motion in different ways, according to their different qualities, and thus likewise set in motion the nerves of his hand, and the points of origin of these nerves in his brain; and this is what occasions the soul's perception of various qualities in the bodies, corresponding to the various sorts of disturbance that they produce in the brain.

[DISCOURSE V]. You see, then, that sensation does not require that the soul should contemplate any images resembling the objects of sensation. For all that, the objects we look at do in fact produce very perfect images in the back of the eyes. [. . .]

Further, the images of objects are not only produced in the back of the eye but also sent on to the brain. [. . .]

[DISCOURSE VI]. And when it is thus transmitted to the inside of our head, the picture still retains some degree of its resemblance to the objects from which it originates. But we must not think that it is by means of this resemblance that the picture makes us aware of the objects—as though we had another pair of eyes to see it, inside our brain; I have several times made this point; rather, we must hold that the movements by which the image is formed act directly on our soul *qua* united to the body, and are ordained by Nature to give it such sensations.

I will explain this in more detail. The perceived qualities of seen objects can all be brought under six main heads: light, colour, position, distance, size and shape. First, then, as regards light and colour (the only qualities belonging specially to the sense of sight): it must be held that our soul is of such a nature that a sensation of light is determined by the strength of the disturbance that occurs at the points of origin of the optic nerve-fibres in the brain; and one of colour, by the kind of disturbance. In the same way, the disturbance of the nerves that supply the ears determines the hearing of sounds; the disturbance of the nerves in the tongue determines the tasting of flavours; and in general, disturbance of nerve anywhere in the body determines, if it is moderate, a feeling of enjoyment, and if it is too violent, a pain. But there need be no resemblance here between the ideas conceived by the soul and the disturbances that cause them.

Source: *The Dioptrics*, in the *Philosophical Writings of Descartes*, trans. Anscombe and Geach (Nelson). (Extracts.)

39 (i) Primary and Secondary Qualities (1690)

JOHN LOCKE

To discover the nature of our *ideas* the better, and to discourse of them intelligibly, it will be convenient to distinguish them as they are ideas or perceptions in our minds, and as they are modifications of matter in the bodies that cause such perceptions in us: that so we may not think (as perhaps usually is done) that they are exactly the images and resemblances of something inherent in the subject; most of those of sensation being in the mind no more the likeness of something existing without us, than the names that stand for them are the likeness of our ideas, which yet upon hearing they are apt to excite in us.

Whatsoever the mind perceives *in itself*, or is the immediate object of perception, thought, or understanding, that I call *idea*; and the power to produce any idea in our mind, I call *quality* of the subject wherein that power is. Thus a snowball having the power to produce in us the ideas of white, cold, and round, the power to produce those ideas in us, as they are in the snowball, I call qualities; and as they are sensations or perceptions in our understandings, I call them ideas; which *ideas*, if I speak of sometimes as in the things themselves, I would be understood to mean those qualities in the objects which produce them in us.

Qualities thus considered in bodies are:

First, such as are utterly inseparable from the body, in what state soever it be; and such as in all the alterations and changes it suffers, all the force can be used upon it, it constantly keeps; and such as sense constantly finds in every particle of matter which has bulk enough to be perceived; and the mind finds inseparable from every particle of matter, though less than to make itself singly be perceived by our senses: e.g. take a grain of wheat, divide it into two parts; each part has still solidity, extension, figure, and mobility: divide it again, and it retains still the same qualities; and so divide it on, till the parts become insensible; they must retain still each of them all those qualities. For division can never take away either solidity, extension, figure, or mobility from any body, but only makes two or more distinct separate masses of matter, of that which was but one before; all which distinct masses, reckoned as so many distinct bodies, after division, makes a certain number. These I call *original* or *primary qualities* of body, which I think we may observe to produce simple ideas in us, viz, solidity, extension, figure, motion or rest, and number.

Secondly, such qualities which in truth are nothing in the objects themselves but powers to produce various sensations in us by their primary qualities, i.e. by the bulk, figure, texture, and motion of their insensible parts, as colours, sounds, tastes, etc. These I call *secondary qualities*. To these might be added a *third* sort, which are allowed to be barely powers; though they are as much real qualities in the subject as those which I, to comply with the common way of speaking, call qualities, but for distinction, secondary qualities. For the power in fire to produce a new colour, or consistency, in *wax* or *clay*, by its primary qualities, is as much a quality in fire, as the power it has to produce in *me* a new idea or sensation of warmth or burning, which I felt not before, by the same primary qualities, viz. the bulk, texture, and motion of its insensible parts.

The next thing to be considered is, how bodies produce ideas in us; and that is manifestly by impulse, the only way which we can conceive bodies to operate in.

If then external objects be not united to our minds when they produce ideas therein; and yet we perceive these *original* qualities in such of them as singly fall under our senses, it is evident that some motion must be thence continued by our nerves, or animal spirits, by some parts of our bodies, to the brains or the seat of sensation, there to produce in our minds the particular ideas we have of them. And since the extension, figure, number, and motion of bodies of an observable bigness, may be perceived at a distance by the sight, it is evident some singly imperceptible bodies must come from them to the eyes, and thereby convey to the brain some motion; which produces these ideas which we have of them in us.

After the same manner that the ideas of these original qualities are produced in us, we may conceive that the ideas of *secondary* qualities are also produced, viz. by the operation of insensible particles on our senses. For, it being manifest that there are bodies and good store of bodies, each whereof are so small, that we cannot by any of our senses discover either their bulk, figure, or motion—as is evident in the particles of the air and water, and others extremely smaller than those; perhaps as much smaller than the particles of air and water, as the particles of air and water are smaller than peas or hail-stones—let us suppose at present that the different motions and figures, bulk and number, of such particles, affecting the several organs of our senses, produce in us those different sensations which we have from the colours and smells of bodies; v.g. that a violet, by the impulse of such insensible particles of matter, of peculiar figures and bulks, and in different degrees and modifications of their motions, causes the ideas of the blue colour and sweet scent of that flower to be produced in our minds. It being no more impossible to conceive that God should annex such ideas to such motions, with which they have no similitude, than that he should annex the idea of pain to the motion of a piece of steel dividing our flesh, with which that idea hath no resemblance.

What I have said concerning colours and smells may be understood also of tastes and sounds, and other the like sensible qualities; which, whatever reality we by mistake attribute to them, are in truth nothing in the objects themselves, but powers to produce various sensations in us; and depend on those primary qualities, viz. bulk, figure, texture, and motion of parts.

From whence I think it easy to draw this observation—that the ideas of primary qualities of bodies are resemblances of them, and their patterns do really exist in the bodies themselves, but the ideas produced in us by these secondary qualities have no resemblance of them at all. There is nothing like our ideas, existing in the bodies themselves. They are, in the bodies we denominate from them, only a power to produce those sensations in us: and what is sweet, blue, or warm in idea, is but the certain bulk, figure, and motion of the insensible parts, in the bodies themselves, which we call so.

Flame is denominated hot and light; snow, white and cold; and manna, white and sweet, from the ideas they produce in us. Which qualities are commonly thought to be the same in those bodies that those ideas are in us, the one the perfect resemblance of the other, as they are in a mirror, and it would by most men be judged very extravagant if one should say otherwise. And yet he that will consider that the same fire that at one distance produces in us the sensation of warmth does, at a nearer approach, produce in us the far different sensation of pain, ought to bethink himself what reason he has to say—that this idea of warmth, which was produced in him by the fire, is *actually in the fire*; and his idea of pain, which the same fire produced in him the same way, is *not* in the fire. Why are whiteness and coldness in snow, and pain not, when it produces the one and the other idea in us; and can do neither, but by the bulk, figure, number, and motion of its solid parts?

The particular bulk, number, figure, and motion of the parts of fire or snow are really in them, whether any one's senses perceive them or no: and therefore they may be called *real* qualities, because they really exist in those bodies. But light, heat, whiteness, or coldness, are no more really in them than sickness or pain is in manna. Take away the sensation of them; let not the eyes see light or colours, nor the ears hear sounds; let the palate not taste, nor the nose smell, and all colours, tastes, odours, and sounds, as they are such particular ideas, vanish and cease, and are reduced to their causes, i.e. bulk, figure, and motion of parts.

A piece of manna of a sensible bulk is able to produce in us the idea of a round or square figure; and by being removed from one place to another, the idea of motion. This idea of motion represents it as it really is in manna moving: a circle or square are the same, whether in idea or existence, in the mind or in the manna. And this, both motion and figure, are really in the manna, whether we take notice of them or no: this everybody is ready to agree to. Besides, manna, by the bulk, figure, texture, and motion of its parts, has a power to produce the sensations of sickness, and sometimes of acute pains or gripings in us. That these ideas of sickness and pain are *not* in the manna, but effects of its operations on us, and are nowhere when we feel them not; this also every one readily agrees to. And yet men are hardly to be brought to think that sweetness and whiteness are not really in manna; which are but the effects of the operations of manna, by the motion, size, and figure of its particles, on the eyes and palate: as the pain and sickness caused by manna are confessedly nothing but the effects of its operations on the stomach and guts, by the size, motion, and figure of its insensible parts.

(ii) Sensation and Judgement in Perception (1690)

We are further to consider concerning perception, that the ideas we receive by sensation are often altered by the judgment, without our taking notice of it. When we set before our eyes a round globe of any uniform colour, v.g. gold, alabaster, or jet, it is certain that the idea thereby imprinted on our mind is of a flat circle, variously shadowed, with several degrees of light and brightness coming to our eyes. But we having, by use, been accustomed to perceive what kind of appearance convex bodies are wont to make in us; what alterations are made in the reflections of light by the difference of the sensible figures of bodies; the judgment presently, by an habitual custom, alters the appearances into their causes. So that from that which is truly variety of shadow or colour, collecting the figure, it makes it pass for a mark of figure, and frames to itself the perception of a convex figure and an uniform colour; when the idea we receive from thence is only a plane variously coloured, as is evident in painting.

But this is not, I think, usual in any of our ideas, but those received by sight. Because sight, the most comprehensive of all our senses, conveying to our minds the ideas of light and colours, which are peculiar only to that sense; and also the far different ideas of space, figure, and motion, the several varieties whereof change the appearance of its proper object, viz. light and colours; we bring ourselves by use to judge of the one by the other. This, in many cases by a settled habit, in things whereof we have frequent experience, is performed so constantly and so quick, that we take that for the perception of our sensation which is an idea formed by our judgment; so that one, viz. that of sensation, serves only to excite the other, and is scarce taken notice of itself; as a man who reads or hears with attention and understanding, takes little notice of the characters or sounds, but of the ideas that are excited in him by them.

Nor need we wonder that this is done with so little notice, if we consider how quick the actions of the mind are performed. For, as itself is thought to take up no space, to have no extension; so its actions seem to require no time, but many of them seem to be crowded into an instant. I speak this in comparison to the actions of the body. Any one may easily observe this in his own thoughts, who will take the pains to reflect on them. How, as it were in an instant, do our minds, with one glance, see all the parts of a demonstration, which may very well be called a long one, if we consider the time it will require to put it into words, and step by step show it another? Secondly, we shall not be so much surprised that this is done in us with so little notice, if we consider how the facility which we get of doing things, by a custom of doing, makes them often pass in us without our notice.

(iii) Knowledge of Exterior Causes of Sensations (1690)

The knowledge of our own being we have by intuition. The existence of a God, reason clearly makes known to us, as has been shown.

The knowledge of the existence of *any other thing* we can have only by *sensation*: for there being no necessary connection of real existence with any *idea* a man hath in his memory; nor of any other existence but that of God with the existence of any particular man: no particular man can know the existence of any other being, but only when, by actual operating upon him, it makes itself perceived by him. For, the having the idea of anything in our mind, no more proves the existence of that thing, than the picture of a man evidences his being in the world, or the visions of a dream make thereby a true history.

It is therefore the *actual receiving* of ideas from without that gives us notice of the existence of other things, and makes us know, that something doth exist at that time without us, which causes that idea in us; though perhaps we neither know nor consider how it does it. For it takes not from the certainty of our senses, and the ideas we receive by them, that we know not the manner wherein they are produced: v.g. whilst I write this, I have, by the paper affecting my eyes, that idea produced in my mind, which, whatever object causes, I call *white*; by which I know that that quality or accident (i.e. whose appearance before my eyes always causes that idea) doth really exist, and hath a being without me.

The notice we have by our senses of the existing of things without us, though it be not altogether so certain as our intuitive knowledge, or the deductions of our reason employed about the clear abstract ideas of our own minds; yet it is an assurance that deserves the name of *knowledge*. If we persuade ourselves that our faculties act and inform us right concerning the existence of those objects that affect them, it cannot pass for an ill-grounded confidence: for I think nobody can, in earnest, be so sceptical as to be uncertain of the existence of those things which he sees and feels. At least, he that can doubt so far (whatever he may have with his own thoughts), will never have any controversy with me; since he can never be sure I say anything contrary to his own opinion. As to myself, I think God has given me assurance enough of the existence of things without me: since, by their different application, I can produce in myself both pleasure and pain, which is one great concernment of my present state. This is certain: the confidence that our faculties do not herein deceive us, is the greatest assurance we are capable of concerning the existence of material beings. For we cannot act anything but by our faculties; nor talk of knowledge itself, but by the help of those faculties which are fitted to apprehend even what knowledge is.

We are further confirmed in this assurance by other concurrent reasons:

I. It is plain those perceptions are produced in us by exterior causes affecting our senses: because those that want the *organs* of any sense, never can have the ideas belonging to that sense produced in their minds. The organs themselves do not produce them: for then the eyes of a man in the dark would produce colours, and his nose smell roses in the winter: but we see nobody gets the relish of a pineapple, till he goes to the Indies, where it is, and tastes it.

II. Because sometimes I find that *I cannot avoid the having those ideas produced in my mind.* For though, when my eyes are shut, or windows fast, I can at pleasure recall to my mind the ideas of light, or the sun, which former sensations had lodged in my memory; so I can at pleasure lay by *that* idea, and take into my view that of the smell of a rose, or taste of sugar. But, if I turn my eyes at noon towards the sun, I cannot avoid the ideas which the light or sun then produces in me. So that there is a manifest difference between the ideas laid up in my memory (over which, if they were there only, I should have constantly the same power to dispose of them, and lay them by at pleasure), and those which force themselves upon me, and I cannot avoid having. And therefore it must needs be some exterior cause, and the brisk acting of some objects without me, whose efficacy I cannot resist, that produces those ideas in my mind, whether I will or no.

III. Add to this, that many of those ideas are *produced in us with pain*, which afterwards we remember without the least offence. Thus, the pain of heat or cold, when the idea of it is revived in our minds, gives us no disturbance; which, when felt, was very troublesome; and is again, when actually repeated: which is occasioned by the disorder the external object causes in our bodies when applied to them: and we remember the pains of hunger, thirst, or the headache, without any pain at all; which would either never disturb us, or else constantly do it, as often as we thought of it, were there nothing more but ideas floating in our minds, and appearances entertaining our fancies, without the real existence of things affecting us from abroad.

IV. Our *senses* in many cases *bear witness to the truth of each other's report* concerning the existence of sensible things without us. He that *sees* a fire may, if he doubt whether it be anything more than a bare fancy, *feel* it too; and be convinced, by putting his hand in it. Which certainly could never be put into such exquisite pain by a bare idea or phantom, unless that the pain be a fancy too: which yet he cannot, when the burn is well, by raising the idea of it, bring upon himself again.

Thus I see, whilst I write this, I can change the appearance of the paper; and by designing the letters, tell *beforehand* what new idea it shall exhibit the very next moment, by barely drawing my pen over it: which will neither appear (let me fancy as much as I will) if my hands stand still; or though I move my pen, if my eyes be shut: nor, when those characters are once made on the paper, can I choose afterwards but see them as they are; that is, have the ideas of such letters as I have made. Whence it is manifest, that they are not barely the sport and play of my own imagination, when I find that the characters that were made at the pleasure of my own thoughts, do not obey them; nor yet cease to be, whenever I shall fancy it, but continue to affect my senses constantly and regularly, according to the figures I made them. To which if we will add, that the sight of those shall, from another man, draw such sounds as I beforehand design they shall stand for, there will be little reason left to doubt that those words I write do really exist without me, when they cause a long series of regular sounds to affect my ears, which could not be the effect of my imagination, nor could my memory retain them in that order.

But yet, if after all this any one will be so sceptical as to distrust his senses, and to affirm that all we see and hear, feel and taste, think and do, during our whole being, is but the series and deluding appearances of a long dream, I make him this answer, That the certainty of things existing in *rerum natura*, when we have the testimony of our senses for it, is not only as great as our frame can attain to, but as our condition needs. For he that sees a candle burning, and hath experimented the force of its flame by putting his finger in it, will little doubt that this is something existing without him, which does him harm, and puts him to great pain: which is assurance enough, when no man requires greater certainty to govern his actions by than what is as certain as his actions themselves.

But this knowledge extends as far as the present testimony of our senses, employed about particular objects that do then affect them, and no further. For if I saw such a collection of simple ideas as is wont to be called *man*, existing together one minute since, and am now alone, I cannot be certain that the same man exists now, since there is no necessary connection of his existence a minute since with his existence now: by a thousand ways he may cease to be, since I had the testimony of my senses for his existence. And, therefore, though it be highly probable that millions of men do now exist, yet, whilst I am alone, writing this, I have not that certainty of it which we strictly call knowledge; though the great likelihood of it puts me past doubt, and it be reasonable for me to do several things upon the confidence that there are men (and men also of my acquaintance, with whom I have to do) now in the world: but this is but probability, not knowledge.

Whereby yet we may observe how foolish and vain a thing it is for a man of a narrow knowledge, who having reason given him to judge of the different evidence and probability of things, and to be swayed accordingly; how vain, I say, it is to expect demonstration and certainty in things not capable of it; and refuse assent to very rational propositions, and act contrary to very plain and clear truths, because they cannot be made out so evident as to surmount every the least (I will not say reason, but) pretence of doubting. He that, in the ordinary affairs of life, would admit of nothing but direct plain demonstration, would be sure of

nothing in this world but of perishing quickly. The wholesomeness
of his meat or drink would not give him reason to venture on it:
and I would fain know what it is he could do upon such grounds
as are capable of no doubt, no objection.

Source: An Essay Concerning Human Understanding, Bk. II, Chs.
8 and 9 (extracts), Bk. IV, Ch. 11 (extract).

40 (i) Immaterialism (1710)

GEORGE BERKELEY

1 It is evident to any one who takes a survey of the objects of
human knowledge, that they are either ideas actually imprinted
on the senses, or else such as are perceived by attending to the
passions and operations of the mind, or lastly ideas formed by
help of memory and imagination, either compounding, dividing,
or barely representing those originally perceived in the aforesaid
ways. By sight I have the ideas of light and colours with their
several degrees and variations. By touch I perceive, for example,
hard and soft, heat and cold, motion and resistance, and of all
these more and less either as to quantity or degree. Smelling
furnishes me with odours; the palate with tastes, and hearing
conveys sounds to the mind in all their variety of tone and composition. And as several of these are observed to accompany each
other, they come to be marked by one name, and so to be reputed
as one thing. Thus, for example, a certain colour, taste, smell,
figure and consistence having been observed to go together, are
accounted one distinct thing, signified by the name *apple.* Other
collections of ideas constitute a stone, a tree, a book, and the like
sensible things; which, as they are pleasing or disagreeable, excite
the passions of love, hatred, joy, grief, and so forth. [. . .]
    3 That neither our thoughts, nor passions, nor ideas formed by
the imagination, exist without the mind, is what every body will
allow. And it seems no less evident that the various sensations or
ideas imprinted on the sense, however blended or combined
together (that is, whatever objects they compose) cannot exist
otherwise than in a mind perceiving them. I think an intuitive
knowledge may be obtained of this, by any one that shall attend

to what is meant by the term *exist* when applied to sensible things. The table I write on, I say, exists, that is, I see and feel it; and if I were out of my study I should say it existed, meaning thereby that if I was in my study I might perceive it, or that some other spirit actually does perceive it. There was an odour, that is, it was smelled; there was a sound, that is to say, it was heard; a colour or figure, and it was perceived by sight or touch. This is all that I can understand by these and the like expressions. For as to what is said of the absolute existence of unthinking things without any relation to their being perceived, that seems perfectly unintelligible. Their *esse* is *percipi*, nor is it possible they should have any existence, out of the minds or thinking things which perceive them.

4 It is indeed an opinion strangely prevailing amongst men, that houses, mountains, rivers, and in a word all sensible objects have an existence natural or real, distinct from their being perceived by the understanding. But with how great an assurance and acquiescence soever this principle may be entertained in the world; yet whoever shall find in his heart to call it in question, may, if I mistake not, perceive it to involve a manifest contradiction. For what are the forementioned objects but the things we perceive by sense, and what do we perceive besides our own ideas or sensations; and is it not plainly repugnant that any one of these or any combination of them should exist unperceived? [...]

8 But say you, though the ideas themselves do not exist without the mind, yet there may be things like them whereof they are copies or resemblances, which things exist without the mind, in an unthinking substance. I answer, an idea can be like nothing but an idea; a colour or figure can be like nothing but another colour or figure. If we look but ever so little into our thoughts, we shall find it impossible for us to conceive a likeness except only between our ideas. Again, I ask whether those supposed originals or external things, of which our ideas are the pictures or representations, be themselves perceivable or no? If they are, then they are ideas, and we have gained our point; but if you say they are not, I appeal to anyone whether it be sense, to assert a colour is like something which is invisible; hard or soft, like something which is intangible; and so of the rest.

9 Some there are who make a distinction betwixt *primary* and *secondary* qualities: by the former, they mean extension, figure, motion, rest, solidity or impenetrability and number: by the latter

they denote all other sensible qualities, as colours, sounds, tastes, and so forth. The ideas we have of these they acknowledge not to be the resemblances of any thing existing without the mind or unperceived; but they will have our ideas of the primary qualities to be patterns or images of things which exist without the mind, in an unthinking substance which they call *matter*. By matter therefore we are to understand an inert, senseless substance, in which extension, figure, and motion, do actually subsist. But it is evident from what we have already shewn, that extension, figure and motion are only ideas existing in the mind, and that an idea can be like nothing but another idea, and that consequently neither they nor their archetypes can exist in an unperceiving substance. Hence it is plain, that the very notion of what is called *matter* or *corporeal substance*, involves a contradiction in it.

10 They who assert that figure, motion, and the rest of the primary or original qualities do exist without the mind, in unthinking substances, do at the same time acknowledge that colours, sounds, heat, cold, and such like secondary qualities, do not, which they tell us are sensations existing in the mind alone, that depend on and are occasioned by the different size, texture and motion of the minute particles of matter. This they take for an undoubted truth, which they can demonstrate beyond all exception. Now if it be certain, that those original qualities are inseparably united with the other sensible qualities, and not, even in thought, capable of being abstracted from them, it plainly follows that they exist only in the mind. But I desire any one to reflect and try, whether he can by any abstraction of thought, conceive the extension and motion of a body, without all other sensible qualities. For my own part, I see evidently that it is not in my power to frame an idea of a body extended and moved, but I must withal give it some colour or other sensible quality which is acknowledged to exist only in the mind. In short, extension, figure, and motion, abstracted from all other qualities, are inconceivable. Where therefore the other sensible qualities are, there must these be also, to wit, in the mind and nowhere else. [. . .]

18 But though it were possible that solid, figured, moveable substances may exist without the mind, corresponding to the ideas we have of bodies, yet how is it possible for us to know this? Either we must know it by sense, or by reason. As for our senses, by them we have the knowledge only of our sensations, ideas, or those things that are immediately perceived by sense, call them

what you will: but they do not inform us that things exist without the mind, or unperceived, like to those which are perceived. This the materialists themselves acknowledge. It remains therefore that if we have any knowledge at all of external things, it must be by reason, inferring their existence from what is immediately perceived by sense. But what reason can induce us to believe the existence of bodies without the mind, from what we perceive, since the very patrons of matter themselves do not pretend, there is any necessary connexion betwixt them and our ideas? I say it is granted on all hands (and what happens in dreams, phrensies, and the like, puts it beyond dispute) that it is possible we might be affected with all the ideas we have now, though no bodies existed without, resembling them. Hence it is evident the supposition of external bodies is not necessary for the producing our ideas: since it is granted they are produced sometimes, and might possibly be produced always in the same order we see them in at present, without their concurrence.

19 But though we might possibly have all our sensations without them, yet perhaps it may be thought easier to conceive and explain the manner of their production, by supposing external bodies in their likeness rather than otherwise; and so it might be at least probable there are such things as bodies that excite their ideas in our minds. But neither can this be said; for though we give the materialists their external bodies, they by their own confession are never the nearer knowing how our ideas are produced: since they own themselves unable to comprehend in what manner body can act upon spirit, or how it is possible it should imprint any idea in the mind. Hence it is evident the production of ideas or sensations in our minds, can be no reason why we should suppose matter or corporeal substances, since that is acknowledged to remain equally inexplicable with, or without this supposition. If therefore it were possible for bodies to exist without the mind, yet to hold they do so, must needs be a very precarious opinion; since it is to suppose, without any reason at all, that God has created innumerable beings that are entirely useless, and serve to no manner of purpose.

Source: The Principles of Human Knowledge, Secs. 1, 3, 4, 8–10, 18, 19.

(ii) Heat and Pain (1713)

PHILONOUS. What mean you by sensible things?

HYLAS. Those things which are perceived by the senses. Can you imagine that I mean any thing else?

PHILONOUS. Pardon me, Hylas, if I am desirous clearly to apprehend your notions, since this may much shorten our inquiry. Suffer me then to ask you this farther question. Are those things only perceived by the senses which are perceived immediately? Or may those things properly be said to be *sensible*, which are perceived mediately, or not without the intervention of others?

HYLAS. I do not sufficiently understand you.

PHILONOUS. In reading a book, what I immediately perceive are the letters, but mediately, or by means of these, are suggested to my mind the notions of God, virtue, truth, etc. Now, that the letters are truly sensible things, or perceived by sense, there is no doubt: but I would know whether you take the things suggested by them to be so too.

HYLAS. No certainly, it were absurd to think *God* or *Virtue* sensible things, though they may be signified and suggested to the mind by sensible marks, with which they have an arbitrary connexion.

PHILONOUS. It seems then, that by *sensible things* you mean those only which can be perceived immediately by sense.

HYLAS. Right.

PHILONOUS. Doth it not follow from this, that though I see one part of the sky red, and another blue, and that my reason doth thence evidently conclude there must be some cause of that diversity of colours, yet that cause cannot be said to be a sensible thing, or perceived by the sense of seeing?

HYLAS. It doth.

PHILONOUS. In like manner, though I hear variety of sounds, yet I cannot be said to hear the causes of those sounds.

HYLAS. You cannot.

PHILONOUS. And when by my touch I perceive a thing to be hot and heavy, I cannot say with any truth or propriety, that I feel the cause of its heat or weight.

HYLAS. To prevent any more questions of this kind, I tell you once for all, that by *sensible things* I mean those only which are perceived by sense, and that in truth the senses perceive nothing which they do not perceive immediately: for they make no inferences. The deducing therefore of causes or occasions from effects and appearances, which alone are perceived by sense, entirely relates to reason.

PHILONOUS. This point then is agreed between us, that *sensible things are those only which are immediately perceived by sense.* You will farther inform me, whether we immediately perceive by sight any thing beside light, and colours, and figures: or by hearing, any thing but sounds: by the palate, any thing beside tastes: by the smell, beside odours: or by the touch, more than tangible qualities.

HYLAS. We do not.

PHILONOUS. It seems therefore, that if you take away all sensible qualities, there remains nothing sensible.

HYLAS. I grant it.

PHILONOUS. Sensible things therefore are nothing else but so many sensible qualities, or combinations of sensible qualities.

HYLAS. Nothing else.

PHILONOUS. Heat then is a sensible thing.

HYLAS. Certainly.

PHILONOUS. Doth the reality of sensible things consist in being perceived? or, is it something distinct from their being perceived, and that bears no relation to the mind?

HYLAS. To *exist* is one thing, and to be *perceived* is another.

PHILONOUS. I speak with regard to sensible things only: and of these I ask, whether by their real existence you mean a subsistence exterior to the mind, and distinct from their being perceived?

HYLAS. I mean a real absolute being, distinct from, and without any relation to their being perceived.

PHILONOUS. Heat therefore, if it be allowed a real being, must exist without the mind.

HYLAS. It must.

PHILONOUS. Tell me, Hylas, is this real existence equally compatible to all degrees of heat, which we perceive: or is there any reason why we should attribute it to some, and deny it others? And if there be, pray let me know that reason.

HYLAS. Whatever degree of heat we perceive by sense, we may be sure the same exists in the object that occasions it.

PHILONOUS. What, the greatest as well as the least?

HYLAS. I tell you, the reason is plainly the same in respect of both: they are both perceived by sense; nay, the greater degree of heat is more sensibly perceived; and consequently, if there is any difference, we are more certain of its real existence than we can be of the reality of a lesser degree.

PHILONOUS. But is not the most vehement and intense degree of heat a very great pain?

HYLAS. No one can deny it.

PHILONOUS. And is any unperceiving thing capable of pain or pleasure?

HYLAS. No certainly.

PHILONOUS. Is your material substance a senseless being, or a being endowed with sense and perception?

HYLAS. It is senseless, without doubt.

PHILONOUS. It cannot therefore be the subject of pain.

HYLAS. By no means.

PHILONOUS. Nor consequently of the greatest heat perceived by sense, since you acknowledge this to be no small pain.

HYLAS. I grant it.

PHILONOUS. What shall we say then of your external object; is it a material substance, or no?

HYLAS. It is a material substance with the sensible qualities inhering in it.

PHILONOUS. How then can a great heat exist in it, since you own it cannot in a material substance? I desire you would clear this point.

HYLAS. Hold, Philonous, I fear I was out in yielding intense heat to be a pain. It should seem rather, that pain is something distinct from heat, and the consequence or effect of it.

PHILONOUS. Upon putting your hand near the fire, do you perceive one simple uniform sensation, or two distinct sensations?

HYLAS. But one simple sensation.

PHILONOUS. Is not the heat immediately perceived?

HYLAS. It is.

PHILONOUS. And the pain?

HYLAS. True.

PHILONOUS. Seeing therefore they are both immediately perceived at the same time, and the fire affects you only with one simple, or uncompounded idea, it follows that this same simple idea is both the intense heat immediately perceived, and the pain; and consequently, that the intense heat immediately perceived, is nothing distinct from a particular sort of pain.

HYLAS. It seems so.

PHILONOUS. Again, try in your thoughts, Hylas, if you can conceive a vehement sensation to be without pain, or pleasure.

HYLAS. I cannot.

PHILONOUS. Or can you frame to yourself an idea of sensible pain or pleasure in general, abstracted from every particular idea of heat, cold, tastes, smells? etc.

HYLAS. I do not find that I can.

PHILONOUS. Doth it not therefore follow, that sensible pain is nothing distinct from those sensations or ideas, in an intense degree?

HYLAS. It is undeniable; and to speak the truth, I begin to suspect a very great heat cannot exist but in a mind perceiving it. [. . .]

Source: Three Dialogues (extract from First Dialogue).

41 The Meaning of 'White' (1843)

J. S. MILL

A Sensation is to be carefully distinguished from the object which causes the sensation; our sensation of white from a white object: nor is it less to be distinguished from the attribute whiteness, which we ascribe to the object in consequence of its exciting the sensation. Unfortunately for clearness and due discrimination in considering these subjects, our sensations seldom receive separate names. We have a name for the objects which produce in us a certain sensation: the word *white*. We have a name for the quality in those objects, to which we ascribe the sensation: the name *whiteness*. But when we speak of the sensation itself (as we have not occasion to do this often except in our scientific speculations), language, which adapts itself for the most part only to the common uses of life, has provided us with no single-worded or immediate designation; we must employ a circumlocution, and say, The sensation of white, or The sensation of whiteness; we must denominate the sensation either from the object, or from the attribute, by which it is excited. Yet the sensation, though it

never *does*, might very well be *conceived* to exist, without anything whatever to excite it. We can conceive it as arising spon-
taneously in the mind. But if it so arose, we should have no name
to denote it which would not be a misnomer. [...]

In the case of sensations, another distinction has also to be kept in
view, which is often confounded, and never without mischievous
consequences. This is, the distinction between the sensation itself,
and the state of the bodily organs which precedes the sensation,
and which constitutes the physical agency by which it is produced. One of the sources of confusion on this subject is the
division commonly made of feelings into Bodily and Mental.
Philosophically speaking, there is no foundation at all for this
distinction; even sensations are states of the sentient mind, not
states of the body, as distinguished from it. What I am conscious
of when I see the colour blue, is a feeling of blue colour, which is
one thing; the picture on my retina, or the phenomenon of hitherto mysterious nature which takes place in my optic nerve or in my
brain, is another thing, of which I am not at all conscious, and
which scientific investigation alone could have apprised me of.
These are states of my body: but the sensation of blue, which is
the consequence of these states of body, is not a state of body:
that which perceives and is conscious is called Mind. When
sensations are called bodily feelings, it is only as being the class
of feelings which are immediately occasioned by bodily states;
whereas the other kinds of feelings, thoughts, for instance, or
emotions, are immediately excited not by anything acting upon
the bodily organs, but by sensations, or by previous thoughts.
This, however, is a distinction not in our feelings, but in the
agency which produces our feelings: all of them when actually
produced are states of mind.

Besides the affection of our bodily organs from without, and
the sensation thereby produced in our minds, many writers admit
a third link in the chain of phenomena, which they call a Perception, and which consists in the recognition of an external
object as the exciting cause of the sensation. [...]

In these so-called perceptions, or direct recognitions by the
mind, of objects, whether physical or spiritual, which are external
to itself, I can see only cases of belief; but of belief which claims
to be intuitive, or independent of external evidence. When a stone
lies before me, I am conscious of certain sensations which I
receive from it; but if I say that these sensations come to me

from an external object which I *perceive*, the meaning of these words is, that receiving the sensations, I intuitively *believe* that an external cause of those sensations exists. The laws of intuitive belief, and the conditions under which it is legitimate, are a subject which, as we have already so often remarked, belongs not to logic, but to the science of the ultimate laws of the human mind. [. . .]

A body, according to the received doctrine of modern metaphysicians, may be defined, the external cause to which we ascribe our sensations. When I see and touch a piece of gold, I am conscious of a sensation of yellow colour, and sensations of hardness and weight; and by varying the mode of handling, I may add to these sensations many others completely distinct from them. The sensations are all of which I am directly conscious; but I consider them as produced by something not only existing independently of my will, but external to my bodily organs and to my mind. This external something I call a body.

It may be asked, how come we to ascribe our sensations to any external cause? And is there sufficient ground for so ascribing them? It is known, that there are metaphysicians who have raised a controversy on the point; maintaining that we are not warranted in referring our sensations to a cause such as we understand by the word Body, or to any external cause whatever. Though we have no concern here with this controversy, nor with the metaphysical niceties on which it turns, one of the best ways of showing what is meant by Substance is, to consider what position it is necessary to take up, in order to maintain its existence against opponents.

It is certain, then, that a part of our notion of a body consists of the notion of a number of sensations of our own, or of other sentient beings, habitually occurring simultaneously. My conception of the table at which I am writing is compounded of its visible form and size which are complex sensations of sight; its tangible form and size, which are complex sensations of our organs of touch and of our muscles; its weight, which is also a sensation of touch and of the muscles; its colour, which is a sensation of sight; its hardness, which is a sensation of the muscles; its composition, which is another word for all the varieties of sensation which we receive under various circumstances from the wood of which it is made, and so forth. All or most of these various sensations frequently are, and, as we learn by experience, always might be, experienced simultaneously, or in many different orders of succession at our own choice: and hence the thought of any one of them makes us think of the others, and the whole becomes mentally amalgamated into one mixed state of consciousness, which, in the language of the school of Locke and Hartley, is termed a Complex Idea.

Now, there are philosophers who have argued as follows. If we conceive an orange to be divested of its natural colour without acquiring any new one; to lose its softness without becoming hard, its roundness without becoming square or pentagonal, or of any other regular or irregular figure whatever; to be deprived of size, of weight, of taste, of smell; to lose all its mechanical and all its chemical properties, and acquire no new ones; to become in short, invisible, intangible, imperceptible not only by all our senses, but by the senses of all other sentient beings, real or possible; nothing, say these thinkers, would remain. For of what nature, they ask, could be the residuum? and by what token could it manifest its presence? To the unreflecting its existence seems to rest on the evidence of the senses. But to the senses nothing is apparent except the sensations. We know, indeed, that these sensations are bound together by some law; they do not come together at random, but according to a systematic order, which is part of the order established in the universe. When we experience one of these sensations, we usually experience the others also, or know that we have it in our power to experience them. But a fixed law of connection, making the sensations occur together, does not, say these philosophers, necessarily require what is called a substratum to support them. The conception of a substratum is but one of many possible forms in which that connection presents itself to our imagination; a mode of, as it were, realizing the idea. If there be such a substratum, suppose it at this instant miraculously annihilated, and let the sensations continue to occur in the same order, and how would the substratum be missed? By what signs should we be able to discover that its existence had terminated? Should we not have as much reason to believe that it still existed as we now have? And if we should not then be warranted in believing it, how can we be so now? A body, therefore, according, to these metaphysicians, is not anything intrinsically different from the sensations which the body is said to produce in us; it is, in short, a set of sensations, or rather, of possibilities of sensation, joined together according to a fixed law.

The controversies to which these speculations have given rise, and the doctrines which have been developed in the attempt to find a conclusive answer to them, have been fruitful of important consequences to the Science of Mind. The sensations (it was answered) which we are conscious of, and which we receive, not at random, but joined together in a certain uniform manner, imply not only a law or laws of connection, but a cause external to our mind, which cause, by its own laws, determines the laws according to which the sensations are connected and experienced. The schoolmen used to call this external cause by the name we have already employed, a *substratum*; and its attributes (as they expressed themselves) *inherent*, literally *stuck*, in it. To this substratum the name Matter is usually given in philosophical discussions. It was soon, however, acknowledged by all who reflected on the subject, that the existence of matter cannot be proved by extrinsic evidence. The answer, therefore, now usually made to Berkeley and his followers, is, that the belief is intuitive; that mankind, in all ages, have felt themselves compelled, by a necessity of their nature, to refer their sensations to an external cause: that even those who deny it in theory, yield to the necessity in practice, and both in speech, thought, and feeling, do, equally with the vulgar, acknowledge their sensations to be the effects of something external to them: this knowledge, therefore, it is affirmed, is as evidently intuitive as our knowledge of our sensations themselves is intuitive. And here the question merges in the fundamental problem of metaphysics properly so called: to which science we leave it.

But although the extreme doctrine of the Idealist metaphysicians, that objects are nothing but our sensations and the laws which connect them, has not been generally adopted by subsequent thinkers; the point of most real importance is one on which those metaphysicians are now very generally considered to have made out their case: viz., that *all we know* of objects, is the sensations which they give us, and the order of the occurrence of those sensations. Kant himself, on this point, is as explicit as Berkeley or Locke. However firmly convinced that there exists an universe of 'Things in themselves,' totally distinct from the universe of phenomena, or of things as they appear to our senses; and even when bringing into use a technical expression (*Noumenon*) to denote what the thing is in itself, as contrasted with the *representation* of it in our minds; he allows that this representation (the matter of which, he says, consists of our sensations, though the form is given by the laws of the mind itself) is all we know of the object: and that the real nature of the Thing is, and by the constitution of our faculties ever must remain, at least in the present state of existence, an impenetrable mystery to us. [...]

There is not the slightest reason for believing that what we call the sensible qualities of the object are a type of anything inherent in itself, or bear any affinity to its own nature. A cause does not, as such, resemble its effects; an east wind is not like the feeling of cold, nor heat like the steam of boiling water. Why then should matter resemble our sensations? Why should the inmost nature of fire and water resemble the impressions made by those objects upon our senses? Or on what principle are we authorized to deduce from the effects, anything concerning the cause, except that it is a cause adequate to produce those effects? It may, therefore, safely be laid down as a truth both obvious in itself, and admitted by all whom it is at present necessary to take into consideration, that, of the outward world, we know and can know absolutely nothing, except the sensations which we experience from it. [...]

[...] If we know not, and cannot know, anything of bodies but the sensations which they excite in us or in others, those sensations must be all that we can, at bottom, mean by their attributes; and the distinction which we verbally make between the properties of things and the sensations we receive from them, must originate in the convenience of discourse rather than in the nature of what is signified by the terms.

Attributes are usually distributed under the three heads of Quality, Quantity, and Relation. We shall come to the two latter presently: in the first place we shall confine ourselves to the former.

Let us take, then, as our example, one of what are termed the sensible qualities of objects, and let that example be whiteness. When we ascribe whiteness to any substance, as, for instance, snow; when we say that snow has the quality whiteness, what do we really assert? Simply, that when snow is present to our organs, we have a particular sensation, which we are accustomed to call the sensation of white. But how do I know that snow is present? Obviously by the sensations which I derive from it, and not otherwise. I infer that the object is present, because it gives me a certain assemblage or series of sensations. And when I ascribe to it the attribute whiteness, my meaning is only, that, of the sensations composing this group or series, that which I call the sensation of white colour is one.

This is one view which may be taken of the subject. But there is also another and a different view. It may be said, that it is true we *know* nothing of sensible objects, except the sensations they excite in us; that the fact of our receiving from snow the particular sensation which is called a sensation of white, is the *ground* on which we ascribe to that substance the quality whiteness; the sole proof of its possessing that quality. But because one thing may be the sole evidence of the existence of another thing, it does not follow that the two are one and the same. The attribute whiteness (it may be said) is not the fact of receiving the sensation, but something in the object itself; a *power* inherent in it; something *in virtue* of which the object produces the sensation. And when we affirm that snow possesses the attribute whiteness, we do not merely assert that the presence of snow produces in us that sensation, but that it does so through, and by reason of, that power or quality.

For the purposes of logic it is not of material importance which of these opinions we adopt. [...]

It is as easy to comprehend that the object should produce the sensation directly and at once, as that it should produce the same sensation by the aid of something else called the *power* of producing it.

But, as the difficulties which may be felt in adopting this view of the subject cannot be removed without discussions transcending the bounds of our science, I content myself with a passing indication, and shall, for the purposes of logic, adopt a language compatible with either view of the nature of qualities. I shall say, —what at least admits of no dispute,—that the quality of whiteness ascribed to the object snow, is *grounded* on its exciting in us the sensation of white; and adopting the language already used by the school logicians in the case of the kind of attributes called Relations, I shall term the sensation of white the *foundation* of the quality whiteness. For logical purposes the sensation is the only essential part of what is meant by the word; the only part which we ever can be concerned in proving. When that is proved, the quality is proved; if an object excites a sensation, it has, of course, the power of exciting it. [...]

It is sometimes said, that all propositions whatever, of which the predicate is a general name, do, in point of fact, affirm or deny resemblance.

There is some slight degree of foundation for this remark, but no more than a slight degree. The arrangement of things into classes, such as the class *metal,* or the class *man,* is grounded indeed on a resemblance among the things which are placed in the same class, but not on a mere general resemblance: the resemblance it is grounded on consists in the possession by all those things of certain common peculiarities; and those peculiarities it is which the terms connote, and which the propositions consequently assert; not the resemblance. For though when I say, Gold is a metal, I say by implication that if there be any other metals it must resemble them, yet if there were no other metals I might still assert the proposition with the same meaning as at present, namely, that gold has the various properties implied in the word metal; just as it might be said, Christians are men, even if there were no men who were not Christians. Propositions, therefore, in which objects are referred to a class, because they possess the attributes constituting the class, are so far from asserting nothing but resemblance, that they do not, properly speaking, assert resemblance at all.

But we remarked some time ago . . . that there is sometimes a convenience in extending the boundaries of a class so as to include things which possess in a very inferior degree, if in any, some of the characteristic properties of the class,—provided they resemble that class more than any other, insomuch that the general propositions which are true of the class will be nearer to being true of those things than any other equally general propositions. For instance, there are substances called metals which have very few of the properties by which metals are commonly recognised; and almost every great family of plants or animals has a few anomalous genera or species on its borders, which are admitted into it by a sort of courtesy, and concerning which it has been matter of discussion to what family they properly belonged. Now when the class-name is predicated of any object of this description, we do, by so predicating it, affirm resemblance and nothing more. [. . .]

There is still another exceptional case, in which, though the predicate is the name of a class, yet in predicating it we affirm nothing but resemblance, the class being founded not on resemblance in any given particular, but on general unanalysable resemblance. The classes in question are those into which our simple sensations, or rather simple feelings, are divided. Sensations of white, for instance, are classed together, not because we can take them to pieces, and say they are alike in this, and not alike in that, but because we feel them to be alike altogether, though in different degrees. When, therefore, I say, The colour I saw yesterday was a white colour, or, The sensation I feel is one of tightness, in both cases the attribute I affirm of the colour or of the other sensation is mere resemblance—simple *likeness* to sensations which I have had before, and which have had those names bestowed upon them. The names of feelings, like other concrete general names, are connotative; but they connote a mere resemblance. When predicated of any individual feeling, the information they convey is that of its likeness to the other feelings which we have been accustomed to call by the same name. [. . .]

One necessary part of the theory of Names and of Propositions remains to be treated of in this place: the theory of Definitions. [. . .]

The simplest and most correct notion of a Definition is, a proposition declaratory of the meaning of a word; namely, either the meaning which it bears in common acceptation, or that which the speaker or writer, for the particular purposes of his discourse, intends to annex to it.

The definition of a word being the proposition which enunciates its meaning, words which have no meaning are unsusceptible of definition. Proper names, therefore, cannot be defined. A proper name being a mere mark put upon an individual, and of which it is the characteristic property to be destitute of meaning, its meaning cannot of course be declared; though we may indicate by language, as we might indicate still more conveniently by pointing with the finger, upon what individual that particular mark has been, or is intended to be, put. [. . .]

In the case of connotative names, the meaning, as has been so often observed, is the connotation; and the definition of a connotative name is the proposition which declares its connotation. This might be done either directly or indirectly. The direct mode would be by a proposition in this form: 'Man' (or whatsoever the word may be) 'is a name connoting such and such attributes,' or 'is a name which, when predicated of anything, signifies the possession of such and such attributes by that thing.' Or thus: Man is everything which possesses such and such attributes; Man is everything which possesses corporeity, organisation, life, rationality, and certain peculiarities of external form.

This form of definition is the most precise and least equivocal of any; but it is not brief enough, and is besides too technical for common discourse. The more usual mode of declaring the connotation of a name is to predicate of it another name or names of known signification, which connote the same aggregation of attributes. [. . .]

When, on the other hand, the abstract name does not express a complication of attributes, but a single attribute, we must remember that every attribute is grounded on some fact or phenomenon, from which, and which alone, it derives its meaning. To that fact or phenomenon, called in a former chapter the foundation of the attribute, we must, therefore, have recourse for its definition. Now, the foundation of the attribute may be a phenomenon of any degree of complexity consisting of many different parts, either co-existent or in succession. To obtain a definition of the attribute, we must analyse the phenomenon into these parts. Eloquence, for example, is the name of one attribute only; but this attribute is grounded on external effects of a complicated nature, flowing from acts of the person to whom we ascribe the attribute; and by resolving this phenomenon of causation into its two parts, the cause and the effect, we obtain a definition of eloquence, viz. the power of influencing the feelings by speech or writing.

A name, therefore, whether concrete or abstract, admits of definition, provided we are able to analyse, that is, to distinguish into parts, the attribute or set of attributes which constitute the meaning both of the concrete name and of the corresponding abstract: if a set of attributes, by enumerating them; if a single attribute, by dissecting the fact or phenomenon (whether of perception or of internal consciousness) which is the foundation of the attribute. But, farther, even when the fact is one of our simple feelings or states of consciousness, and therefore unsusceptible of analysis, the names both of the object and of the attribute still admit of definition: or rather, would do so if all our simple feelings had names. Whiteness may be defined, the property or power, of exciting the sensation of white. A white object may be defined, an object which excites the sensation of white. The only names which are unsusceptible of definition, because their meaning is unsusceptible of analysis, are the names of the simple feelings themselves. These are in the same condition as proper names. They are not indeed, like proper names, unmeaning; for the words *sensation of white* signify, that the sensation which I so denominate resembles other sensations which I remember to have had before, and to have called by that name. But as we have no words by which to recall those former sensations, except the very word which we seek to define or some other which, being exactly synonymous with it, requires definition as much, words cannot unfold the signification of this class of names; and we are obliged to make a direct appeal to the personal experience of the individual whom we address.

Source: A System of Logic, Bk. I, Chs. 3, 5 and 8. (Extracts.) Longman.

UNIVERSALS AND REALITY

12 The Philosophical Economy of the Theory of Ideas (1936)

H. F. CHERNISS

The objection with which in the *Metaphysics*[1] Aristotle introduces his criticism of the theory of Ideas expresses a difficulty which has tended to alienate the sympathy of most students who approach the study of Plato. The hypothesis, Aristotle says, is a superfluous duplication of the phenomenal world; it is as if one should think it impossible to count a number of objects until that number had first been multiplied. This objection, even tacitly entertained, distorts the motivation of the hypothesis; that it misrepresents Plato's express attitude towards scientific problems, the well-known statement of Eudemus quoted by Simplicius on the authority of Sosigenes amply proves.[2] The complications of the planetary movements had to be explained, Plato asserted, by working out an hypothesis of a definite number of fixed and regular motions which would 'save the phenomena'. This same attitude is expressed in the *Phaedo* where Socrates explains the method of 'hypothesis' which he used to account for the apparently disordered world of phenomena;[3] the result of this method, he says, was the Theory of Ideas.[4]

The phenomena for which Plato had to account were of three kinds, ethical, epistemological, and ontological. In each of these spheres there had been developed by the end of the fifth century doctrines so extremely paradoxical that there seemed to be no

[1] *Met.*, 990a 34ff. It is repeated almost exactly at 1078b 34–6.
[2] Simplicius, *in De Caelo*, p. 488, 18–24 (Heiberg).
[3] *Phd.*, 99d 4–100a 8.
[4] *Phd.*, 100b 1–102a 1.

possibility of reconciling them with one another or any one of them with the observable facts of human experience.[5] The dialogues of Plato, I believe, will furnish evidence to show that he considered it necessary to find a single hypothesis which would at once solve the problems of these several spheres and also create a rationally unified cosmos by establishing the connection among the separate phases of experience.

The interests of Socrates,[6] the subject-matter of the early dialogues, the 'practical' tone of Plato's writings throughout make it highly probable that he took his start from the ethical problems of his day. It is unnecessary to labour the point that he considered it fundamentally important to establish an absolute ethical standard; that the bearing on this point of the 'inconclusive', 'exploratory' dialogues could not have been obscure to his contemporaries is obvious to anyone who looks at such evidence of the time as is furnished by the Δισσοὶ Λόγοι (which discusses the relativity of good and evil, fair and foul, just and unjust, true and false, and the possibility of teaching wisdom and virtue) or by the papyrus fragment of Antiphon the Sophist[7] (where conventional justice is called adventitious and generally contradictory to natural justice which is defined as that which is truly advantageous to each individual). The necessity for an absolute standard of ethics which would not depend upon the contradictory phenomena of conventional conduct but would be a measure of human activities instead of being measured by them was forcibly demonstrated by the plight into which Democritus had fallen. He had bitterly opposed the relativism of Protagoras;[8] yet two of his own ethical fragments show how vulnerable he must have been to counter-attack. 'They know and seek fair things,' he said, 'who are naturally disposed to them.'[9] And,

---

[5] Note the criticism and warning in *Phd.*, 101e: ἅμα δ' οὐκ ἂν φύροιο ὥσπερ οἱ ἀντιλογικοὶ περί τε τῆς ἀρχῆς διαλεγόμενος καὶ τῶν ἐξ ἐκείνης ὡρμημένων, εἴπερ βούλοιό τι τῶν ὄντων εὑρεῖν· ἐκείνοις μὲν γὰρ ἴσως οὐδὲ εἷς περὶ τούτου λόγος οὐδὲ φροντίς. ἱκανοὶ γὰρ ὑπὸ σοφίας ὁμοῦ πάντα κυκῶντες ὅμως δύνασθαι αὐτοὶ αὑτοῖς ἀρέσκειν. They do not keep the 'universes of discourse' clearly defined but think it is legitimate, for example, to drag an epistemological difficulty into an ethical problem before they have completely canvassed the ethical phenomena and have set up an hypothesis to explain them. An example of this 'childish' confusion is outlined in the *Phil.*, (15d–16a; 17a).

[6] Cf. e.g. Aristotle, *Met.*, 987b 1ff.

[7] *Oxyrh. Pap.*, XI, 1364; Diels, *Fragmente der Vorsokratiker*, 4th ed., vol. 11, pp. xxxii ff.

[8] Plutarch, *Adv. Colot.*, 1108f–1109a.

[9] Democritus, *fragment 56* (Diels): τὰ καλὰ γνωρίζουσι καὶ ζηλοῦσιν οἱ εὐφυέες πρὸς αὐτά.

attempting to reconcile conventional law and natural good, he remarked, 'The law seeks to benefit the life of men but can do so only when they themselves desire to fare well. For to those who obey it it indicates their proper goodness.'[10] This bald assertion of a difference between fair and foul things, virtuous and vicious actions offers no standard whereby to determine the difference, no reason for the similarity of all fair things qua fair and for their difference from all that are foul. So long as these are only characteristics of material individuals no standard can be found, for to measure individuals against one another is to succumb to relativism. To compare and contrast one must have a definite standard of reference which must itself be underivative lest it become just another example of the characteristic in question and so lead to an infinite regress. The 'dialogues of search', by demonstrating the hopelessness of all other expedients, show that the definitions requisite to normative ethics are possible only on the assumption that there exist, apart from phenomena, substantive objects of these definitions which alone are the source of the values attaching to phenomenal existence.[11] The possibility of ethical distinctions, then, implies objective differences which can be accounted for only by the hypothesis of substantive ideas.

While this hypothesis makes an ethical system possible in the abstract, the problems raised by conscious human activity involve the construction of a complete ethical theory in the questions of epistemology. That a consistent and practical ethical theory depends upon an adequate epistemology, Plato demonstrates in the *Meno*. The subject of that dialogue is *virtue*, but it is with one of the popular practical questions about virtue that Meno opens the discussion. Socrates protests that such questions as the teachability of virtue must wait upon a satisfactory definition of virtue;[12] but Meno's failure to produce a definition makes him fall back upon the 'eristic argument' that one cannot search for

---

[10] Democritus, *fragment* 248 (Diels): ὁ νόμος βούλεται μὲν εὐεργετεῖν βίον ἀνθρώπων. δύναται δὲ ὅταν αὐτοὶ βούλωνται πάσχειν εὖ. τοῖσι γὰρ πειθομένοισι τὴν ἰδίην ἀρετὴν ἐνδείκνυται.

[11] *Euth.*, 15c 11–e 2; *Laches* 199e (cf. 200e–201a); *Lysis*, 222e (N.B. 218c–220b 5; necessity of finding a πρῶτον φίλον which is the final cause of πάντα φίλα); *Charm.*, (176a); *Hippias Minor* (376b: if *anyone* errs voluntarily, it must be the good man [who, of course, as good would not err at all]). Cf. *Prot.*, (361c: the difficulties into which the arguments has led show that it is necessary first to discover what ἀρετή is and *then* discuss its teachability).

[12] *Men.*, 71a 3–7. It is in the light of this that I find the key to the riddles of the *Protagoras* in Socrates' remarks at the end of that dialogue (*Pro.*, 361c 2–d).

either the known or the unknown.[13] To the implication here that
ethical problems are not susceptible of investigation Socrates
answers that one can escape this difficulty only by supposing that
learning or discovering is really recollection of that which has
already been *directly* known.[14] Here Socrates is not concerned
with the details of the process; his contention is simply that, since
determination of the characteristics of virtue presupposes a definition of its essential nature and to give such a definition presupposes knowledge of the essence, we must assume that essential
virtue exists and has been directly known unless we are to surrender all possibility of considering ethical problems. Socrates is
forced by Meno's insistence to discuss his question anyway, but
his repeated objection that such questions demand a prior determination of the nature of virtue itself is a warning and an
explanation of the paradoxical outcome of the consequent discussion.[15]

   If men act virtuously without being able to teach virtue (that
is, without being able to give a consistent account of the causes
of their actions), it is because they have 'right opinions' and so
are virtuous by a kind of 'divine grace'.[16] But such right opinions,
though having results speciously identical with those of knowledge, are unstable, for they are haphazard, being unconnected
by a chain of causality with the final cause. The recognition of
this causal relationship, however, is knowledge and this is just
recollection.[17] Consequently until one bases his reasoning upon
the knowledge of essential virtue, there can be no adequate
solution of the problems of ethics.[18] So it is that by argument and
example the *Meno* demonstrates how, having to distinguish knowledge and right opinion in order to save the phenomena of moral
activity, the ethical philosopher is forced to face the problems of
epistemology.

   But Plato was not satisfied with having proved that considerations of ethics require the assumption of substantive ideas and an
epistemology consistent with such an hypothesis. The pragmatic
relativism of Protagoras' ethics was, after all, a necessary result
of his subjective realism; and Plato had before him the example
of Democritus who, though insisting upon the reality of definite
moral standards, could not finally refute Protagoras since he had

---

[13] *Men.*, 80e–81a.
[14] *Men.*, 81d 4–5. Note the word used for acquiring the knowledge in the
first place: ἑωρακυῖα (81c 6).
[15] *Men.*, 86c 6–87b 5.   [16] *Men.*, 99a–d.
[17] *Men.*, 97e–98b.   [18] *Men.*, 100b.

no adequate reason for giving mind the sovereignty over sensations. There is a winsome sadness in his confession of defeat expressed in the reply he makes the sensations give to the strictures of mind: 'unhappy Intelligence, with evidence we give you you attempt our overthrow; your victory is your defeat'.[19] The saving of the phenomena of intellection and sensation is the primary duty of epistemology; if, however, it should appear that these phenomena can be saved in their own right only by setting up the same hypothesis as was found to be essential for ethics, the coincidence of results would by the principle of scientific economy enunciated in Plato's phrasing of the astronomical problem lend added validity to the hypothesis in each sphere.

The epistemological necessity for the existence of the Ideas is proved by the same indirect method as was used in establishing the ethical necessity. Since the phenomena to be explained have first to be determined, it is essential to proceed by analysis of the psychological activities, to decide the nature of these activities and their objects. In brief, the argument turns upon the determination of intellection as an activity different from sensation and opinion. In the *Timaeus*,[20] in an avowedly brief and casual proof of the separate existence of Ideas, it is stated that if intellection is other than right opinion it follows that there exist separate substantive Ideas as the objects of intellection. The indications of the essential difference of intellection and right opinion are there said to be three. Knowledge is produced by instruction, is always accompanied by the ability to render a true account or proof, and cannot be shaken by persuasive means, whereas right opinion is the result of persuasion, is incapable of accounting for itself, and is susceptible of alteration by external influence. The difference here mentioned is vividly exemplified in the myth of Er[21] by the horrible choice of the soul concerning whom it is said: 'he was one of those who had come from heaven, having in his former life lived in a well-ordered city and shared in virtue out of habit without philosophy'.[22] The *Theaetetus*, in its attempt to define knowledge, treats as the last possibility considered the suggestion that 'true opinion' may be a constitutive element of knowledge, may in conjunction with a λόγος or 'account' *be* knowledge itself.[23] As this proposal is tested, it is shown that, of

[19] Democritus, *fragment* 125.
[20] *Tim.*, 51d–e.   [21] *Rep.*, 619b ff.
[22] In the parallel passage of the *Phd.* (82a–b) 'philosophy' is glossed by 'intelligence': ἄνευ φιλοσοφίας τε καὶ νοῦ.
[23] *Tht.*, 201c 8 ff.

the various possible meanings which λόγος might here have, the most satisfactory is 'knowledge of the proper difference of the object known'.[24] But if this 'knowledge of the difference' is not to be, in turn, mere 'right opinion' about the difference, an empty tautology, the definition is vitiated by a 'circulus in definiendo'.[25] In short, if 'true opinion' and knowledge are not identical, the former can not be an essential element of the latter, either. The common assumption of a relationship between 'right opinion' and knowledge is due to the external similarity of their results,[26] but the rightness of any particular opinion is simply accidental as Plato succinctly shows.[27] Right opinion is still essentially opinion; and this, the *Theaetetus* has already proved, cannot be knowledge, for it involves the possibility of error or wrong opinion which can be explained only as a mistaken reference to something known, although it is difficult to see how—if the term of reference be known—a mistaken identification is possible.[28] Opinion, then, is different from knowledge and secondary to it, for no satisfactory account of error can be given until the process of intellection has been explained.[29] Similarly the earlier part of the *Theaetetus* proved that knowledge can not be sensation or derived from sensation,[30] because sensation itself implies a central faculty to which all individual perceptions are referred and which passes judgement on them all.[31] As in the *Republic*[32] the proof that knowledge and opinion are different faculties is conclusive evidence for the fact that the objects with which they are concerned must be different, so here from the observation that the mind functioning directly without any intermediate organ contemplates the notions that are applicable to all things[33] proceeds the conclusion that knowledge is not to be found in the perceptions but in the reflection upon them, since only in this process is it possible to grasp reality and meaning.[34] The attempt of the *Theaetetus* to define knowledge fails, and this failure demonstrates that the λόγος, the essential characteristic of knowledge, cannot be explained by any theory which takes phenomena to be the objects of intellection. That this is the purpose of the dialogue is revealed by the *Timaeus* passage above which shows that the λόγος is the δεσμός of the *Meno*,[35] the mark which distin-

24 *Tht.*, 208d.
26 *Tht.*, 200e 4–6.
28 *Tht.*, 187b 4–200d 4.
30 Cf. *Tht.*, 186e 9–187a 6.
32 *Rep.*, 477e–478b 2.
34 *Tht.*, 186d 2 ff.

25 *Tht.*, 209d 4–210a 9.
27 *Tht.*, 201a–c.
29 *Tht.*, 200b–d.
31 *Tht.*, 184b 5–186e 10.
33 *Tht.*, 185e 1–2.
35 *Men.*, 98a.

guishes knowledge from right opinion in that dialogue and which was there identified with ἀνάμνησις. The _Theaetetus_, then, is an attempt to prove that the theory of Ideas is a necessary hypothesis for the solution of the problems of epistemology; the constructive doctrine of the *Sophist* demonstrates that it is a sufficient hypothesis for that purpose.[36] The process of abstraction and generalisation which Aristotle thought sufficient to account for knowledge[37] was recognised by Plato,[38] but he considered it to be inadequate. In the *Parmenides*,[39] after advancing all his objections to the hypothesis, Parmenides is made to assert that it is still necessary to assume the existence of Ideas if thought and reasoning are to be saved; and in the *Phaedo*[40] Socrates outlines the theory of abstraction almost in the very words which Aristotle was to use, connects it with the theories of the mechanistic physics, and rejects it in favour of the theory of separate Ideas. The possibility of abstraction itself, if it is to have any meaning, Plato believes, requires the independent reality of the object apprehended by the intellect. That is the basis of his curt refutation of mentalism in the *Parmenides*.[41] So the process of abstraction and analysis outlined in the *Philebus*, which is there said to be possible because of the participation of the phenomena in real Ideas,[42] and which in a simple example of its use in the *Republic*[43] is called 'our customary method', is in the *Phaedrus*[44] designated as ἀνάμνησις and said to require the substantial existence of the Ideas and previous direct knowledge of them by the intellect. The successful 'recollection' of the Ideas by means of the dialectical process is in the *Republic*[45] said to constitute intellection as distinguished from opinion, and the man who is capable of such activity is there described in terms parallel to the 'mythical' description of the 'wingéd intellect' of the *Phaedrus*.[46]

The nature of the mental processes, then, can be explained only by the hypothesis of Ideas. Since no mere addition to right opinion from the sphere with which it itself deals can produce knowledge or make intelligible the fact of error and since no

---

[36] Cf. *Soph.*, 258d–264b and note the triumphant tone of 264b 5–7.

[37] *De Anima* 432a 3–14; *Post. Anal.*, 100a 3–b 17; cf. *Met.*, A, 1.

[38] *Charm.*, 159a 1–3; *Phil.*, 38b 12–13.

[39] *Parm.*, 135b 5–c 3.   [40] *Phd.*, 96b.   [41] *Parm.*, 132b–c.

[42] *Phil.*, 16c 10 ff. N.B. 16d 2: εὑρήσειν γὰρ ἐνοῦσαν.

[43] *Rep.*, 596a.

[44] *Phdr.*, 249b 5–c 4. Cf. the extended demonstration of *Phd.*, 74a 9–77a 5 which is based upon epistemological considerations.

[45] *Rep.*, 479e–480a.   [46] *Phdr.*, 249c.

combination of sensations can account for apperception, knowledge cannot be synthetic or derivative. Knowledge as a special
faculty dealing *directly* with its own objects must be assumed in
order not only to explain the fact of cognition but also to make
possible opinion and sensation as they are given by experience.
The special faculty of knowledge, however, is characterised by
direct contact of subject and object; since phenomena cannot
enter into such a relationship with the subject, mediating organs
being required in their case, <u>it is necessary that the objects</u> of
<u>knowledge be real entities existing apart from the phenomenal</u>
<u>world and that the mind have been affected by them</u> before the
mental processes dealing with phenomena occur. Only so can one
avoid the self-contradictory sensationalism of Protagoras, the
psychological nihilism of Gorgias, and the dilemma of Democritus.

The effort to save the phenomena of mental activity leads to
the same hypothesis as did the attempt to explain human conduct,
and the ethical hypothesis is supported by the independent requirements of epistemology. There is, however, another sphere
naturally prior to knowledge and sensation and by which finally
all epistemological theories must be judged. The Ideas are necessary to account for the data of mental processes; but the physical
world and its characteristics are not dependent upon these
mental processes, and it is no more sufficient to assume an ontology which will fit the requirements of epistemology than it is to
construct an epistemology in order to account for the phenomena
of ethics. It is with this in mind that Timaeus, when in a physical
discourse he uses a résumé of the epistemological proof of the
existence of Ideas, apologises for his procedure with the excuse
that the magnitude of his main subject requires him to give the
briefest possible demonstration.[47] The very language of this passage shows that Plato considered it as a requirement of sound
method to develop his ontological hypothesis according to the
data of the physical world itself. This requirement is explained in
the *Theaetetus* where a detailed theory of psychological relativism is expounded[48] by way of considering the thesis that knowledge is sensation. Such a doctrine, in spite of the objections that
can be brought against its epistemological and ethical consequences, may still present a correct account of the nature of
existence as nothing but a flux of motions. What seem to be
individual objects and characteristics would then be merely the

[47] *Tim.*, 51c 5 ff.   [48] *Tht.*, 156a–160e.

transitory resultants of the component motions. In that case, knowledge would really be vivid sensations which are the functions of clashing and passing movements.[49] To argue that no practical ethics or adequate epistemology can be developed from such an account is pointless, for there could be no *naturally* valid criterion by which to evaluate the different moments of evidence.[50] Such a theory as that of Ideas would be a merely pragmatic hypothesis, and distinctions of good and bad, true and false would be at best only conventional and artificial. It is, then, necessary that the study of ontology be undertaken independently of the requirements of ethics and epistemology to discover what hypothesis will explain the data of physical phenomena as such.[51] The data with which the investigation has to work are the constantly shifting phenomena of the physical world, and Plato accepts this unceasing flux as a characteristic of all phenomenal existence.[52] This flux, however, is the datum which has to be explained, and his contention is simply that change itself is intelligible and possible only if there exist entities which are not themselves involved in the change. The argument in the *Theaetetus*[53] attempts to show that the constant flux of phenomena involves alteration as well as local motion but that alteration requires the permanent subsistence of immutable abstract qualities. The relativism that asserts the constant change of everything, however, makes attributes and perceptions the simultaneous resultants of the meeting of agent and patient, while agent and patient themselves are merely complexes of change without independent existence,[54] with the result that not only are all things constantly changing their characteristics but the characteristics themselves are constantly altering, and 'whiteness' can no more be really 'whiteness' than any other colour.[55] Similarly, if the qualities themselves are always altering, the sensations which are defined by these constantly altering qualities are undifferentiated.[56] Such an account of the world involves the denial not only of fixed states and determinable processes but also of the laws of contradiction and the excluded middle.[57] The data of phenomenal change, then, logically require the hypothesis of immutable and immaterial ideas. The argument occurs again at the end of the *Cratylus* (where, however, it is connected with

---

[49] *Tht.*, 179c.   [50] *Tht.*, 158b–e.   [51] *Tht.*, 179d.
[52] Cf. *Tim.*, 27d 5–28a 4.   [53] *Tht.*, 181c–183b.
[54] *Tht.*, 182b.   [55] *Tht.*, 182d 1–5.
[56] *Tht.*, 182d 8–e5.   [57] *Tht.*, 183a 4–b5.

one form of the epistemological proof);[58] and Aristotle accuses the Protagoreans, in the same terms as does Plato, of denying the laws of logic.[59] In a passage obviously influenced by the *Theaetetus*,[60] he explains the difficulties of the relativists as due to their failure to recognise immaterial existences and to note the distinction between quantitative and qualitative change. Like Plato, Aristotle felt that a logical account of physical nature required some hypothesis of qualitative existence as underived from quantitative distinctions.

The digression on mensuration in the *Politicus*[61] has the same intention. There Plato distinguishes between quantitative and qualitative 'measurement', the former being only relative measurement and the latter measurement against a norm,[62] and castigates those who think all the world susceptible of quantitative measurement; their error lies in the supposition that all difference can be reduced to quantitative distinctions.[63] For this reason in the *Timaeus*, where the quantitative determinations of the minima of phenomenal air, fire, water, and earth are elaborated in great detail,[64] Plato still insists that there must be substantive Ideas of air, fire, water, and earth, apart from phenomena, immutable, the objects of intellection only,[65] and that phenomenal objects are what they are because they are imitations of these real Ideas.[66] Indications of the ontological necessity of the hypothesis are not lacking in this dialogue either. The most certain and evident characteristic of phenomena is their instability; they are all involved in the process of generation[67] and so imply a cause external to themselves.[68] Apart from the 'mythical' form of the explanation to which this leads, the argument is the same as the indirect proof of the *Theaetetus*. The instability of phenomena can be explained only by assuming a world of Ideas as the source of phenomenal characteristics. To dispense with such a super-phenomenal world is not only to identify right opinion and knowledge but, in fact, to say that phenomena are stable.[69] This brief remark of Timaeus sums up the results of the demonstration in

---

[58] *Crat.*, 439d 3–440c 1.
[59] *Met.*, 1008a 31–34; cf. 1009a 6–12.
[60] *Met.*, 1010a 1–37.   [61] *Pol.*, 283d–287a.
[62] *Pol.*, 283d 7–284b 2.
[63] *Pol.*, 284e 11–285c 2; cf. Rodier, *Études de philosophie grecque*, p. 48, note 1.
[64] *Tim.*, 53c 4–55c 5; 55d 7–57c 6.   [65] *Tim.*, 51a 7–52a 4.
[66] *Tim.*, 50c, 51a 7–b 1 (cf. Shorey in *Class. Phil.*, XXIII [1928], p. 358).
[67] *Tim.*, 28b 8–c 2.   [68] *Tim.*, 28c 2–3.   [69] *Tim.*, 51d 6–7.

the *Theaetetus* which shows that the relativistic ontology transgresses the law of the excluded middle and so can no more say that all is in motion than that all is at rest. To do away with stable qualities is tantamount to denying the possibility of change.[70] Yet it is the possibility of phenomenal alteration that was to be saved, for phenomena have no stability at all;[71] they are fleeting phrases without persistent substantiality,[72] but such they can be only if apart from them there are substances of which somehow the phenomena partake.[73]

The physical phenomena, then, considered in themselves and not as objects of sensation or cognition still can be saved only by the hypothesis of separate, substantive Ideas. That the necessary and sufficient hypothesis for this sphere turns out to be the very one needed for ethics and epistemology makes it possible to consider the three spheres of existence, cognition, and value as phases of a single unified cosmos.

The apparently disparate phenomena of these three orders, like the seemingly anomalous paths of the planets, had to be accounted for by a single, simple hypothesis which would not only make intelligible the appearances taken separately but at the same time establish the interconnection of them all. The problem which Plato set others in astronomy he set himself in philosophy; the resulting theory of Ideas indicates by its economy that it proceeded from the same skill of formulation which charted for all time the course of astronomical hypothesis.

Source: 'The Philosophical Economy of the Theory of Ideas', *American Journal of Philology*, 1936.

[70] Aristotle reproduces the argument in his own language in *Metaphysics*, 1010a 35–7.

[71] Cf. *Tim.*, 49d 4 ff. (βεβαιότητα-d) and 51d 5–7.

[72] *Tim.*, 49c 7–50a 4.

[73] *Tim.*, 50b–c. That the mere configuration of space is not enough to produce phenomenal fire, etc., 51b 4–6 shows (N.B. καθ' ὅσον ἂν μιμήματα τούτων δέχηται). All this, I think, makes Shorey's interpretation of 56b 3–5 certain (*Class. Phil.*, XXIII [1928], pp. 357–8). To interpret στερεὸν γεγονός here as 'having received a third dimension' would be tautological, for the pyramid is *eo ipso* three-dimensional. Cf. also A. Rivaud in his introduction to his edition of the *Timaeus* (p. 26) in the Budé series.

43 Are there Universals? (*1939*)

J. L. AUSTIN

People (philosophers) speak of 'universals' as though these were entities which they often stumbled across, in some familiar way which needs no explanation. But they are not so. On the contrary, it is not so very long since these alleged entities were calculated into existence by a transcendental argument: and in those days, anyone bold enough to say there 'were' universals kept the argument always ready, to produce if challenged. I do not know if it is upon this argument that Mr. Mackinnon and Mr. Maclagan[1] are relying. It may be that they do claim to stumble across 'universals' in some easy manner: or it may be that they rely upon some other argument which is admittedly transcendental.[2] But I propose to consider, not very fully, that celebrated argument which, above all, seems suited to prove the existence of 'universals' in the most ordinary sense of that word: it runs as follows:

It is assumed that we do 'sense' things, which are many or different.[3] Whether these things are 'material objects' or what are commonly called 'sense-data', is not here relevant: in fact, the argument can be made to apply to the objects of any kind of 'acquaintance', even non-sensuous,—although such applications were not originally envisaged. It is assumed, further, that we make a practice of calling many different sensa by the same single name: we say '*This* is grey', and '*That* is grey', when the sensa denoted by 'this' and by 'that' are not identical. And finally it is assumed that this practice is 'justifiable' or indispensable. Then we proceed to ask: How is such a practice possible? And answer:

(*a*) Since we use the same single *name* in each case, there must surely be some single identical thing 'there' in each case:

[1] The two previous speakers in the symposium of which the paper reprinted here formed a part. (Ed.)

[2] For there are in fact several: see below.

[3] There is a constant and harmful ambiguity here: the sensa are commonly different *both* 'numerically' *and* 'qualitatively.' (the former, of course, always). The 'universal' is alleged to be single and identical in *both* ways. Hence, from the start, that fatal confusion of the problem of 'genus and species' with the problem of 'universal and particular'.

something of which the name is the name: something, therefore, which is 'common' to all sensa called by that name. Let this entity, whatever it may be, be called a 'universal'.

(b) Since it was admitted that the things we sense are many or different, it follows that this 'universal', which is single and identical, is *not sensed*.

Let us consider this argument.

(1) This is a *transcendental*[4] argument: if there were not in existence something other than sensa, we should not be able to do what we *are* able to do, (viz. name things). Let us not consider here whether, in general, such a form of argument is permissible or fruitful: but it is important to notice the following points:

(i) The 'universal' is emphatically *not* anything we stumble across. We can claim only to know *that*, not *what*, it is. 'Universal' *means* that which will provide the solution to a certain problem: that x which is present, one and identical, in the different sensa which we call by the same name. Unfortunately, as so often happens, succeeding generations of philosophers fell naturally into the habit of supposing that they were perfectly well acquainted with these entities in their own right: they have any amount to tell us about them (partly this was due to a confusion of 'universals' in our present sense with 'universals' in other senses, as we shall see). For instance, we are told that they are 'objects of thought': and myths are invented, about our 'contemplation' of universals: and so on.

(ii) On the same grounds, it must be held that to ask a whole series of questions which have constantly been asked is nonsensical. For instance: 'How is the universal related to the particulars?' 'Could there be universals without instances?': and many others. For a 'universal' is *defined* as something which is related to certain sensa in a certain way. We might as well worry about what is the relation between a man and his aunt, and as to whether there can be aunts without nephews (or nieces).

(iii) Here, however, a point to which I have already twice referred in anticipation, must be made: this will unfortunately be a digression. There are *other* transcendental

---

[4] In Kant's sense. But it is also 'transcendental' in another sense, that of proving the existence of a class of entities different in kind from sensa.

arguments for 'the existence of universals'. I shall mention one: A true statement is one which corresponds with reality: the statements of the scientist are true: therefore there are realities which correspond to those statements. Sensa do not correspond to the statements of the scientist (exactly *why*, is rather too obscure to discuss here): therefore there must exist other objects, real but not sensible, which do correspond to the statements of the scientist. Let these be called 'universals'.

That this argument begs many questions, is evident. Are all sciences alike? Is all truth correspondence? Does no science make statements about sensa? Some, for instance, would distinguish 'a priori' sciences from 'empirical' sciences: and hold that the 'truth' of the former is *not* correspondence, while the statements of the latter *are* about sensa. Of course, too, the assumption that the sciences are true is a large one.[5] But all this cannot be entered into.

What it is important to notice for our purposes is, that here too the argument is *transcendental*. The 'universal' is an x, which is to solve our problem for us: we know only that it is non-sensible, and in addition must possess certain characters, the lack of which prohibits sensa from corresponding to the statements of the scientist. But we do not stumble across these 'universals': though, needless to say, philosophers soon take to talking as though they did.

Now it must be asked: What conceivable ground have we for *identifying* the 'universals' of our original argument with the 'universals' of this second argument? Except that both are non-sensible, nothing more is known in which they are alike. Is it not odd to suppose that *any two* distinct transcendental arguments could possibly be known each to prove the existence of the *same* kind of thing? Hence the oddity of speaking of 'arguments for the existence of universals': in the first place, no two of these arguments are known to be arguments for the existence of the same thing: and in the second place, the phrase is misleading because it suggests that we know what a 'universal' is quite apart from the argument for its existence—whereas in fact

[5] Even Plato once decided that he ought not to make it. It has been suggested to me that the argument should be formulated in terms of 'having meaning' rather than of 'being true'. I doubt if this would be any improvement.

'universal' *means*, in each case, simply 'the entity which this argument proves to exist'.

As a matter of fact, we can, indirectly show that the objects 'proved' to exist by the two arguments so far mentioned are *not* the same. For firstly, the variety of 'universals' proved to exist in the case of the first argument is strangely greater than in the case of the second argument: the former proves a 'universal' to exist corresponding to every general name, the latter only does so when the name is that of an object studied by the scientist.[6] But it might still be thought, that the 'universals' proved to exist by the second argument do, nevertheless, form part of the class of 'universals' proved to exist by the first argument: e.g. 'circularity' or 'straightness' could be proved to exist by either argument. Yet in fact, no clearer cases could be chosen for demonstrating that the two kinds of 'universals' are distinct: for, if 'circularity' is to be proved to exist by the first argument, then I must be able to say truly of certain sensa 'this is circular': whereas, the 'circularity' which is to be proved to exist by the second argument must be such that it cannot be truly predicated of *any* sensa.[7]

The purpose of this digression is to point out that, apart altogether from questions as to whether the 'arguments for the existence of universals' are good and as to whether they permit us to talk further about universals, an immeasurable confusion arises from the fact that 'universal' may mean at any moment any one of a number of different things. For example, if 'universal' is being used in the sense of the second argument, it is good enough sense to ask 'How are universals related to particulars?' though any answer would be difficult to find. (The answer that particulars

[6] It is to be remembered that, if we are to argue that 'science' is not about sensa, very little can be recognised as 'science'.

[7] It cannot be sense to say that sensible circles are more or less 'like' the universal 'circularity': a particular can be like nothing but another particular. Nor can I agree with Mr. Maclagan that, on his account, the 'sensible figure' could be an approximation to the 'geometrical figure': for what is sensed can be like nothing but something else which is sensed. But I must allow that 'non-sensuous perception' 'intuitive acquaintance' and so on seem to me to be contradictions in terms, attempts to have things both ways. I find confirmation of this, when Mr. Maclagan says a sensible circle might be *more* than an 'approximation' to a geometrical circle: i.e., as I understand him, it would *be* a geometrical circle, although we didn't know it. Thus he is making the objects of intuition the same in kind as the objects of sense—indeed interchangeable.—I wonder if Mr. Maclagan's non-sensuous intuition is such that we can say on occasion, '*This is* a (geometrical) circle'? For whatever reason, we do not ever, I think, speak so. Yet surely, if we are 'acquainted' with geometrical circles, we ought to be able to do this.

are 'approximations' to universals not only implies that the two
are the *same* in kind whereas they were said to be different, but
also again exposes the difference between this argument and the
other; since it would be absurd to say, of some non-scientific
object like a bed, that there was no sensible bed which was *really*
a bed, but all sensible beds were only more or less remote 'approximations' to beds. Again, to ask 'Are there universals without
instances?' is now absurd for the reason that a 'universal', in the
sense of the second argument, is not the sort of thing which 'has
instances' at all (indeed, someone will certainly be found to *apply*
the first argument *to* the objects 'proved' to exist by the second
argument).

(2) So far, we have not investigated the validity of our argument.

(i) It is to be observed, that if the argument holds in its first
part (*a*), it certainly also holds in its second part (*b*). If
there 'are universals', then they are not sensed: the whole
point of the argument is, that there must exist something
of a kind quite different from sensa. Nevertheless, a fatal
mistake has been made by many philosophers: they accept
the *first* part of the argument ('there are universals'), which
as we shall shortly see is wrong, and they *reject* the second
part, which is a necessary corollary of the first. Of course,
the talk is at first still to the effect that universals are
'thought': but theories are soon formed as to how we
'abstract universals from particulars' and then 'see universals in particulars'.[8] Undoubtedly, there are 'reasons'
of a kind for constructing these theories and rejecting the
'separation' of universals, of which the following will be
the most pleasing to self-refuting nominalists: if we accept
both (*a*) and (*b*), it becomes difficult to give any account of
how I come to classify together the various things called
'grey'; true, if and when I am correct in classifying a certain sensum as 'grey', then the universal must be 'in' it:
but it is not *sensed* 'in' it: how then am I to decide whether
it is or isn't there, or even guess it?[9] Hence we depart
from the argument in its pristine form, and embark on
mythologies: and by the time we have finished, we may

[8] Do we smell universals in particulars too?
[9] In *this* sense of 'giving an explanation of naming', the theory gives
none.

well have reached the position of so many philosophers,
and hold that what I *do* sense are 'universals', what I do
not sense are 'particulars',[10] which, considering the meanings of the words, comprises two self-contradictions.

(ii) Finally, it must be pointed out that the first part of the
argument (*a*), is wrong. Indeed, it is so artless that it is
difficult to state it plausibly. Clearly it depends on a
suppressed premiss which there is no reason whatever to
accept, namely, that words are essentially 'proper names',
*unum nomen unum nominatum.** But why, if 'one identical' word is used, *must* there be 'one identical' object
present which it denotes? Why should it not be the whole
function of a word to denote many things?[11] Why should
not words be by nature 'general'?—However, it is in any
case simply false that we use the *same* name for different
things: 'grey' and 'grey' are *not* the same, they are two
similar symbols (tokens), just as the things denoted by
'this' and by 'that' are similar things. In this matter, the
'words' are in a position precisely analogous to that of the
objects denoted by them.[12]

But, it may be objected, by the 'same single' word it was never
meant that it is *numerically* identical. In what sense, then, was it
meant? If it meant 'qualitatively identical', then it is clear that
the sense in which there is an identical 'type' of the tokens is just
like the sense in which the sensa share in an identical common
character: hence the former cannot be taken as self-explanatory
while the latter is admitted obscure. If it meant that all these
tokens 'have the same meaning', then we cannot *assume* that it is
the business of similar tokens to 'mean' something which is
numerically self-identical, without begging our whole question in
the manner already pointed out.

But, it will be further said, I do *sense* something identical in
different sensa. How this could be I do not understand; but if it is
true, it is clear that this identical something is not an entity
different in kind from sensa.

[10] Other theories: that the particular *is* just a cluster of universals: that the
universal *is* a particular of a special sort (an image).

* Roughly, 'one name for one thing named'—Ed.

[11] Many *similar* things, on a plausible view: but other views might be
held.

[12] There are ways, of course, in which they are not so analogous: for
instance, that one token is of the same type as another, is determined by
convention as well as by similarity.

I conclude that this argument does not prove 'the existence of universals'; and that, if it did, nothing more could be said about them than is said in the course of the argument itself, except that they are certainly quite different from 'universals' in other senses of that word, i.e. as 'proved' to exist by other transcendental arguments.

In a certain sense, it perhaps is *sometimes* not harmful to talk about 'universals' or 'concepts'; just as it is *sometimes* convenient to talk about 'propositions', and as it is very often convenient to use 'material object language'. To say something about 'concepts' is sometimes a convenient way of saying something complicated about sensa (or even about other objects of acquaintance, if there are any), including symbols and images, and about our use of them:[13] though very different methods of translation will have to be employed on different occasions. But on the whole there is remarkably little to be said in favour of 'universals', even as an admitted logical construction: the plain man did not use it, until he acquired the habit from philosophers, and the errors into which that habit leads are very common and numerous. For example, in addition to those already noted, the error of taking a single *word* or *term*, instead of a sentence, as that which 'has meaning'; hence, given some word like 'resemblance', we search for what *it* denotes (cp III). Or again, we confuse the view that all sentences are about sensa, with the view that every word or term denotes a sensum. Or again, and this most concerns us, we think of the 'abstracted' universal as a solid piece of property of ours, and enquire into its 'origin'.

I should like, then, to learn from Mr. Mackinnon and Mr. Maclagan, 'what a concept is'.

Source: 'Are there *a priori* concepts?', *Proceedings of the Aristotelian Society*, Suppl. Volume 1939. (Extract.)

---

[13] But we must 'be careful'. We must not say e.g., 'a universal is an image': Berkeley probably did not make this mistake, but Hume probably did: hence Hume is led, whereas Berkeley is not, into a theory about 'the origin' of our ideas.

44 Of Words (1690)

JOHN LOCKE

Naming.—When children have by repeated sensations got ideas fixed in their memories, they begin by degrees to learn the use of signs. And when they have got the skill to apply the organs of speech to the framing of articulate sounds, they begin to make use of words to signify their ideas to others. These verbal signs they sometimes borrow from others, and sometimes make themselves, as one may observe among the new and unusual names children often give to things in their first use of language.

Abstraction.—The use of words then being to stand as outward marks of our internal ideas, and those ideas being taken from particular things, if every particular idea that we take in should have a distinct name, names must be endless. To prevent this, the mind makes the particular ideas, received from particular objects, to become general; which is done by considering them as they are in the mind such appearances, separate from all other existences and the circumstances of real existence, as time, place, or any other concomitant ideas. This is called *abstraction*, whereby ideas taken from particular beings become general representatives of all of the same kind; and their names general names, applicable to whatever exists comformable to such abstract ideas. Such precise, naked appearances in the mind, without considering how, whence, or with what others they came there, the understanding lays up (with names commonly annexed to them) as the standards to rank real existences into sorts, as they agree with these patterns, and to denominate them accordingly. Thus, the same colour being observed today in chalk or snow, which the mind yesterday received from milk, it considers that appearance alone, makes it

a representative of all of that kind; and having given it the name
whiteness, it by that sound signifies the same quality wheresoever
to be imagined or met with; and thus universals, whether ideas or
terms, are made.

Of the signification of words

The use of words is to be sensible marks of ideas, and the ideas
they stand for are their proper and immediate signification. The
use men have of these marks being either to record their own
thoughts for the assistance of their own memory; or, as it were,
to bring out their ideas, and lay them before the view of others:
words in their primary and immediate signification stand for
nothing but *the ideas in the mind of him that uses them*, how
imperfectly soever or carelessly those ideas are collected from
the things which they are supposed to represent. But though
words, as they are used by men, can properly and immediately
signify nothing but the ideas that are in the mind of the speaker,
yet they in their thoughts give them a secret reference to two
other things. *First*, they suppose their words to be marks of the
ideas in the minds also of other men with whom they communicate. *Secondly*, because men would not be thought to talk barely
of their own imaginations, but of things as really they are, therefore they often suppose their words to stand also for the reality
of things.

Of general terms

The greatest part of words general.—All things that exist being
particulars, it may perhaps be thought reasonable that words,
which ought to be conformed to things, should be so too, I mean
in their signification: but yet we find the quite contrary. The far
greatest part of words, that make all languages, are general terms:
which has not been the effect of neglect or chance, but of reason
and necessity.
  For every particular thing to have a name is impossible.—First,
It is impossible that every particular thing should have a distinct
peculiar name. For the signification and use of words depending
on that connexion which the mind makes between its ideas and
the sounds it uses as signs of them, it is necessary, in the applica-

tion of names to things, that the mind should have distinct ideas of the things, and retain also the particular name that belongs to every one, with its peculiar appropriation to that idea. But it is beyond the power of human capacity to frame and retain distinct ideas of all the particular things we meet with: every bird and beast men saw, every tree and plant that affected the senses, could not find a place in the most capacious understanding. If it be looked on as an instance of a prodigious memory, that some generals have been able to call every soldier in their army by his proper name: we may easily find a reason why men have never attempted to give names to each sheep in their flock, or crow that flies over their heads; much less to call every leaf of plants or grain of sand that came in their way by a peculiar name.

And useless.—Secondly, If it were possible, it would yet be useless, because it would not serve to the chief end of language. Men would in vain heap up names of particular things, that would not serve them to communicate their thoughts. Men learn names, and use them in talk with others, only that they may be understood: which is then only done when by use or consent the sound I make by the organs of speech excites in another man's mind who hears it, the idea I apply it to in mine when I speak it. This cannot be done by names applied to particular things, whereof I alone having the ideas in my mind, the names of them could not be significant or intelligible to another who was not acquainted with all those very particular things which had fallen under my notice.

How general words are made.—The next thing to be considered is, how general words come to be made. For since all things that exist are only particulars, how come we by general terms, or where find we those general natures they are supposed to stand for? Words become general by being made the signs of general ideas: and ideas become general by separating from them the circumstances of time and place, and any other ideas that may determine them to this or that particular existence. By this way of abstraction they are made capable of representing more individuals than one; each of which, having in it a conformity to that abstract idea, is (as we call it) of that sort.

But to deduce this a little more distinctly, it will not perhaps be amiss to trace our notions and names from their beginning, and observe by what degrees we proceed, and by what steps we enlarge our ideas from our first infancy. There is nothing more evident than that the ideas of the persons children converse with

are, like the persons themselves, only particular. The ideas of the
nurse and the mother are well framed in their minds; and, like
pictures of them there, represent only those individuals; and the
names of *nurse* and *mamma* the child uses, determine themselves
to those persons. Afterwards, when time and a larger acquaintance
has made them observe that there are a great many other things
in the world, that, in some common agreements of shape and
several other qualities, resemble their father and mother and
those persons they have been used to, they frame an idea which
they find those many particulars do partake in; and to that they
give, with others, the name *man*, for example. And thus they come
to have a general name, and a general idea. Wherein they make
nothing new, but only leave out of the complex idea they had of
Peter and James, Mary and Jane, that which is peculiar to each,
and retain only what is common to them all.

Source: An Essay Concerning Human Understanding (O.U.P.).
Bk. II, Ch. 11, (extracts), Bk. III, Chs. 2 and 3 (extracts).

45 Abstractionism and Concept-formation (1957)

PETER GEACH

I shall use 'abstractionism' as a name for the doctrine that a
concept is acquired by a process of singling out in attention some
one feature given in direct experience—*abstracting* it—and
ignoring the other features simultaneously given—*abstracting
from* them. The abstractionist would wish to maintain that all
acts of judgment are to be accounted for as exercises of concepts
got by abstraction; but he is often driven into allowing exceptions
for certain kinds of concepts, because in their case abstractionism
is palpably unreasonable. My own view is that abstractionism is
wholly mistaken; that no concept at all is acquired by the
supposed process of abstraction.

My refutation of abstractionism will make no appeal to the
empirical data collected by professional child psychologists. My

procedure may thus appear to many readers arrogantly *a priori*. Surely the origins of anything have to be discovered empirically; what is the use of arguing without information? But since acquiring a concept is a process of becoming able *to do something*, an enquiry as to the origin of a concept may be vitiated from the start by wrong analysis of *what is done* when the concept is exercised; and such an error may be shown without any empirical data as to concept-formation in children. Again, as Wittgenstein remarked, the connexion between *learning* and *being able* to do something is not just an empirical one; for we should plainly not be willing to call *any* process that ended in ability to do something 'learning' to do it. Of course we cannot work out in our heads how abilities are acquired; but there are conceivable ways of acquiring them to which we should unhesitatingly refuse to apply the term 'learning'. If, as in a story of Stephen Leacock's, a boy could come to know Latin by submitting to a brain operation, he would not have *learned* Latin from the surgeon. Now abstractionism is a theory of how certain mental performances are *learned*; the discussion I am entering upon is designed to show that the processes alleged by abstractionists would not be a *learning* of how to make these mental acts. Moreover, I shall try to show that the whole idea of abstraction—of discriminative attention to some feature given in experience—is thoroughly incoherent; if I succeed, no notice need any longer be taken of claims that abstractionism has experimental support. No experiment can either justify or straighten out a confusion of thought; if we are in a muddle when we design an experiment, it is only to be expected that we should ask Nature cross questions and she return crooked answers.

Abstractionism has played an important role in the history of philosophy; but it is not this that concerns us—the doctrine is very much alive.[1]

Abstractionism and Logical Concepts

Abstractionists rarely attempt an abstractionist account of logical concepts, like those of *some*, *or*, and *not*; they will usually admit

---

[1] See H. H. Price, *Thinking and Experience*, London: Hutchinson, 1953, and G. Humphrey, *Thinking*, London: Methuen, 1951.

that such concepts are a special case to which abstractionism does not apply. There have, however, been some attempts to explain even logical concepts as obtained by abstraction.[2] These attempts appeal to 'inner sense' as the material from which logical concepts are to be extracted. Such an appeal could hardly be avoided; for logical concepts are not to be explained as the result of performing abstraction upon any sense-experience. In the sensible world you will find no specimens of alternativeness and negativeness from which you could form by abstraction the concept of *or* or of *not*. The sort of concept applicable in the sensible world that is plausibly representable as got by abstraction is the sort that could in favourable circumstances be conveyed by ostensive definition; the word answering to the concept could be used to label a specimen of what the concept applies to, or a picture of such a specimen. But nowhere in the sensible world could you find anything, nor could you draw any picture, that could suitably be labelled 'or' or 'not'. Hence the abstractionist appeals to 'inner sense' as the source of logical concepts: 'or' gets its meaning through our performing abstraction upon experiences of hesitation, and 'not' is similarly related to experiences of frustration or inhibition (stopping oneself from doing things) and so on. So far as I can tell, these abstractionist views as to logical concepts being got out of inner experiences are based upon the feelings that happen to be aroused in a particular writer when he says a logical word over and over to himself—a magical rite of evoking its meaning.[3] To many people, such recitation of the word 'or' suggests a feeling of dithering between alternatives; to me, on the other hand, it naturally suggests a threat— '——, or else ——!' Would an abstractionist be willing to say on that account that my concept of *or* was different from the others'? He surely ought to say so, on his own premises. But in fact the coherency of other men's language, and the possibility of communicating with them, should be conclusive proof that all have the same logical concepts . . . idiosyncratic feelings produced by logical words are neither here nor there. Of course in the living use of such words, as opposed to the recitation of them, such feelings may be wholly absent, without the words' being in any way deprived of meaning by their absence. I very much doubt

[2] As in B. Russell, *An Inquiry into Meaning and Truth*, London: George Allen and Unwin, 1940, and Price, *op. cit.*

[3] For a conspicuous example of this, see William James, *The Principles of Psychology*, London: Macmillan, 1901, Vol. I, pp. 245–6, 252–3.

whether anybody either dithers or feels threatened when he contemplates the statement that every number is odd *or* even.

Russell's attempted account of 'every S is P' is highly instructive. A judgment that a definite individual, A, is a swan and is not white would consist in my applying my concept *swan* to A but stopping myself from applying my concept *white* to A. I can now abstract what would be common to the possible judgments that A is a swan and not white, that B is a swan and not white, and so on; this gives me the content of a possible judgment that *something* is a swan and not white. If I now inhibit myself from making this judgment (whose content is derived, by abstraction, from the contents of certain possible judgments that would themselves involve my inhibiting myself from doing something) then I am judging that *nothing* is a swan without being white, i.e. that *every* swan is white. Russell thinks it is quite fair play to use inhibition of an inhibition as part of his apparatus; has not Pavlov studied pre-verbal forms of this operation in dogs? (Russell, p. 255; *cf.* also pp. 88–90 on 'some'.)

A professional psychologist may well protest that Russell's account just exhibits the characteristic weaknesses of a logician trying to do psychology, and is too obviously wrong to be of any interest. But the logical part of Russell's analysis is right: 'every S is P' does mean the same as 'no S is not P', and this is the negation of 'some S is not P'. The trouble arises rather from Russell's abstractionist accounts of negation and 'some'; since his account as a whole is clearly wrong, and the logical part of it is right, we ought to reject abstractionism about logical concepts.

The attempt to relate logical words to inner experiences and feelings thus breaks down. For a convinced abstractionist, though, a possible alternative would be to deny that there are special logical concepts corresponding to the logical words. This is especially plausible as regards negation. Is it not a mere blind copying of language-structures to suppose that use of the term 'not red' brings into play two distinct concepts—the concept *not* and the concept *red*? Surely what I exercise in using the term 'not red' is simply the concept *red*; knowing what *is* red and knowing what *is not* red are inseparable—*eadem est scientia oppositorum*. The abstractionist might thus say that the problem how we get a concept of *not* is spurious; only concepts expressed in positive terms need to be explained, and for these abstractionism has not been shown to be inadequate. If concepts were fundamentally capacities for recognition, as abstractionists think they are, this argument would be decisive; for clearly we recognize the presence and the absence of a characteristic by one and the same capacity. (See Price, p. 123.[4]) But even apart from this special view as to the nature of concepts, it seems undeniable that in some sense the concept *red* is the very same mental capacity as the concept *not red*; and thus there seems to be no place for a special concept of negation—putting 'not' before 'red' would simply serve to distinguish a special exercise of the concept *red*.

If, however, we relate the concept *not* to judgments expressed in language, then I think we can see a justification for saying that there is such a distinct concept, since ability to use the word 'not' intelligently is certainly a distinct mental ability. Again, students of elementary logic show ability to understand the word 'not' in logical schemata, such as: 'if every P is M, and some S is not M, then some S is not P'. If 'not' in 'not red' were merely a signal for a special exercise of the concept *red*, our grasp of its meaning in such schemata would be inexplicable. We cannot say that 'not' in 'not M' is merely a signal for a special use of the concept expressed by 'M'; for the schematic letter 'M' does not express a concept, as 'red' does.

Even if we consider non-linguistic performances in which concepts are exercised, we can still, I think, distinguish between exercise of the concept *red and not red* and exercise of the concept *not* as such. To sort a lot of pebbles into red ones and ones that are not red could be simply an exercise of the concept *red and not red*; and here it would be plainly silly to distinguish a concept of *red* and one of *not red* as distinct abilities. But now suppose that the sorter goes over his two heaps when the sorting is done, to see if there are any misplaced pebbles: the act of transferring a pebble to *the other* heap is an exercise of the concept of negation.

In describing the way that the concept *not* would show itself in the sorter's behaviour, I found it natural to use the word 'other' (= Latin '*alter*', not '*alius*': 'the other of two'). This concept of *other* is near akin to the concept of negation; and is equally inexplicable on abstractionist lines. There does not even seem to be a characteristic feeling of otherness; and there is certainly no

---

[4] Oddly enough, on the very next page of his work Price slides into the view that negation is understood through abstraction performed on 'inner' experiences of frustration: 'Disappointed expectation', he says, 'is what brings *not* into our lives'.

feature common to all the things that are other. Yet this concept is easily and early arrived at; a child understands the use of 'other hand' and 'other foot' before it understands 'right' and 'left', for which an abstractionist account is plausible.

The logical concepts must then, I think, be recognized as distinct mental abilities; and if so they do not admit of any abstractionist explanation. [. . .]

Abstractionism and Arithmetical Concepts

There are very many concepts, of a more homely appearance than the logical concepts, for which abstractionism is no less unworkable. Number-concepts are one example. We are indeed often taught arithmetic in childhood by such procedures as putting three apples with two apples; and then later on we hear of the addition of 'abstract units'—'3 + 2 = 5' means, we are told, that three abstract units and two more make five in all. This is surely because abstractionism has invaded pedagogic theory and practice; the talk about 'abstract units' presumably means that '3 + 2 = 5' is taken as expressing the result of abstraction from the nature of the concrete units added, e.g. from their being apples. But this is one of the contexts in which the abstractionist talk of 'discriminative attention' is most obviously a muddled and indefensible way of talking. It may well be all right to say: 'Don't bother about the shapes of the things I show you, just attend to their colours'; this is the sort of case that makes abstractionism plausible. But it is certainly a self-contradictory instruction to say: 'Don't bother about what kind of things they are, just attend to their number'. For a number is essentially a number *of* a kind of things; things are numerable only as belonging to a kind of things.[5] What number I find may vary, without my observations' varying, because I am considering a different kind of things; the same auditory experience may give me the number 2 if what I have in mind is *heroic couplets*, 4 if it is *lines of verse*, 40 if it is *syllables*, 25 if it is *words*; if I have no special kind of thing in mind, no number will suggest itself to me at all. (Of course, if I

[5] This truism is certainly what Frege intended to bring out in saying that a number attaches to a *Begriff*. What makes the truism worth enunciating is that people who would verbally assent to it are often sufficiently muddle-headed to say other things that are incompatible with it.

am shown a lot of apples and just told to count, the kind of things I shall think of will most likely be *apples*; but it need not be.) Thus number-concepts just cannot be got by concentrating on the number and abstracting from the kind of things that are being counted. Before applying a number-concept we must first apply the concept of some kind of things to the things that we count. This shows why number-concepts cannot be among the first to be acquired, and why there are languages of primitive peoples that are rich in words for kinds of things (corresponding to common nouns and adjectives in English) but very poor in numeral words.

Moreover, the elementary arithmetical operations cannot be coherently explained as being performed on collections of abstract units, or as what operations on concrete collections look like when we abstract from the special natures of such collections. Such an account superficially appears adequate for addition and subtraction; for multiplication and division it will not do at all. It sounds plausible to say that '$3 + 2 = 5$' and '$5 - 2 = 3$' describe features of putting-together and taking-away operations performable on pennies and conkers; features that we apprehend on their own account by abstracting from the pennies and the conkers. It is perhaps a bit less plausible to say that, by taking an operation performed on concrete units and abstracting from the concrete units, we can conceive an operation upon that many abstract units; still, whatever 'abstract unit' means, surely 'three conkers and two more are five conkers' remains true when for 'conkers' we substitute 'abstract units'. But it does not in the same way look like sense to talk of getting six abstract units by multiplying two abstract units by three abstract units, or of getting two abstract units by dividing three abstract units into six abstract units; nor are there any operations with pennies that would enable us to give such talk a sense when once we had abstracted from the pennies. To talk of raising two abstract units to the power of three abstract units is, if possible, even worse nonsense; and no manipulations of three pennies will teach a child what the exponent '3' means. In teaching arithmetic, the idea that the number *n* consists of *n* abstract units is not just logically open to exception, or lacking in rigour; it is quite unusable in practice.

Even at the level of school arithmetic, a child needs to master a way of talking about the number *n* which has nothing to do with groups of *n* concrete or abstract units—viz. in expressions of the form 'doing a thing *n* times over'. Exponentiation has to be explained this way; 2 to the power of 3 is 1 multiplied 3 times over by 2 ($1 \times 2 \times 2 \times 2$). The same thing is clear for multiplication and division. '$2 \times 3 = 6$' means that to add 2 to anything 3 times over is to add 6; '13 divided by 5 gives 2, remainder 3' means that from 13 you can subtract 5 *twice* over, the result being 3. Now this account could be used, instead of the nonsense about concrete and abstract units, for addition and subtraction too. Adding 5 to 7 can be explained as performing 5 times over upon the number 7 the operation of *going on to the next number*—(7), 8, 9, 10, 11, 12. Subtraction is similarly explicable in terms of counting backwards. 'This may be more correct logically than talking about abstract units', someone will protest, 'but it is too difficult for children—it is psychologically unsound'. But if a child finds 'doing a thing so many times over' too difficult to understand, it will never acquire genuine number-concepts and never be able to do arithmetic at all. And learning to say number words when presented with groups of apples varying in number is not even to start learning what 'to do a thing so many times over' means. To teach a child this, one would count, or get the child to count, while some action was repeatedly done.

Now the way counting is learned is wholly contrary to abstractionist preconceptions. What an abstractionist might call 'abstract counting'—i.e. recitation of the successive numerals without counting any objects—is logically and temporally prior to counting objects; the series of numerals has to be learned before it can be applied. The first numerals ('one' to 'twenty' in English) must indeed be learned parrotwise to begin with, like 'eany-meany-miny-mo'; but success in counting beyond this point depends on the child's practical grasp of a rule by which it could go on forming numerals indefinitely. (Such practical grasp of a rule of course does not imply ability to formulate it.) Young children sometimes amuse themselves by counting up to large numbers (several thousands); they have never heard their elders do this, and quite likely they will never in their lives have occasion to count so high for any practical purpose; the exercise of going on in the series of numerals is one that they find pleasurable on its own account. The ability to do this is not yet possession of full-blown number-concepts, because the series of numerals has not yet any application; but the performance is a characteristic *intellectual* performance. Moreover, the pattern of the numeral series that is thus grasped by the child exists nowhere in nature outside human languages; so the human race cannot possibly have discerned this pattern by abstracting it from some natural context. The practices of counting objects, and again of counting the repeated performances of some action or operation, are developed on the basis of this 'abstract counting'; what has to be mastered here is the establishment of one-one correspondence between the numerals and the things or performances being counted—e.g. one gets the child to go on to the next numeral when and only when it goes up another stair of the staircase. The abstractionist doctrine that 'abstract numbers' are understood by abstracting from the special nature of the things numbered puts the cart before the horse.

Abstractionism and Relational Concepts

Other concepts, less near akin to logical concepts than number-concepts are, turn out to resist abstractionist explanations. Consider the concepts *big* and *small*. Is there a common identifiable feature shared by a big elephant, a big rat, and a big flea, and which they do not share with a small elephant, a small rat, and a small flea? Can I pick this feature out by discriminative attention, abstracting from what kind of thing it is that I am calling big or small? Certainly not; I cannot rightly apply the term 'big' or 'small' unless I am meaning a big or small thing of a certain kind. A big flea or rat is a small animal, and a small elephant is a big animal. There can be no question of ignoring the kind of thing to which 'big' or 'small' is referred and forming a concept of *big* or *small* by abstraction. It has indeed been pointed out that I can recognize a thing as big or small of its kind without any explicit mental reference to the standard size of that kind of thing (PRICE, p. 65); but though I need not have the standard size in mind, reference to the kind of thing is inherent in any use of 'big' and 'small'.

Relational concepts in general raise difficulties of which abstractionists are usually unaware—they lump relations together with attributes as 'recurrent characteristics' that we can recognize (*cf.* PRICE, p. 10). The trouble is that a relation neither exists nor can be observed apart from its converse relation; what is more, the concept of a relation and of its converse is one and the same indivisible mental capacity, and we cannot exercise this capacity without actually thinking of both relations together; *relativa sunt simul natura et intellectu.* It is difficult, in view of this, to give *any* account of our understanding the difference between 'the knife is to the left of the book' and 'the knife is to the right of the book'. But I do not see how an abstractionist account of it is even possible; for all that is obtainable by abstraction, one would think, is ability to recognize the 'recurrent characteristic' of right-left ordering, not ability to tell which thing is to the left and which to the right. If we are to concentrate upon the 'recurrent characteristic', and 'abstract from' the terms between which the relations hold, what else can be the result? Yet surely it is only if there is at least an ability to tell which thing is to the right and which to the left, that we can say there exists a concept of *right* and *left*.

Abstractionism and Colour-Concepts

These examples so far show only that abstractionism does not cover the whole field of concepts. I wish to maintain a far stronger conclusion—that there is no concept at all of which an abstractionist account is adequate. If there were any truth in abstractionism, it would at any rate be adequate for concepts of simple sensible qualities, for concepts like *red* and *round*. Now if I possess the concept *red*, then I can perform acts of judgment expressible in sentences containing the word 'red'. This ability, however, certainly cannot be learned by any kind of attention to red patches for any length of time; even if after a course of attending to red patches the ability turned out to be present, we should still be justified in refusing to say it had been *learned* that way. We can say this quite as confidently as we can say that the ordinary use of the word 'red' cannot be learned by hearing the word 'red' uttered ceremonially in the presence of a red object—simply on this account, that such a ceremony is not the ordinary use of the word 'red'.

Price has the rare merit among abstractionists of having pointed out that ceremonious ostensive definition normally plays a rather small part in the learning of language. His own theory is that we learn the sense of words like 'cat' and 'black' by a double process of abstraction; that

the common feature, e.g. 'cat', in these otherwise unlike utterances is gradually correlated with a common factor in observed environmental situations which are otherwise unlike. Similarly 'black' gradually sorts itself out from another range of utterances which are otherwise unlike, and is correlated with a visible quality experienced in otherwise unlike situations. (Price, p. 215.)

This is much more plausible than the usual stuff about ostensive definition, but I think it is still open to two fatal objections. First, it is integral to the use of a general term that we are not confined to using it in situations including some object to which the term applies; we can use the terms 'black' and 'cat' in situations not including any black object or any cat. How could this part of the use be got by abstraction? And such use is part of the very beginnings of language; the child calls out 'pot' in an 'environmental situation' in which the pot is conspicuous by its absence. Secondly, it is of course not enough, even when language is being used to describe the immediate situation, that we should utter a lot of words corresponding to several features of the situation; but the abstraction that Price appeals to could scarcely account for our doing anything more than this.

It is indeed hard to see at first sight what account other than an abstractionist account could possibly be given for such concepts as colour-concepts; and for this very reason such concepts are the abstractionists' favoured examples. The reason, surely, why men born blind cannot have colour-concepts is that they have no colour-sensations; and does not this imply that men who can see form their colour-concepts by attending to certain features given in their visual experiences?

In the first place, it is not true that men born blind can form no colour-concepts of any sort. A man born blind can use the word 'red' with a considerable measure of intelligence; he can show a practical grasp of the logic of the word.[6] What is more, he may, if he is intelligent, grasp something of the aesthetic significance of red and its place in human life—like Locke's blind man who said he thought scarlet must be like the sound of a trumpet. Of course a man born blind cannot have our colour-

---

[6] 'Red' has, for example, a very considerable logical resemblance to 'hot'; both redness and heat admit of degrees, a surface can be red all over and hot all over, there can be redness or heat throughout a volume, etc., etc. A blind man could show that he had a concept of *red* akin to our own by using 'red' and 'hot' in logically similar ways; he need not be able to formulate the logical similarities.

concepts; but this, it turns out, proves nothing whatsoever. If it is logically impossible that a man blind from birth should have colour-concepts quite like those of a sighted man, then the unlikeness cannot be regarded as a remarkable empirical fact, throwing light upon the origin of concepts. Now concepts are mental capacities; somebody who is enabled by his colour-concepts to do what somebody else cannot do has a specifically different capacity and thus a different concept. A part of a sighted man's colour-concepts is his ability to apply them to visual experiences; and a man blind from birth necessarily lacks this ability. There is sufficient similarity between the abilities of men blind from birth and of sighted men, who alike use colour-words intelligently, for us to be justified in speaking of 'colour-concepts' in both cases; what dissimilarity there is is a logical consequence of the blind man's having always been blind, and calls for no abstractionist explanation. If we supposed that men blind from birth could (logically) have the same colour-concepts as sighted men, their not having them would call for explanation; but such a supposition would be just a muddle. Different men may use tools that are quite similar in dissimilar ways; but a concept is not externally related to its applications, as a tool is to its uses; a man who can do different things with his concept has a concept that is to some extent different from the other fellow's.

In point of fact, abstractionism goes to wreck even over colour-concepts, as may be shown by a further argument. Let us consider chromatic colour, i.e. colour other than white, grey, and black. The concept *chromatic colour*, in spite of my having had to explain the term by using a string of words, is surely no less 'simple', no less a concept of something 'given in direct experience', than the concept *red*. (One common meaning of the adjective 'coloured' is the possession of chromatic colour—'coloured chalks', 'coloured glass', 'penny plain, twopence coloured'.) Now it is quite impossible that I should form this concept, *chromatic colour*, by discriminative attention to a feature given in my visual experience. In looking at a red window-pane I have not two sensations, one of redness and one barely of chromatic colour; there are not, for that matter, two distinct sense-given features, one of them making my sensation to be barely a sensation of chromatic colour, the other making it a sensation of redness. If I abstract from what differentiates red from other chromatic colours I am abstracting from red itself; red is not chromatic colour *plus* a *differentia*, so that we can concentrate our attention upon chromatic colour and abstract from the *differentia*.

The difficulty I have just raised resembles one raised by Locke (*Essay*, III. iv. 6) about the relation between the concepts *red* and *colour*—'colour' having for him the wider sense of the word, covering also white, black, and grey. Locke observed that 'red' cannot be defined by adding a *differentia* to 'coloured', and inferred that the concept *coloured* cannot be reached by abstracting from the distinctive marks of the various colours. His solution is that the word 'coloured' stands for 'the way' that all the 'ideas' of the several colours 'got into the mind'; 'it signifies no more but such ideas as are produced in the mind only by the sight and have entrance only through the eyes'. Presumably his view is that all 'ideas' with this common origin have a peculiar feel or look, which is manifest to 'inner sense' and can be singled out abstractively; at least, I can think of no other interpretation that makes his view plausible. Even so, this is a pretty obvious makeshift. But I would rather not discuss Locke's actual problem, because (using the word 'colour' in his way) we should encounter special, and for the moment irrelevant, difficulties about the concept *colour*. It is clear, however, that the concept *chromatic colour* stands on the same footing as the concept *red*, and does not raise any of these peculiar difficulties; clear, too, that no such account as Locke gives for the concept *colour* will fit. Failing to account for so simple a concept as *chromatic colour*, abstractionism must be pronounced finally bankrupt.

Making Concepts is not a Finding of Recurrent Features

At this point we feel inclined—indeed, almost forced—to say that the mind makes a distinction between redness and chromatic colour, although there are not two distinct features to be found in the red glass or in my visual sensation. And here, I think, we are approaching the true solution.

'If the glass has not two distinct attributes, redness and chromatic colour, how can these attributes be distinct anywhere? and then how can anything be chromatically coloured without being red?' This objection, natural as it is, rests upon a false Platonistic logic; an attribute is being thought of as an identifiable object. It would be better to follow Frege's example and compare attributes to mathematical functions.[7] 'The square of' and 'the double of' stand for distinct functions, and in general the square of x is different from the double of x; but if x is 2 then the square of x *is* the double of x, and the two are not in this case distinguishable even in thought. Similarly, since what is chromatically coloured is often not red, 'the chromatic colour of x' or 'x's being chromatically coloured' does not in general stand for the same thing as 'the redness of x'; but if x is red, then it is by one and the same feature of x that x is made red and chromatically coloured; the two functions, so to speak, assume the same value for the argument x.

'If there are two distinct features to be found in my mental representation, and only one in the pane of glass, then my mind represents things otherwise than they are, i.e. represents them falsely. It would follow that the conceptual way of thinking distorts reality.' How can we get over this difficulty?

The statement 'An understanding which understands a thing otherwise than the thing is, is wrong' is ambiguous; the qualification of the verb 'understands' by the adverb 'otherwise' may relate either to the thing that is understood or to the person who understands. If it relates to the thing that is understood, then the statement is true, its meaning being this: Any understanding that understands a thing *to be* otherwise than it is, is wrong. But this meaning is inapplicable to the case we are considering. For when our understanding frames a proposition about the colour of the glass, it does not assert that this colour is complex, but on the contrary that it is simple.—If, however, the qualification is taken to refer to the person who understands, then the statement is false; for the way it is with our understanding when we understand is different from the way it is with the thing we understand, in its actual existence. When our understanding understands things that are simple, it may understand them in its own complex fashion without understanding them *to be* complex.

The last paragraph is a translation from Aquinas (Ia q. 13 art. 12 ad 3 um), modified so as to fit my chosen example. It appears to me to be a decisive solution to the problem of conceptual thought's 'falsifying' reality. We can now say something that goes

---

[7] The use of this analogy does not commit us to the whole of Frege's apparatus. Readers who are interested in the development of the analogy may care to refer to my paper 'Form and Existence' (*Proc. Arist. Soc.*, 1954–1955).

for all concepts without exception. Having a concept never means being able to recognize some feature we have found in direct experience; the mind *makes* concepts, and this concept-formation and the subsequent use of the concepts formed never is a mere recognition or finding; but this does not in the least prevent us from applying concepts in our sense-experience and knowing sometimes that we apply them rightly. In all cases it is a matter of fitting a concept to my experience, not of picking out the feature I am interested in from among other features given simultaneously. Suppose I look at a lot of billiard balls on a table, and form the judgment that some of them are red and some are not. If I state this judgment in words, 'red' may plausibly be taken to report a feature of what I see, but 'some' and 'not' certainly cannot. But it would be perverse to infer that my distorting conceptual thought represents the reality as exhibiting features, somehood and nottishness, which are not really there; and no less perverse to argue that, since my judgment is correct, there must be somehood and nottishness *in rebus*. We must resist the perennial philosophical temptation to think that if a thought is to be true of reality, then it must copy it feature by feature, like a map. Even the use of the word 'red' is not to be explained in terms of reporting or copying real features; for, as we saw, the terms 'red' and '(chromatically) coloured' *may* answer to the same feature of the same thing; and again, what is logically distinctive in the use of colour-words is certainly not to be reached, by an act of abstraction, from the seeing of red things.

In rejecting abstractionism, we deny a privileged position to 'sensory' concepts, e.g. colour-concepts. These concepts are indeed specially involved in the procedure of describing one's sensations; geometrical concepts and colour-concepts enter into the description of visual sensations in a way that other concepts do not. If I look at a tomato, there is some justification for saying: 'what I actually see can be *completely* described in terms of colour, shape, and size, without mentioning any other characteristics'. There is however no reason to think that this gives 'sensory' concepts an epistemological primacy over others; for the description of sensations is a highly sophisticated exercise of concepts, and is secondary to the application of 'sensory' concepts to the material environment. In this primary, outward-looking application, 'sensory' concepts have not in fact any privileged position; a child with only a few concepts and only a small understanding of language may easily possess concepts like *door* and *book* (and even the logical concept *other*, as in 'other hand', 'other foot') before it has any colour-concepts at all.

About psychological investigations designed to prove that concepts are formed by abstraction, I think it is safe to say that either what is studied is not the formation of concepts, or it is manifest on a little consideration that the concepts were not formed by abstraction. The first criticism applies to such experiments as getting rats to 'recognize triangles as such', i.e. training them to react similarly to triangles of various shapes and sizes. The psychologist may well say: 'the rats are able to perfect a type of behaviour which is fully described by the implications in our use of the term "concept"'; but 'our' (the experimenters') use of the term is then wholly different from its use in this book. (See Humphrey, p. 254). This is not merely a verbal point, the psychologist's explanation of such a phrase as 'the concept of triangularity' is what it is now fashionable to call a persuasive definition, not a mere Humpty-Dumpty pronunciamento. He can scarcely deny that human beings show their possession of the concept *triangle* by behaviour very different from rats'; but he invites us to regard this difference as unimportant.

Consider, on the other side, a study of genuine conception-formation by Smoke (Humphrey, pp. 252-3, 275-6). On cards three inches square, figures of various sorts were drawn; some of these were *pogs*, a *pog* being a blue rectangle enclosing a blue circle that touches only one long side of the rectangle. (Humphrey describes '*pog*' as a 'nonsense name'; this is a self-contradictory expression, and is clearly wrong; '*pog*' is merely not part of ordinary language.) The subject was shown a number of *pogs*, was given the verbal instruction 'Try to find out everything a figure must be if it is to be called a *pog*', and was told to raise his hand when he thought he knew what a *pog* was. His claim to knowledge was then tested by getting him to try (i) to pick out further *pogs*, (ii) to draw a *pog*, (iii) to define '*pog*' in words. Many subjects who failed at test (iii) succeeded at test (i). Humphrey thinks that this experiment shows 'that a subject can form and utilize a concept without verbalization'.

What Humphrey appears not to notice is that the verbal instruction given to the subject requires for its understanding some highly sophisticated concepts (the concept of *name*, the concept implicit in 'everything that a thing must be if . . .'); such concepts are not among the first to be acquired, and the experiment does nothing to show that *they* are acquired 'without verbalization'. Again, the verbal instructions, and the whole set-up of the experiment, already delineate many of the logical peculiarities of the word '*pog*'; the word is not a mere nonsense-syllable at the start of the experiment (as Humphrey's tendentious term 'nonsense name' suggests). '*Pog*' is to be a common noun, used to refer to a certain design of colours and shapes; a subject who has grasped this much already has an inchoate concept of a *pog*, and with one who had not grasped this much the experiment would not succeed. (The 'grasp' that I mean is a matter of partly knowing *how* to use the word '*pog*', not of knowing, explicitly judging, *that* the word is to be a common noun, etc.) So the experiment does not show that the subject can abstractively form the concept *pog* from scratch, independently of 'verbalization'.

Are we to say that subjects who can recognize *pogs* but cannot verbally define the term '*pog*' possess the concept *pog*? This certainly seems reasonable; how many of us could give a watertight definition of 'chair' or 'money', words that we should certainly wish to say express concepts? Defining a term is normally a particular exercise of the corresponding concept rather than a way of getting the concept,[8] and performance of this exercise is not a necessary condition of having the concept. But though the subject may acquire the concept *pog* without being able to give a verbal definition of '*pog*', in the experimental set-up described the concept is acquired only against the background of a considerable command of language; to speak of 'forming concepts without verbalization' merely obscures the matter.

As I remarked before in reference to aphasia, I do not wish so to use the term 'concept' that every concept necessarily involves some linguistic capacity. But Smoke's experiments certainly do not show that concepts can be formed *from scratch* by abstraction —by discriminative attention to features given in sense-experience —and that language is of no importance in their formation. Linguistic capacities, for an abstractionist, are necessarily an external, adventitious aspect of the possession of concepts. 'Fundamentally a concept is a recognitional capacity' for the abstractionist (PRICE, p. 355); so a depreciation of linguistic performances is an essential part of the abstractionist programme. Smoke has supplied no experimental support for such depreciation.

Source: Mental Acts (Routledge and Kegan Paul) Ch. 6 (extract), Chs. 7–11.

[8] As Aquinas already recognized: Ia q. 85 art. 2 ad 3 um.

Index

Aeschylus 234
Anscombe, G. E. M. 131n, 135n
Antiphon the Sophist 380
Aquinas, Thomas 413, 416n
d'Argenson, Marquis 150n
Aristotle 150–1, 156–70, 232–5, 263, 314–21, 379, 380n, 385, 388, 389n
Austen, Jane 326
Austin, J. L. 219–31, 389–96
Ayer, A. J. 35–42, 236

Bacon 95
Benn, S. I. 154–9
Bentham 143
Berkeley, Edmund C. 26n
Berkeley, George 360–3, 364–7, 371, 396n
Berlin, I. 160n
Black, M. 136n
Boyle's Law 188–91
Braithwaite, R. B. 186–98
Brentano 145–6
Broad, C. D. 198n
Butler, Bishop 188, 329

Caligula, Emperor 150
Campbell, C. A. 56–8
Cantor, G. 111
Carritt, E. F. 157n
Cherniss, J. F. 379–89
Christ 144, 145
Christoffel, E. B. 110
Cohen, L. J. 301n
Columbus 107
Cook Wilson, J. 333n
Crosland, C. A. R. 176n

Dedekind, R. 111
Democritus 6, 380–3, 386
Dennis, Nigel 62

Descartes, René 59–61, 73, 100, 219n, 344–51

Epicurus 235
Eubulides, antinomy of liar 271
Euclid 96, 280

Fischer, K. 103n
Foot, Philippa 115–35, 136, 137n, 138, 144
Frege, G. 101–9, 110–11, 280, 301, 405n, 412–13

Galileo 343
Gasking, D. 202n
Geach, Peter T. 59–61, 226n, 400–416
Glaucon 303–14
God 18, 146, 215, 234, 344
Gödel, Kurt 283
Goldbach 185
Gorgias 386
Grotius 150

Handford, S. A. 228n
Hare, R. M. 117, 161n
Hart, H. L. A. 201–10
Helmholtz, H. 110
Herbart 103
Hilbert, D. 109–14
Hobbes, Thomas 150, 211–16, 236
Hobhouse, L. T. 156
Honoré, A. M. 201–10
Hume, David 16, 19, 43–51, 52, 54, 62–9, 130–1, 181–2, 183, 187, 189, 216–19, 236, 396n
Humphrey, G. 401n, 415–16

James, William 60–1, 402n
Johnson, W. E. 187

417

Kant, Immanuel 56, 151–4, 159, 165–7, 371–2
Keynes, J. N. 188n
Kneale, William 182–6, 192n, 329–342
Kotarbiński, Tadeusz 272
Kronecker, L. 110

Laplace 237
Leacock, Stephen 401
Leibniz 219n
Lewis, David K. 5
Locke, John 182, 351–60, 397–400, 412
Łukasiewicz, Jan 270

McGovern, Patrick J. 26n
MacKay, D. M. 26n
Mackinnon 390, 396
Maclagan 390, 396
McTaggart, J. McT. E. 51–6
Magellan 115
Malebranche 18
Marill, T. 25n
Messick, Samuel 27n
Mill, John Stuart 89–101, 106, 197, 199–201, 202, 203, 367–77
Moore, G. E. 140, 219–31, 239–261
Mounce, H. O. 135–48

Neisser, Ulric 27n
Newton, Isaac 66
Nietzsche 129

Paul, St. 145–6
Pears, David 62–9, 189n, 231–8
Peirce, C. S. 291, 300
Peters, R. S. 136n, 154–9, 211n
Philetas of Cos 271
Phillips, D. Z. 135–48
Plato 130, 219n, 234, 303–14, 316n, 379–89, 392n
Plutarch 151n, 380n
Polus 320
Price, H. H. 333n, 401n, 404, 409–410
Protagoras 380, 382, 386
Ptolemy 100

Putnam, Hilary 26n, 28–9
Pythagoras 105

Quine, W. V. 287–302

Ramsey, F. P. 189n
Reichenbach, Hans 189n
Reid 200
Rhees, Rush 145n
Ross Ashby, W. 26n
Rousseau, J. J. 149–51
Russell, Bertrand 31–5, 51, 402n, 403
Ryle, Gilbert 2n, 321–9

Santayana, George 22
Schröder, E. 107
Scriven, Michael 26n, 30
Shaffer, Jerome 1–24, 24–31
Shaftesbury, Lord 46n
Shearn, Martin 36n, 40n
Shoemaker 70
Simplicius 379n
Smart, J. J. C. 10
Smoke 415–16
Socrates 129, 131–2, 379–82
Sorel, Georges 145–6
Spinoza 19
Stevenson 117
Stewart, Dugald 91–2
Strawson, P. F. 83n
Stricker 105

Tarski, Alfred 261–87, 299–300
Thrasymachus 129, 131–2
Timaeus 386, 388–9
Tomkins, Silvanus S. 27n
Turing, A. M. 25–6

Warnock, Mary 136n
Watanobe, Satosi 29n
Watling, John 38n, 41n
Weinberg, J. R. 189n
Williams, Bernard 69–87, 159–79
Wittgenstein, L. 118n, 140
Wollheim, Richard 136n, 160n
Wright, G. H. von 136n

Young, Michael 178n